Evidence

Evidence

Inns of Court School of Law
The City Law School, City University, London

OXFORD
UNIVERSITY PRESS

OXFORD
UNIVERSITY PRESS

Great Clarendon Street, Oxford OX2 6DP

Oxford University Press is a department of the University of Oxford.
It furthers the University's objective of excellence in research, scholarship,
and education by publishing worldwide in

Oxford New York

Auckland Cape Town Dar es Salaam Hong Kong Karachi
Kuala Lumpur Madrid Melbourne Mexico City Nairobi
New Delhi Shanghai Taipei Toronto

With offices in

Argentina Austria Brazil Chile Czech Republic France Greece
Guatemala Hungary Italy Japan Poland Portugal Singapore
South Korea Switzerland Thailand Turkey Ukraine Vietnam

Oxford is a registered trade mark of Oxford University Press
in the UK and in certain other countries

Published in the United States
by Oxford University Press Inc., New York

British Library Cataloguing in Publication Data

Data available

Library of Congress Cataloging in Publication Data

Data available

Typeset by Newgen Imaging Systems (P) Ltd., Chennai, India
Printed in Great Britain
on acid-free paper by
Ashford Colour Press, Gosport, Hampshire

ISBN 0–19–928952–2   978–0–19–928952–3

10 9 8 7 6 5 4 3 2 1

FOREWORD

I am delighted to write this Foreword to the Manuals which are written by practitioners and staff of the Inns of Court School of Law (ICSL).

The Manuals are designed primarily to support training on the Bar Vocational Course (BVC). They now cover a wide range, embracing both the compulsory and the optional subjects of the BVC. They provide an outstanding resource for all those concerned to teach and acquire legal skills wherever the BVC is taught.

The Manuals for the compulsory subjects are updated and revised annually. The Manuals for the optional subjects are revised every two years. In a new and important development, the publishers will maintain a website for the Manuals which will be used to keep them up-to-date throughout the academic year.

The Manuals, continually updated, exemplify the practical and professional approach that is central to the BVC. I congratulate the staff of the ICSL who have produced them to an excellent standard, and Oxford University Press for its commitment in securing their publication. As my predecessor the Hon. Mr Justice Gross so aptly said in a previous Foreword, the Manuals are an important ingredient in the constant drive to raise standards in the public interest.

The Hon. Mr Justice Etherton
Chairman of the Advisory Board of the Institute of Law
City University, London
May 2006

OUTLINE CONTENTS

DETAILED CONTENTS

PREFACE

The law of evidence regulates the means by which facts may be proved in courts of law. It is for this reason that mastery of its basic principles and rules is essential to the practitioner. All too often, both before a trial and during its conduct in court, the rules of evidence must be applied on the spur of the moment, without the opportunity to consult books or articles. Perhaps instructions have been belatedly received. Perhaps a problem arises at the trial itself: during examination in chief, cross-examination or re-examination; when the admissibility of an item of evidence is suddenly questioned; or when it becomes necessary to deal with a judicial intervention or to make submissions about the contents of a summing-up.

This Manual, by its combination of text, materials, examples and problems, aims to develop not only a knowledge of evidence law, but also understanding of the ways in which it is applied in practice.

The law is stated as at 28 March 2006.

TABLE OF CASES

TABLE OF STATUTES

International legislation

TABLE OF SECONDARY LEGISLATION

Fundamentals of evidence

1.1 What is evidence?

Before looking at the rules of evidence (ie, the law governing what evidence will or will not be allowed into court) it is useful to be clear about some of the matters of fundamental importance in understanding how evidence works. The subject matter of this chapter is therefore of considerable importance. You will find that the key terms that are being referred to in this chapter are used throughout this book.

1.1.1 Facts and law

The legal sanctions that the court can impose depend upon the proven facts of the case. Therefore, for example, before a judge in the Crown Court can impose a sentence on a defendant, the defendant must be proven to have committed an offence. Further, the type of sentence imposed on the defendant depends on which offence or offences that defendant is proven to have committed: in effect, which factual allegations the court has accepted. Likewise a civil court could not award damages to a claimant for three breaches of contract if the claimant had only proven a single breach. Furthermore, the amount of any damages awarded would depend on how much loss the claimant could prove flowed from that breach.

It will be seen therefore that the court's power to exercise legal sanctions and to apply legal rules depends on *proof* of particular facts. The function of the law is to establish which facts have to be proven in any given case.

1.1.2 Proof

The word 'proof' is used commonly in evidential discussion. Later, in this and the next chapter, you will be introduced to concepts such as 'burden of proof', 'standard or proof' and 'probative value'. Before defining these terms, it is worth attempting a working definition of the key word 'proof'.

The legal meaning of proof is not so different from its ordinary meaning. In ordinary speech 'proof' is most commonly used to mean *either* the process of convincing a person of a particular conclusion by the use of facts and logic *or* successfully convincing a person of a particular conclusion in that way. Therefore if A says to B, 'Prove it,' A means that B should produce facts and make arguments on the point in question and that the facts and arguments produced should be such as will convince A. It is worth noting the following points:

(a) Proof is achieved by combining facts and arguments.

(b) There is an implicit standard below which a conclusion would be 'unproven'. Some things are more difficult to prove than others. The more improbable the desired conclusion the harder it will be to prove it. By 'harder' we mean that more facts and better arguments will be required to convince the person to reach the conclusion in question.

(c) Facts and arguments are not all equally valuable in proving conclusions. We expect anyone deciding whether something is proven to treat facts and arguments differently for a variety of reasons. Some have less relevance or bearing on the matter in question. Some facts relied upon may be less reliable than others, whether because the source of the fact is suspect or because there is an impression that the fact does not give the whole picture.

(d) There is always someone who has to decide whether something has been proven. Proof requires a tribunal to determine whether something is proven.

The approach of the courts to proof is essentially the same. However, as one might expect from the formal nature of courts, proof is subject to a system of rules and practices. These rules and practices are at the heart of the rules of evidence and most of this Manual will examine how the formal process of proof is based on these rules and practices. It is therefore worth considering some of the ways in which the points noted above are applied in a formal, legal setting.

1.1.2.1   Facts and arguments

The legal process of proof in court requires a combination of facts and arguments to prove cases. The rules of evidence and of court procedure draw a distinction between facts, which are proven by the evidence (usually the calling of witnesses) and arguments, which are advanced later on by the advocates in the case. For example, an advocate in a Crown Court trial should not comment on the evidence given by a witness while conducting cross-examination (see the *Advocacy Manual*). Rather, he or she will make comments upon that evidence (ie, make arguments about it) during a closing speech after all of the facts have been put before the jury (see the *Civil Litigation* and *Criminal Litigation Manuals*).

1.1.2.2   Standards of proof

Every allegation in a case must be established to a particular 'standard of proof'. The standard for any particular allegation is set by the law. It is in this context that phrases you may have heard before such as 'beyond reasonable doubt' and 'on the balance of probabilities' are used. The law has also regulated who must prove facts. The 'prove it' demand is generally imposed upon the party bringing the case (ie, the claimant in civil cases and the prosecution in criminal cases) but, given the complexity of the litigation process, this is not always so. The requirement that a party prove a particular conclusion is called the 'burden of proof'. We shall examine the burden and standard of proof more closely in **Chapter 2**.

1.1.2.3   Facts and arguments are variable

The rules of evidence recognise that facts are not all equally useful in proving conclusions. While the rules of evidence generally seek to admit all facts that might prove a conclusion ('relevant facts') there are numerous safeguards that aim to prevent the trial process being undermined by the reception of weak evidence.

The formalised trial process has rules for how facts are proven (see **1.7** below) and there are also rules preventing some facts from being proven if the source of the fact in question is in some way potentially unreliable (for example, 'hearsay' evidence, **Chapters 11** and **12** and the requirement that an expert is proven to be an expert witness before expert opinion evidence can be given: see **Chapter 16**).

We shall see that some of these rules aim to prevent parties from wasting the time and resources of the court with facts that have little value in deciding the issues of the case (for example, rules that limit the extent to which parties can prove that witnesses are of bad character: see **Chapters 8 and 10**). Other rules seek to prevent the court from being distracted from deciding the real issues of the case. There is therefore a process of filtering out some facts from cases. This is more frequently the case in criminal trials than in civil trials.

At the heart of this filtering process is the concept of 'weight' (see **1.3.2** below), which is simply a way of evaluating the capacity of some facts, or combinations of facts and arguments, to prove conclusions. The weight to be attached to any fact is significant in two ways. First, it often determines whether the court will admit evidence of the fact at all (for example, where the fact adduced prove the bad character of a criminal defendant: see **Chapter 9**). Secondly, it is used to decide whether the fact is sufficient to reach a particular standard of proof (ie, to prove a particular conclusion: see **Chapter 2**).

1.1.2.4   The tribunal of fact

A general term for the person or persons who must decide whether the facts in question are proven is 'the tribunal of fact' or the 'fact-finder'. Quite who this is depends on which court a party is appearing in. The tribunal of fact in a Crown Court trial is the jury. In the Crown Court the jury is responsible for reaching factual decisions and the judge for deciding legal issues. This raises an important distinction that we will return to later (**1.8**). The 'law-decider' is generally referred to as the 'tribunal of law'. The legal decisions include matters such as the appropriate sentence for a person who has been found guilty of an offence or the effect of the frustration of a contract. However, legal decisions also include decisions such as whether particular facts (ie, evidence) should be put in front of a tribunal of fact at all. Therefore the tribunal of law may occasionally have to examine the facts (and particularly the weight to be attached to the facts) to decide legal issues. For example, a judge deciding whether a confession was obtained unlawfully would have to decide the *factual* questions surrounding the circumstances in which it was obtained in order to reach a *legal* conclusion as to the admissibility of the confessions.

The tribunal of fact and the tribunal of law are often the same person or persons. Most civil cases are heard by a single judge who determines both the facts of the case and the legal issues. This is also so with criminal cases heard in the magistrates' court. Although the fact-finder and the tribunal of law are the same in many cases, the distinction between tribunals of fact and law is important.

1.1.3   Evidence

Facts and arguments combine to prove conclusions and this is so in cases brought before the courts as much as anywhere else. However, not all things asserted as 'facts' are accepted as such by other people. The term 'fact' is slightly misleading. The meaning given to the word by the *Oxford English Dictionary* is, '*Something that has really occurred or is actually the case; . . . hence, a particular truth known by actual observation or authentic testimony, as opposed to what is merely inferred*'. Although there is no formal definition of the term in law, the word is most correctly used to illustrate matters that are accepted by the tribunal of fact to have occurred. The tribunal of fact will consider various matters put before it and decide whether the alleged thing is true or not (ie, whether the alleged thing is a 'fact'). The matters it receives to reach that decision are 'evidence of that fact'. Looking again at the definition given above, a tribunal of fact will not be relying on 'actual observation' and so will have to rely on 'authentic testimony' to reach its conclusions.

We shall see that testimony is given a particular meaning at law but for the time being we can take testimony to mean evidence and note that evidence establishes facts.

It is worth noting at this point that evidence will not only prove a fact but that a proven fact may combine with other evidence (or proven facts) to prove some other fact. In other words a fact may be evidence of another fact.

In essence, evidence is that which proves facts and the 'proof' is the process of converting evidence into facts.

1.2   Facts in issue

It was noted above that all issues in a case must be proven. These are often termed the 'facts in issue'. Identifying the facts in issue is not as straightforward as it might first appear. First, what the facts in issue are in a particular case depends on the relevant law. Secondly, because of the adversarial nature of litigation in England and Wales, the parties to a case will make allegations and counter-allegations. A defendant may either challenge the allegations of the prosecution (in criminal cases) or claimant (in civil cases) or may raise some entirely different legal defence. Clearly, these counter-allegations have to be resolved. Finally, quite what the facts in issue are at trial is affected by rules of procedure (ie, rules dictating how the trial process will run). This means that there are differences between civil and criminal cases.

1.2.1   Criminal cases

1.2.1.1   General principle

In criminal cases, whether in the Crown Court or a magistrates' court, a trial starts with a process of arraignment or plea. The defendant is accused formally of the commission of an offence and asked to plead to it. If the plea is 'not guilty', *all* of the elements of the offence are put in issue (ie, the defendant has required the prosecution to prove them all). Furthermore the defendant may raise defences during trial which will also be put in issue.

Therefore every element of the offence for which a defendant is being tried must be established in criminal cases. In addition any defence alleged and for which some evidence is admitted (see the 'evidential burden' in **Chapter 2**) will become a fact in issue. In *R v Sims* [1946] KB 531, CCA, Lord Goddard CJ said (at p 539):

The prosecution has to prove the whole of their case including the identity of the accused, the nature of the act and the existence of any necessary knowledge or intent.

Therefore the facts in issue in a criminal case are:

- the identity of the culprit;
- the *actus reus* of the offence;
- the *mens rea* of the offence; and
- any defences raised at trial.

1.2.2   Civil cases

1.2.2.1   General principle

In civil cases, the process of making allegations begins much earlier and is more sophisticated than in criminal cases. Cases are initiated by the 'statement of case' process (see *Civil*

Litigation Manual). The claimant will make detailed allegations of some particular civil wrong (such as a breach of contract) in his or her 'particulars of claim'. The defendant will respond by way of a defence (assuming the defendant does not fully admit liability at this point). The defence will respond to each particular allegation made by the claimant.

The Civil Procedure Rules 1998 (CPR), r 16.5(1), provides:

In his defence, the defendant must state—

(a) *which of the allegations . . . he denies;*

(b) *which allegations he is unable to admit or deny, but which he requires the claimant to prove; and*

(c) *which allegations he admits.*

Denial of an allegation puts the denying party under an obligation to state reasons for denial (CPR, r 16.5(2)). The requirement to prove allegation stated in paragraph (b) recognises that there may be allegations made by a claimant that a defendant is simply not able to form a judgment upon (particularly matters such as loss and damage that may be within the personal knowledge of the claimant).

In so far as a party admits an allegation made by another party, it ceases to be a fact in issue. Otherwise the allegation remains a fact in issue.

In addition to responding to the case alleged by a claimant a defendant may raise new issues that would constitute a defence. For example, even if a defendant admits to having entered into a contract with the claimant, he might allege the existence of a frustrating event (ie, raise the defence of frustration). This would be done in his defence and would raise a new fact in issue.

There is therefore much more flexibility as to what may or not be a fact in issue in a civil case. First of all, the parties have far more control over what might be a fact in issue before trial. Secondly, there is a greater variety of subject matter being litigated in civil courts. While all criminal cases are composed of an *actus reus* and a *mens rea*, civil cases are not so strictly categorised. Each area of substantive civil law will have different potential facts in issue.

1.2.3 Significance of facts in issue

It might be wondered why a lawyer will bother to identify the facts in issue in a case. In fact many lawyers who have experience in particular areas probably identify the facts in issue by instinct. The phrase 'facts in issue' is in fact not used widely in the courts. However, it is useful in understanding how evidence proves cases. By identifying the facts in issue in a case, three things are achieved:

(a) A list of issues are identified so that it is possible to go on to determine *who* it is that must prove which issue. In other words identifying the facts in issue is the first step in determining who bears the various *burdens of proof* in a case. This is dealt with in more detail in **Chapter 2**.

(b) This list places limits on the evidence that should and can be admitted at trial. The courts will not entertain evidence that does not assist in resolving the matters in dispute (ie, the facts in issue). In other words the facts in issue determine the *relevance* of evidence. Relevance in turn is one of the factors that determines the *admissibility* of evidence: evidence that is not relevant to one or more fact in issue is inadmissible at trial.

(c) A lawyer is thereby better able to analyse the case, to identify evidence to be admitted and to formulate arguments about evidence.

1.3 Proof concepts

The rules of evidence are based on four very important concepts: relevance, weight, probative value and prejudicial effect. One or more of these concepts underpins every rule of evidence.

1.3.1 Relevance

As noted in **1.2.3** above, the concept of relevance is fundamental to all evidence. Evidence must be relevant for it to be admissible in both civil and criminal cases. Furthermore, a clear understanding of the relevance of a particular piece of evidence is necessary in applying other rules of admissibility such as the rule against hearsay.

1.3.1.1 Definition

There have been a number of attempts to define relevance. In *DPP v Kilbourne* [1973] AC 729, Lord Simon said (at p 756):

Evidence is relevant if it is logically probative or disprobative of some matter which requires proof. It is sufficient to say . . . that relevant (ie logically probative or disprobative) evidence is evidence which makes the matter . . . more or less probable.

Note the stress upon logic in the above except. Relevance does not stem from intuition or feelings about a particular piece of evidence but from how one might rationalise and explain it. An advocate will often highlight the relevance of particular pieces of evidence in his or her closing speech in order to persuade them to reach a particular conclusion.

A slightly more complicated definition was given by Stephen in his *Digest of the Law of Evidence*, where it was said:

Any two facts to which it was applied are so related to each other that according to the common course of events one either taken by itself or in connection with other facts proves or renders probable the . . . existence or non-existence of the other.

It follows that evidence does not have to *prove* a matter to be relevant. Rather, it has to *assist* in proving a matter. As Stephen makes clear, one fact (the item of evidence) has a relationship with another fact (the conclusion from the item of evidence) because it at least renders probable the conclusion. Note, however, that the requirement that the fact is rendered 'probable' is arguably stricter than lord Simon's 'makes . . . more or less probable.'

In *R v Randall* [2004] 1 WLR 56 Lord Steyn noted that a judge, in determining the issue of relevance, 'has to decide whether the evidence is capable of increasing or decreasing the existence of a fact in issue'. Lord Steyn also adopted the observation in Keane, *The Modern Law of Evidence*, 6th edn (2005) that the question of relevance 'is typically a matter of degree to be determined, for the most part by common sense and experience'. Relevance is therefore not a rule of law. There are no cases that set precedents for what will or will not be relevant in any particular situation.

1.3.1.2 Direct and circumstantial evidence

Relevant facts may tend to prove or disprove a fact in issue either directly or indirectly. Classic examples of direct evidence include:

(a) testimony by a witness about his or her own perception of a fact in issue, for example, that he saw the accused stab the deceased to prove directly that a stabbing took place;

(b) the production to the court of some object, the existence of which is in issue, for example, a lease to prove the existence of the lease;

Circumstantial evidence does not involve the immediate perception of a fact in issue, but is evidence from which the existence or non-existence of a fact in issue can be inferred. Examples include:

(a) evidence of opportunity, ie, evidence of presence at the time and place of the act in question;

(b) certain types of evidence of identity, eg, that DNA samples taken from the accused match those found at the scene of the crime; and

(c) evidence of facts providing a motive for a person to have done a particular act.

In none of these situations does the evidence prove the defendant's commission of the offence alone; they will only do so when combined with other evidence.

1.3.1.3   Sufficiency of relevance

It is sometimes said that a fact is 'not very relevant' or 'of marginal relevance' or that one fact is 'more' relevant than another. On the other hand, if relevance is determined by a strictly logical test of whether something makes a 'matter . . . more or less probable' (per Lord Simon in *DPP v Kilbourne* [1973] AC 729), then relevance is a quality a piece of evidence either does or does not have.

Consider an example in a civil case:

Arthur is being sued for negligence and breach of contract in respect of building works he has carried out for Amy. Amy wishes to show that he has been successfully sued in respect of a road accident in which he was alleged to have driven carelessly.

If we were to adopt a literal approach to Lord Simon's test we might say that the driving case is relevant to the building works case. Our argument would be that the previous case shows that Arthur has previously been less than careful. We would say that Arthur is therefore a relatively careless person and that this would show, to some small extent, that he may have been careless when carrying out work for Amy. By a very small degree it renders more probable the conclusion that Arthur was negligent on this occasion.

In fact, a court would probably be unwilling to accept this evidence and this would be on the grounds that it is not relevant. It would therefore appear that the courts have qualified the strictness of the test for relevance by introducing the concept of 'sufficiency of relevance', ie that evidence must display a suffcent degree of relevance before it will be admitted.

Consider the following examples:

- In *R v Whitehead* (1848) 3 Car & Kir 202, a doctor was tried for manslaughter of one patient. Evidence that the doctor had treated other patients skilfully was held to be irrelevant. Only evidence of the skill used in treating the patient who died was held to be relevant.

- In *Hart v Lancashire and Yorkshire Railway Co* (1869) 21 LT 261 the defendants were sued for negligently causing an accident. It was alleged that the accident had been caused by the changing of railway points. Evidence that the defendant company had altered its practice in changing railway points after an accident was held to be irrelevant.

- *Hollingham v Head* (1858) 27 LJ CP 241 was a breach of contract case in which the defendant sought to prove certain terms of the contract that would excuse him from liability. To prove that those terms were incorporated into the contract with the defendant, he sought to adduce evidence that the plaintiff had entered into contracts with other persons on those same terms. The Court of Common Pleas held that evidence of contracting behaviour with other parties was irrelevant.

- *R v Blastland* [1986] AC 41 concerned the murder and buggery of a boy. The defendant wished to adduce evidence that showed that, before the victim's body had been found, another person, M, had spoken about the murder of a boy. The House of Lords held that evidence that showed that M knew of the murder was irrelevant to the issue in the case, namely whether the defendant was the murderer.

- In *R v Kearley* [1992] 2 AC 228, the House of Lords considered the relevance of statements made by third parties. In that case the police had raided a flat and, while they were searching it, they received repeated calls to the flat by people asking for the defendant and requesting drugs. In so far as the callers made statements that the defendant sold drugs, these statements would be inadmissible as hearsay evidence. However, the fact that the callers *believed* drugs were sold at the premises would make it an exception to the hearsay rule. The House of Lords recognised this but, as in *R v Blastland*, said that the state of mind of the maker of the statement was not relevant in this case.

Do you agree with these judgments? Do you think that the evidence was excluded because it did not render the conclusion more or less likely or because it was not sufficiently effective in doing so?

In these cases, the courts often justified the conclusion that there was no relevance to the evidence by identifying or describing a test that is slightly different to that identified in *Kilbourne*. In *Hollingham v Head* the court said that the previous contracting behaviour was not relevant because it supported no *reasonable* inference as to how the parties had contracted. This stricter test may be compared with Stephen's use of the phrase 'renders probable' noted above. The evidence does not simply have to be relevant, but it has to be sufficiently relevant to permit the tribunal of fact reasonably to draw an inference as to the existence of the term in the contract. In cases such as *Blastland* and *Kearley* it is not difficult to formulate arguments on the relevance of the evidence as follows:

Blastland:

- M said that the boy had been murdered before this was generally known.
- Therefore M had some peculiar knowledge of the death of the boy.
- Therefore M may have murdered the boy.
- Therefore the defendant may not have murdered the boy.

Kearley:

- Callers requested drugs at the defendant's flat.
- Therefore callers expected to receive drugs at the defendant's flat.
- Therefore the callers may have received drugs at the defendant's flat in the past.
- Therefore the defendant may have been selling drugs from his flat in the past.
- Therefore the defendant may still have been selling drugs from his flat.

Neither of these logical arguments is without its flaws but both of them are sustainable. Nonetheless the House of Lords on both occasions concluded that the evidence represented by the first bullet point was not relevant to the conclusion in the final bullet point. This must be because the logic in each case is *insufficiently* strong or, in evidential terms, the evidence is *insufficiently* relevant.

The rationale for the restriction of evidence of marginal relevance is that it would increase the issues that have to be litigated, with the resulting increase in cost and complexity of the trial process (see *R v Patel* [1951] 2 All ER 29).

Thus, the test for relevance is not simply whether the evidence might tend to prove or disprove a fact in issue. Evidence must be capable of proving or disproving it to a sufficient degree. There is no clear statement of *how* relevant evidence has to be. In part this is because relevance is, as Lord Steyn affirmed in *R v Randall* [2004] 1 WLR 56, not an issue of law but a matter of logic, common sense or experience. This means that relevance cannot be assessed by reference to precedent but only on the basis of the facts of each one.

1.3.1.4   Conditional relevance

We have seen that some evidence does not have relevance on its own. Rather, its relevance depends on its relationship to other evidence in the case. As a result, the court may admit evidence conditionally (or '*de bene esse*') upon the proof of such facts as render that evidence relevant. If the other evidence is not adduced, the judge will have to direct the jury to ignore the evidence that was conditionally admitted (or a civil judge or magistrate would have to disregard it). In extreme cases (where it will not be possible for the tribunal of fact to ignore it) the trial may have to be discontinued.

1.3.1.5   Importance of argument

To recap, the relevance of evidence is a matter of logic or of common sense. Relevance is a filter upon evidence; no evidence that is deemed irrelevant will be admitted. The test is whether it will increase or decrease the probability of a fact in issue being proved (or possibly whether it is sufficiently likely to do so or likely to do so to a sufficient extent). This will be a matter of argument or explanation. In many cases the relevance of direct evidence or circumstantial evidence will be so clear that the argument does not need to be stated. Generally, however, some argument will have to be made at some point during the course of the trial. Given that relevance is not a matter of law but a matter of logic, it is not possible to lay down any rules about such arguments. However, the following points should be borne in mind:

(a) Evidence is not simply 'relevant'. Rather, it is relevant to something. Identifying to which facts in issue evidence is relevant is necessary to constructing convincing arguments.

(b) Evidence need not be directly relevant to a fact in issue. Instead, the evidence may be relevant to a fact which, in turn, is relevant to a fact in issue.

(c) It is not only necessary to identify *what* evidence is relevant to, it is necessary to identify *how* or *why* that evidence is relevant to that issue. This requires the drawing on logic or common sense to construct generalisations about human behaviour.

(d) Finally and most importantly, evidence is relevant if it is *capable* of leading to a particular conclusion, not if it *will* necessarily lead to that conclusion.

1.3.2   Weight

We have seen in the preceding section that the *relevance* of evidence concerns what conclusions the evidence is capable of proving or disproving. The *weight* of the evidence concerns the extent to which the evidence does prove or disprove the conclusion. While it is still possible to disagree about what something is capable of proving, this is not likely in most cases and, even where it is, the disagreement is usually based on logical analysis or 'common sense'. Weight is far more subjective. Among 12 jurors, some may be inclined to reach a particular conclusion from a particular piece of evidence, and others may not. There might be difficulty articulating why they do or do not do so. In so far as they can, they might draw on concepts such as 'belief' or 'feelings' or 'instinct'. However, they may also draw on 'logic' and 'common sense'.

1.3.2.1 Importance of weight at trial

Weight is generally a matter for the tribunal of fact. Once the tribunal of law decides to admit evidence, it is a matter for the tribunal of fact to decide how much weight to attach to it.

There are a number of ways in which weight will influence what a lawyer does:

(a) A lawyer may seek to *influence* the weight to be attached to evidence by the tribunal of fact. An advocate cross-examining a witness is generally seeking to reduce the weight to be attached to the evidence of that witness. An advocate must therefore be aware of how particular evidence or questions might affect the weight that might be attached to other evidence in the case.

(b) Lawyers do not only fight cases at trial. Many cases are settled before trial. Defendants in criminal proceedings plead guilty in the face of strong evidence and civil litigants compromise their claims in the face of strong opposition. Therefore lawyers must be able to *assess* the weight of evidence for both parties so that they can give clear advice about the prospects of success.

(c) Lawyers will often have to *argue* about the weight to be attached to evidence. This arises in a number of different ways:

   (i) In both civil and criminal cases advocates will make submissions or speeches to the tribunal of fact. In doing so they seek to persuade the tribunal to reach the desired conclusions by emphasising the weight of the favourable evidence, and attacking the apparent weight of the less favourable. This is only possible if the advocate understands the strengths and weaknesses of the evidence as presented.

   (ii) As will be seen in later chapters of this Manual (such as **Chapter 9** on character evidence and later in this chapter), some evidence is excluded in part owing to its lack of weight. To conduct arguments about the probative force of evidence, the weight of that evidence must be understood and explained.

   (iii) The failure to call sufficient evidence (ie, evidence of sufficient weight) on a particular issue or as a whole has procedural consequences. The most dramatic is the submission of no case to answer (see the *Criminal Litigation and Sentencing Manual*). Furthermore, as will be seen in **Chapter 2**, a party is only required to disprove an issue once the opposing party has called evidence of sufficient weight to put the matter in issue.

1.3.2.2 Challenges to the weight of evidence

A distinction may be drawn between evidence that is relevant to the facts in issue and evidence that is relevant to the credibility of a witness. For example, where an eye-witness to a criminal offence is shown to have poor eyesight and a grudge against the defendant these would be matters going, not to the facts in issue, but to the credibility of the witness. Evidence affecting credibility is also known as collateral evidence and includes:

(a) challenges to the truthfulness of particular witnesses;

(b) challenges to the ability of the particular witnesses to give an accurate account;

(c) challenges to the strength or validity of the arguments or generalisations made about the evidence;

(d) alternative explanations about the evidence;

Guidance on the weight to be attached to evidence is occasionally given in case law (eg, *R v Turnbull* [1977] QB 224 on identification, see **Chapter 15**) or by statute law (eg, Civil

Evidence Act 1995, **Chapter 11**) on what might influence the weight to be attached to the evidence.

1.3.2.3 Collateral evidence

Both civil and criminal courts seek to limit the extent to which collateral evidence will be admitted. While clearly of use to the tribunal of fact, to allow collateral facts to be admitted on all occasions could lead to a great deal of evidence being admitted that does not directly bear on the issues in the case. This concern about keeping cases focused on the factual disputes has led to a general rule of limitation concerning collateral evidence, namely the rule of finality. This will be examined in detail in **Chapter 6**.

1.3.3 Probative value and prejudicial effect

Probative value and prejudicial effect are often balanced one against the other. As will be seen below (**1.5.2**) in a criminal case where the probative value of evidence is outweighed by its prejudicial effect, that evidence may be excluded (ie, it will never go before the jury). What, then, do these two concepts mean?

Probative value is a combination of relevance (what something might prove) and weight (whether it does prove it). Probative value is essentially an evaluation of the extent to which an item of evidence proves a case in a rational way.

Prejudicial effect is an evaluation of the *risk* that the evidence in question will be used by the tribunal in an inappropriate way, for example, becoming distracted from deciding the case to the requisite standard of proof (such as beyond reasonable doubt) or taking into consideration irrelevant or immaterial matters. Prejudicial effect includes an overwillingness on the part of the tribunal of fact to convict (or make some other adverse finding) contrary either to the relevance or the weight that ought to be attached to the evidence before it.

In so far as these concepts are to be compared and balanced, no real guidance has been provided on when one outweighs the other. As will be seen at **1.5.2**, the balance is exercised as a judicial discretion and therefore rules about how the test ought to be applied have been avoided.

1.4 Proof of facts without evidence

One party or another must prove each and every fact in issue. This is usually done by adducing evidence at court. Most of this Manual concerns the restrictions on the admissibility of that evidence. However, before examining such matters, it should be recognised that there are rules of practice and procedure that allow the court to reach conclusions on some facts in issue (or even on some very small details of a case) without calling evidence. Two of these will be examined: formal admissions and judicial notice. This section will also deal with the question of the extent to which the tribunal of fact or law can rely upon its own personal knowledge to fill evidential gaps in the case.

1.4.1 Formal admissions

Both the civil and criminal courts have rules of procedure that allow the parties to reduce the number of facts in issue in a case that have to proved by evidence. These rules allow a party formally to admit a fact in issue or a fact that might assist in proving a fact in issue.

Formal admission of this sort determines that particular matter: it is proved and no further evidence will be admitted to prove or disprove it.

Formal admissions are often made to enable cases to be disposed of more quickly and efficiently where there is no serious dispute on the matters admitted. Occasionally, however, a party might see a tactical advantage in admitting a particular fact rather than running extra risks in requiring the other side to call damaging evidence to prove it.

Note the distinction between formal and informal admissions.

(a) A *formal* admission is the result of a rule of procedure. The effect of the formal admission is that the particular issue is finally resolved: the admission is conclusive of that fact. Evidence that proves or disproves that issue alone is not relevant and will not be admitted.

(b) In contrast a party may make an *informal* admission, for example, by admitting to another person (including a police officer in a police station) particular relevant facts. This latter type of admission, commonly known as a confession, is only evidence of that particular fact. It is still possible for the tribunal of fact to disregard it. For detailed analysis of the rules of evidence concerning informal admissions, see **Chapter 13**.

1.4.1.1   Criminal cases

Formal admissions are governed by the Criminal Justice Act 1967. Section 10(1) provides:

Subject to the provisions of this section, any fact of which oral evidence may be given . . . may be admitted . . ., and the admission by any party of any such fact under this section shall, as against that party, be conclusive evidence . . . of the fact admitted.

Section 10(2) sets out how such formal admissions are made. In essence the section provides that formal admissions:

- can be made by the defendant (or the prosecutor if a private person) himself (s 10(1));
- can be made at trial or before trial (s 10(2)(a));
- can be made orally in court. If made on behalf of the defendant they must be made by the defendant's solicitor or barrister (s 10(2)(b), (d));
- can be made in writing either in court or outside of court. The written formal admission must be signed either by the defendant (or prosecutor) in person or, if the party making the admission is a company, by an appropriate officer of that company (s 10(2)(c)).

A formal admission may be withdrawn with leave of the court (s 10(4)). *R v Kolton* [2000] Crim LR 761 suggests that this will only happen rarely. The court will expect evidence from both the party making the admission and their legal representatives that shows the admission to have been made by mistake or misunderstanding.

1.4.1.2   Civil cases

Statements of case may formally admit facts in issue. However the Civil Procedure Rules (CPR) also provide for situations in which parties may wish to admit facts once the statement of case process has ended. CPR, r 14.1, states:

(1) A party may admit the truth of the whole or any part of another party's case.

(2) He may do this by giving notice in writing (such as in a statement of case or by letter).

(3) The court may allow a party to amend or withdraw an admission.

Such admissions can be made voluntarily by a party, usually to save costs and time. Furthermore, there are various provisions of the CPR that allow one party to request or demand of another party admissions on particular points or issues such as the 'notice to admit facts' (r 32.18) and the rules relating to written requests or court orders to provide additional information (rr 18.1 and 26.5(3) respectively).

1.4.2 Judicial notice

In some cases a judge may take judicial notice of a fact. Where this happens there is no longer any requirement to prove the fact in question. The matter is accepted by the court without evidence being adduced.

1.4.2.1 Judicial notice without enquiry

There are some matters that are so obvious or so far beyond dispute that it would be a waste of court resources for them to have to be proved every time a case is litigated. In such situations it is possible for a judge to 'take notice' of the fact and to dispense with any requirement that it be proved.

Where a fact is so commonly agreed as to be beyond serious dispute, a judge may take notice of it without hearing any evidence. Famous examples include:

- *R v Luffe* (1807) 8 East 193 (two weeks is too short a period for human gestation).
- *Dennis v A J White and Co* [1916] 2 KB 1 (that the streets of London are full of traffic).
- *Nye v Niblett* [1918] 1 KB 23 (cats are ordinarily kept for domestic purposes).
- *Green v Bannister* [2003] EWCA Civ 1819 (the existence of a 'blind spot' that cannot be observed in a car's wing mirror).

Some matters are taken on judicial notice by virtue of legislation. For example:

- Acts of Parliament do not have to be proved by evidence. It is not necessary to prove an Act's content or that it was passed by both Houses of Parliament (Interpretation Act 1978, ss 3, 22(1)).
- European Community Treaties, the Official Journal of the Communities and decisions of the European Court are taken on judicial notice (European Communities Act 1972, s 3(2)).
- A judicial or official document that appears to have been signed and stamped by a judge of the Supreme Court shall be taken on judicial notice to have been signed or stamped by him (Evidence Act 1845, s 2).

1.4.2.2 Judicial notice after enquiry

Where a fact is not quite so notorious or widely known, it is still possible for judicial notice of that fact to be taken. However, in such cases, the judge will conduct an investigation. This will happen when the matter is one that is easily resolved by reference to sources of great reliability (such as ministerial certificates, learned works, etc).

This enquiry is not a trial on the matter. The rules of evidence do not regulate what the judge may consult and it is not possible to call evidence to rebut the judge's findings. Furthermore, the conclusions of the judge in the particular case constitute a binding legal precedent on the point.

This form of judicial notice will take place in relation to the following types of information:

(a) Facts of a general nature that can be readily demonstrated by reference to authoritative extraneous sources such as diaries, atlases, encyclopaedia, etc. In *McQuaker v Goddard* [1940] 1 KB 687, a judge resolved that a camel was a domestic creature by consulting books and hearing expert evidence.

(b) Facts of a political nature. Judicial notice can be taken of these following enquiry of political sources. In *R v Bottrill, ex p Kuechenmeister* [1947] 1 KB 41, judicial notice was taken of the fact that the country was still at war with Germany after examining a certificate from the Foreign Secretary to that effect.

(c) Customs and professional practices following consultation of suitably qualified experts in that field or area. For example, in *Heather v P-E Consulting Group Ltd* [1973] Ch 189 judicial notice was taken of accountancy practices.

1.4.3 Personal knowledge

To what extent can a judge take judicial notice of something within his own personal knowledge? May a juror or a magistrate do so? The general rule is that neither the judge or juror may apply their personal knowledge of facts (*Palmer v Crone* [1927] 1 KB 804) and jurors should be warned not to take steps to acquire such knowledge during trial (for example, by visiting the scene of an alleged crime) (*R v Oliver* [1996] 2 Cr App R 514). In *Bowman v DPP* [1991] RTR 263, the use of personal knowledge was distinguished from judicial notice. It was also stated that any personal knowledge ought to be identified so as to allow comment by parties to the case.

However, the courts have allowed judges to use their general knowledge and magistrates may use their local knowledge in reaching decisions (for example, *Paul v DPP* (1989) 90 Cr App R 173). In *Wetherhall v Harrison* [1976] QB 773, the Divisional Court drew a distinction between judges, on the one hand, and jurors and magistrates, on the other. They said that the former ought not to use their personal knowledge but the latter could. The rationale was in part to facilitate the sharing of their personal experiences and local knowledge.

There are no clear rules on the extent to which personal knowledge of matters not established by evidence can be used. In part, this is due to the difficulty of separating the personal knowledge of a judge from judicial notice in many cases. So far as personal knowledge of jurors and lay magistrates is concerned, as their deliberations take place away from the public gaze it will rarely be apparent that they have not resorted to personal knowledge or experience.

In *Hammington v Berker Sportcraft Ltd* [1980] ICR 248, it was stated that the tribunal of fact should only be able to rely on personal knowledge if the parties had been given the opportunity to deal with the evidence during the trial.

1.5 Admissibility

So far, we have considered how evidence proves cases. However, we shall see in the rest of this Manual that many of the rules of evidence are concerned with whether evidence that could prove a relevant fact will be admitted. The starting point is that any item of evidence if sufficiently relevant is admissible unless there is a specific rule that it is not admissible. In other words, the vast majority of the rules of evidence are about the *inadmissibility* of evidence: the rules of evidence are a series of filters keeping evidence out of court rather than a series of principles letting it in.

For example, an item of evidence might be relevant in a particular criminal case but because it is hearsay evidence it is *inadmissible*.

1.5.1 Preliminary facts

Some rules of evidence simply state that evidence of a particular class is admissible or inadmissible as a matter of law or logic. An example of this is hearsay evidence. It is not necessary to determine whether or not the evidence was obtained in any particular way. The court can determine the admissibility of this evidence without having to hear any evidence as to how it was obtained, for example.

However, some rules of evidence state that evidence will not be admissible if it was obtained in particular circumstances (such as the exclusion of confession evidence obtained by oppression under s 76(2)(a) of the Police and Criminal Evidence Act 1984) or that evidence will only be admitted if certain matters are proved (for example, a witness cannot give expert opinion evidence until he or she is accepted as an expert). Therefore, admissibility depends on proof of particular facts. The facts that lead to the admission or exclusion of evidence are not ordinary facts in the case. They do not go to prove the issues themselves. They are a necessary step for the admission of other evidence. They are called '*preliminary facts*' because they have to be proved before the evidence to which they relate can be admitted. The process of determining these factual disputes is called a 'trial within a trial' or a '*voir dire*'.

1.6 Exclusion

There is no general judicial discretion to *include* evidence that is rendered inadmissible by a rule of evidence (see *Sparks v R* [1964] AC 964, PC and *Myers v DPP* [1965] AC 1001, HL).

However, there is a power to exclude otherwise admissible evidence in both civil and criminal cases.

1.6.1 Civil cases

The general exclusionary discretion is contained in CPR, r 32.1, which provides:

 (1) *The court may control the evidence by giving directions as to—*
  (a) *the issues on which it requires evidence;*
  (b) *the nature of the evidence which it requires to decide those issues; and*
  (c) *the way in which the evidence is to be placed before the court.*
 (2) *The court may use its power under this rule to exclude evidence that would otherwise be admissible.*
 (3) *The court may limit cross examination.*

This power should be exercised to give effect to the 'overriding objective' (see *Civil Litigation Manual*).

1.6.2 Criminal cases

There are important discretions to exclude evidence in criminal cases. There are two types of discretion that must be considered:

- discretion to exclude prejudicial evidence;
- discretion to exclude evidence obtained unfairly.

1.6.2.1   Discretion to exclude prejudicial evidence

In *R v Sang* [1980] AC 402, it was held that a trial judge had a discretion to exclude evidence tendered by the prosecution if its prejudicial effect outweighed its probative value. This discretion was an aspect of the judge's duty to regulate the trial process. It is important to be clear about the two important concepts.

Probative value. This has already been referred to above (**1.3.3**). Probative value is the likely effect of the evidence on the minds of a tribunal of fact that is acting rationally.

Prejudicial effect. This is the use of evidence in an irrational way. The prejudicial effect could either be the capacity of the evidence to tempt the tribunal of fact to convict on inadequate evidence (for example, because the evidence causes the jury to be disgusted with the defendant's alleged conduct), or to reach false conclusions on the evidence in question (for example, evidence that the defendant has committed offences in the past might be given too much weight in deciding his or her guilt for the present offence).

The discretion to exclude prejudicial evidence is useful in situations in which evidence might prove more than one thing. On the one hand, it will have probative value but, on the other, it will have one or more prejudicial effects.

Note that this principle does not oblige the judge to exclude such evidence, it is a matter of judicial discretion. The judge would have to weigh up the probative value of the evidence and compare it to the risk of prejudice.

The exclusionary discretion only applies to evidence tendered by the prosecution not evidence tendered by a co-accused (*R v Lobban* [1995] 2 All ER 602). The discretion exists to protect the accused from wrongful conviction. Thus, where a defendant seeks to exclude evidence adduced by a co-defendant, the judge would not be able to act without potentially increasing the risk of the wrongful conviction of the co-defendant. Therefore, the judge has no discretion to intervene in such a situation.

This discretion applies to any evidence that may lead the jury to follow an impermissible line of reasoning. *R v Lobban*, for example, concerned prejudice deriving from the admissibility of statements made in confessions, whereas the common application is still likely to be for evidence of previous bad character by a defendant.

1.6.2.2   Discretion to exclude unfairly obtained evidence

There is a statutory discretion under s 78 of the Police and Criminal Evidence Act 1984 ('PACE 1984') to exclude evidence as follows:

> *(1)   In any proceedings the court may refuse to allow evidence on which the prosecution proposes to rely to be given if it appears to the court that, having regard to all the circumstances, including the circumstances in which the evidence was obtained, the admission of the evidence would have such an adverse effect on the fairness of the proceedings that the court ought not to admit it.*

The detail of this discretion will be considered in **Chapter 13**. However, some preliminary points are worth noting.

(a) There is some overlap between this and the common law power noted above and it seems that the courts are increasingly advised to exercise the common law discretion under the authority of s 78 (*Attorney-General's Reference (No 1 of 2003)* [2003] EWCA Crim 1286). However, the main difference is that the common law discretion is limited to balancing the probative value of the evidence and the irrational ways in which a jury may evaluate that same evidence. In exercising its discretion under s 78, both the probative value and the way in which the evidence might be misused may be taken into consideration, but s 78 goes much further. The court is required to consider the effect on the fairness of the proceedings and to examine how the evidence was obtained. This means that potentially probative evidence that would not lead to prejudicial thinking on the part of the jury could be excluded if it would have an adverse effect on the fairness of proceedings for other reasons. Examples of such exclusion include tricks played on the accused and/or his legal advisers with a view to obtaining confessions (*R v Mason* [1988] 1 WLR 139); denial of the accused's right to legal advice (*R v Samuel* [1988] QB 615) and the improper use of undercover surveillance (*R v Loosely* [2001] 4 All ER 897).

(b) This discretion only applies before evidence is admitted. Once it has been admitted, the defence will have to rely on the common law discretion to exclude the evidence that is preserved by s 82(3) (see *R v Sat-Bhambra* (1989) 88 Cr App R 55).

1.6.2.3 Appealing a refusal to exercise a discretion to exclude

As the exclusion of the evidence in both of these situations is discretionary, it will be very difficult to overturn a judge's decision on such a matter on appeal. In such situations the court will not intervene unless the discretion was exercised perversely by either refusing to exercise a discretion or erring in principle: see *R v Cook* [1959] 2 QB 340 and *R v Uniacke* [2003] EWCA Crim 30. However, the failure by a judge to apply (or show the application of) the concepts of relevance and weight or other matters relevant to the discretion in question may lead to his or her exercise of discretion being overturned.

1.6.2.4 Other discretions

Various statutes have created discretions to exclude particular classes of otherwise admissible evidence. For example, the Criminal Justice Act 2003 ('CJA 2003'), s 101(3) allows the judge to exclude evidence of the defendant's bad character. Section 126 of the same Act provides the court with a discretion to exclude hearsay evidence.

1.7 Adducing evidence

An advocate can only advance arguments based on evidence that has been presented to court by legitimate means. The three bases of putting evidence before the court ('adducing evidence') are:

- testimony;
- documentary evidence;
- real evidence.

1.7.1 Testimony

This is evidence that is given by a witness. Usually the witness will attend court, swear an oath or affirm, stand in the witness box and give his or her evidence orally. Each statement of fact by the witness is evidence of that fact. Having been given by a witness, the evidence becomes 'testimony'.

There are rules of procedure that allow parties to rely on written witness statements in place of calling the witness. In criminal cases this is, for example, by virtue of s 9 of the

Criminal Justice Act 1967 (see **4.3.1.1**). In civil cases, CPR, r 35(2) permits a witness's statement to stand as his or her evidence in chief unless the court orders otherwise (see **4.3.2**).

1.7.2   Documentary evidence

Documentary evidence is evidence that is contained in a document. In contrast to the exceptional practices set out in **1.7.1** above, the contents of the documents are not treated as the testimony of the maker.

Documentary evidence must be 'proved' by a witness. This means that the origin and relevance of the document must be established. It does not mean that the author of the document must in all cases be established. An anonymous note found lying at the scene of a crime might be admissible to prove certain facts without actually establishing who wrote it (although such proof may often be necessary to establish the relevance of the document to the proceedings in question). What proof in this sense requires is that it is established that the document has some bearing on the case in question.

The admissibility of documentary evidence is governed by the rules regulating hearsay in **Chapters 11 and 12**.

1.7.3   Real evidence

Real evidence derives evidential value from the physical nature of an object. The item is produced in court (as an exhibit) or the court will visit the item, for example, when the court goes to the place where an incident took place (often referred to as the *locus in quo*) to view it. The significance of real evidence is that the tribunal of fact can reach conclusions based on the physical characteristics of the item or place rather than any words narrated. Therefore, a book could be both documentary evidence (by reading and interpreting it) and real evidence (by examining its physical characteristics). Furthermore, a witness in court would be giving testimonial evidence but the witness would also be real evidence himself in so far as the tribunal of fact evaluates him as a person while giving evidence to determine, for example, whether they appear to be telling the truth or whether (where relevant to an issue in the case) they have particular physical characteristics.

1.8   Tribunals of fact and law

1.8.1   General rule: distinction between tribunal of law and tribunal of fact

The general rule is that the tribunal of fact in any given case will decide the facts and that the tribunal of law will decide the law. In the Crown Court, this distinction is clear to see. The judge, as tribunal of law, deals with legal issues and will often do so in the absence of the jury. The jury deals with factual issues and the judge is under a duty to remind jurors that it is their function, not his, to decide factual issues (*R v Jackson* [1992] Crim LR 214). The direction is a follows:

It is my job to tell you what the law is and how to apply it to the issues of fact that you have to decide and to remind you of the important evidence on these issues. As to the law, you must accept what I tell you. As to the facts, you alone are the judges. It is for you to decide what evidence you accept and what evidence you reject or of which you are unsure. If I appear to have a view of the evidence or of the facts with which you do not agree, reject my view. If I mention or emphasise evidence that you regard as unimportant, disregard that evidence. If I do not mention what you regard as important, follow your own view and take that evidence into account.

1.8.2 Exceptions to the general rule

The tribunal of law will decide factual matters in the following cases.

1.8.2.1 Summing up to the jury

The judge is not completely barred from considering and commenting upon the evidence in a case. As noted in **1.8.1**, it was said in *R v Jackson* [1992] Crim LR 214 that the judge should direct the jury on their respective functions. However, you will see by referring back to the detail of the direction that the judge could (indeed should) remind the jury of the evidence and review it. Clearly, this will involve some evaluation and consideration of the evidence. It is probably true to say, however, that the judge is not in fact *deciding* factual issues.

Where the judge strays too far in commenting or sifting the facts of a case, there may be a ground for appeal. See *Blackstone's Criminal Practice* or *Archbold*.

1.8.2.2 Preliminary facts and the *voir dire*

As noted at **1.5.1** some questions as to the admissibility of evidence must be resolved by the proof of particular facts ('preliminary facts'). As the admissibility issue is an issue of law, the tribunal of law must determine it and will therefore have to decide whether facts relevant to admissibility have been established. For example, by virtue of s 76(2)(a) of the Police and Criminal Evidence Act 1984, a confession is only admissible if the prosecution proves that it was not obtained by oppression. As the consequence of proving this issue is the admissibility or inadmissibility of a confession it must be resolved by the judge and it is therefore the judge who will have to decide whether there was in fact oppressive conduct that led to the confession.

Generally, the process of establishing the admissibility of evidence should be something of which the jury is unaware as their awareness of the evidence could lead to prejudice against a party if it was subsequently excluded. Therefore, the determination of admissibility is achieved by a 'trial within a trial' or *voir dire*, which takes place in the absence of the jury. As its name suggests, this is a trial to resolve a preliminary issue during or at the start of the main trial to which it relates. Both parties can call witnesses on the matter in question and make submissions. The judge will then decide the issue and give reasons for the conclusion reached. In this respect, the judge is clearly exercising the role of a fact-finder. For further details of the *voir dire* process, see the **Criminal Litigation Manual**, *Blackstone's Criminal Practice*, or *Archbold*.

Not all determinations of preliminary issues take place in the absence of the jury. Many matters (such as whether a witness is qualified to give expert evidence) are conducted in the presence of the jury. This is generally the case where the matter would not take long to resolve and where the jury would not be likely to reach prejudicial conclusions from knowing of the existence of the evidence.

1.8.2.3 Sufficiency of evidence

As will be seen in **Chapter 2**, one party or another must call sufficient evidence to put a matter in dispute at trial ('discharging the evidential burden'). This is a question of law that must be resolved by analysis of the evidence.

In criminal cases the prosecution have to prove that there is a case for the defence to meet on all of the elements of the offence. The test is that set out in *R v Galbraith* [1981] 1 WLR 1039, CA:

(1) *If there is no evidence that the crime alleged has been committed by the defendant, there is no difficulty — the judge will stop the case.*

(2) *The difficulty arises where there is some evidence but it is of a tenuous character, for example, because of inherent weakness or vagueness or because it is inconsistent with other evidence . . . where the judge concludes that the prosecution evidence, taken at its highest is such that a jury properly directed could not properly convict on it, it is his duty on a submission being made to stop the case.*

This is determined at the end of the prosecution case and in the absence of the jury. Furthermore, the jury should not be told that the submission took place (*R v Smith* (1987) 85 Cr App R 197, CA). For further details on submissions of no case to answer, see the **Criminal Litigation and Sentencing Manual**.

In civil cases with a jury, the judge has a discretion to rule that a party has no case to answer without that party calling evidence (*Young v Rank* [1950] 2 KB 510). Again, this discretion is exercised, the evidence having been evaluated that has been called by the other party.

1.8.2.4   The meaning of words

In *Brutus v Cozens* [1973] AC 854, HL, it was stated that, generally, the meaning of words is a question of fact for the jury to determine. However, Lord Reid envisaged that words might require judicial interpretation if it is shown that they are being used in an unusual way in the statute in question or if there is an issue as to whether the jury reached a perverse interpretation of the word in question.

1.8.2.5   Other special cases

There are particular situations in which the law has given the judge the responsibility of determining questions of fact. For example:

(a) In libel cases it is for the judge to determine whether a document is *capable* of bearing a defamatory meaning. It is then a matter for the jury whether the document does bear the defamatory meaning (*Nevill v Fine Arts and General Insurance Co Ltd* [1897] AC 68 and *Jameel v Wall Street Journal Europe* [2003] EWCA Civ 1694).

(b) Under the Perjury Act 1911, s 1(1), a person commits perjury if he or she makes a false statement that is 'material' to a proceeding. It is a question of law whether a statement was in fact material (s 11(6)).

(c) Questions of foreign law are questions of fact to be determined after consideration of evidence. However, in criminal cases under s 15 of the Administration of Justice Act 1920 and in civil cases under s 69(5) of the Supreme Court Act 1981 and s 68 of the County Courts Act 1984, it is for the judge rather than the jury to decide this issue.

1.8.3   When the same person or persons are tribunal of law and tribunal of fact

In a magistrates' court and in civil courts where a jury is not used, the functions of the tribunal of law and the tribunal of fact are exercised by the same person or persons. Therefore, a county court judge or a magistrate will determine both legal and factual issues. This often makes the process much simpler and more efficient but it also poses two practical difficulties for a lawyer:

(a) It can be difficult to determine the basis upon which a decision has been reached. In jury trials, while the same difficulty can arise, the appellate courts will consider the way in which the jury were directed by the judge to determine how they might have reached their decisions and to decide whether there is a valid basis of appeal due to an error. Where the same person or persons are both tribunal of law and tribunal of fact there is no practical requirement for the tribunal of law to tell the tribunal of fact how to apply legal concepts. Therefore, there is nothing upon which to base an appeal. To solve this difficulty, the rules of procedure for various courts set rules requiring the court to give reasons for its answers. Quite how much reasoning is required varies by the type of court. See the *Criminal Litigation and Sentencing Manual* and the *Civil Litigation Manual* for detail on the giving of reasons.

(b) The same person or persons will both determine that evidence is inadmissible and will, at some later point, decide the factual issues in the case. In jury trials, where evidence is to be excluded, the decision to exclude evidence will be made in the absence of the jury. If the application succeeds, the jury will not have heard the evidence and will not have to discount it. Where there is no jury this is not possible. Magistrates, for example, may decide to exclude a confession under the Police and Criminal Evidence Act 1984, s 78, and will then have to proceed on the assumption that they never heard it. Clearly, there is a risk that the bench will not be able to disregard that evidence completely. However, it does appear to be an implicit feature of these court processes that the magistrates, or the judge in a civil court, will be able to ignore evidence in such circumstances.

2

Burden and standard of proof

This chapter considers which parties bear the burden of proving or disproving facts in issue, and to what standard.

2.1 Introduction

2.1.1 Burden of Proof

The law of evidence recognises two principal burdens:

- the legal burden; and
- the evidential burden.

2.1.1.1 Legal burden

The legal burden is the obligation placed on a party to prove a fact in issue. Whether a party has discharged the legal burden is a question to be determined by the tribunal of fact at the end of the trial. The legal burden is also known as the 'persuasive burden' and the 'burden of proof'.

2.1.1.2 Evidential burden

The evidential burden is the obligation on a party to adduce sufficient evidence to raise a fact in issue, ie make a particular issue a live issue at trial. Whether a party has discharged the evidential burden is a question of law for the judge. The judge will assess whether the amount and quality of the evidence adduced by a party is sufficient to raise a fact in issue. If the court decides it is not sufficient, then the fact in issue has not been raised and the judge will not let the fact in issue go before the tribunal of fact.

A party bearing a legal burden also, by necessity, bears an evidential burden, since a party cannot discharge a legal burden without also discharging an evidential burden.

2.1.2 Standard of proof

The standard of proof is the degree of cogency or persuasiveness required of the evidence in order to discharge a burden of proof.

2.2 Criminal proceedings

The presumption of innocence in criminal law means that the legal burden in criminal cases properly lies with the prosecution, and that a high standard of proof is required.

2.2.1 Incidence of the legal burden

2.2.1.1 General rule

The general rule is that the prosecution, who bring criminal proceedings against a defendant, bear the legal burden to prove all elements of the offence(s) on which the defendant is tried. In *Woolmington v DPP* [1935] AC 462, HL, Lord Sankey LC stated:

> Throughout the web of the English criminal law one golden thread is always to be seen, that it is the duty of the prosecution to prove the prisoner's guilt subject to what I have already said as to the defence of insanity and subject also to any statutory exception... No matter what the charge or where the trial, the principle that the prosecution must prove the guilt of the prisoner is part of the common law of England and no attempt to whittle it down can be entertained.

2.2.1.2 Exceptions

Defence of insanity

The only common law exception to the general rule is the defence of insanity. Where this defence is raised, the legal burden of proving that the defendant was insane is borne by the defence: *M'Naghten's Case* (1843) 10 Cl & F 200, *R v Smith* (1910) 6 Cr App R 19, *Sodeman v The King* [1936] 2 All ER 1138. For all other common law defences only an evidential burden is borne by the defence (see **2.2.2** below).

Express statutory exceptions

A number of statutory defences purport to place a legal burden on the defence ('a reverse burden'). For example, the Homicide Act 1957, s 2 makes it a defence to murder for the defendant to prove that he was suffering from an abnormality of the mind, which substantially impaired his mental responsibility for acts or omissions in doing or being a party to the killing.

Implied statutory exceptions

Reverse burdens may also be implied by statute. The Magistrates' Courts Act 1980, s 101 provides:

> *Where the defendant... relies for his defence on any exception, exemption, proviso, excuse, or qualification, whether or not it accompanies the description of the offence or matter of complaint in the enactment creating the offence or on which the complaint is founded, the burden of proving the exception, exemption, proviso, excuse or qualification shall be on him: and this notwithstanding that the information or complaint contains an allegation negativing the exception, exemption, proviso, excuse, or qualification.*

For example, in a trial for the offence of driving a vehicle without a licence, it is for the driver to prove that he was the holder of a current driving licence (*John v Humphreys* [1955] 1 WLR 325).

On its wording, s 101 of the 1980 Act is confined to summary trials. The position in trials on indictment was set out in *R v Edwards* [1975] QB 27, where the Court of Appeal held that a similar principle existed at common law. The court stated that there was an exception to the fundamental rule that the prosecution must prove every element of the offence charged. The exception is limited to offences arising under enactments which prohibit the doing of an act save in specified circumstances, or by persons of specified classes or with specified qualifications, or with the licence or permission of specified authorities. Where the accused seeks to rely on such a proviso, exemption, excuse or qualification, he will bear a legal burden.

Whether a statutory provision impliedly places the legal burden of proof on the accused is a question of statutory construction for the court. Such questions are not always easy to resolve. It is an offence under s 155(1) of the Factories Act 1961 not to comply with s 29(1) of the Act which requires that any workplace 'shall, so far as is reasonably practicable be made and kept safe for any person working therein'. In *Nimmo v Alexander Cowan and Sons Ltd* [1968] AC 107, HL, the question arose as to whether the phrase 'so far as is reasonably practicable' placed a legal burden on the defendant or the plaintiff in the case of proceedings brought for a statutory tort under the Factories Act 1960, s 29(1). Their Lordships held, by a majority, that it was for the plaintiff to prove that the workplace was not safe and for the defendant to prove that it was not reasonably practicable for him to do more in keeping his workplace safe than he had done.

In *R v Hunt* [1987] AC 352, where the defendant was prosecuted for possession of morphine under the Misuse of Drugs Act 1971, s 5. The Misuse of Drugs Regulations 1973, Sch 1, para 3, provide that s 5 shall have no effect in relation to any preparation of morphine containing not more than 0.2% of morphine. The House of Lords held that on its proper construction the statute required the prosecution to prove that the substance in question contained more than 0.2% of morphine. Lord Griffiths gave the following general guidance:

. . . if the linguistic construction of the statute did not clearly indicate on whom the burden should lie the court should look to other considerations to determine the intention of Parliament, such as the mischief at which the Act was aimed and practical considerations affecting the burden of proof and, in particular, the ease or difficulty that the respective parties would encounter in discharging the burden.

Presumption of innocence

The European Convention on Human Rights (ECHR), Article 6(2) provides that:

Everyone charged with a criminal offence shall be presumed innocent until proved guilty according to law.

The compatibility of the imposition of a legal burden on the defence with the presumption of innocence under the ECHR, Article 6(2) has been the subject of a number of recent decisions by the House of Lords and the Court of Appeal. The leading authority is *Attorney-General's Reference (No 4 of 2002)* [2005] 1 AC 264, from which the following principles may be distilled:

(a) The defendant has a right to a fair trial.

(b) The presumption of innocence is an important, but not an absolute right and so derogations from the principle are permitted.

(c) The ECHR requires a balance to be struck between the rights of the individual and the wider interests of the community.

(d) There is an obligation on the state to justify any derogation from the presumption of innocence.

(e) For a reverse burden of proof to be acceptable there must be a compelling reason why it is fair and reasonable to deny the accused person the protection normally guaranteed to everyone by the presumption of innocence.

(f) In determining whether the imposition of a reverse burden is justified, the courts should have regard to:

    (i)   the seriousness of the punishment which may flow from conviction;

    (ii) the extent and nature of the factual matters required to be proved by the accused, and their importance relative to the matters required to be proved by the prosecution;

    (iii) the extent to which the burden on the accused relates to facts which, if they exist, are readily provable by him as matters within his own knowledge or to which he has ready access;

    (iv) the particular social problem or mischief which the measure has been enacted to address.

(g) Where an infringement of Article 6(2) cannot be justified, the courts should where possible, 'read down' the offending provision under the Human Rights Act 1998, s 3 so that it imposes only an evidential burden on the defendant. The interpretative obligation under s 3 of the 1998 Act is a strong one; it places a duty on the court to strive to find a possible interpretation compatible with the ECHR. It applies even if there is no ambiguity in the language of the provision and it will sometimes be necessary to adopt an interpretation which linguistically may appear strained.

(h) Where it is not possible to read down the provision, the court should make a declaration of incompatibility. However, this is a measure of last resort.

The following is a brief survey of whether burdens imposed by statute are legal or evidential, in the light of decisions so far:

Statutes imposing a legal burden

(a) Road Traffic Act 1988, s 5(2): where the accused is charged with an offence of being in charge of a motor vehicle on a road or other public place under s 5(1)(b) of the Act, the statutory defence provided by s 5(2), that there was no likelihood of him driving (*Attorney-General's Reference (No 4 of 2002)* [2005] 1 AC 264).

(b) Criminal Justice Act 1988, s 139(4): where the accused is charged with possession of a bladed article in a public place under s 139, the defence provided by s 139(4), that he had a good reason or lawful authority for being in possession of the article (*L v DPP* [2003] QB 137; *R v Matthews* [2004] QB 690).

(c) Trademarks Act 1994, s 95(2): where the accused is charged with unauthorised use of a trademark under s 92, the statutory defence provided by s 95(2), that he believed on reasonable grounds that his use of a sign was not infringing trademark (*R v Johnston* [2003] 1 WLR 1736, HL).

(d) Insolvency Act 1986, s 352: where the accused is bankrupt and is charged under s 353(1) with failing to inform the official receiver that property belonging to his estate has been disposed, the statutory defence contained in s 352, that he had no intention to defraud or conceal the state of his affairs (*Attorney-General's Reference (No 1 of 2004)* [2004] 1 WLR 2111).

(e) Protection From Eviction Act 1977, s 1(2): where a defendant landlord is charged with unlawful eviction, the statutory defence provided by s 1(2), that he believed the occupier had ceased to reside at the premises (*Attorney-General's Reference (No 1 of 2004)* [2004] 1 WLR 2111).

(f) Homicide Act 1957, s 4(1): where a defendant is charged with murder, the defence provided by s 4(1) of the Homicide Act 1957, that he survived a suicide pact (*Attorney-General's reference (No 1 of 2004)* [2004] 1 WLR 2111).

(g) Criminal Justice and Public Order Act 1994, s 51(7): where a defendant charged with witness intimidation under s 51(1), the defence of proving that this was not done with the relevant intention (*Attorney-General's Reference (No 1 of 2004)* [2004] 1 WLR 2111).

Statutes imposing an evidential burden

(a) Misuse of Drugs Act 1971, s 5(3): where a defendant is charged with possession of drugs with intent to supply under s 5(3), the statutory defence under s 28(2) and (3), that he neither believed, suspected nor had reason to suspect that the substance he had was a controlled drug (*R v Lambert* [2001] 3 All ER 547).

(b) Terrorism Act 2000, s 11(1): where a defendant is charged with membership of a proscribed organisation under s 11(1), the statutory defence provided by s 11(2), that the organisation was not proscribed on the last time he was or professed to be a member and he had not taken part in any of its activities whilst it was proscribed (*Attorney-General's Reference (No 4 of 2002)* [2005] 1 AC 264).

(c) Insolvency Act 1986, s 352: where a bankrupt defendant is charged under s 353(2) with making a gift, transfer or creating a charge on property before the expiry of a five-year period from the start of the bankruptcy, the statutory defence contained in s 352 (*Attorney-General's Reference (No 1 of 2004)* [2004] 1 WLR 2111).

2.2.2 Incidence of the evidential burden

The general rule is that a party bearing the legal burden on a particular issue usually bears the evidential burden. However, certain common law and statutory criminal defences place only an evidential burden on the accused. Once the accused has adduced sufficient evidence to discharge the evidential burden, the legal burden of disproving the defence is on the prosecution.

Examples of such common law defences include:

- self-defence (*R v Lobell* [1957] 1 QB 547, CCA);
- duress (*R v Gill* (1963) 47 Cr App R 166, CCA);
- non-insane automatism (*Bratty v Attorney-General for Northern Ireland* [1963] AC 386, HL);
- intoxication (*R v Foote* [1964] Crim L R 405);
- provocation (*Mancini v DPP* [1942] AC 1, HL).

Examples of such statutory defences include:

- Criminal Law Act 1967, s 3, which permits the use of reasonable force to prevent the commission of a crime or effect or assist in the lawful arrest of offenders, suspected offenders or those lawfully at large;
- Sexual Offences Act 2003, s 75 (see 3.5.6);
- various terrorism offences: see Terrorism Act 2000, ss 118(1)–(5), 12(4), 39(5)(a), 54, 57, 77 and Northern Ireland (Emergency Provisions) Act 1996, ss 13, 32 and 33 (possession of information offences).

Even where such defences are not specifically raised, if there is sufficient evidence of such a defence, whether adduced by the prosecution or the defence, then the judge must leave the issue to the jury (*Palmer v The Queen* [1971] AC 814) and legal burden to disprove the defence will be on the prosecution (*Bullard v R* [1957] AC 635, PC). This remains the case even if the defence in question has been expressly disclaimed by the defence

(*R v Kachikwu* (1968) 52 Cr App R 538, CA) or is inconsistent with the defence which the accused has in fact raised (*R v Newell* [1989] Crim LR 906).

2.2.3   Standard of proof

2.2.3.1   Legal burden

Borne by the prosecution

The standard of proof to which the prosecution must prove its case has been variously described as 'beyond reasonable doubt' (*Woolmington v DPP* [1935] AC 462, HL), and 'making the jury sure' (*R v Kritz* [1950] 1 KB 82). It was described in *Miller v Minister of Pensions* [1947] 2 All ER 372 per Denning J in the following terms:

It need not reach certainty, but it must carry a high degree of probability. Proof beyond reasonable doubt does not mean proof beyond the shadow of doubt. The law would fail to protect the community if it admitted fanciful possibilities to deflect the course of justice. If the evidence is so strong against a man as to leave only a remote possibility in his favour which can be dismissed with the sentence 'of course it is possible, but not in the least probable', the case is proved beyond reasonable doubt, but nothing short of that will suffice.

Thus, if there is a reasonable doubt about the defendant's guilt, the standard of proof has not been met and the defendant must be acquitted. Although judges are not required slavishly to follow a formula when directing juries on the standard of proof, they must make it clear that the prosecution must prove its case beyond reasonable doubt, or to the extent that the jury is sure. The Judicial Studies Board has provided the following specimen direction to assist judges:

How does the prosecution succeed in proving the defendant's guilt? The answer is—by making you sure of it. Nothing less than that will do. If after considering all the evidence you are sure that the defendant is guilty, you must return a verdict of 'Guilty'. If you are not sure, your verdict must be 'Not Guilty'. (See www.jsboard.co.uk, specimen direction 2).

Borne by the defence

Where the defence bear the legal burden in relation to a fact in issue in a criminal trial the standard of proof is the balance of probabilities (*R v Carr-Briant* [1943] KB 607).

2.2.3.2   Evidential burden

Where either the prosecution or the defence bear the legal burden on an issue, the evidential burden may be described as the obligation to adduce such evidence as would be sufficient, if believed and left uncontradicted, to justify as a possibility a finding by the jury in their favour (*Jayasena v R* [1970] AC 618).

Where the defendant bears the evidential burden alone, he must adduce such evidence as would, if believed and left uncontradicted, induce a reasonable doubt in the mind of the jury as to whether his version might not be true (*Bratty v Attorney-General for Northern Ireland* [1963] AC 386, HL).

2.2.4   Preliminary matters in criminal cases and the burden and standard of proof

The admissibility of certain types of evidence, such as a confession alleged to have been obtained by oppression, falls to be dealt with as preliminary matters in criminal proceedings. Generally, the party seeking to have such evidence admitted will have the burden of proving its admissibility in accordance with the standard imposed by the relevant rules of evidence (*R v Sartori* [1961] Crim LR 397; *R v Yacoob* (1981) 72 Cr App R 313). Thus, where the prosecution seek to adduce evidence of a confession challenged on the basis that it was obtained by oppression, then PACE 1984, s 76(2) requires the prosecution to prove beyond reasonable doubt that it was not so obtained. Where a defendant seeks to adduce the confession of a co-defendant, and oppression is raised, then the defendant is required by the Police and Criminal Evidence Act 1984, s 76A to disprove oppression on the balance of probabilities. See **Chapter 13**.

2.3   Civil proceedings

2.3.1   Incidence of the legal burden

2.3.1.1   Common law

In civil cases, at common law, the general rule is that the legal burden on any fact in issue is borne by the party asserting and not denying: he who asserts must prove not he who denies (*Joseph Constantine Steamship Line Ltd v Imperial Smelting Corporation Ltd* [1942] AC 154; *Re H (Minors) (Sexual Abuse: Standard of Proof)* [1996] AC 563, HL). Accordingly, the claimant usually bears the legal burden (and by necessity an evidential burden) of proving all the elements of his claim. Similarly, the defendant bears the legal (and evidential) burden of proving any defence and /or counter claim against the claimant. This general rule includes negative assertions: 'if the assertion of a negative is an essential part of the plaintiff's case, the proof of the assertion still rests upon the plaintiff' (per Bowen LJ, *Abrath v North Eastern Railway Company* (1883) 11 QBD 440, CA, at 457). So, for example, where a builder alleges breach of contract because he has not been paid for building works, he must prove not only that there was a contract for building works which were performed (positive assertions), but also that he has not been paid (a negative assertion).

The incidence of the legal burden is usually apparent from the statements of case *(BHP Billiton Petroleum Ltd v Dalmine SpA* [2003] BLR 271). However, sometimes a party may try to avoid a legal burden by drafting his statement of case in such a way as to make assertions of his own look like assertions of his opponent. Consider *Soward v Leggatt* (1856) 7 C & P 613. A landlord claimed that his tenant 'did not repair' the premises. The tenant claimed that he 'did well and sufficiently repair'. It was held that the landlord could as easily have pleaded that the defendant tenant 'allowed the house to become dilapidated'. The reality was that the landlord was alleging breach of covenant and, therefore, it was for him to prove it, not for the defendant to prove that there had been no breach.

However, difficulties arise when it is unclear whether a particular fact in issue is properly classified as a part of the claimant's cause in action or the defendant's defence. Where this situation arises, it is for the court to determine who bears the burden of proof. In such cases the courts will determine the issue by reference to policy considerations and, in particular, the ease or difficulty that the respective parties would encounter in discharging the burden. Thus, in *Joseph Constantine Steamship Line Ltd v Imperial Smelting Corporation Ltd* [1942] AC 154, HL, the plaintiffs were charterers of a ship who claimed damages from the owners for failure to load. However, the ship had exploded before it could be loaded and the defendant owners relied on the defence of frustration. The defence of frustration is not available where the frustrating event was the fault of the party seeking to rely on it. Therefore, the charterers argued that the defendant owners could not rely on frustration unless they proved that the explosion was not their fault. The House of Lords held that once the defence of frustration was raised, the burden of proving that the frustration was due to the negligence of the defendant owners was on the charterers.

In bailment cases it has been held that once the bailor has proved bailment, the bailee has the burden of proving that the goods were lost or damaged without fault on his or her part (*Coldman v Hill* [1919] 1 KB 443; *Levison v Patent Steam Carpet Cleaning Ltd* [1978] QB 69). The rationale for this is that it would be too onerous for the bailor to prove fault on the part of the bailee.

2.3.1.2 Agreement

In contract cases, which party bears the legal burden on a certain issue may be fixed by the express terms of the contract. Where the terms of the contract are silent as to who bears the burden on a particular issue, it is a matter of construction for the courts. In *Munro, Brice and Co v War Risks Association Ltd* [1918] 2 KB 78, a marine insurance policy against loss by perils of the sea contained an exemption clause excepting loss by capture, seizure and consequences of hostilities. The insured ship left port and was never heard of again. It was held that it was for the claimant to show the loss was by the perils of the sea and for the defendant underwriters to show that the loss came within an exception, ie was by capture, seizure, or consequences of hostilities.

However, contrast *Munro, Brice and Co* with *Hurst v Evans* [1917] 1 KB 352 which concerned a policy of insurance against loss of or damage to jewellery unless caused by breakage or by theft or dishonesty committed by any servant of the assured. A robbery occurred during which jewellery was taken and damaged. The plaintiff claimed under the policy of insurance and, when this was refused, brought an action for damages. The defendant insurance company relied on the exemption clause arguing that the loss was caused by the theft or dishonesty of one of the plaintiff's employees. It was held that the plaintiff bore the legal burden of proving that they were not stolen or damaged by his servants or agents. This decision was clearly influenced by policy considerations, the judge stating that to hold that the burden was on the defendant, on the facts of the case, would 'produce absurd results'.

Where the claimant relies upon a proviso to an exemption clause, the courts have held that it is for the claimant to prove that the facts of the case bring it within proviso. In *The Glendarroch* [1894] P 226, the plaintiffs sued for damage to goods shipped on *The Glendarroch*. The defendant shippers claimed that the case fell within an exemption clause excepting damage caused by perils of the sea. The plaintiffs argued that the loss did not come within the exemption clause as it was due to the fault of negligent navigation on the part of the defendant shippers. The Court of Appeal held that it was for the plaintiffs to prove the contract and non-delivery; for the defendants to bring the case within the exemption clause (perils of the sea); but for the plaintiffs to bring the case within the proviso to the exemption clause (defendants' negligence).

2.3.1.3 Statute

The incidence of the legal burden may be fixed by statute. For example, if, in proceedings referred to in the Consumer Credit Act 1974, s 139(1), the debtor or any surety alleges that the credit bargain is extortionate within the meaning of ss 137 and 138 of the Act, then, under s 171(1), it is for the creditor to prove the contrary.

2.3.2 Standard of proof

In *Miller v Minister of Pensions* [1947] 2 All ER 372, Denning J described the standard of proof in civil cases as follows:

If the evidence is such that the tribunal can say; 'We think it more probable than not', the burden is discharged, but, if the probabilities are equal, it is not.

There are, however, some exceptional cases where the criminal standard of proof is required:

(a) Contempt of court (*Re Bramblevale Ltd* [1970] Ch 128, CA; *Dean v Dean* [1987] 1 FLR 517, CA)

(b) Where a person's livelihood is at stake (*R v Milk Marketing Board, ex p Austin The Times*, 21 March 1983)

(c) Allegations of misconduct amounting to a criminal offence in disciplinary hearings (*Re A Solicitor* [1993] QB 69, DC; *R (on the application of S) v Governing Body of YP School* [2003] EWCA Civ 1306)

(d) Where statute requires the criminal standard of proof (*Judd v Minister of Pensions and National Insurance* [1966] 2 QB 580).

In civil cases where allegations are made of misconduct so serious that it could form the basis of a criminal prosecution, a higher degree of probability may be required, although the standard remains the balance of probabilities, a higher degree of probability may be required. The more serious the allegation, the less likely it is to be true and so the stronger should be the evidence before the court concludes that it is proved on the balance of probabilities (*Re H (Minors) (Sexual Abuse: Standard of Proof)* [1996] AC 563, HL; *Hornal v Neuberger Products Ltd* [1957] 1 QB 247; *R v Home Secretary, ex p Khawaja* [1984] AC 74, HL).

Presumptions

3.1 Introduction

There are two types of presumption:

- presumptions with proof of basic facts; and
- presumptions without proof of basic facts

3.2 Presumptions with proof of basic facts

This type of presumption is an evidential device that permits a court to conclude the existence of a fact ('the presumed fact') on the proof of a preliminary fact ('the basic fact'). For example, where it is proved that two persons went through a marriage ceremony with the intention to marry ('the basic fact'), the court may presume that all the formalities required for a valid marriage were complied with ('the presumed fact'). This type of presumption operates as an evidential shortcut enabling a party to prove a fact in issue without having to call any further evidence on the point.

Presumptions with proof of basic facts may be sub-divided into three categories:

(a) irrebuttable presumptions of law;

(b) rebuttable presumptions of law; and

(c) presumptions of fact.

3.3 Irrebuttable presumptions of law

Definition: Upon proof of the preliminary fact, the court *must* conclude the existence of the presumed fact, and no evidence may be adduced to the contrary. Thus, the presumption is said to be irrebuttable. In practice, irrebuttable presumptions are simply rules of substantive law. The following examples may be given:

3.3.1 Civil Evidence Act 1968, s 13(1)

Section 13(1) of the Civil Evidence Act 1968 provides:

In an action for libel or slander in which the question whether a person did or did not commit a criminal offence is relevant to an issue arising in the action, proof that at the time when that issue falls to be determined, that person stands convicted of that offence shall be conclusive evidence that he committed that offence; and his conviction thereof shall be admissible in evidence accordingly.

3.3.2   Children and Young Persons Act 1933, s 50

Section 50 of the Children and Young Persons Act 1933 provides:

It shall be conclusively presumed that no child under the age of 10 years can be guilty of an offence.

3.3.3   Sexual Offences Act 2003, s 76

Section 76 of the Sexual Offences Act 2003 provides:

(1)   If in proceedings for an offence to which this section applies it is proved that the defendant did the relevant act and that any of the circumstances specified in subsection (2) existed, it is to be conclusively presumed—

(a)   that the complainant did not consent to the relevant act, and

(b)   that the defendant did not believe that the complainant consented to the relevant act.

(2)   The circumstances are that—

(a)   the defendant intentionally deceived the complainant as to the nature or purpose of the relevant act;

(b)   the defendant intentionally induced the complainant to consent to the relevant act by impersonating a person known personally to the complainant.

Section 76 of the Sexual Offences Act 2003 applies to offences under ss 1 to 4 of that Act. Commentators have argued that this provision might contravene the ECHR, Article 6(2) as it deprives the defendant of the opportunity to put forward a defence, namely that the victim was aware of the deception but consented nonetheless. However, the point has yet to be tested on appeal.

3.4   Rebuttable presumptions of law

Definition: Upon proof of the preliminary fact the court must conclude the existence of the presumed fact, unless sufficient evidence to the contrary is adduced. For this reason, the presumption is said to be rebuttable.

3.4.1   Civil proceedings

In civil proceedings rebuttable presumptions of law may be further divided into:

(a) *Evidential presumptions.* An evidential presumption places only an evidential burden on the party against whom it operates. Thus, in order to rebut the existence of the presumed fact, the party disputing it need only adduce some evidence on the point.

(b) *Persuasive presumptions.* A persuasive presumption places a persuasive, or legal, burden on the party against whom it operates. Thus, in order to rebut the existence of the presumed fact, the party disputing it must disprove it.

3.4.2   Criminal proceedings

In criminal proceedings the position is slightly different. As noted in **Chapter 2**, the prosecution bear the burden of proving the accused's guilt. As a result, where the prosecution rely on a common law rebuttable presumption, only an evidential burden can be placed on the defendant. Similarly, where the defendant relies upon a common law rebuttable presumption, a legal burden must be placed on the prosecution. Statutory presumptions, on the other hand, may operate so as to place a legal burden on the accused.

The prosecution are further restricted in the use of presumptions in that they cannot rely on a presumption to prove facts which are central to an offence (*Dillon v R* [1982] AC 484, PC).

3.4.3 Presumption of marriage

There are two presumptions of marriage:

3.4.3.1 Formal validity

Where it is proved that the parties to the marriage went through a marriage ceremony with the intention to marry, it is presumed that the marriage complied with the formalities required for a valid marriage (*Piers v Piers* (1849) 2 HL Cas 331; *Mahadervan v Mahadervan* [1964] P 233). There is little authority on the point but it is thought that this presumption applies to both civil and criminal proceedings. In civil proceedings it operates as a persuasive presumption.

3.4.3.2 Essential validity

Where it is proved that a formally valid marriage ceremony was conducted, it is presumed that the parties to the marriage had the requisite capacity and gave their consent. Again, it is thought that this presumption applies to both civil and criminal proceedings. In so far as it applies to civil proceedings it is probably a persuasive presumption although the authorities are not entirely clear on the point (*Re Peete* [1952] 2 All ER 599 and *Taylor v Taylor* [1967] P 25).

3.4.4 Presumption of legitimacy

Where paternity is in dispute, and it is proved that a child was either conceived whilst the mother was married (*Maturin v Attorney-General* [1938] 2 All ER 214) or born to her whilst she was lawfully married (*The Poulett Peerage Case* [1903] AC 395), it is presumed that the child is the legitimate offspring of the parties to the marriage. This presumption applies to civil proceedings only. It is expressly made a persuasive presumption by the Family Law Reform Act 1969, s 26.

3.4.5 Presumptions of death

3.4.5.1 Common law

In *Chard v Chard* [1956] P 259 it was held that the court must presume a person's death where it is proved that:

(a) there is no acceptable affirmative evidence that the person was alive during a seven-year period;

(b) there are several people who would be expected to have heard from the person during that seven-year period;

(c) those people have not heard from that person; and

(d) all due enquiries that are appropriate have been made in respect of the person.

There is conflicting authority as to the date on which the fact of the deceased's death may be presumed. Some authorities suggest that the presumption allows the court to conclude that the deceased died at the end of the seven-year period (*Re Phené's Trusts* (1870) LR 5 Ch App 139; *Chipchase v Chipchase* [1939] P 391). Other authority suggests that death can only be presumed to have occurred on the date of trial (*Lal Chand Marwari v Manhant Ramrup Gir* (1925) 42 TLR 159, PC).

This presumption applies in both civil and criminal proceedings. In civil proceedings it is probably only an evidential presumption (*Prudential Assurance v Edmonds* (1877) 2 App Cas 487, HL). This is also implicit from the first of the basic facts identified in *Chard v Chard*.

3.4.5.2   Matrimonial Causes Act 1973, s 19(3)

Section 19(3) of the Matrimonial Causes Act 1973 provides:

. . . the fact that for a period of seven years or more the other party to the marriage has been continually absent from the petitioner and the petitioner has no reason to believe that the other party has been living within that time shall be evidence that the other party is dead until the contrary is proved.

This is a persuasive presumption and applies in matrimonial proceedings only.

3.4.5.3   Law of Property Act 1925, s 184

Section 184 of the Law of Property Act 1925 provides:

In all cases where . . . two or more persons have died in circumstances rendering it uncertain which of them survived the other or others, such deaths shall (subject to any order of the court) . . . be presumed to have occurred in order of seniority, and accordingly the younger shall be deemed to have survived the elder.

This is a persuasive presumption that applies in any civil proceedings concerning claims to property. An example of its application may be found in *Hickman v Peacey* [1945] AC 304 where the residents of a house were all killed from a bomb explosion.

3.4.6   Sexual Offences Act 2003, s 75

Section 75 of the Sexual Offences Act 2003 provides:

(1)   If in proceedings for an offence to which this section applies it is proved—
  (a)   that the defendant did the relevant act,
  (b)   that any of the circumstances specified in subsection (2) existed, and
  (c)   that the defendant knew that those circumstances existed,

  the complainant is to be taken not to have consented to the relevant act unless sufficient evidence is adduced to raise an issue as to whether he consented, and the defendant is to be taken not to have reasonably believed that the complainant consented unless sufficient evidence is adduced to raise an issue as to whether he reasonably believed it.

The circumstances set out in s 75(2) include:

- the use of violence against the complainant at, or immediately before, the commission of the relevant act (s 75(2)(a));

- the complainant's inability to communicate consent to the defendant owing to his or her physical disability (s 75(2)(e)); and

- the administration of a substance to the complainant which was capable of causing or enabling the complainant to be stupefied or overpowered at the time of the relevant act (s 75(2)(f)).

The wording of the provision ('*unless sufficient evidence is produced*') and the fact that the burden is borne by the defence clearly make this an evidential presumption. As a result, it is thought that this provision is compatible with the Human Rights Act 1998. This provision only applies to offences under ss 1 to 4 of the 2003 Act.

3.4.7   Presumption of official regularity

Where it is proved that a person has acted in a judicial, official or public capacity, it will be presumed that the person had been properly appointed and that the act complied with all necessary formalities. This presumption applies in both civil and criminal proceedings. In civil proceedings it operates as a persuasive presumption. Two examples may be given. In *R v Cresswell* (1873) 1 QBD 446, it was proved that a building had been used for marriage ceremonies, and so it was presumed that the building had been duly consecrated. In *R v Roberts* (1878) 14 Cox CC 101, CCR, it was proved that a person had acted as a deputy county court judge, and so it was presumed that that person had been properly appointed.

3.5   Presumptions of fact

Definition: Upon proof of the preliminary fact, the court may conclude the existence of the presumed fact. Presumptions of fact are no more than commonly occurring examples of inferences that may be drawn on the basis of circumstantial evidence.

There are two key differences between presumptions of law and presumptions of fact. First of all, a presumption of fact does not require the court to conclude the existence of the presumed fact; rather, it simply permits it to do so. Secondly, a presumption of fact has no effect on the burden of proof; instead, it places a 'tactical' burden on the party against whom it operates. In other words, because the presumption permits the tribunal of fact to find in favour of one party on a certain issue, it places a tactical obligation on the other party to call evidence on that point, because if it fails to do so, there is a danger that it may lose on that issue.

3.5.1   Presumption of intention

Section 8 of the Criminal Justice Act 1967 provides:

A court or jury, in determining whether a person has committed an offence,—

(a) *shall not be bound in law to infer that he intended or foresaw a result of his actions by reason only of its being a natural and probable consequence of those actions; but*

(b) *shall decide whether he did intend or foresee that result by reference to all the evidence, drawing such inferences from the evidence as appear proper in the circumstances.*

The effect of this provision is that the tribunal of fact is not obliged to conclude that a defendant intended or foresaw the natural and probable consequence of his or her actions, but is permitted to infer that the defendant did so in the light of all the evidence. This presumption obviously only applies in criminal proceedings.

3.5.2 Presumption of guilty knowledge

This presumption applies where a person is charged with theft, handling stolen goods or an offence which has theft as an ingredient, such as burglary. Where evidence is given that the accused was found in possession of the property soon after it had been stolen, and he either offered no explanation as to how it came to be in his possession, or offered an explanation that the tribunal of fact finds to be untrue, then the tribunal of fact may infer that the accused was either the thief, a handler of stolen goods or the burglar. This presumption is more commonly known by practitioners as the doctrine of recent possession.

3.5.3 Presumption of continuance of life

Where a person is proved to have been alive on a particular date, they may be presumed to have been alive on a subsequent date. Whether the presumption will be made in a particular case depends on factors such as the age and health of the person and the circumstances in which he or she was last seen. Clearly, the longer it is since the person was seen, the less likely it is that the tribunal of fact will reach the conclusion that he or she is still alive. This presumption applies in both civil and criminal proceedings.

3.6 *Res ipsa loquitur*

In *Scott v London and St Katherine Docks Co* (1865) 3 Hurl & C 596, it was held that, per Erle CJ:

. . . where the thing is shown to be under the management of the defendant or his servants, and the accident is such as in the ordinary course of things does not happen if those who have management use proper care, it affords reasonable evidence, in the absence of explanation by the defendants, that the accident arose from want of care.

Thus, in a claim for negligence, where it is shown that:

(a) something is under the control of the defendant;

(b) that thing caused an accident; and

(c) the accident would not have happened if the thing had been properly managed,

then it may be presumed that the accident arose due to the negligence of the defendant. There is contradictory authority as to whether the doctrine of *res ipsa loquitur* is properly classified as a presumption of fact (see, for example, *Ng Chun Pui v Lee Chuen Tat* [1988] RTR 298, PC), a persuasive presumption (see, for example, *Woods v Duncan* [1946] AC 401) or an evidential presumption (see, for example, *The Kite* [1933] P 154). It has been argued that this presumption defies classification; the strength of the inference of negligence that may be drawn in a particular case will differ depending on the facts, and so the presumption can operate so as to place either a tactical, evidential or legal burden on the other party.

3.7 Conflicting presumptions

Where two presumptions of equal strength apply to the facts of a case, the one leading to a conclusion which conflicts with that of the other, the authorities are unclear as to the approach that the court should adopt. *Monckton v Tarr* (1930) 2 BWCC 504, CA is authority for the view that conflicting presumptions of equal strength should cancel out each other. However, *Taylor v Taylor* [1967] P 25 suggests that the court may choose between the different presumed facts by a comparison of their likelihood, or even on the basis of policy considerations.

3.8 Presumptions without proof of basic facts

This type of presumption, in contrast to those examined so far, is not a 'true' presumption in that it does not require that a basic, or preliminary, fact be proved before the presumption can be made. It is simply a way of stating where the burden of proof lies in certain situations. The most common examples of this type of presumption are:

3.8.1 Presumption of innocence

The presumption of innocence requires that in a criminal trial the court must conclude that the defendant is innocent unless the contrary is proved. It is simply a way of expressing the common law rule that the prosecution bears the legal burden of proving the accused's guilt beyond reasonable doubt.

3.8.2 Presumption of sanity

The presumption of sanity requires that in a criminal trial the court must conclude that the defendant is sane until the contrary is proved. It is simply a way of expressing the common law rule that where the defence of insanity has been raised, the accused bears the legal burden of proving it.

3.8.3 Presumption of mechanical regularity

Where a mechanical device is of a type that is ordinarily in working order, the court must conclude that it was working on the particular instance in question. A party wishing to prove that such a device was not working properly bears an evidential burden. This presumption has been used to prove that mechanical devices such as traffic lights (*Tingle Jacobs and Co v Kennedy* [1964] 1 WLR 638) and speedometers (*Nicholas v Penny* [1950] 2 KB 466) were operating properly. This presumption applies to both civil and criminal proceedings.

4

Witnesses

The most common way for evidence to be adduced is through the testimony of a witness. In this chapter we will consider the rules that determine which persons may give evidence, when a person may be compelled to give evidence and how a person's evidence will be given.

4.1 Competence and compellability

A witness is said to be 'competent' if he can as a matter of law be called by a party to give evidence. A witness is said to be 'compellable' if, being competent, he can as a matter of law be compelled by the court to give evidence. A compellable witness who, having been ordered to attend court, refuses to do so, or on attending court, refuses to give sworn evidence is liable to be imprisoned for contempt of court (in proceedings before the High Court or the Crown Court), committed to prison (in proceedings before a magistrates' court) or fined up to £1,000 (in proceedings before a county court).

4.1.1 General rule

The general rule at common law has two limbs:

- all persons are competent; and
- all competent persons are compellable.

In criminal proceedings the first limb of the general rule has been put on a statutory footing in the Youth Justice and Criminal Evidence Act 1999 ('the YJCEA 1999'), s 53(1), which provides:

At every stage in criminal proceedings all persons are (whatever their age) competent to give evidence.

The rule that all persons are competent and that all competent witnesses are compellable is subject to a number of statutory and common law exceptions in both criminal and civil proceedings. We shall consider each in turn.

4.1.2 Exceptions in criminal proceedings

4.1.2.1 Children and persons of unsound mind

As noted at **4.1.1** above, all persons, whatever their age, are competent to give evidence in criminal proceedings. Thus, a child witness is not prevented from giving evidence by virtue of his or her age. However, the YJCEA 1999, s 53(3) provides:

A person is not competent to give evidence in criminal proceedings if it appears to the court that he is not a person who is able to—
   (a) understand questions put to him, and
   (b) give answers to them which can be understood.

This exception applies to all witnesses but will most commonly affect children and persons of unsound mind.

4.1.2.2   The accused

For the prosecution
Section 53(4) of the YJCEA 1999 provides:

A person charged in criminal proceedings is not competent to give evidence in the proceedings for the prosecution (whether he is the only person charged, or is one of two or more persons charged in the proceedings).

However, s 53(5) states that '*a person charged in criminal proceedings*' does not include a person who is not, or is no longer, liable to be convicted of any offence in the proceedings. An accused is thus competent to give evidence for the prosecution:

- on pleading guilty;
- on acquittal;
- where separate trials are ordered; or
- where a *nolle prosequi* has been entered on the direction of the Attorney-General.

Where the accused pleads guilty and intends to give evidence for the prosecution against his former co-accused, there is a danger that he may tailor his evidence in the hope of receiving a more lenient sentence. Thus, the court has a discretion to sentence him before he gives evidence (*R v Palmer* (1993) 99 Cr App R 83). A similar situation arises where the prosecution wish to call an accomplice against whom proceedings are pending. There is a rule of practice, but not law, that the prosecution should only be allowed to call such witnesses where they have given an undertaking to discontinue proceedings or not to prosecute him (*R v Pipe* (1966) 51 Cr App R 17; *R v Turner* (1975) 61 Cr App R 67). As it is only a rule of practice, it is ultimately a matter of judicial discretion whether or not to allow the accomplice to be called.

For the accused
By virtue of YJCEA 1999, s 53(1), the accused is competent to give evidence on his or her own behalf. However, he is not compellable. Section 1(1) of the Criminal Evidence Act 1898, provides:

A person charged in criminal proceedings shall not be called as a witness in the proceedings except upon his own application.

Where the accused does elect to give evidence, two important consequences follow. First, any evidence that the accused may give is admissible against any co-accused (*R v Rudd* (1948) 32 Cr App R 138). Secondly, he is open to cross-examination by both the prosecution and any co-accused. Thus, while an accused is neither competent nor compellable for the prosecution when appearing in his own defence, he may be cross-examined by the prosecution about the guilt of the co-accused (*R v Paul* [1920] 2 KB 183).

If an accused decides not to testify, it should be the invariable practice of counsel to record the decision and to cause the accused to sign the record, giving a clear indication that he has by his own will decided not to testify bearing in mind the advice, if any, given to him by his counsel (*R v Bevan* (1993) 98 Cr App R 354, CA; *R v Chatroodi* [2001] All ER (D) 259 (Feb)). In practice, this is done by endorsing the decision on the brief itself.

For the co-accused

The accused is competent as a witness for a co-accused (YJCEA 1999, s 53(1)) but is not compellable (Criminal Evidence Act 1898, s 1(1)). Once the accused is no longer a '*person charged*' in the proceedings, he or she will become compellable. An accused ceases to be a person charged:

- on pleading guilty;
- on acquittal;
- where separate trials are ordered; or
- where a *nolle prosequi* has been entered on the direction of the Attorney-General.

4.1.2.3   Spouse or civil partner of the accused

Competence

A spouse or civil partner is competent for any party in criminal proceedings (YJCEA 1999, s 53(1)). However, as a person charged in the proceedings is not competent to give evidence for the prosecution, where the accused and the spouse or civil partner are both charged in the proceedings, neither will be competent for the prosecution (s 53(4)).

Compellability

The compellability of the spouse or civil partner of the accused is governed by PACE 1984, s 80:

(2)   *In any proceedings the spouse or civil partner of a person charged in the proceedings shall, subject to subsection (4) below, be compellable to give evidence on behalf of that person.*

(2A) *In any proceedings the spouse or civil partner of a person charged in the proceedings shall, subject to subsection (4) below, be compellable—*

   (a) *to give evidence on behalf of any other person charged in the proceedings but only in respect of any specified offence with which that other person is charged; or*

   (b) *to give evidence for the prosecution but only in respect of any specified offence with which any person is charged in the proceedings.*

(3)   *In relation to the spouse or civil partner of a person charged in any proceedings, an offence is a specified offence for the purposes of subsection (2A) above if—*

   (a) *it involves an assault on, or injury or a threat of injury to, the spouse or civil partner or a person who was at the material time under the age of 16;*

   (b) *it is a sexual offence alleged to have been committed in respect of a person who was at the material time under that age; or*

   (c) *it consists of attempting or conspiring to commit, or of aiding, abetting, counselling, procuring or inciting the commission of, an offence falling within paragraph (a) or (b) above.*

(4)   *No person who is charged in any proceedings shall be compellable by virtue of subsection (2) or (2A) above to give evidence in the proceedings.*

(4A) *References in this section to a person charged in any proceedings do not include a person who is not, or is no longer, liable to be convicted of any offence in the proceedings (whether as a result of pleading guilty or for any other reason).*

(5)   *In any proceedings a person who has been but is no longer married to the accused shall be compellable to give evidence as if that person and the accused had never been married.*

(5A) *In any proceedings a person who has been but is no longer the civil partner of the accused shall be compellable to give evidence as if that person and the accused had never been civil partners.*

(6)   *Where in any proceedings the age of any person at any time is material for the purposes of subsection (3) above, his age at the material time shall for the purposes of that provision be deemed to be or to have been that which appears to the court to be or to have been his age at that time.*

(7)   *In subsection (3)(b) above 'sexual offence' means an offence under the Sexual Offences Act 1956, the Indecency with Children Act 1960, the Protection of Children Act 1978 or Part 1 of the Sexual Offences Act 2003.*

For the prosecution

A spouse or civil partner, subject to one exception, is compellable to give evidence on behalf of the prosecution against the accused or any co-accused, in respect of any specified offences (Police and Criminal Evidence Act 1984, s 80(2A)(b)). Section 80(3)(a) to (c) provides that an offence is a specified offence if:

- it involves an assault on, or injury or threat of injury to, the spouse or civil partner (s 80(3)(a));

- it involves an assault on, or injury or threat of injury to, a person under the age of 16 (s 80(3)(a));

- it is a sexual offence committed in relation to a person under the age of 16 (s 80(3)(b)); or

- it is an offence that consists of attempting or conspiring to commit, or of aiding, abetting, counselling, procuring or inciting the commission of any of the above offences (s 80(3)(c)).

The drafting of s 80 gives rise to an apparent problem. This stems from the use of the word 'involves' in s 80(3)(a). The question arises whether the test is legal or factual, ie whether s 80(3) refers to those offences which include assault, injury or threat of injury as an element of the offence, or whether it also includes those offences which involve assault, injury or threat of injury, on the facts alone.

The exception referred to above is that where the spouse or civil partner is charged in the same proceedings, he is not compellable unless he is no longer likely to be convicted (s 80(4), (4A)).

For the accused

The spouse or civil partner of the accused is generally compellable for the accused (Police and Criminal Evidence Act 1984, s 80(2)). The only exception is that where the spouse or civil partner is charged in the same proceedings, he is not compellable unless he is no longer likely to be convicted (s 80(4), (4A)).

For the co-accused

A spouse or civil partner is compellable to give evidence on behalf of any co-accused, but only in respect of specified offences (Police and Criminal Evidence Act 1984, s 80(2A)(a)). Where the spouse or civil partner is charged in the same proceedings, he is not compellable unless he is no longer likely to be convicted (s 80(4), (4A)).

Former spouse or civil partner

Under the Police and Criminal Evidence Act 1984, s 80(5) and (5A), the provisions of s 80 do not apply where the spouse is no longer married to the accused or the civil partnership has ended. If a marriage is void *ab initio* there never was a spouse. Thus in *R v Khan* (1987) 84 Cr App R 44, CA, it was held that a woman with whom a man had gone through a bigamous ceremony of marriage was a competent witness against him for the prosecution. (This case was decided at a time when s 80(5) governed competence as well as compellability.) On the other hand, parties who are married remain married where they are judicially separated, or simply not cohabiting (whether by reason of an informal arrangement, a separation agreement or a non-cohabitation order).

Cohabitees

In *R v Pearce* [2002] 1 WLR 1553, it was held that the Police and Criminal Evidence Act 1984, s 80 does not cover the cohabitee of an accused who is not married to the accused.

4.1.2.4 Heads of state

The Sovereign and the sovereign or head of foreign states are competent (YJCEA 1999, s 53(1)) but not compellable. Furthermore, diplomats and consular officials, and their staff, have immunity from compellability pursuant to a wide variety of statutory provisions.

4.1.2.5 Bankers

Bankers and bank officials are competent (YJCEA 1999, s 53(1)). Their compellability is governed by the Bankers' Books Evidence Act 1879. Section 6 of that Act provides that bankers and bank officials shall not be compellable, in legal proceedings to which the bank is not a party, to produce any banker's book the contents of which may be proved under the Act, or to appear as witnesses to prove the matters recorded therein, unless by order of a judge.

4.1.2.6 Judges

Judges and masters are competent (YJCEA 1999, s 53(1)) but cannot be compelled to give evidence relating to judicial function.

4.1.3. Procedure

Where there is an issue regarding the competence of a witness it should be determined at the beginning of the trial (*R v Yacoob* (1981) 72 Cr App R 313, CA). It is determined by the court in the absence of the jury (YJCEA 1999, ss 53(3) and 54(4)). It may be raised either by a party to the proceedings or by the court of its own motion (s 54(1)). The party calling the witness must satisfy the court, on the balance of probabilities, that the witness is competent to give evidence in criminal proceedings (s 54(2)). Any questioning of the witness is conducted by the court in the presence of the parties (s 54(6)).

The parties may call expert evidence (s 54(5)). Under different provisions of the YJCEA 1999 the court has the power to make special measures directions to facilitate the giving of evidence by a vulnerable or incapacitated witness (see **4.9** below). The court, in determining competence under s 53(3), is required to treat the witness as if they have the benefit of any special measures directions that the court would make if the witness were to give evidence at trial (s 54(3)).

4.1.4 Exceptions in civil proceedings

The general rule in civil proceedings is that all persons are competent and that all competent persons are compellable. The only exceptions to this rule are children, persons of unsound mind, the Sovereign, foreign heads of state, diplomats, bankers and judges.

4.1.4.1 Children

Section 96 of the Children Act 1989 provides:

(1) *Subsection (2) applies where a child who is called as a witness in any civil proceedings does not, in the opinion of the court, understand the nature of an oath.*

(2) *The child's evidence may be heard by the court if, in its opinion—*

> (a) he understands that it is his duty to speak the truth; and
>
> (b) he has sufficient understanding to justify his evidence being heard.

A 'child', for these purposes, is a person under the age of 18 (s 105). The court must first determine whether or not a child witness understands the oath (s 96(1)). In deciding this issue the courts are likely to be guided by the decision of the Court of Appeal in *R v Hayes* [1977] 1 WLR 238. *Hayes* is a criminal case that was decided at a time when the position in criminal proceedings was similar to that provided by s 96. The test laid down in *Hayes* was:

> Whether the child has a sufficient appreciation of the solemnity of the occasion and the added responsibility to tell the truth, which is involved in taking an oath, over and above the duty to tell the truth which is an ordinary duty of normal social conduct.

In civil proceedings, if a child fails this test, he or she may only give evidence if the conditions in s 96(2) are satisfied and any evidence must be given unsworn.

On matters of procedure, the courts are also likely to draw on previous criminal authority. As the competence of the witness is a matter for the judge, he should put to the child preliminary questions so as to be able to form an opinion (*R v Surgenor* (1940) 27 Cr App R 175). Whether a child is sufficiently young to warrant examination to see whether he can give sworn evidence is a matter for the judge to decide on the particular facts of the case. However, in *R v Khan* (1981) 73 Cr App R 190, CA, it was held that although much depends on the type of child before the court, as a general working rule inquiry is necessary in the case of a child under the age of 14.

4.1.4.2 Persons of unsound mind

In civil cases the competence of a person of unsound mind is determined by his or her ability to understand the nature and sanction of the oath. If such a witness does not understand the nature of the oath then he cannot testify (*R v Hill* (1851) 2 Den 254). In determining whether such a witness understands the nature of the oath, the courts have adopted the test in *R v Hayes* [1977] 1 WLR 238 (see 4.1.4.1 above). If the witness understands the nature of the oath, and is therefore competent to testify, it is a matter for the tribunal of fact to decide how much weight should be attached to his evidence (*R v Hill* (1851) 2 Den 254).

4.1.4.3 Heads of state, bankers and judges

The rules concerning the competence and compellability of the Sovereign, foreign heads of state, diplomats, bankers and judges in criminal proceedings (see **4.1.2.4** to **4.1.2.6** above) apply equally to civil proceedings with one exception, namely that in civil proceedings competence is determined by the common law and not the YJCEA 1999.

4.2 Oaths and affirmations

4.2.1 Sworn evidence

Generally, evidence given by a witness in both civil and criminal proceedings will be given on oath. Evidence given on oath is known as sworn evidence. The present law is governed by the Oaths Act 1978.

Section 1(1) of the 1978 Act directs the form and manner in which oaths are to be administered and taken by Christians and Jews. In *R v Chapman* [1980] Crim LR 42 it was held that failure to comply with s 1(1), which was directive only, did not necessarily invalidate the whole taking of the oath. The oath was valid if taken in a way binding and intended to be binding upon the conscience of the witness.

Section 1(3) of the 1978 Act provides that for those of other religious beliefs the oath shall be administered 'in any lawful manner'. An oath is lawfully administered where:

- it appears to the court that the oath is binding on the conscience of the witness; and
- the witness considers the oath to be binding on his or her conscience.

In *R v Kemble* [1990] 1 WLR 1111, CA, the evidence of a Muslim witness was held to have been lawfully administered even though it had been administered on the New Testament, whereas Islam requires that a binding oath must be made on a copy of the Koran that is written in Arabic.

To prevent persons with no religious belief from taking an oath and later alleging that, because of their beliefs, the oath was of no effect, s 4(2) of the 1978 Act provides that the fact that a person taking an oath has no religious belief does not prevent it from being binding on him. Section 5(1) permits any person who objects to being sworn to make a solemn affirmation instead of taking an oath. A solemn affirmation is of the same force and effect as an oath (s 5(4)).

4.2.2   Criminal proceedings

The ability to give sworn evidence is governed by the YJCEA 1999 s 55. Section 55(2) provides:

The witness may not be sworn ... unless—
   (a) he has attained the age of 14, and
   (b) he has sufficient appreciation of the solemnity of the occasion and of the particular responsibility to tell the truth which is involved in taking the oath.

Under the YJCEA 1999, s 55(3) and (8), a person who is able to give intelligible testimony, ie

- is able to understand questions put to him or her; and
- is able to give answers that can be understood,

is presumed to have sufficient appreciation of the solemnity of the occasion and of the responsibility to tell the truth. If evidence to the contrary is adduced, it is for the party seeking to have the witness sworn to prove, on a balance of probabilities, that the witness has attained the age of 14 and has a sufficient appreciation of the matters mentioned (s 55(4)). The preliminary facts required to trigger the presumption in s 55(3) are the same as the requirements of the test for competence in s 53(3) (see **4.1.2.1**). Thus, the combined effect of s 53(3) and s 55(3) is that a competent witness who is at least 14 years of age will be presumed capable of giving sworn evidence.

Section 55 of the YJCEA 1999 provides that the determination of whether a witness may be sworn (which can be raised by either party or the court) must take place in the absence of the jury (s 55(5)), but in the presence of the parties (s 55(7)). Expert evidence can be received (s 55(6)).

A witness who is not permitted to give sworn evidence by virtue of the YJCEA 1999, s 55(2) must give his or her evidence unsworn (s 56(2)) and a court may properly receive unsworn evidence in such circumstances (s 56(4)).

Children and persons of unsound mind are the types of witness who most commonly give evidence unsworn. The amount of weight to be attached to the evidence of such a witness is a matter for the jury. Clearly, if the evidence is so tainted with insanity as to be unworthy of credit, the jury will properly disregard it (*R v Hill* (1851) 2 Den 254). Equally, however, a person suffering from a mental illness may be a perfectly reliable witness. In *R v Barratt* [1996] Crim LR 495, CA, the witness was suffering from a fixed belief in paranoia and held bizarre beliefs about certain aspects of her private life, but the court could see no reason to suppose that on matters not affected by her condition, her evidence was not as reliable as that of any other witness.

4.2.3   Civil proceedings

The general rule is that a witness who is not sworn cannot give evidence at all and a judgment based on such evidence will be set aside as a nullity (*R v Marsham, ex p Lawrence* [1912] 2 KB 362). However, a person may give unsworn evidence if:

- The case is brought on the small claims track and the court does not require evidence on oath (CPR, r 27.8(4)).

- The witness is producing a document that can be identified by another witness on oath (*Perry v Gibson* (1834) 1 Ad & El 48).

- The evidence is of the terms of an agreement between parties and the witness is counsel for one of the parties (*Hickman v Berens* [1895] 2 Ch 638); or

- The witness is a child and is not competent to give sworn testimony (Children Act 1989, s 96).

Unlike criminal cases, there is no general power on the part of the civil courts to accept the unsworn testimony of a person suffering from a mental illness or other mental disability.

4.3   Form of witness evidence

The general rule is that evidence must be given orally by a witness who is present in court. However, there are a number of exceptions to this rule.

4.3.1   Criminal proceedings

In criminal proceedings the exceptions are that:

- evidence may be read with the agreement of both parties (Criminal Justice Act 1967, s 9);

- evidence may be given through a live link (CJA 2003, s 51; YJCEA 1999, s 24; Criminal Justice Act 1988, s 32); and

- evidence may be given by a pre-recorded video (Criminal Justice Act 2003, s 137; YJCEA 1999, ss 27 and 28)

4.3.1.1   Evidence read by agreement

By virtue of the Criminal Justice Act 1967, s 9, a written statement shall be admissible to the same extent as oral evidence by the maker of the statement where:

(a) The statement purports to be signed by the maker (s 9(2)(a)).

(b) The statement contains a declaration by that person to the effect that it is true to the best of his knowledge and belief and that he made the statement knowing that if it were tendered in evidence, he would be liable to prosecution if he wilfully stated in it anything which he knew to be false or did not believe to be true (s 9(2)(b)).

(c) A copy of the statement has been served on each of the other parties (s 9(2)(c)).

(d) Within seven days of service none of the parties have served a notice objecting to the statement being tendered in evidence (s 9(2)(d)).

A party wishing to rely on this provision must therefore serve the statement at least seven days in advance of the hearing. This provision is commonly relied upon where a witness does not give controversial evidence.

4.3.1.2   Evidence through a live link

Criminal Justice Act 2003, s 51

Under the CJA 2003, s 51, the court has a general power to direct that a witness, other than the defendant, give evidence through a live link. The witness must be in the United Kingdom at the time when the evidence is given (s 56(2)). The live link will usually be a closed-circuit television link, but could be any technology with the same effect, such as video-conferencing facilities or the Internet. Evidence may only be given through a live link where it is in the interests of the efficient or effective administration of justice for the witness to do so. In deciding whether to make a direction the court must consider all the circumstances in the case, including:

(a) the availability of the witness;

(b) the need for the witness to attend in person;

(c) the importance of the witness's evidence to the proceedings;

(d) the views of the witness; and

(e) whether a direction might tend to inhibit any party to the proceedings from effectively testing the witness's evidence.

Criminal Justice Act 1988, s 32

Under the Criminal Justice Act 1988, s 32, a witness who is outside the United Kingdom may give his or her evidence by live television link but only in the following proceedings:

• trials on indictment;

• appeals to the criminal division Court of Appeal;

• references by the Criminal Cases Review Commission;

• proceedings in youth courts; and

• appeals to the Crown Court arising out of proceedings in the youth court.

The Criminal Justice Act 1988, s 32 is presently only in force in relation to proceedings for offences involving the killing of any person and certain offences involving serious fraud.

Special measures directions

Under the YJCEA 1999, s 19, the court has the power to make a 'special measures direction' in respect of certain types of vulnerable witness. Where the court makes a special measures direction, it may order that the witness may give evidence by live link (YJCEA 1999, s 24). Special measures directions will be considered in more detail at **4.9**.

4.3.1.3 Pre-recorded video evidence

Criminal Justice Act 2003, s 137

Under s 137 of the CJA 2003 the court has a general power to direct that all, or part, of the pre-recorded video evidence of a witness, other than the defendant, shall stand as a witness's evidence-in-chief where:

(a) a person is called as a witness in proceedings for an offence that is either triable on indictment only or is a prescribed either-way offence (s 137(1)(a));

(b) that person witnessed the offence, part of the offence, or events closely connected with the offence (s 137(1)(b));

(c) the witness has given a video-recorded account of those events at a time when they were still fresh in his memory (s 137(1)(c),(d) and (e));

(d) the witness's recollection of the events in question is likely to have been significantly better when he gave that account (s 137(3)(b)(i));

(e) the witness in oral evidence in the proceedings asserts the truth of the statements made by him in the recorded account (s 137(2)); and it is in the interests of justice for the recording to be admitted (s 137(3)(b)(ii)) having regard to:

    (i) the interval between the time of the events in question and the time when the recorded account was made (s 137(4)(a));

    (ii) any factors that might affect the reliability of what the witness said in that account (s 137(4)(b));

    (iii) the quality of the recording (s 137(4)(c)); and

    (iv) any views of the witness as to whether his evidence in chief should be given orally or by means of the recording (s 137(4)(d)).

It does not matter if the statements in the recorded account were not made on oath (s 137(5)). Once a video recording has been admitted, the witness may not give evidence-in-chief otherwise than by means of the recording as to any matter which, in the opinion of the court, has been dealt with adequately in the recorded account (s 138).

Special measures directions

When making a special measures direction under YJCEA 1999, s 19, the court may also direct that a pre-recorded video interview with a witness stands as his or her evidence-in-chief (YJCEA 1999, s 27) and that cross-examination or re-examination be pre-recorded (YJCEA 1999, s 28). See **4.9**.

Where the prosecution rely on a pre-recorded video of a child's evidence-in-chief, the judge may allow the jury to have transcripts of the recording if this would assist them in following the recording. The judge should make it clear that the transcript is only for that limited purpose and should give them directions both at the time, and during summing up, so as to safeguard against the risk of disproportionate weight being given to the transcript (*R v Welstead* [1996] 1 Cr App R 59, CA). The judge has a discretion to permit a jury to view a video of a child's evidence again in court (*R v Rawlings* [1995] 1 WLR 178). However, the judge must always warn the jury not to attach disproportionate weight to the evidence and remind them of the cross-examination and re-examination of the witness. It is submitted that these principles will also apply to evidence adduced under s 137.

4.3.2 Civil proceedings

Under CPR, r 32.2, the general rule is that any fact which needs to be established by the evidence of a witness is to be proved:

(a) at trial, by his oral evidence given in public; and

(b) at any other hearing, by his evidence in writing.

However, this provision is subject to any provision to the contrary contained in the CPR or elsewhere, or to any order of the court (CPR, r 32.2(2)). For example, under CPR, r 32.3, the court may allow a witness to give evidence through a video link or by other means.

Under CPR, r 35(1), where a party has served a witness statement, and wishes to rely at trial on the evidence of the witness who made the statement, the witness must be called to give oral evidence unless the court orders otherwise or the statement is put in as hearsay evidence. By r 35(2), where a witness is called to give oral evidence under r 35(1), his witness statement shall stand as his evidence-in-chief unless the court orders otherwise. However, the court may permit a witness to amplify his witness statement and give evidence in relation to new matters that have arisen since the witness statement was served if it considers that there is a good reason for not confining the evidence of the witness to the contents of his statement (r 32.5(3), (4)).

For details of the formal requirements of witness statements and discussion of other procedural issues such as disclosure, see the *Civil Litigation Manual* and *Blackstone's Civil Practice*.

4.4 Power of a party to choose its witnesses

4.4.1 No property in a witness

In both criminal and civil proceedings a party may call any witness even if the witness has previously agreed to give evidence for the opposing party. In *Harmony Shipping Co SA v Saudi Europe Line Ltd* [1979] 1 WLR 1380, CA, a handwriting expert was approached by the plaintiffs to authenticate a particular document. The expert's view was that it was a forgery (which was unfavourable to their case). Later, the defendants asked him to advise on the same issue and, forgetting his previous involvement in the case, he expressed the same view as before. On discovering that the plaintiffs had already retained him, the expert refused to accept any further instructions from the defendants. The defendants then issued a subpoena against him. The Court of Appeal held that, as there is no property in a witness, the expert witness was compellable on behalf of the defendants. It should be noted that any communications between the expert and the plaintiffs might have been protected by legal professional privilege (see **Chapter 18**). However, in *Harmony Shipping* it was not the communications that were in issue but the evidence.

4.4.2 Criminal proceedings

4.4.2.1 The accused

The accused may call such witnesses to support his or her case as he thinks fit (subject to the rules of competence and compellability). Although, once a witness has given evidence for the prosecution, he cannot be called to give evidence for the defence (*R v Kelly* (1985) *The Times,* 27 July, CA).

4.4.2.2   The prosecution

As for the prosecution, the relevant rules for trials on indictment were set out in *R v Russell-Jones* [1995] 3 All ER 239, CA:

(a) The prosecution must bring to court all the witnesses whose statements have been served as witnesses on whom the prosecution intends to rely, if the defence want them to attend. (In deciding which statements to serve, the prosecution have an unfettered discretion, but must normally disclose material statements not served.)

(b) The prosecution enjoy a discretion, which must be exercised in the interests of justice to promote a fair trial, whether to call, or tender for cross-examination, any witnesses it requires to attend.

(c) The prosecution ought normally to call, or offer to call, all the witnesses who give direct evidence of the primary facts of the case, even if there are inconsistencies between one witness and another, unless for good reason the prosecutor regards the witnesses' evidence as unworthy of belief.

(d) It is for the prosecution to decide which witnesses can give direct evidence of the primary facts.

(e) The prosecutor is also the primary judge of whether or not a witness is unworthy of belief.

(f) The prosecutor is not obliged to proffer a witness merely in order to give the defence material to attack the credit of other prosecution witnesses.

In *R v Haringey Justices, ex p DPP* [1996] QB 351, DC, it was held that the principles set out in *Russell-Jones* also apply to criminal trials in magistrates' courts. However, a question arose as to the point at which the procedure in a magistrates' court is equivalent to the service of statements in proceedings on indictment (see (a) above). The court concluded that, in the case of an offence triable either way, that point was reached when the prosecution served copies of witness statements by way of advanced information, but that in other cases the prosecutor should retain an unfettered discretion until the case starts. Following the incorporation of the ECHR into domestic law by the Human Rights Act 1998, the Attorney-General issued guidelines on the Disclosure of Information in Criminal Proceedings. The guidelines are persuasive authority but do not have the force of law. One of the principal aims of the guidelines is to ensure that defendants receive a fair trial within the meaning of Article 6(1) of the ECHR. Paragraph 57 of the guidelines provides:

> The prosecutor should ... provide to the defence all evidence upon which the Crown proposes to rely in a summary trial. Such provision should allow the accused and their legal advisers sufficient time properly to consider the evidence before it is called.

There is conflicting authority as to whether the trial judge has the power to direct the prosecution to call a witness. In *R v Sterk* [1972] Crim LR 391, prosecution counsel referred to a witness in opening but later formed the view that he was unreliable and declined to call him. The Court of Appeal held that the judge should have ordered the prosecution at least to tender the witness for cross-examination. However, in *R v Oliva* [1965] 1 WLR 1028 it was held that the judge has a discretion to invite the prosecution to call a witness, but that if they refuse the ultimate sanction is for the judge to call the witness himself. This approach was followed in *R v Haringey Justices, ex p DPP* [1996] QB 351, DC.

4.4.3   Civil proceedings

Prior to the implementation of the Civil Procedure Rules, parties to civil proceedings had an unfettered choice as to which witnesses they would call (*Briscoe v Briscoe* [1968] P 501). However, CPR, r 32.1 provides that:

> *(1)   The court may control the evidence by giving direction as to—*
>
> > *(a)   the issues on which it requires evidence;*
> >
> > *(b)   the nature of the evidence which it requires to decide those issues;*
> >
> > *(c)   the way in which the evidence is to be placed before the court.*
>
> *(2)   The court may use its power under this rule to exclude evidence that would otherwise be admissible.*

The judge, nevertheless, has no power to order a party to call a particular witness (*Society of Lloyd's v Jaffray* (2000) *The Times,* 3 August).

4.5   Order of witnesses

Parties are generally free to call witnesses in the order of their choice. The only major restriction concerns the order of defence witnesses in criminal trials. PACE 1984, s 79 provides that:

> *If at the trial of any person for an offence—*
>
> > *(a) the defence intends to call two or more witnesses to the facts of the case; and*
> >
> > *(b) those witnesses include the accused,*
>
> *the accused shall be called before the other witness or witnesses unless the court in its discretion otherwise directs.*

The court may exercise its discretion to permit the defence to call a witness to fact other than the defendant first where, for example:

(a) the witness's evidence relates to some formal or uncontroversial matter; or

(b) the witness's evidence concerns events which occurred before the time of the events about which the accused will give evidence and the defence case will be more readily understood if told in chronological order.

Section 79 of PACE 1984 is of no application to persons who are not witnesses to fact, eg, expert witnesses.

4.6   Calling a witness after the close of the case

The general rule is that a party must adduce all of its evidence before the close of its case. Thus, a party will generally not be allowed at some later stage to remedy defects in its case, or contradict the evidence of the other party, by adducing additional evidence.

4.6.1   Criminal proceedings

In criminal proceedings there are two well-established exceptions to this general rule.

(a) Matters arising *ex improviso.* Where a matter arises which could not reasonably have been foreseen, then the judge has a discretion to allow a party who has already closed its case to call evidence in rebuttal (*R v Scott* (1984) 79 Cr App R 49; *R v Hutchinson* (1985) 82 Cr App R 51, CA).

(b) Formal evidence omitted through inadvertence or oversight. The court will normally allow evidence in rebuttal to be called in order to make good a purely formal omission. For example, in *Price v Humphries* [1958] 2 QB 353, DC, the prosecutor failed to prove that the Director of Public Prosecutions had given leave to bring the proceedings.

However, the discretion of the trial judge to permit the prosecution to call evidence after the close of its case is not restricted to the above exceptions. It has been held that the judge has a wider discretion, the limits of which should not be precisely defined, but which should be exercised only rarely outside the two established exceptions (*R v Francis* [1991] 1 WLR 1264, CA), especially when the evidence is tendered after the case for the accused has begun (*R v Munnery* [1990] 94 Cr Appr 164, CA). In *Francis*, evidence having been given that at a group identification the man standing at position number 20 was identified, the prosecution were allowed to recall the inspector in charge of the identification procedure to say that it was the appellant who was standing at position number 20. Counsel for the prosecution was under the impression that the name of the person standing in that position was not in issue. In *Jolly v DPP* [2000] Crim LR 471, DC, the Divisional Court held that it was now 'beyond argument' that there was a general discretion to permit the calling of evidence after the close of the prosecution case which must be exercised having regard to the interests of justice and to any possible prejudice to the defendant. The court stated that the discretion would be sparingly exercised but it doubted whether it assisted the court any longer to speak in terms of exceptional circumstances. Each case had to be considered on its own facts.

There is a sacrosanct rule that once the jury has retired to consider its verdict, no witnesses may be called or recalled (*R v Owen* [1952] 2 QB 362). However, the judge has a discretion to permit witnesses to be called up to that point and witnesses have even been called while the judge is summing up the case (*R v Sanderson* [1953] 1 WLR 392).

4.6.2 Civil proceedings

A similar approach to that taken in criminal proceedings has been followed in civil cases. In *Stocznia Gdanska SA v Latvian Shipping Co* (2000) LTL 12/2/2001, the claimants made an application to adduce further evidence after the close of the trial but before judgment had been handed down. It was held that the claimants ought to be allowed to adduce it as to ignore it would neither be just nor in accordance with the overriding objective (CPR, r 1.1).

4.7 Judge's powers to call and examine witnesses

4.7.1 Criminal proceedings

In criminal proceedings in the Crown Court the judge, without the consent of either party, may call and examine any witnesses not called by the parties (*R v Chapman* (1838) 8 Car & P 558; *R v Harris* [1927] 2 KB 587). Magistrates have a similar power (*R v Haringey Justices, ex p DPP* [1996] QB 351, DC).

4.7.2 Civil proceedings

Prior to the implementation of the CPR, apart from cases for civil contempt, the judge could not call a witness without the consent of the parties (*Re Enoch and Zaretsky, Bock and Co's Arbitration* [1910] 1 KB 327, CA). Under CPR, r 32.1, the court now has the power to direct the nature of the evidence which it requires to decide an issue and the way in which such evidence is to be placed before the court. Thus, the judge has the power to direct that a witness give evidence without the consent of either party.

4.8   Securing the attendance of witnesses

4.8.1   Criminal proceedings

Where the prosecution or defence anticipate that a witness will not attend the Crown Court voluntarily, they may apply for a witness summons under the Criminal Procedure (Attendance of Witnesses) Act 1965, s 2. The party seeking the summons must show that the witness is likely to be able to give material evidence, or produce a material exhibit, but will not voluntarily attend as a witness or will not voluntarily produce the exhibit and that it would be in the interests of justice for a summons to be issued. Failure to comply with a witness summons may be summarily punished as contempt of court by up to three months' imprisonment (s 3).

In a magistrates' court the attendance of witnesses may be secured by a witness summons or a warrant under the Magistrates' Court Act 1980, s 97. A witness summons may be issued where the witness is likely to be able to give material evidence, or produce a material exhibit, but will not voluntarily attend as a witness or will not voluntarily produce the exhibit. However, should the witness fail to attend court in answer to the summons, the court may issue a warrant for his or her arrest (s 97(3)). Refusal to be sworn or give evidence may be punished by up to one month's imprisonment and/or a fine of up to £2,500 (s 97(4)).

4.8.2   Civil proceedings

The attendance of a witness in a civil case is secured by the issuing of a witness summons under CPR, r 34. A civil witness summons may similarly require a witness to attend court to give evidence or to produce a document. Failure to obey a witness summons issued by the High Court is contempt of court and the contemnor may be committed to prison for up to two years and/or fined (*Wyatt v Wingford* (1729) 2 Ld Raym 1528; Contempt of Court Act 1981, s 14(1)). Refusal to be sworn or give evidence also amounts to contempt of court (*R v Daye* [1908] 2 KB 333). A person failing to answer to a witness summons issued by a county court may be fined up to £1,000 (County Courts Act 1984, s 55(1) and (2)). Refusal to be sworn or give evidence may also be punished by a fine (s 55(1)).

4.9   Special measures directions

The YJCEA 1999 introduced in criminal proceedings a statutory regime of 'special measures directions'. A special measures direction is an order that may be made by the court, either of its own motion or on application by either party, which is intended to protect vulnerable and intimidated witnesses and facilitate the giving of their evidence.

4.9.1   Eligibility

A witness will be eligible in principle for a special measures direction if he comes within any of the following three categories:

(a) he is under the age of 17 at the time of the hearing (s 16(1)(a));

(b) the court considers that the quality of evidence given by the witness is likely to be diminished because the witness:

    (i)   suffers from a mental disorder within the meaning of the Mental Health Act 1983;

    (ii) has a significant impairment of intelligence and social functioning; or

    (iii) has a physical disability or is suffering from a physical disorder (s 16(1)(b)).

(c) The court considers that the quality of evidence given by the witness is likely to be diminished by reason of fear or distress on the part of the witness in connection with testifying in the proceedings (s 17(1)). In determining this issue, s 17(2) requires the court to take into account factors such as:

    (i)   the nature and alleged circumstances of the offence;

    (ii) the age of the witness;

    (iii) the social and cultural background and ethnic origins of the witness;

    (iv) the religious beliefs and political opinions of the witness; and

    (v) the behaviour of the accused, his family or associates towards the witness.

The accused is not eligible for a special measures direction (YJCEA 1999, ss 16(1) and 17(1)). In *R (S) v Waltham Forest Youth Court* [2004] 2 Cr App R 335, it was held that non-availability of special measures directions to the accused did not breach ECHR, Article 6.

4.9.2 Availability

Witnesses who are eligible for a special measures direction by virtue of their age (s 16(1)(a)) or physical or mental incapacity (s 16(1)(b)) may have any of the special measures directions available under ss 23 to 30. Witnesses who are eligible by virtue of their fear or distress (s 17(1)) may have any of the special measures directions available under ss 23–28. See Table 4.1.

Table 4.1 Special measures directions

Section authorising direction	Special measures direction available	Available		Limits
		s 16	s 17	
23	Witness prevented from seeing accused by screen or other means	Yes	Yes	
24	Evidence given by live link	Yes	Yes	
25	Exclusion of specified person from court	Yes	Yes	Only if: • sexual offence; or • reasonable grounds for believing that person other than accused has sought or will seek to intimidate the witness about testifying.
26	Wigs and gowns not worn	Yes	Yes	
27	Pre-recorded video interview with witness to stand as evidence in chief	Yes	Yes	
28	Cross-examination or re-examination to be pre-recorded	Yes	Yes	Only if s 27 direction has been made.
29	Examination of witness through interpreter or court-approved intermediary	Yes	No	
30	Use of devices to enable communication between witness and others during examination	Yes	No	

Where the court determines that a witness is eligible, it must then go on to consider:

(a) whether any of the special measures available (or any combination of them) would be likely to improve the quality of evidence given by the witness (s 19(2)(a)); and, if so,

(b) which of those special measures (or any combination of them) would be likely to maximise so far as practicable the quality of the witness's evidence (s 19(2)(b)).

The court must have regard to all the circumstances of the case and, in particular, the views of the witness and the extent to which any special measure might tend to inhibit the witness's evidence being effectively tested by a party to the proceedings (s 19(3)).

4.9.3 Child witnesses

A 'child witness' is a witness who is eligible for a special measures direction because he is under 17 years of age (ss 16(1)(a) and 21(1)(a)). Section 21(3) of the YJCEA 1999 provides that, in relation to a child witness, the court must make a special measures direction that:

(a) provides for any video-recorded interview to stand as evidence-in-chief under s 27 of the YJCEA 1999 (s 21(3)(a)); and

(b) provides for any evidence which is not given by means of a video recording (whether in-chief or otherwise) to be given by means of a live link under s 24 of the YJCEA 1999 (s 21(3)(b)).

However, the court need not make such a special measures direction where:

(a) having regard to all the circumstances it is in the interests of justice not to admit a video recording of the witness's evidence-in-chief (s 21(4)(b)); or

(b) the court is satisfied that neither direction would be likely to maximise the quality of the witness's evidence so far as is practicable (for example, where some other special measures available would have that effect) (s 21(4)(c)).

4.9.4 Child witnesses in need of special protection

Under the YJCEA 1999, s 21(1)(b) a child witness is 'in need of special protection' where he or she is a witness to one or more of the offences specified in YJCEA 1999, s 35(3), namely:

(a) sexual offences under either Part 1 of the Sexual Offences Act 2003 or the Protection of Children Act 1978 (s 35(3)(a));

(b) kidnapping, false imprisonment or child abduction (s 35(3)(b));

(c) child cruelty (s 35(3)(c)); or

(d) any other offence involving an assault on, or injury, or threat of injury to any person (s 35(3)(d)).

4.9.4.1 Offences other than sexual offences

Where a child witness is deemed to be in need of special protection by virtue of being a witness to an offence other than a sexual offence (categories (b) to (d)), the court must make a special measures direction that:

(a) provides for any video-recorded interview to stand as evidence-in-chief under s 27 of the YJCEA 1999 (s 21(3)(a)); and

(b) provides for any evidence which is not given by means of video recording (whether in-chief or otherwise) to be given by means of a live link under s 24 of the YJCEA 1999 (s 21(3)(b)).

However, the court need not make such a special measures direction where, having regard to all the circumstances, it is in the interests of justice not to admit a video recording of the witness's evidence-in-chief (s 21(4)(b)).

4.9.4.2 Sexual offences

By virtue of s 21(3) and (6) of the YJCEA 1999, where a child witness is deemed in need of special protection because of his or her being a witness to a sexual offence (category (a) above), the court must make a special measures direction that:

(a) provides for any video-recorded interview to stand as evidence-in-chief under s 27 of the YJCEA 1999 (s 21(3)(a));

(b) provides for video-recorded cross-examination (otherwise than by the accused in person) and re-examination to be admitted under s 28 of the YJCEA 1999 (s 21(6)(a) and (b)); and

(c) provides for any evidence which is not given by means of a video recording (whether in-chief or otherwise) to be given by means of a live link under s 24 of the YJCEA 1999 (s 21(3)(b)).

However, the court need not make such a special measures direction where:

- having regard to all the circumstances it is in the interests of justice not to admit a video recording of the witness's evidence-in-chief (s 21(4)(b)); or

- the witness has informed the court that he does not want a special measure under s 28 (video recording of cross-examination and re-examination) to apply (s 21(7)(b)).

4.9.5 Procedure

The procedure for applying for a special measures direction is set out in the Criminal Procedure Rules, r 29. In the case of an application to a magistrates' court, the application must be made in writing within 14 days of the defendant indicating an intention to plead not guilty. In the case of an application to the Crown Court, the application must be made in writing within 28 days of the service of the documents containing the evidence. The application must be sent to the court and a copy to every other party to the proceedings. If a party wishes to oppose the application, they must give written notice to the applicant and the court within 14 days of the date on which they were served with the application.

4.9.6 Warning to jury

On a trial on indictment where evidence has been given in accordance with a special measures direction, the judge must give the jury such warning (if any) as the judge considers necessary to ensure that the direction given in relation to the witness does not prejudice the accused (s 32).

5

Corroboration and suspect witnesses

5.1 Introduction

The general rule is that a court's decision may properly be based on the evidence of a single witness. However, in criminal proceedings the law of evidence recognises two exceptions to this rule:

- offences requiring corroboration; and
- suspect witnesses.

5.2 Offences requiring corroboration

Corroboration is required before a person can be convicted of the following offences.

5.2.1 Perjury

Section 13 of the Perjury Act 1911 provides:

A person shall not be liable to be convicted of any offence against this Act, or of any offence declared by any other Act to be perjury or subornation of perjury, or to be punishable as perjury or subornation of perjury, solely upon the evidence of one witness as to the falsity of any statement alleged to be false.

The jury must be directed by the judge to look for evidence which is capable of corroborating the evidence given by the main witness as to the falsity of the statement made by the accused; if they can find none, they should acquit the accused (*R v Rider* (1986) 83 Cr App R 207). Corroboration need not be by the testimony of a witness and may take the form of documentary evidence.

5.2.2 Speeding

Section 89(1) of the Road Traffic Regulation Act 1984 creates the offence of speeding. Subsection (2) provides:

A person prosecuted for such an offence shall not be liable to be convicted solely on the evidence of one witness to the effect that, in the opinion of that witness, the person prosecuted was driving the vehicle at a speed exceeding a specified limit.

The need for corroboration arises from the possible inaccuracy of a witness's evidence as to the speed of the vehicle. However, in most cases evidence of the vehicle's speed comes from a reading taken by an automatic camera or radar gun. As this is factual evidence, rather than opinion evidence, s 89(2) of the 1984 Act will not apply.

5.2.3 Attempt

Where an accused is charged with attempting to commit either of the two preceding offences, the same requirement for corroboration applies to the trial for the attempt as it would in a trial for the completed offence (Criminal Attempts Act 1981, s 2(1) and (2)(g)).

5.3 Suspect witnesses

A witness is said to be suspect where there is a danger that he may give unreliable evidence.

5.3.1 Children, complainants in sexual cases and accomplices

Historically, the common law recognised three categories of suspect witness. The judge was required to warn the jury of the danger of convicting the accused on the basis of such a witness's uncorroborated evidence. The three categories were:

- complainants in sexual cases;
- children; and
- accomplices giving evidence for the prosecution.

The requirement on the judge to give such warnings to the jury was abrogated by the Criminal Justice Act 1988, s 34 (in the case of children) and the Criminal Justice and Public Order Act 1994, s 32 (in the case of complainants in sexual offences and accomplices).

Following the abolition of the requirement to give corroboration warnings for complainants in sexual offences and accomplices, the Court of Appeal gave guidance on how the court should approach the evidence of unreliable witnesses in *R v Makanjuola* [1995] 2 Cr App R 469. Lord Taylor of Gosforth CJ summarised the new position in eight points:

(a) Section 32(1) [of the Criminal Justice and Public Order Act 1994] abrogated the requirement to give a corroboration direction in respect of an alleged accomplice or a complainant of a sexual offence, simply because a witness falls into one of those categories.

(b) It is a matter for the judge's discretion what, if any, warning he considers appropriate in respect of such a witness as indeed in respect of any other witness in whatever type of case. Whether he chooses to give a warning and in what terms will depend on the circumstances of the case, the issues raised and the content and quality of the witness's evidence.

(c) In some cases, it may be appropriate for the judge to warn the jury to exercise some caution before acting upon the unsupported evidence of a witness. This will not be so simply because the witness is a complainant of a sexual offence nor will it necessarily be so because the witness is alleged to be an accomplice. There will need to be an evidential basis for suggesting that the evidence of the witness may be unreliable. An evidential basis does not include mere suggestion by cross-examining counsel.

(d) If any question arises as to whether the judge should give a special warning in respect of a witness, it is desirable that the question be resolved by discussion with counsel in the absence of the jury before final speeches.

(e) Where the judge does decide to give some warning in respect of a witness, it will be appropriate to do so as part of the judge's review of the evidence and his comments as to how the jury should evaluate it rather than as a set-piece legal direction.

(f) Where some warning is required, it will be for the judge to decide the strength and terms of the warning. It does not have to be invested with the whole florid regime of the old corroboration rules.

(g) Attempts to reimpose the straightjacket of the old corroboration rules are strongly to be deprecated.

(h) Finally, the Court of Appeal will be disinclined to interfere with a trial judge's exercise of his discretion save in a case where that exercise is unreasonable in the *Wednesbury* sense.

Lord Taylor gave further guidance as follows:

The judge will often consider that no special warning is required at all. Where, however, the witness has been shown to be unreliable, he or she may consider it necessary to urge caution. In a more extreme case, if the witness is shown to have lied, to have made previous false complaints, or to bear the defendant some grudge, a stronger warning may be thought appropriate and the judge may suggest it would be wise to look for some supporting material before acting on the impugned witness's evidence. We stress that these observations are merely illustrative of some, not all, of the factors which the judges may take into account in measuring where a witness stands in the scale of reliability and what response they should make at that level in their directions to the jury.

The crucial factor is that the judge always has a discretion whether to warn or not. He has to decide:

- whether any warning is appropriate; and
- what form the warning should take.

The decision will depend on the issues raised in the trial, the circumstances of the case and the judge's view of the content and quality of the witness's evidence. In those cases where the judge suggests that the jury might look for supporting material, he ought to identify for the jury any evidence which is capable of being supporting evidence and also any evidence which a jury might think offers support but which in law cannot do so (*R v B (MT)* [2000] Crim LR 181).

5.3.2 Analogous cases

The common law also recognised several further categories of witness which, while not requiring a full corroboration warning from the judge, nevertheless required a warning as to a special need for caution. They became known collectively as the 'analogous cases' and included categories such as co-defendants and witnesses tainted by an improper motive. In *R v Muncaster* [1999] Crim LR 409, CA, it was held that the guidance in *R v Makanjuola* applied equally to these cases.

5.3.2.1 Co-defendants

There is a danger that a co-defendant who gives evidence incriminating his co-accused has a purpose of his own to serve. Following *Makanjuola* and *Muncaster*, whether any warning is given, and the terms of any warning, are at the discretion of the judge. However, it has been held that it is desirable, as a matter of practice, for the jury to be warned of the need to have caution when relying on such evidence (*R v Knowlden* (1981) 77 Cr App R 94; *R v Cheema* [1994] 1 WLR 147, CA). In *Jones* [2004] 1 Cr App R 5, CA, it was suggested that the direction should consist of four parts:

(a) the jury should consider the case for and against each defendant separately;

(b) the jury should decide the case on all the evidence, including the evidence of each defendant's co-defendant;

(c) when considering the evidence of co-defendants, the jury should bear in mind that he may have an interest to serve or, as it is often put, an axe to grind; and

(d) the jury should assess the evidence of co-defendants in the same way as the evidence of any other witness.

In *R v Petkar* [2004] 1 Cr App R 270, CA, the court followed *Jones* but raised concerns that such a direction might devalue the testimony of both defendants. In that case the failure of the trial judge to give any form of warning was not fatal to the safety of the conviction because it was obvious that both accused had axes to grind.

5.3.2.2 Witnesses with improper motive

A judge should warn a jury to treat with caution the evidence of a witness where there is material to suggest that a witness's evidence may be tainted by improper motive (*R v Beck* [1982] 1 WLR 461). Evidence given by a fellow prisoner of a cell confession allegedly made by the accused is inherently unreliable and, while it is undesirable to restrict the circumstances in which a judge might warn the jury to exercise caution in regard to a particular witness's evidence, and the terms in which any such warning might be given, the judge in such a case ought to draw the attention of the jury to any indications that the evidence might be tainted by improper motive and their possible significance. He should then advise the jury to be cautious before accepting his evidence (*Benedetto v R* [2003] 1 WLR 1545, PC).

5.4 Identification witnesses

The Court of Appeal has recognised that identification evidence is also potentially unreliable and has taken a similar approach to that taken in relation to suspect witnesses. Whenever the prosecution case rests wholly or substantially on the correctness of one or more identifications of the accused, which the defence allege to be mistaken, the judge should warn the jury of the special need for caution. Where the quality of the identifying evidence is poor, the judge should withdraw the case from the jury unless there is evidence to support the reliability of the identification. The judge should identify to the jury the evidence which he adjudges to be capable of being supporting evidence and any evidence which the jury might think was supporting but which does not have that quality (*R v Turnbull* [1977] QB 224). Identification evidence will be considered further at **Chapter 15**.

5.5 Confessions by mentally handicapped defendants

Section 77(1) of PACE 1984 requires the trial judge to warn the jury of the special need for caution before convicting a defendant where the prosecution evidence depends wholly or substantially on a confession by a defendant suffering from a mental handicap and the confession was not made in the presence of an independent person. The same requirement applies to summary trials (s 77(2)) and trials on indictment without a jury (s 77(2A)). 'Independent person' does not include a police officer or a person employed for or engaged on police purposes (s 77(3)). 'Mentally handicapped' means a state of arrested or incomplete development of mind which includes significant impairment of intelligence and social functioning (s 77(3)).

The warning should be given by the trial judge when summing up the case. However, where the prosecution case depends wholly upon confession evidence, the accused suffers from a significant degree of mental handicap, and, in the opinion of the judge, the confession evidence is unconvincing to a point where the jury, properly directed by the judge, could not properly convict in reliance on that evidence, then the judge should withdraw the case from the jury (*R v Mackenzie* (1993) 96 Cr App R 98).

Examination-in-chief

Examination-in-chief is the questioning of a witness by the party calling him or her.

6.1 Leading questions

6.1.1 General rule

Leading questions are those questions that either suggest the answer sought or assume the existence of a fact not yet established. For example, in a case where the prosecution case is that A stole money from B, a question that suggests the answer sought would be:

'Did you see A taking money from B's wallet?'

A question that assumes the existence of a fact not yet established would be:

'How much money did you see A take from B?'

The rationale of this rule is to prevent the witness from being led into giving answers that are favourable only to the party calling him and thereby giving a distorted account of the events. If evidence is elicited by leading questions, it remains admissible, but the weight to be attached to it may be reduced (*Moor v Moor* [1954] 1 WLR 927).

6.1.2 Exceptions to the rule

There are three main exceptions to the rule:

(a) Introductory matters. Leading questions may be asked in relation to matters that are introductory, such as the witness's name and occupation.

(b) Undisputed matters. Where a matter is not in dispute, leading questions may be asked.

(c) Hostile witnesses. Where the court has given leave for the party to treat its own witness as hostile, leading questions may be put (see **6.5.2**).

6.2 Refreshing memory out of court

The rules regarding the circumstances in which a witness is permitted to refresh his memory out of court apply to both civil and criminal proceedings.

In *R v Richardson* [1971] 2 QB 484, the Court of Appeal approved the practice of permitting a witness to refresh his memory from a copy of his witness statement before giving evidence.

The court recognised that requiring witnesses to give evidence without the opportunity to do so would reduce their testimony in the witness box to more of a test of memory than of truthfulness. It would tend to create difficulties for the honest witness but would be likely to do little to hamper dishonest witnesses. The court warned that it would be wrong for several witnesses to be handed their statements in circumstances which enabled one to compare with another what each had said. Likewise, such statements should not be read to witnesses in each other's presence (*R v Skinner* (1993) 99 Cr App R 212, CA).

Where prosecution witnesses in a criminal trial have refreshed their memory before giving evidence, it is desirable that the defence should be informed (*Worley v Bentley* [1976] 2 All ER 449). However, a failure to do so will not, by itself, be a ground for acquittal (*R v Westwell* [1976] 2 All ER 812). The defence are entitled to inspect and cross-examine the witness on a document used to refresh his memory. Where such cross-examination extends to matters contained in the document to which the witness has not referred, then the party calling the witness is entitled to put the whole of the document in evidence so that the court may see the document on which the witness has been cross-examined.

In *R v Da Silva* [1990] 1 ALL ER 29 it was held that the judge has a discretion to permit a witness who has started to give evidence to refresh his memory from a witness statement where the witness indicates:

(a) that he cannot now recall the details of events because of the lapse of time since they took place;

(b) that he made a statement much nearer the time of the events and that the contents of the statement represent his recollection at the time he made it;

(c) that he had not read the statement before coming into court; and

(d) that he wishes to have an opportunity to read the statement before continuing to give evidence.

The witness may either withdraw from the witness box or remain there to read the statement. However, there must be no communication with the witness during that time. The statement must be removed when the witness comes to give evidence and he should not be permitted to refer to it again (*R v Da Silva* [1990] 1 All ER 29). It would appear from *R v South Ribble Magistrates' Court, ex p Cochrane* [1996] 2 Cr App R 544, DC that the conditions set out in *Da Silva* are not strict requirements; whether to allow a witness to refresh their memory from a statement once they have started to give evidence is always a matter of discretion for the court. In *ex p Cochrane*, a witness who had read his statement before giving evidence, but had not taken it in properly, was allowed to refresh his memory. The court could see no logical distinction between a witness in that position and someone who has not read his statement at all. In criminal proceedings, where the requirements of the CJA 2003, s 139 are satisfied, a witness may be permitted to refresh his memory from his witness statement during the course of his evidence (see further **6.3.2**)

6.3   Refreshing memory in court

6.3.1   Civil proceedings

In the vast majority of cases a witness's witness statement will stand as his evidence-in-chief (CPR, r 32.5(2)). However, a witness may nevertheless benefit from being able to refresh his memory while giving evidence. The witness will be permitted to refresh his memory from any document where:

(a) the document was made or verified at the time of the events in question or so shortly thereafter that the facts were still fresh in the witness's memory;

(b) the document is produced in court for inspection by the court and any other party; and

(c) that, in cases where the witness has no recollection of the events in question but simply swears to the accuracy of the contents of the document, it is the original or, if the original is not available, an accurate copy.

6.3.2   Criminal proceedings

Criminal proceedings were formerly subject to the common law rules. However, the CJA 2003, s 139 provides:

> *(1)   A person giving oral evidence in criminal proceedings about any matter may, at any stage in the course of doing so, refresh his memory of it from a document made or verified by him at an earlier time if—*
>
> > *(a)   he states in his oral evidence that the document records his recollection of the matter at that earlier time; and*
> >
> > *(b)   his recollection of the matter is likely to have been significantly better at that time than it is at the time of his oral evidence.*

Once those matters are proved there is a presumption that the witness will be permitted to refresh his memory from the document.

6.3.3   Stage of proceedings

A witness may be allowed to refresh his or her memory at any stage of the proceedings, even in re-examination (*R v Sutton* [1991] Crim LR 836, CA; CJA 2003, s 139(1)).

6.3.4   Present recollection revived and past recollection recorded

The common law rule has been held to apply both in cases of 'present recollection revived' and 'past recollection recorded'. 'Present recollection revived' describes the situation where a witness uses a document to refresh his memory. Past recollection recorded refers to the situation where the witness has no actual recollection of the past event and simply swears to the accuracy of the record in the document. An example may be found in *Maugham v Hubbard* (1828) 8 B & C 14 where an issue arose as to whether a sum of money had been paid. A witness was permitted to prove receipt of the money by looking at a written acknowledgement initialled by himself and stating in evidence that, on the basis of seeing his initials, he was sure that he had received the money, although he had no actual recollection of doing so.

Section 139 of the CJA 2003 applies only to 'present recollection revived'. Documents which would formerly have been used to refresh memory in cases of 'past recollection recorded' may now be admissible under s 120(1), (4) and (6) of the 2003 Act:

> *(1)   This section applies where a person (the witness) is called to give evidence in criminal proceedings.*
>
> . . .

> (4)   A previous statement by the witness is admissible as evidence of any matter stated of which oral evidence by him would be admissible if,—
>   (a) any of the following conditions is satisfied, and
>   (b) while giving evidence the witness indicates that to the best of his knowledge and belief he made the statement, and that to the best of his belief it states the truth.
> . . .
> (6)   The second condition is that the statement was made by the witness when the matters stated were fresh in his memory but he does not remember them, and cannot reasonably be expected to remember them, well enough to give oral evidence of them in the proceedings.

6.3.5   Making and verifying

At common law and under s 139 of the 2003 Act a memory-refreshing document must either be made by the witness or made by another and verified by the witness. The witness must have verified the accuracy of the contents of the document when the facts were still fresh in his memory (*Eleftheriou v Eleftheriou* [1993] Crim LR 947).

Verification may be visual or aural. In *Anderson v Whalley* (1852) 3 Car & Kir 54, it was held that entries in a ship's log made by the mate and inspected by the captain could be used by the latter to refresh his memory. In *R v Kelsey* (1982) 74 Cr App R 213, it was held that a witness could refresh his memory from a note dictated to a police officer and read back to the witness where the police officer was called to prove that the note was the one he had taken down and read back.

6.3.6   Contemporaneity

At common law, the memory-refreshing document must have been made at the time of the events recorded or so shortly after that those events were still fresh in the witness's memory. The Court of Appeal has stated that the concept of contemporaneity contains 'a measure of elasticity and should not be taken to confine a witness to an over-short period' (*R v Richardson* [1971] 2 QB 484).

Section 139 of the 2003 Act contains no requirement that the memory-refreshing document be made contemporaneously or while the events were still fresh in the memory.

6.3.7   Originals and copies

At common law and under the CJA 2003, s 139, there is no requirement that the memory-refreshing document be the original. A witness may refresh his memory from a copy of the original document. Thus, in *Topham v McGregor* (1844) Car & K 320, a witness was permitted to refresh his memory from an accurate copy of a newspaper article, the original having been destroyed. In *R v Chisnell* [1992] Crim LR 507, an officer was allowed to refresh his memory from a statement made nine months after the events it recorded, where the court was satisfied that it was an accurate transcription of a contemporaneous note which had subsequently been lost.

Similarly, a witness may be permitted to refresh his memory from a document based on an original note and containing substantially what was in it. In *R v Cheng* (1976) 63 Cr App R 20, a police officer made a statement based upon notes that he had made shortly after the defendant's arrest. By the time of the trial the original notes had been lost but the officer was permitted to refresh his memory from the statement because the statement substantially reproduced what was in the original notes, even if it was not an exact copy. In *Attorney-General's Reference (No. 3 of 1979)* (1979) 69 Cr App R 411, the court allowed a witness to refresh his memory from a document that he had compiled from jottings taken during the course of an interview, the events being fresh in his mind at the time he made the note, even though he was unable to decipher the jottings at trial and the note was not a complete record of the interview.

At common law, in cases of 'past recollection recorded' (see *Maugham v Hubbard* (1828) 8 B & C 14 above), then the original must be produced (*Doe d Church & Philips v Perkins* (1790) 3 TR 749). However, if the original is not available, an accurate copy can be used (*Topham v McGregor*).

6.3.8   Inspection

A memory-refreshing document must be made available for inspection by any other parties to the proceedings, who may then cross-examine the witness on its contents. A memory-refreshing document may go before the jury if it would assist them in determining an issue at the trial. In *R v Bass* [1953] 1 QB 680, two police officers read identical accounts of a confession allegedly made by the defendant. The defendant disputed making the confession. The officers denied that they had collaborated in preparing their notes of the interview. It was held that the jury should have been allowed to inspect the notebooks as it may have assisted the jury in evaluating the credibility and accuracy of the officers' evidence.

In *R v Sekhon* (1987) 85 Cr App R 19 the Court of Appeal identified two other circumstances in which a memory-refreshing document may go before a jury:

(a) where it is difficult for the jury to follow the cross-examination of the witness who has refreshed his memory, without having the record before them; and

(b) where it is convenient to use the record as an aide-memoire as to the witness's evidence where that evidence is long and involved.

6.3.9   Cross-examination

A party to the proceedings may cross-examine a witness on the contents of a document he has used to refresh his memory. However, where cross-examination goes beyond those parts used by the witness to refresh his memory, the party calling the witness is entitled to put the document in evidence (*Gregory v Tavernor* (1833) 6 Car & P 280; *Senat v Senat* [1965] P 172). Similarly, where cross-examination involves a suggestion that the witness has fabricated his evidence, which will usually involve, either expressly or impliedly, an allegation that the memory-refreshing document is concocted, the memory-refreshing document may then be admissible as evidence to rebut this suggestion and to show whether or not it is a genuine contemporaneous record which has not subsequently been altered (*R v Sekhon* (1987) 85 Cr App R 19).

Where a memory-refreshing document is put in evidence following cross-examination it is evidence of consistency and/or the truth of the matters stated in it (Civil Evidence Act 1995, ss 1 and 6(4) and (5); CJA 2003, s 120(3)). The CJA 2003, s 120 provides:

(1)   This section applies where a person (the witness) is called to give evidence in criminal proceedings.

. . .

(3)   A statement made by the witness in a document—
(a)   which is used by him to refresh his memory while giving evidence.
(b)   on which he is cross-examined, and
(c)   which as a consequence is received in evidence in the proceedings, is admissible of any matter stated of which oral evidence by him would be admissible.

Section 120(3) only applies to statements made by a witness. Thus, where a witness has only verified the memory-refreshing document it could not be admitted as evidence of the truth of the matters stated under s 120(3).

6.4   Previous consistent statements

The general rule, in both civil and criminal proceedings, is that a witness may not be asked in examination-in-chief about a previous oral or written statement, consistent with his testimony, in order to show his consistency (*R v Gregson* [2003] 2 Cr App R 34). Nor may a party seek to adduce evidence of such a statement through another witness. The rationale for the rule is that such evidence is too easy for a witness to fabricate. It has also been suggested that such evidence is, in any event, superfluous as a witness's evidence should be taken as true until there is a reason for impeaching it.

Two examples may be given. In *Corke v Corke* [1958] P 93, the Court of Appeal held that a wife, whose husband had accused her of having committed adultery with a lodger, should not have been permitted to adduce evidence that she had telephoned her doctor immediately after the accusation had been made, requesting him to come at once and examine both her and the lodger, with a view to establishing their innocence of misconduct. In *R v Roberts* [1942] 1 All ER 187, the accused was charged with the murder of a girl by shooting her. At the trial he gave evidence that the gun went off accidentally while he was trying to make up a quarrel with the girl. Two days after the alleged offence, the accused had told his father that his defence would be one of accident. The Court of Appeal held that proof of this conversation was not permissible if tendered to bolster the credibility of the accused by showing his consistency.

There are a number of exceptions to the rule in both civil and criminal proceedings.

6.4.1   Exceptions in civil proceedings

Section 6 of the Civil Evidence Act 1995 provides:

> (2)   *A party who has called or intends to call a person as a witness in civil proceedings may not in those proceedings adduce evidence of a previous statement made by that person except—*
>   (a)   *with leave of the court, or*
>   (b)   *for the purpose of rebutting a suggestion that his evidence has been fabricated.*
>   . . .
> (4)   *Nothing in this Act affects any of the rules of law as to the circumstances in which, where a person called as a witness in civil proceedings is cross-examined on a document used by him to refresh his memory, that document may be made evidence in the proceedings.*

Therefore, there are three exceptions to the general rule in civil proceedings:

- the statement is admissible with the leave of the court (s 6(2)(a));
- the statement is admissible to rebut an allegation of recent fabrication (s 6(2)(b)); and
- the statement is admissible as a memory-refreshing document (s 6(4)).

6.4.1.1   Leave of the court

Under the Civil Evidence Act 1995, s 6(2)(a), the court has a wide discretion to admit previous consistent statements where it would be just to do so. In *Morris v Stratford-on-Avon Rural District Council* [1973] 1 WLR 1059, a decision under the equivalent provision in the

Civil Evidence Act 1968, the trial was held five years after the accident which gave rise to the action. A witness whose recollection of the facts was hazy was allowed to adduce in his evidence-in-chief a statement that he had made to an insurance company nine months after the accident.

6.4.1.2   Evidence in rebuttal of an allegation of recent fabrication

The mere fact that the cross-examination of a witness suggests that the witness is not worthy of belief does not allow the proof of a previous statement by the witness to reinforce his credibility. This is so even if the cross-examination exposes a previous inconsistency or contradiction between his evidence and a statement made on a previous occasion (*R v Coll* (1889) 25 LR Ir 522; *R v Beattie* (1998) 89 Cr App R 302). However, where it is suggested that the witness has recently fabricated his evidence, evidence is admissible in rebuttal to show that on an earlier occasion the witness made a statement consistent with that testimony (*R v Oyesiku* (1971) 56 Cr App R 240, CA; *Fox v General Medical Council* [1960] 1 WLR 1017). For example, in *Flanaghan v Fahy* [1918] 2 IR 361, it was put to a witness, who had testified that a certain document was a forgery, that he had invented his evidence because of the hostility which existed between him and the defendant. The witness was then allowed to call evidence to show that he had told someone else that it was a forgery before the cause of the hostility between him and the defendant arose.

In *R v Oyesiku* (1971) 56 Cr App R 240, the Court of Appeal approved the judgment of Dixon CJ in the Australian case *Nominal Defendant v Clement* (1961) 104 CLR 476 in which he held that:

(a) where it is suggested that the witness's account is a recent invention or reconstruction, even though not with conscious dishonesty, a previous consistent statement is admissible;

(b) the previous statement must have been made either contemporaneously with the event or at a time sufficiently early to be inconsistent with the suggestion that his evidence is a recent invention or reconstruction;

(c) the judge must exercise great care in determining whether a previous statement is admissible. In particular, he must be satisfied that:

    (i) the account given by the witness has been attacked on the ground of recent invention or reconstruction or that foundation for such an attack has been laid;

    (ii) the contents of the previous statement are in fact to the like effect as the account given by the witness in evidence; and

    (iii) having regard to the time and circumstances in which it was made, it rationally tends to the answer the attack.

The facts in *R v Oyesiku* were as follows. After the defendant had been arrested, and while he was still in custody, his wife made a written statement to his solicitor. At trial, prosecution counsel suggested in cross-examination that she had made up her evidence to help her husband. The Court of Appeal held that in re-examination she had properly been permitted to adduce evidence of her previous consistent statement. However, the conviction was quashed as the trial judge had not allowed the document to go before the jury which would have assisted them in determining the extent to which the previous statement answered the attack.

A previous consistent statement can be proved either during the re-examination of the witness or by calling the other person to whom the statement was made (*R v Wilmot* (1989) 89 Cr App R 341).

6.4.1.3   Memory-refreshing document

See **6.3.1** above.

6.4.1.4   Evidential status of a previous consistent statement

A previous consistent statement admissible under the Civil Evidence Act 1995, s 6 is admissible as evidence of consistency and the truth of the matters stated (ss 1 and 6(5)).

6.4.2   Exceptions in criminal proceedings

Memory-refreshing documents
See **6.3.2** above.

6.4.2.1   Previous identifications

At common law, evidence of a previous identification of the accused by a witness out of court is permissible (*R v Christie* [1914] AC 545). However, the common law rules have been superseded by the CJA 2003, s 120 which provides:

(1)   *This section applies where a person (the witness) is called to give evidence in criminal proceedings.*
. . .
(4)   *A previous statement by the witness is admissible as evidence of any matter stated of which oral evidence by him would be admissible if,—*
    (a)   *any of the following conditions is satisfied, and*
    (b)   *while giving evidence the witness indicates that to the best of his knowledge and belief he made the statement, and that to the best of his belief it states the truth.*
. . .
(5)   *the first condition is that the statement identifies or describes a person, object or place.*

6.4.2.2   Recent complaint

For a long time it was a part of the common law that where a complainant, in the case of a sexual offence, made a voluntary complaint shortly after the alleged incident, then evidence could be given of the complaint. Such evidence was not evidence of the matters stated, but evidence of consistency between the complainant's conduct and his testimony, and to disprove consent (*R v Lillyman* [1896] 2 QB 167, CCR). Again, the common law has now been superseded by the CJA 2003, s 120 which provides:

(1)   *This section applies where a person (the witness) is called to give evidence in criminal proceedings.*
. . .
(4)   *A previous statement by the witness is admissible as evidence of any matter stated of which oral evidence by him would be admissible if,—*
    (a)   *any of the following conditions is satisfied, and*
    (b)   *while giving evidence the witness indicates that to the best of his knowledge and belief he made the statement, and that to the best of his belief it states the truth.*
. . .
(7)   *The third condition is that—*
    (a)   *the witness claims to be a person against whom an offence has been committed,*
    (b)   *the offence is one to which the proceedings relate,*
    (c)   *the statement consists of a complaint made by the witness (whether to a person in authority or not) about conduct which would, if proved, constitute the offence or part of the offence,*
    (d)   *the complaint was made as soon as could reasonably be expected after the alleged conduct,*
    (e)   *the complaint was not made as a result of a threat or a promise, and*
    (f)   *before the statement is adduced the witness gives oral evidence in connection with its subject matter.*
(8)   *For the purpose of subsection (7) the fact that the complaint was elicited (for example, by a leading question) is irrelevant unless a threat or promise was involved.*

Section 120(7) broadens the previous common law exception so as to permit evidence of recent complaint in relation to any offence, not just a sexual offence. Previously, evidence of a complaint elicited as the result of a leading question was inadmissible (*R v Osborne* [1905] 1 KB 551). However, the CJA 2003 now expressly permits the admission of complaints made in answer to such questions as long as no threat or promise was involved (s 120(8)). Of course, such questioning may nevertheless affect the weight that the tribunal of fact attaches to the evidence.

A recent complaint is evidence of the truth of the matters stated, consistency between a complainant's conduct and his evidence at trial and, where consent is in issue, lack of consent (s 120(4)).

6.4.2.3 Statements in rebuttal of recent fabrication

The common law rules that govern the admissibility of statements in rebuttal of recent fabrication in civil proceedings apply equally to criminal proceedings (see **6.4.1.2**). In criminal proceedings such a statement will be admissible as evidence of consistency and as evidence of any matter stated of which oral evidence by that witness would be admissible (CJA 2003, s 120(2)).

6.4.2.4 Statements upon accusation

An accusation of involvement in a criminal offence will most often be made by police officers in an informal conversation with the suspect, on arrest or in interview. The law of evidence recognises three types of statement that could be made by a person when confronted by such an accusation:

- an admission;
- an exculpatory statement;
- a mixed statement.

(a) Admissions
A statement which contains an admission is admissible as a confession under PACE 1984, s 76(1) as evidence of the facts stated. Confessions will be considered further in **Chapter 13**.

(b) Exculpatory statements
An exculpatory statement is a statement denying any involvement in the offence. It is admissible as evidence of the attitude and reaction of the accused when taxed with incriminating facts and, thus, evidence of the consistency of the accused's defence, but it is not evidence of the truth of the matters stated (*R v Storey* (1968) 52 Cr App R 334).

In *R v Storey*, the prosecution lead evidence was that, when a quantity of cannabis had been found in the accused's flat, she had explained that it belonged to a man who had brought it there against her will. The defence relied on this statement in a submission of no case to answer. The Court of Appeal upheld the judge's ruling that the statement was not evidence of the facts stated, it was evidence of the reaction of the accused which formed part of the general picture to be considered by the jury.

In *R v Pearce* (1979) 69 Cr App R 365, it was held that this exception to the rule against previous consistent statements is not limited to statements made on the first encounter with the police. However, the longer the time that has elapsed after the first encounter the less the weight which will be attached to the denial.

Where a previous exculpatory statement adds nothing to the evidence already before the court it may be excluded on the basis that it is not relevant and is, therefore, inadmissible. This was the reasoning of the Court of Appeal in *R v Tooke* (1989) 90 Cr App R 417, when upholding the trial judge's decision to exclude a spontaneous written statement made to the police within an hour of the incident because during the course of the trial, a statement made at the scene to the same effect had already been admitted. The Court recognised that in such a case it is not an easy task for the judge to decide, in his discretion, where the dividing line falls.

(c) Mixed statements

A mixed statement is one that is partly incriminatory and partly exculpatory. For example, 'I hit W, but only because I was trying to defend myself.' The whole of a mixed statement is admissible, because it would obviously be unfair for the prosecution to exclude those parts that are favourable to the accused, while relying on those parts favourable to the prosecution (*R v Storey* (1968) 52 Cr App R 334). Moreover, the whole statement is to be taken into consideration in determining where the truth lies. While it could be argued that the exculpatory parts should be admitted as evidence of reaction only, and not as evidence of the truth of the matters stated, it is considered too difficult to explain this legal nicety to a jury. However, the judge may point out that the incriminating parts are likely to be true (otherwise why say them?), whereas excuses do not have the same weight (*R v Sharp* [1988] IWCR 7, HL; *R v Aziz* [1996] AC 41, HL).

In *R v Garrod* [1997] Crim LR 445, the Court of Appeal addressed the question of how to identify when a statement contained enough in the nature of admissions to justify calling it 'mixed'. The court, acknowledging that many statements could be said to contain some admissions of relevant fact, as well a statement of innocence and a denial of guilt, held that a statement should be regarded as mixed if it contained an admission of fact which was significant to any issue in the case, ie capable of adding some degree of weight to the prosecution case on an issue which was relevant to guilt.

In *R v Aziz* [1996] AC 41, HL, it was held that mixed statements are only admissible as evidence of the truth of the matters stated if tendered by the prosecution. However, where the prosecution tender a mixed statement but do not rely on it as proof of any part of their case against the accused, the accused may rely upon it for the truth of its contents (*Western v DPP* [1997] 1 Cr App R 474, DC).

6.4.2.5   *Res gestae* statements

Under the doctrine of *res gestae*, evidence is admissible of any act or statement so closely associated in time, place and circumstances with some matter in issue that it can be said to be a part of the same transaction. A *res gestae* statement is admitted for the truth of its contents. In *R v Fowkes* (1856) *The Times*, 8 March, the defendant was charged with murder. The son of the victim and another person present at the scene were permitted to give evidence that on seeing a face at the window through which a shot was fired, the son had said, 'There's Butcher' (a name by which the defendant was known). The doctrine of *res gestae* will be considered in greater detail at 12.3.3.

6.5   Unfavourable and hostile witnesses

A party may not impeach the credibility of its own witness, whether by:

* asking leading questions; or
* asking about or calling evidence to prove prior inconsistent statements, prior discreditable conduct, bad character, previous convictions or bias.

6.5.1   Unfavourable witnesses

An unfavourable witness is one who either fails to prove that which he was expected to prove ('fails to come up to proof') or who gives evidence unfavourable to the party by whom he has been called. In accordance with the general rule, the party calling the witness may not impeach his credibility but may only call other witnesses to prove the matters that the unfavourable witness failed to prove (*Ewer v Ambrose* (1825) 3 B & C 746).

6.5.2   Hostile witnesses

A hostile witness is one who, in the opinion of the judge, '*is not desirous of telling the truth to the court at the instance of the party calling him*' (Stephen, *Digest of the Law of Evidence*, 12th edn, Article 147).

In criminal proceedings, the prosecution may call a person even if he has shown that he is likely to be a hostile witness, for example, by retracting an earlier statement and/or making a second statement (*R v Mann* (1972) 56 Cr App R 750, CA).

An application for leave to treat a witness as hostile must be made to the judge and, in criminal proceedings, should generally be made in the presence of the jury (*R v Darby* [1989] Crim LR 817, CA; *R v Khan* [2003] Crim LR 428 CA). Normally, the application will be made during examination-in-chief. However, in rare cases in which a witness shows hostility in re-examination, an application can be made at this later stage (*R v Powell* [1985] 1 WLR 1364). The judge should have regard to the demeanour of the witness, the evidence the witness gives, the evidence the witness does not give and the witness's willingness to cooperate. If a witness gives evidence contrary to an earlier statement or fails to give the evidence expected, the party calling the witness and the judge should not immediately proceed to treat him as hostile, unless that is the only appropriate course because of the degree of hostility, but should consider first inviting the witness to refresh his memory from appropriate material (*R v Maw* [1994] Crim LR 841, CA).

Where the judge grants leave to treat a witness as hostile, the party calling the witness may, at common law, ask leading questions (*R v Thompson* (1976) 64 Cr App R 96, CA).

Section 3 of the Criminal Procedure Act 1865, which applies in both civil and criminal proceedings, makes provision for the party calling a hostile witness to prove previous inconsistent statements made by that witness. Section 3 provides that:

A party producing a witness shall not be allowed to impeach his credit by general evidence of bad character, but he may, in case the witness shall in the opinion of the judge prove adverse, contradict him by other evidence, or, by leave of the judge, prove that he has made at other times a statement inconsistent with his present testimony; but before such last-mentioned proof can be given the circumstances of the supposed statement, sufficient to designate the particular occasion, must be mentioned to the witness, and he must be asked whether or not he has made such a statement.

The first part of s 3 of the 1865 Act merely restates the common law rule that a party cannot impeach its own witness. The remainder of the provision applies only to adverse witnesses. In *Greenough v Eccles* (1859) 5 CB NS 786, it was held that 'adverse' means hostile. Thus, the section allows a party calling a hostile witness:

- to contradict the witness, in the same manner as an unfavourable witness, by calling other evidence; or

- to prove a previous inconsistent statement against the witness.

If the witness, under cross-examination on the previous inconsistent statement, confirms its contents, then that will stand as his evidence and can be accepted by the tribunal of fact subject to assessment of the witness's credibility (*R v Maw*). Where the witness does not admit the truth of the previous statement, the statement is admissible as evidence of the matters stated in both civil proceedings (Civil Evidence Act 1995, ss 1 and 6(3) and (5)) and criminal proceedings (CJA 2003, s 119(1)). Thus, where a witness does not admit making the previous inconsistent statement, and it is proved against him, it will be open to the tribunal of fact to accept either the present testimony of the witness or the previous inconsistent statement and to determine the weight to be attached.

Cross-examination and re-examination

7.1 Cross-examination

Cross-examination is the questioning of a witness by any party other than the party calling him. The purpose of cross-examination is:

- to elicit evidence favourable to the cross-examining party's case;

- to qualify, weaken or cast doubt upon evidence unfavourable to the cross-examining party's case.

7.2 Liability to cross-examination

All witnesses who have been called by a party and taken the oath are liable to cross-examination except:

- those who produce documents without being sworn (*Summers v Mosely* (1834) 2 Cr & M 477);

- those called by mistake who cannot give material evidence (*Wood v Mackinson* (1840) 2 Mood & R 273); and

- those who have been called by the judge, unless the judge grants leave (*Coulson v Disborough* [1894] 2 QB 316).

If a witness dies before being cross-examined his evidence-in-chief is still admissible (*R v Doolin* (1832) 1 Jebb CC 123, IR). Where a witness, in cross-examination, is incapable of giving further evidence, the evidence is admissible and the trial may continue but the judge should warn the jury that if they feel unable to assess that witness's credibility because cross-examination was incomplete, then they should acquit the defendant (*R v Stretton* (1986) 86 Cr App R 7, CA; and *R v Wyatt* [1990] Crim LR 343). However, where a witness, who was unable to continue after his examination-in-chief, gave the only direct evidence on an important part of the prosecution case, it was doubted whether a judicial direction could counteract the prejudice to the defendant who was deprived of the opportunity to test the evidence in cross-examination (*R v Lawless* (1993) 98 Cr App R 342).

In criminal proceedings, a witness is examined-in-chief before being cross-examined. However, sometimes a witness will simply be tendered by the prosecution for cross-examination. This typically happens where a police officer gives evidence of observations he made with a second officer, and the second officer's witness statement does no more than confirm the first officer's evidence in all material details. The prosecution would call the second officer, after the first has given evidence in full, ask the officer sufficient questions to identify him and permit the officer to use any memory-refreshing document, before leaving the witness to be cross-examined by the defence.

In civil proceedings, as the witness statement will usually stand as a witness's evidence-in-chief (CPR, r 32.5(2)), evidence-in-chief would ordinarily consist simply of the witness identifying the witness statement and confirming his belief in the truth of its contents. Cross-examination follows immediately after.

7.3 Restrictions on cross-examination

7.3.1 The accused in criminal proceedings

Generally, a witness called by one party to the proceedings, and liable to cross-examination, may be cross-examined by the accused in person. However, there are a number of restrictions placed upon cross-examination by the accused.

7.3.1.1 Common law

At common law, the judge can restrict both the length of the cross-examination and the issues to which it relates (*R v Brown* [1998] 2 Cr App R 364).

7.3.1.2 The complainant in sexual offences

The YJCEA 1999 places significant restrictions on the accused's ability to cross-examine certain witnesses in person. Section 34 of the YJCEA 1999 provides:

> (1) *No person charged with a sexual offence may in any criminal proceedings cross-examine in person a witness who is the complainant, either—*
>   (a) *in connection with that offence, or*
>   (b) *in connection with any other offence (of whatever nature) with which that person is charged in the proceedings.*

'Sexual offence' is defined in YJCEA 1999, s 62 as any offence under the Sexual Offences Act 2003, Part 1.

7.3.1.3 Child witnesses

Section 35 of the YJCEA 1999 provides:

> (1) *No person charged with an offence to which this section applies may in any criminal proceedings cross-examine in person a protected witness, either—*
>   (a) *in connection with that offence, or*
>   (b) *in connection with any other offence (of whatever nature) with which that person is charged in the proceedings.*

A 'protected witness' is a witness who:

(a) is either the complainant or a witness (s 35(2)(a)) to one or more of the offences specified in YJCEA 1999, s 35(3), namely:
  (i) sexual offences under either Part 1 of the Sexual Offences Act 2003 or the Protection of Children Act 1978 (s 35(3)(a));
  (ii) kidnapping, false imprisonment or child abduction (s 35(3)(b));

(iii) child cruelty (s 35(3)(c)); or

(iv) any other offence involving an assault on, or injury, or threat of injury to any person (s 35(3)(d));

and

(b) either

(i)   where the offence is a sexual offence, the witness is under the age of 17 or falls to be cross-examined having given evidence-in-chief when under that age (s 35(2)(b)), or

(ii) in the case of any other specified offence, the witness is under the age of 14 or falls to be cross-examined having given evidence-in-chief when under that age (s 35(2)(b)).

7.3.1.4   General discretion

Section 36 of the YJCEA 1999 permits the court to make a direction prohibiting the accused from cross-examining a witness in person where neither YJCEA 1999, ss 34 nor 35 operate if:

(2)   . . . it appears to the court—

(a)   that the quality of evidence given by the witness on cross-examination—

(i)   is likely to be diminished if the cross-examination . . . is conducted by the accused in person, and

(ii) would be likely to be improved if a direction were given under this section, and

(b)   that it would not be contrary to the interests of justice to give such a direction.

In determining whether the YJCEA 1999, s 36(2)(a) applies, the court must take into account the various factors set out in s 35(3) including any views expressed by the witness, the nature of the questions likely to be asked and the behaviour of the accused both towards the witness and generally. 'Witness' for the purposes of this section does not include a co-accused (s 36(4)(a)).

7.3.1.5   Procedure

In cases where cross-examination by the accused is prevented under any of the above provisions, YJCEA 1999, s 38 requires that the court must invite the accused to arrange for a legal representative to act for him for the purposes of cross-examining, and require the accused to notify the court whether such a person is to act. If the accused fails to arrange for a legal representative or, failing notification, it appears that there will be no such representative, the court must consider whether it is necessary in the interests of justice for the witness to be cross-examined by a legal representative appointed to represent the accused's interests. If so, the court must appoint a qualified legal representative to cross-examine the witness in the interests of the accused.

Under YJCEA 1999, s 39, a judge is required to give such warning as is necessary (if any) to the jury, in a case where cross-examination in person has been prevented, to ensure that the accused is not prejudiced by any inferences that might be drawn from the fact that he has been prevented from cross-examining, and, where there is a court-appointed legal representative acting, that that person was not acting as the accused's own legal representative.

7.3.2   Judicial discretion

The judge has a common law discretion to prevent counsel from conducting unnecessary or improper cross-examination. Counsel should not waste time by protracted and irrelevant cross-examination but should cross-examine with restraint and the courtesy and consideration which witnesses are entitled to expect (*Mechanical and General Inventions Co Ltd v Austin* [1935] AC 346, HL; *R v Kalia* (1974) 60 Cr App R 200).

In civil proceedings, the court has an additional power to limit cross-examination under CPR, r 32.1(3). (see **1.6.1**)

7.3.3   Code of Conduct for the Bar

There are also a number of rules to be observed which are set out in the Code of Conduct of the Bar of England and Wales, including in particular, the following paragraphs of Part VII (conduct of work):

> *701. A barrister:*
>
> *(a) must in all his professional activities be courteous and act promptly conscientiously diligently and with reasonable competence and take all reasonable and practicable steps to avoid unnecessary expense or waste of the Court's time . . .*
>
> *708. A barrister when conducting proceedings in Court:*
>
> *. . .*
>
> *(e) must not adduce evidence obtained otherwise than from or through the client or devise facts which will assist in advancing the lay client's case;*
>
> *. . .*
>
> *(g) must not make statements or ask questions which are merely scandalous or intended or calculated only to vilify insult or annoy either a witness or some other person;*
>
> *(h) must if possible avoid the naming in open Court of third parties whose character would thereby be impugned;*
>
> *(i) must not by assertion in a speech impugn a witness whom he has had an opportunity to cross-examine unless in cross-examination he has given the witness an opportunity to answer the allegation;*
>
> *(j) must not suggest that a victim, witness or other person is guilty of crime, fraud or misconduct or make any defamatory aspersion on the conduct of any other person or attribute to another person the crime or conduct of which his lay client is accused unless such allegations go to a matter in issue (including the credibility of the witness) which is material to the lay client's case and appear to him to be supported by reasonable grounds.*

While the Code of Conduct is not binding on the court, it does have persuasive force (*R v McFadden* (1975) 62 Cr App R 187, a case concerning the Bar Council Rules which the Code of Conduct replaced).

7.4   Consequences of failing to cross-examine

In *R v Wood Green Crown Court, ex p Taylor* [1995] Crim LR 879, it was held that a party who fails to cross-examine a witness on a fact is deemed to have accepted what the witness says on that fact and therefore cannot invite the tribunal of fact to disbelieve him on that matter. There is therefore a duty to put one's case and it is a fundamental requirement of cross-examination.

However, if it is proposed to invite the jury to disbelieve a witness on a particular matter, it does not follow that it is always necessary to put to the witness explicitly that he is lying, provided that the overall tenor of the cross-examination is designed to show that his account is incapable of belief (*R v Lovelock* [1997] Crim LR 821, CA). It has been held that the rule in *ex p Taylor* does not apply to proceedings before lay justices (*O'Connell v Adams* [1973] CMMLR 3B). If counsel omits to cross-examine on a particular point by reason of inadvertence, the judge has a discretion to allow the witness to be recalled (*R v Wilson* [1977] Crim LR 553, CA).

7.5   Cross-examination and inadmissible evidence

The rules governing the admissibility of evidence apply equally to cross-examination and examination-in-chief. Therefore, questions seeking to elicit evidence that would not be admissible in examination-in-chief cannot be put to a witness in cross-examination. For example, it has been held to be improper for a cross-examining party to attempt to elicit hearsay evidence (*R v Thomson* [1912] 3 KB 19).

Many of the cases in this area concern the use to which admissions and confessions may be put. In *R v Treacy* [1944] 2 All ER 229, it was held that the prosecution should not have been permitted to cross-examine the accused so as to reveal that he had made a confession that had been ruled inadmissible as part of the prosecution case. This rule also obtains in favour of any co-accused of the maker of a confession (*R v Rice* [1963] 1 QB 857). However, where an accused's inadmissible confession is relevant to the defence of the co-accused, and the accused gives evidence inconsistent with it, the co-accused can cross-examine him on it, provided that the judge makes clear to the jury that it is not evidence of the accused's guilt (*R v Rowson* [1986] QB 174, CA; *Lui Mei Lin v R* [1989] 1 All ER 359, PC).

7.6   Cross-examination on documents

Counsel may show a document to a witness during cross-examination, ask the witness to read it to himself and then ask the witness if the contents are true. If the witness admits that they are and he would have been permitted to give oral evidence of the matters stated, then they become the witness's evidence and can be revealed (*R v Gillespie* (1967) 51 Cr App R 172; *R v Cooper* (1985) 82 Cr App R 74).

7.7   Previous inconsistent statements

A previous inconsistent statement is any statement made by the witness prior to giving evidence which is inconsistent with their testimony.

7.7.1   Criminal Procedure Act 1865, ss 4 and 5

Where a previous inconsistent statement is put to the witness and he admits to having made it, then it becomes part of the witness's evidence and no further proof of the statement is required (*R v P (GR)* [1998] Crim LR 663). Where the witness does not admit making the previous statement, its admissibility will be determined, in both criminal and civil proceedings, by the Criminal Procedure Act 1865, ss 4 and 5. Section 4 provides:

If a witness, upon cross-examination as to a former statement made by him relative to the subject matter of the indictment or proceeding, and inconsistent with his present testimony, does not distinctly admit that he has made such statement, proof may be given that he did in fact make it; but before such proof can be given the circumstances of the supposed statement, sufficient to designate the particular occasion, must be mentioned to the witness, and he must be asked whether or not he has made such statement.

In *R v Derby Magistrates' Court, ex P B* [1996] AC 487, HL, Lord Taylor of Gosforth CJ confirmed that s 4 of the 1865 Act applies to both oral and written statements, s 5 of the Act is confined to written statements.

The phrase '*relative to the subject matter of the indictment or proceeding*', which is used in ss 4 and 5 of the 1865 Act, means relevant to the facts in issue as opposed to some collateral matter such as, for example, matters going solely to the credit of the witness (*R v Funderburk* [1990] 1 WLR 587). Thus, where the previous inconsistent statement is relevant only to the credibility of the witness, the 1865 Act does not apply. However, it is not always easy to determine whether an issue is relevant to a fact in issue or merely credibility. This is particularly true where the disputed issue is a sexual one between two persons in private as, in those circumstances, the difference between questions going to credit and questions going to the issue is reduced almost to vanishing point (see **7.8.1** below).

Section 5 of the Criminal Evidence Act 1865 provides:

A witness may be cross-examined as to previous statements made by him in writing, or reduced into writing, relative to the subject matter of the indictment or proceeding, without such writing being shown to him; but if it is intended to contradict such witness by the writing, his attention must, before such contradictory proof can be given, be called to those parts of the writing which are to be used for the purpose of so contradicting him: Provided always, that it shall be competent for the judge, at any time during the trial, to require the production of the writing for his inspection, and he may thereupon make such use of it for the purposes of the trial as he may think fit.

Under s 5 of the 1865 Act, counsel can cross-examine a witness on a document without showing it to the witness. However, even if counsel does not intend to show the writing to the witness with a view to contradicting the witness, the document must be in court because the judge may require the document to be produced (*R v Anderson* (1929) 21 Cr App R 178).

The usual practice is for counsel to hand the document to the witness and ask the witness to read the relevant part to himself. This does not make the document an exhibit. Counsel will then ask the witness whether he still stands by the evidence given to the court. If the witness accepts that the previous inconsistent statement is true, then that becomes part of his evidence. If the witness stands by his evidence, then counsel can choose whether or not to prove the previous statement. If counsel wishes to do so he may prove it by reading, or asking the witness to read, the relevant part to the court. It is then open to the court to examine the document to see the extent of the inconsistency.

Where a witness has been cross-examined on a previous inconsistent statement, then, because under s 5 of the 1865 Act the judge may make such use of it for the purposes of the trial as he may think fit, it is open to the judge to allow the whole of the statement to go before the jury, but the judge has a discretion to allow the jury to see only those parts on which cross-examination was based.

A previous inconsistent statement is admissible, in both criminal proceedings (CJA 2003, s 119(1)) and civil proceedings (Civil Evidence Act 1995, ss 1 and 6(3) and (5)), as evidence of the truth of the previous inconsistent statement and evidence affecting credibility.

7.8   The rule of finality

7.8.1   General rule

A witness's answer to a question concerning a collateral issue is final in that the cross-examining party cannot attempt to call any further evidence to prove the contrary (*Harris v Tippett* (1811) 2 Camp 637). However, the tribunal of fact is under no obligation to accept the answer given by the witness as true. A collateral issue is one that is not directly relevant to the facts in issue in the case. The classic, if somewhat circular, test for identifying a collateral issue was given in *Attorney-General v Hitchcock* (1847) 1 Exch 91 by Pollock CB:

The test whether a matter is collateral or not is this: if the answer of a witness is a matter which you would be allowed on your own part to prove in evidence — if it have such a connection with the issues, that you would be allowed to give it in evidence — then it is a matter on which you may contradict him.

For example, in *R v Burke* (1858) 8 Cox CC 44, in order to undermine the credibility of an Irish witness who was giving evidence through an interpreter, it was suggested in cross-examination that the witness had spoken to two people in English in the court building prior to giving evidence. It was held that this was a collateral issue and, as the witness denied it, evidence to the contrary could not be called. In *R v Marsh* (1985) 83 Cr App R 165, by contrast, a witness's denial that he had threatened the accused was not treated as a collateral issue, part of the defence being that the accused believed that the witness had intended to attack him.

The principal rationale for the rule is that it prevents a proliferation of the issues at trial. However, the rule also recognises that it would be unfair to ambush a witness with questioning on issues that he had not anticipated.

Determining whether a particular issue is a fact in issue or a collateral issue can be very difficult and may require the court to draw some very fine distinctions. In *R v Funderburk* [1990] 1 WLR 587, the Court of Appeal urged a flexible, rather than an overly pedantic, approach to such questions, even recognising that the test may be instinctive and depend upon the prosecutor's and the court's sense of fair play. Where the disputed issue is a sexual one between two persons in private, the difference between questions going to credit and questions going to the issue is reduced almost to vanishing point because sexual intercourse, whether or not consensual, usually takes place in private and leaves few visible traces of having occurred, so that the evidence is often limited to that of the parties and much is likely to turn on the balance of credibility between them.

Whether an issue is collateral or not is a decision to be made by the judge, and it is a decision with which the Court of Appeal will only interfere if it is wrong in principle or clearly wrong on the facts of the case (*R v Somers* [1999] Crim LR 744).

7.8.2 Exceptions

The general rule is subject to four exceptions:

- previous convictions;
- bias;
- reputation for untruthfulness;
- disability affecting reliability.

Where a question concerning any one of the above issues is put to the witness and answered in the negative, the cross-examining party will be permitted to call evidence in rebuttal.

7.8.2.1 Previous convictions

Section 6 of the Criminal Procedure Act 1865, which applies to both civil and criminal proceedings, provides:

If, upon a witness being lawfully questioned as to whether he has been convicted of any offence, he either denies or does not admit the fact, or refuses to answer, it shall be lawful for the cross-examining party to prove such a conviction.

In criminal proceedings, the admissibility of evidence of a witness's previous convictions is governed by the CJA 2003. Thus, the questioning of a witness about a previous conviction is only 'lawful' where the provisions of the CJA 2003 regarding bad character have been satisfied. Section 100 governs the admissibility of the bad character of a witness other than the defendant and s 101 the bad character of the defendant. These provisions will be considered in detail in Chapters 9 and 10. As will be seen, once the requirements of ss 100 and 101 are satisfied, evidence of bad character is admissible even where it is collateral because it is only relevant to the witness's credit. For this reason it is thought that in criminal proceedings this exception to the rule of finality is now of less significance than it has been in the past. In civil proceedings, cross-examination on 'spent convictions' is not permitted unless justice cannot be done in the case except by admitting or requiring such evidence (Rehabilitation of Offenders Act 1974, ss 4(1) and 7(3)). The 1974 Act does not prohibit cross-examination on spent convictions in criminal proceedings; however, paragraph I.6.1 of *Practice Direction (Criminal Proceedings: Consolidation)* [2002] 1 WLR 2870 recommends that both court and advocates should nevertheless give effect to the general intention of Parliament by never referring to a spent conviction when such reference can be reasonably avoided.

7.8.2.2   Bias

Where a witness denies a suggestion of bias or partiality in cross-examination then evidence to contradict the witness may be called in rebuttal in order to show that the witness is prejudiced. For example, in *R v Shaw* (1888) 16 Cox CC 503, the accused was permitted to call evidence to contradict a prosecution witness who denied having threatened to take revenge upon the accused. In *R v Mendy* (1976) 64 Cr App 4, the accused's husband gave evidence on her behalf. The common practice in criminal trials is that witnesses are not allowed into the court room until they give their evidence. In cross-examination he denied having spoken to a man who had been seen in the public gallery taking notes of the evidence during the prosecution case. The prosecution were permitted to call evidence in rebuttal. Following *Thomas v David* (1836) 7 Car & P 350, where a witness denies being the kept mistress of the claimant, the defendant will be permitted to call evidence to prove the nature of their relationship.

It is submitted that in criminal proceedings, following the enactment of the CJA 2003, the exception of bias is only concerned with evidence of bias which falls short of a criminal offence or reprehensible behaviour. Section 99 of the 2003 Act abolished the common law rules governing the admissibility of evidence of bad character in criminal proceedings. As the exception of bias is a common law rule, to the extent that it admitted evidence of bad character it has now been abolished. However, the exception will continue to apply to evidence of bias that does not amount to bad character. The 2003 Act defines bad character as evidence relating to the commission of an offence or other reprehensible behaviour. Thus, the rule now only operates in relation to evidence of bias falling short of this definition. As a result, it is expected that this rule will also be of less significance, in criminal proceedings, than it has been in the past.

7.8.2.3   Evidence of a reputation for untruthfulness

Evidence is admissible that a witness called by one's opponent bears such a general reputation for untruthfulness that he is unworthy of belief. The method by which such evidence must be called was summarised by Edmund Davies LJ in *R v Richardson* (1968) 52 Cr App R 317 as follows:

> (1)   witness X may be asked (a) whether he has knowledge of witness Y's general reputation for untruth-fulness and (b) whether (from such knowledge) he would believe witness Y's evidence; and

(2) *witness X may also express his individual opinion (based upon his personal knowledge) as to whether witness Y is to be believed upon his oath; but.*

(3) *witness X cannot be permitted to indicate during his examination-in-chief the particular facts, circumstances or incidents which formed the basis of his opinion, although he may be cross-examined on them.*

7.8.2.4   Evidence of disability affecting reliability

Medical evidence is admissible to show that a witness suffers from a physical or mental disability that affects the reliability of his evidence (*Toohey v Metropolitan Police Commissioner* [1965] AC 595, HL). Such evidence is not restricted to a general opinion of the unreliability of the witness, but may include evidence of the foundations of, and reasons for, the diagnosis and the extent to which the credibility of the witness is affected.

For example, in *R v Eades* [1972] Crim LR 99, the prosecution were properly allowed to call a consultant psychiatrist to prove that the accused's account of how he had recovered his memory after an accident was not consistent with current medical knowledge.

7.9   Re-examination

After cross-examination a witness may be re-examined by the party calling him. Re-examination is subject to the same rules as evidence-in-chief. Except with leave of the judge, re-examination must be restricted to the matters which arose in cross-examination (*Prince v Samo* (1838) 7 Ad & El 627).

In *R v Beattie* (1989) 89 Cr App R 302, CA, it was held that a party is not entitled, merely by reason of cross-examination on a previous inconsistent statement, to re-examine the witness on a previous statement consistent with the witness's testimony. However, in *R v Ali* [2004] 1 Cr App R 501, the Court of Appeal recognised that the court does have a residual discretion to allow re-examination on a previous consistent statement, to prevent the jury from being positively misled as to the existence of some fact or the terms of an earlier statement.

8

Character evidence: civil cases

8.1 Introduction

Character evidence, in both criminal and civil proceedings, may be defined as evidence of a person's reputation or their disposition to behave in a particular way. It includes evidence of good as well as bad character.

8.2 The relevance of character evidence

Character evidence may be relevant in one of three ways:

(a) Character as a fact issue. The character of a party might itself be a fact in issue in the proceedings. For example, in a defamation action in which the defence is justification, the defendant's character will be a fact in issue.

(b) Character relevant to a fact in issue. The character of a person, while not itself an issue in the proceedings, may be probative of one or more of the facts in issue. For example, where a defendant charged with shoplifting claims he picked up goods but absent-mindedly left the shop without paying for them, evidence of previous convictions for the same offences may be admissible to prove he was acting dishonestly.

(c) Character relevant to credit. The character of a party or witness is relevant to their credibility, eg, where a witness has a previous conviction for perjury.

8.3 Character of parties

In civil proceedings different rules apply depending on whether the evidence relates to the character of a party or a person other than a party such as a witness. We will consider parties first before looking at the rules relating to persons other than parties below.

8.3.1 Character as a fact in issue

The character of a party to a case is admissible if it is a fact in issue in the case. The example of defamation proceedings is given above at **8.2**. Where the defendant pleads justification, the claimant's character is in issue and both parties will be permitted to call evidence relevant to that issue (*Maisel v Financial Times Ltd* (1915) 84 LJKB 2145). Evidence of the claimant's character is also admissible in defamation proceedings on the issue of the quantum of damages: see, generally, *Scott v Sampson* (1882) 8 QBD 491.

8.3.2   Character relevant to a fact in issue

8.3.2.1   Good character

The good character of a party may not be adduced. The rationale for this rule was given by Martin B. in *Attorney-General v Bowman* (1791) 2 Bos & P 532n in which he explained that in criminal proceedings a defendant's good character is admissible because there is a fair and just presumption that a person of good character would not commit a crime whereas no presumption that the defendant did not commit the civil wrong alleged would fairly arise from his good character in the majority of civil cases. The same principle applies to the evidence of the good character of the claimant (*Cornwell v Richardson* (1825) 1 Ry & M 305). It will be noted that neither of these authorities are particularly recent. At least one commentator has argued that evidence of the party's good character should be admissible provided that it meets the ordinary requirement of relevance (see A. Keane, *The Modern Law of Evidence*, Oxford University Press, 6th edn, 2005).

8.3.2.2   Bad character

The character of the defendant, while not itself in issue, may nevertheless be probative of one or more of the issues in the case. For example, in *Hales v Kerr* [1908] 2 KB 601, the plaintiff in an action for negligence alleged that he had contracted an infectious disease through the negligence of the defendant, a barber, in using razors and other appliances in a dirty and unsanitary condition. In support of his case he tendered the evidence of two witnesses who had contracted a similar disease in the defendant's shop. The character of the claimant may also be admitted on the same basis. For example, where proceedings are brought for a residence order to recover the custody of a child, evidence that the applicant has previously assaulted the child and is therefore not a suitable custodian would be admissible.

This type of character evidence is sometimes known as 'similar fact evidence'. However, this phrase is very misleading as it gives the impression that to be admissible the previous misconduct must be factually similar. This is not the case. Similar fact evidence will be admitted as long as it satisfies the ordinary test of relevance. In *Mood Music Publishing Co Ltd v De Wolfe Ltd* [1976] Ch 119, CA, the plaintiffs were music publishers seeking damages for the infringement of their copyright on a piece of music ('Sogno Nostalgico'). They alleged that the defendants, another music publishing company, had copied the plaintiffs' music in producing a piece of music of their own ('Girl in the Dark'). The defendants claimed that any similarity was coincidental. In order to meet this defence, the plaintiffs were permitted to adduce three more scores by the defendants each of which bore a remarkable similarity to music owned by the plaintiffs. The Court of Appeal held that such evidence was admissible as logically probative to disprove the defence of coincidence. Whereas it was possible for there to be one case of coincidental similarity, it was very unlikely that there would be four such coincidences.

This decision was recently upheld by the House of Lords in *O'Brien v Chief Constable of South Wales Police* [2005] 2 WLR 1061, where it was stated per Lord Philips of Worth Matravers:

I would simply apply the test of relevance as the test of admissibility of similar fact evidence in a civil suit. Such evidence is admissible if it is potentially probative of an issue in the act.

Their Lordships held that admissibility of this type of character evidence is a two-stage process. First, the judge must decide if the evidence is relevant. Secondly, if he decides that it is, he then has a discretion (under CPR r 32.1) to refuse to admit it. Per Lord Philips of Worth Matravers:

Evidence of impropriety which reflects adversely on the character of a party may risk causing prejudice that is disproportionate to its relevance, particularly where the trial is taking place before a jury. In such a case the judge will be astute to see that the probative cogency of the evidence justifies the risk of prejudice in the interests of a fair trial. Equally, when considering whether to admit evidence, or permit cross-examination, on matters that are collateral to the central issues, the judge will have regard to the need for proportionality and expedition. He will consider whether the evidence in question is likely to be relatively uncontroversial, or whether its admission is likely to create side issues which will unbalance the trial and make it harder to see the wood from the trees.

8.3.3 Evidence of character relevant to credibility

A party in civil proceedings is treated in the same way as any other witness in so far as evidence relevant to his or her credibility is concerned. Therefore the rules identified at **8.4.2** below apply.

8.4 Persons other than parties to the proceedings

8.4.1 Evidence of character relevant to a fact in issue

8.4.1.1 Good character

Evidence of the good character of a person who is not a party in the proceedings is rarely, if ever, relevant to a fact in issue. In any event, were it to be relevant it would not be admissible by analogy with the rule in *Attorney-General v Bowman* (1791) 2 Bos & P 532n and *Cornwell v Richardson* (1825) 1 Ry & M 305 (see **8.3.2.1** above).

8.4.1.2 Bad character

Evidence of the bad character of a third party may be relevant to a fact in issue in the proceedings. Where it is, the test laid down in *Mood Music Publishing Co Ltd v De Wolfe Ltd* [1976] Ch 119, CA and *O'Brien v Chief Constable of South Wales Police* [2005] 2 WLR 1061, HL, will apply. An example of how the character of a third party may be relevant to a fact in issue in the proceedings arose in *Joy v Philips, Mills & Co Ltd* [1916] 1 KB 849. That case involved a claim for compensation by a deceased workman's dependent father. The deceased, who had been employed as a stable boy by the respondents, was found in their stable clutching a halter, suffering from a kick behind the ear from one of their horses. In order to rebut the claim that the accident had happened in the course of the deceased's employment, the defendant adduced evidence that the deceased had previously hit the horses with a halter and teased them.

8.4.2 Evidence of character relevant to credibility

In most cases, the only persons, other than the parties, whose credibility will be of concern to the court will be the witnesses.

8.4.2.1 Good character

A party calling a witness may wish to adduce evidence of that witness's good character in order to boost the credibility of their testimony. However, in civil proceedings, a party is not permitted to call evidence of the good character of its own witness. In *R v Turner* [1975] QB 834, CA, it was stated per Lawton LJ:

in general evidence can be called to impugn the credibility of a witness but not led in chief to bolster it up.

It is nonetheless a far from uncommon practice for the party calling a witness to seek to bolster their evidence by adducing evidence of their employment, marital status and even, on occasion, their lack of previous convictions.

8.4.2.2 Bad character

A party may discredit an opponent's witnesses by cross-examining him on his bad character as long as the questioning is relevant. However, the judge has a duty to prevent questioning which is improper or oppressive and a general discretion to limit cross-examination under CPR r 32.1(3). In *Hobbs v CT Tinling & Co Ltd* [1929] 2 KB 1 the Court of Appeal gave guidance as to how the court should exercise its discretion to prevent cross-examination as to the credit of a witness:

(1) *Such questions are proper if they are of such a nature that the truth of the imputation conveyed by them would seriously affect the opinion of the Court as to the credibility of the witness on the matter to which he testifies.*

(2) *Such questions are improper if the imputation which they convey relates to matters so remote in time, or of such a character that the truth of the imputation would not affect, or would affect in a slight degree, the opinion of the Court as to the credibility of the witness on the matter to which he testifies.*

(3) *Such questions are improper if there is a great disproportion between the importance of the imputation made against the witness's character and the importance of his evidence.*

Further guidance was given by the Court of Appeal in *R v Sweet-Escott* (1971) 55 Cr App R 316. The question before the court was how far back is it permissible to delve into a witness's past when cross-examining as to credit? The answer given per Lawton LJ was:

Since the purpose of cross-examination as to credit is to show that the witness ought not to be believed on oath, the matters about which he is questioned must relate to his likely standing after cross-examination with the tribunal which is trying him or listening to his evidence.

8.4.2.3 The rule of finality

As the credibility of a witness is not a fact in issue, or of direct relevance to a fact in issue, it is a collateral issue. As a result, the rule of finality applies (see **7.8.1**) and answers given by a witness during cross-examination as to credit cannot be contradicted by the cross-examining party. However, the rule is subject to four exceptions:

- previous convictions;
- evidence of bias;
- evidence of reputation for untruthfulness; and
- evidence of disability affecting reliability.

For further details on the exceptions to the rule of finality, see **7.8.2.**

Character evidence: the defendant in criminal proceedings

9.1 Introduction

This chapter considers the admissibility of evidence of the character of a defendant in criminal proceedings. The rules governing the admissibility of the character of persons other than the defendant will be considered in the following chapter.

9.2 The defendant's good character

In *R v Vye* [1993] 1 WLR 471, CA it was held that evidence of good character may be relevant to either the facts in issue (ie, guilt) and/or credibility. Good character is relevant to guilt as a defendant with a propensity to good behaviour is less likely to have engaged in criminal conduct. It is relevant to credibility as a defendant who is shown to be honest is less likely to give false evidence. The court held that a character direction should, therefore, consist of two limbs:

(1) A direction as to the relevance of the defendant's good character to a defendant's credibility. This direction must to be given when the defendant has testified or made pre-trial answers or statements. Conventionally this is known as the 'first limb' of a character direction; and

(2) A direction as to the relevance of his good character to the likelihood of his having committed the offence charged. This direction is to be given, whether or not he has testified, or made pre-trial answers or statements. It is known as the 'second limb' of a character direction.

The meaning of the phrase 'pre-trial statement and answers' in the first limb of the direction was clarified in *R v Aziz* [1995] 3 All ER 149, where their Lordships held that it referred only to mixed statements, ie statements which are both inculpatory and exculpatory and which are therefore admissible as evidence of the facts they contain (see **6.4.2.4**). Thus, a defendant who does not give evidence and relies only on wholly exculpatory pre-trial answers or statements is not entitled to a first limb direction because such statements would not be admissible as evidence of the facts they contain and therefore there is nothing for the jury to assess in terms of credibility.

A *Vye* direction may be given even if the defendant has previous convictions. Where the previous convictions can only be regarded as irrelevant or of no significance in relation to the offence charged, the authorities suggest that the judge ought to exercise his discretion in favour of treating the defendant as being of 'effective' good character (*R v H* [1994] Crim LR 205; and *R v Aziz* [1995] 3 All ER 149). If he does so, the defendant is entitled to a *Vye* direction (*R v Aziz* [1995] 3 All ER 149; *R v Gray* [2004] 2 Cr App R 30). The judge may qualify the *Vye* direction so as to reflect that the defendant has previous convictions.

Where a defendant of previous good character has been shown at trial to be guilty of criminal conduct, the prima facie rule of practice is to deal with this by qualifying a *Vye* direction rather than by withholding it (*R v Vye* [1993] 1 WLR 471; *R v Durbin* [1995] 2 Cr App R 84; *R v Aziz* [1995] 3 All ER 149; and *R v Gray* [2004] 2 Cr App R 30). In such a case, there is nevertheless a residual discretion to withhold a good character direction, in whole or in part, where it would make no sense, or would be meaningless or absurd or an insult to common sense to do otherwise (*R v Zoppola-Barrazza* [1994] Crim LR 833; *R v Durbin* [1995] 2 Cr App R 84; and *R v Aziz* [1995] 3 All ER 149). For example, in *Zoppola-Barrazza* the defendant, who had no previous convictions, was charged with drug smuggling and in his defence gave evidence of smuggling gold and jewels. The Court of Appeal upheld the trial judge's refusal to give a *Vye* direction.

If a defendant pleads guilty to an offence which is an alternative to that on which he is being tried, and the facts are such that if he is convicted of the greater offence then the guilty plea to the lesser offence will have to be vacated, a good character direction should be given, but should be tailored to take into account the guilty plea (*R v Teasdale* [1993] 4 All ER 290). For example, in *Teasdale* the defendant was charged in an indictment with two offences under the Offences against the Person Act 1861, ss 18 and 47. The counts related to the same incident and were in the alternative. The defendant was of good character apart from the guilty plea to the s 47 offence on the indictment. It was held that a tailored character direction should have been given. However, where the defendant pleads guilty to a count which is not a lesser alternative, it has been held that he then ceases to be a person of good character and the full direction becomes inappropriate (*R v Challenger* [1994] Crim LR 202). The inconsistency of these two decisions has been criticised by both academic commentators and practitioners.

9.2.1 Co-defendants

Where there are two defendants on trial but only one of them is of good character, there is a risk that a good character direction in favour of that defendant will highlight the other defendants absence of good character. In *R v Vye* [1993] 1WLR 471, it was held that where a defendant of good character is jointly tried with a defendant of bad character, the former is still entitled to a full *Vye* direction. As to the defendant of bad character, in some cases the judge may think it best to tell the jury that there has been no evidence about his character and that they must not speculate or treat the absence of information as evidence against him; in other cases the judge may think it best to say nothing about the absence of such information. The proper approach depends on the circumstances of the case, in particular, how great an issue was made of character during the case and speeches.

9.2.2 Proving good character

In *R v Rowton* (1865) Le & CA 520, CCR, it was held that evidence of the defendant's good character must be limited to evidence of his general reputation amongst those to whom he is known; evidence of particular creditable acts and of a witness's opinion as to his good character is inadmissible. This rule has been heavily criticised and in practice has been significantly relaxed. However, *Rowton* has never been overruled and it has been held that the rule in *Rowton* still operates to exclude evidence of previous creditable acts (*R v Redgrave* (1974) Cr App R 10, CA).

9.3 The defendant's bad character

As in civil proceedings, evidence of bad character may be relevant in the following ways:

(a) Character as a fact issue. The character of the defendant may itself be a fact in issue in the proceedings. For example, the Firearms Act 1968, s 21 makes it an offence for a person who has previously been convicted of a criminal offence and sentenced to a term of imprisonment of three or more years to be in possession of a firearm. Therefore, the defendant's bad character is one of the facts in issue that the prosecution must prove in order to secure a conviction.

(b) Character relevant to a fact in issue. The character of the defendant, while not itself an issue in the proceedings, may be probative of one or more of the facts in issue. For example, where a defendant charged with shoplifting claims he absent-mindedly left the shop forgetting to pay, evidence of previous convictions for the same offences may be admissible to prove that he was acting dishonestly.

(c) Character relevant to credit. The character of the defendant is relevant to his credibility. For example, where a defendant has previous convictions which reveal a propensity to be untruthful.

Prior to the implementation of the CJA 2003, the admissibility of the defendant's bad character was governed by both statute and common law. The CJA 2003 repeals the main statutory provisions governing the admissibility of evidence of bad character in criminal proceedings (most notably the Criminal Evidence Act 1898, s 1(3)) and abolishes the common law rules governing the admissibility of evidence of bad character as defined by the 2003 Act. It replaces the old regime with a new statutory framework. While there are some significant changes to the law in this area, the CJA 2003 reflects many of the principles established under the old common law and statutory scheme. For this reason, the previous authorities decided in relation to those principles are likely to be of assistance in interpreting and applying the CJA 2003. In this chapter, therefore, there will be occasional reference to the previous statutes and cases decided under the old law.

The CJA 2003 applies to all trials taking place on or after 15 December 2004 (*R v Bradley* [2005] 1 Cr App R 24).

9.4 Bad character under the Criminal Justice Act 2003

9.4.1 The definition of bad character

Section 98 defines bad character as follows:

References in this Chapter to evidence of a person's 'bad character' are to evidence of, or of a disposition towards, misconduct on his part . . .

The Act also preserves the common law rule that evidence of a person's reputation is admissible for the purpose of proving his bad character (s 99(2) and s 118(1)). Therefore, bad character under the CJA 2003 may be defined as

- evidence of misconduct (ie, specific bad acts);
- evidence of disposition towards misconduct; and
- evidence of reputation for misconduct.

Misconduct is further defined by s 112 as the commission of an offence or other reprehensible behaviour. Therefore, bad character is not limited to previous convictions but includes any reprehensible behaviour by the defendant. See further R. Munday, *'What constitutes "other reprehensible behaviour" under the bad character provisions of the Criminal Justice Act 2003?'* [2005] Crim LR 24.

9.4.2   Bad character not regulated by the Criminal Justice Act 2003

The definition of bad character under the CJA 2003 does not encompass all evidence of misconduct. Section 98 provides that the definition of bad character does not include evidence which:

. . . (a) has to do with the alleged facts of the offence with which the defendant is charged, or

(b) is evidence of misconduct in connection with the investigation or prosecution of the offence.

Therefore, where evidence of misconduct has to do with the alleged facts of the offence, is in connection with the investigation or prosecution of the offence, or where the evidence does not amount to misconduct at all, it is not affected by the Act and its admissibility will be determined under the common law rules. The question of whether the evidence comes within the definition of bad character under the Act is a significant one and will often be the first enquiry when considering the admissibility of evidence of bad character (*R v Edwards* [2005] EWCA Crim 3244, CA).

9.4.2.1   Evidence which has to do with the alleged facts of the offence

Evidence that relates to the commission of the offence for which the defendant is being tried is not affected by the 2003 Act. Clearly, such evidence must be admitted despite the fact that it shows the defendant in a bad light. In cases where the bad character of the defendant is itself an issue in the proceedings, then it would be admissible under s 98(a) of the Act. The example of the Firearms Act 1968, s 21 has already been given (see **9.3**).

9.4.2.2   Evidence of misconduct in connection with the investigation or prosecution

The bad character provisions of the CJA 2003 similarly do not affect the admissibility of evidence of misconduct in connection with the investigation or prosecution of the offence for which the defendant is being tried. For example, the admissibility of evidence that the police obtained the defendant's confession by force or evidence that the defendant has attempted to frighten a witness into not giving evidence would not be affected by the Act.

9.4.2.3   Evidence not amounting to misconduct

As has been noted above at **9.4.1**, references in the CJA 2003 to evidence of a person's 'bad character' are references only to evidence of misconduct or a disposition towards or reputation for misconduct, misconduct being defined as the commission of an offence or other reprehensible behaviour. Therefore, where there is evidence which casts the defendant in a bad light but which does not amount to reprehensible behaviour, its admissibility will not be affected by the Act. Instead, its admissibility will be determined by the common law rules. It is important to note that the common law rules concerning the admissibility of evidence of bad character have only been abolished in relation to bad character as it is defined by s 98 of the Act. They will therefore continue to apply to evidence which casts the defendant in a bad light but which falls short of the statutory definition of bad character. In *R v Weir* [2006] 1 Cr App R 19, CA, the defendant was charged with rape and two counts of indecent assault against A. At the time of the alleged offences A was 13 and M was 39. The Court of Appeal held that evidence of a previous sexual relationship between the defendant, then aged 34, and a 16-year-old girl, and evidence that the defendant had said to another 15-year-old girl, 'Why do you think I'm still single? If only you were a bit older and I a bit younger,' did not amount to misconduct as neither could be said to be reprehensible behaviour. Because the evidence did not amount to 'evidence of bad character' under the 2003 Act the abolition of the common law rules governing the admissibility of 'evidence of bad character' by s 99(1) did not apply. The evidence would therefore have been admissible at common law as it was capable of demonstrating a sexual interest in early or mid-teenage girls much younger than the defendant.

9.4.3   The admissibility of evidence of bad character under the Criminal Justice Act 2003

The CJA 2003 creates seven gateways through which the defendant's bad character may be admitted in evidence. Section 101 provides that:

> (1)   In criminal proceedings evidence of the defendant's bad character is admissible if, but only if—
>   (a)   all parties to the proceedings agree to the evidence being admissible,
>   (b)   the evidence is adduced by the defendant himself or is given in answer to a question by him in cross-examination and intended to elicit it,
>   (c)   it is important explanatory evidence,
>   (d)   it is relevant to an important matter in issue between the defendant and the prosecution,
>   (e)   it has substantial probative value in relation to an important matter in issue between the defendant and a co-defendant,
>   (f)   it is evidence to correct a false impression given by the defendant, or
>   (g)   the defendant has made an attack on another person's character.

In *R v Highton* [2006] 1 Cr App R 7, CA, it was held that a distinction had to be drawn between the admissibility of evidence of bad character, which depended upon it getting through one of the 'gateways' in s 101, and the use to which it could be put once it was admitted. The use to which it could be put depended upon the matters to which it was relevant rather than upon the gateway through which it was admitted. For example, evidence of bad character adduced because the defendant has made an attack on another person's character (s 101(1)(g)), once it has been admitted may subsequently become relevant and admissible in relation to an important matter in issue between the defendant and the prosecution (s 101(1)(d)).

9.5   Agreement of the parties (s 101(1)(a))

Section 101(1) provides:

> (1)   In criminal proceedings evidence of the defendant's bad character is admissible if, but only if—
>   (a)   all parties to the proceedings agree to the evidence being admissible
>
>   . . .

Where the prosecution, the defendant and any co-defendant agree, evidence of the defendant's bad character may be admitted. Both the prosecution and the defendant may use this provision to adduce evidence of the defendant's bad character.

9.6   Evidence adduced by the defendant (s 101(1)(b))

Section 101(1) provides:

(1)   *In criminal proceedings evidence of the defendant's bad character is admissible if, but only if—*

   . . .

   (b) *the evidence is adduced by the defendant himself or is given in answer to a question by him in cross-examination and intended to elicit it*

   . . .

Situations in which the defendant will want to adduce evidence of his own bad character will be rare. However, an example of such a situation would be where the defendant's bad character has not been admitted as part of the prosecution case but in his evidence he attacks the character of another person. In these circumstances the defendant might anticipate that the prosecution will apply to cross-examine the defendant on his bad character under s 101(1)(g) (see **9.11**). Tactically, there would usually be an advantage in the defendant volunteering the evidence himself rather than letting the prosecution elicit it through cross-examination.

Under s 101(1)(b), evidence of bad character can be admitted either by the defendant as part of his case, or as a result of cross-examination. Where it is elicited through cross-examination, it is only admissible if the question is intended to elicit the evidence of bad character. Therefore, if a witness unexpectedly volunteers the evidence, it will not be admissible under s 101(1)(b). In such circumstances, unless the prejudice can be cured by a direction from the judge, a retrial may have to be ordered.

9.7   Important explanatory evidence (s 101(1)(c))

Section 101 provides that:

(1)   *In criminal proceedings evidence of the defendant's bad character is admissible if, but only if—*

   . . .

   (c) *it is important explanatory evidence*

   . . .

The definition of important explanatory evidence is given in s 102 of the Act which provides that:

For the purposes of section 101(1)(c) evidence is important explanatory evidence if—

   (a) *without it, the court or jury would find it impossible or difficult properly to understand other evidence in the case, and*

   (b) *its value for understanding the case as a whole is substantial.*

Both the prosecution and the defence may use this provision to adduce evidence of the defendant's bad character.

At common law there was a rule that evidence of the bad character of the defendant could be admitted where it formed part of a continual background or history relevant to the offence charged, which it was necessary to place before the jury and without which the account placed before the jury would be incomplete or incomprehensible (*R v Pettman* (2 May 1985, unreported). Section 101(1)(c) essentially places this rule on a statutory footing. For this reason, the previous authorities concerning the common law rule will continue to apply.

Decisions under the old law provide useful illustrations of the operation of the rule. In *R v Williams* (1986) 84 Cr App R 299, CA, it was held that on a charge of threatening to kill, evidence of a previous assault was admissible as tending to prove that the defendant intended his victim to take the threat seriously. In *R v M* (T) [2000] 1 WLR 421, CA, the defendant was charged with the rape of his sister. The prosecution was permitted to adduce evidence of previous sexual acts the defendant was forced to carry out on his siblings by other members of the family. The Court of Appeal held that the evidence had properly been admitted because without it the jury would have difficulty understanding the other evidence in the case. For example, it explained how the defendant was able to commit the crimes for which he was being tried without fearing that his acts would be reported to other family members and it explained why his sister did not turn to other members of the family for help. *R v Edwards* [2006] 1 Cr App R 3, CA, provides an example of a case decided under the 2003 Act. In that case an eye-witness was permitted to say that she was able to recognise the defendant because she had purchased heroin from him over a period of approximately one year. The fact that the identification was based on recognition was relevant to the jury's assessment of its accuracy and without the background evidence it would have been impossible or difficult for the jury properly to understand it; its value for understanding the case as a whole was also substantial.

9.7.1 Background evidence and s 98(a)

As has already been noted, under s 98(a) evidence that has to do with the alleged facts of the offence with which the defendant is charged is not evidence of bad character for the purposes of the CJA 2003 (see **9.4.2**). In *R v Edwards* [2005] EWCA Crim 3244, the Court of Appeal recognised that difficult questions can arise as to whether evidence of background or motive falls to be admitted under s 98(a) or s 101(1)(c). *R v McKintosh* [2006] EWCA 193 provides an illustration of the overlap between these two provisions. In that case it was alleged that the defendant had raped the complainant. In her statement she said that during the incident the defendant's accomplice had gone looking for something. She thought he was looking for a gun because approximately one year previously the defendant had threatened her with one. The Court of Appeal held that the evidence of the gun was admissible as evidence of misconduct which had to do with the alleged facts of the offence s 98(a) but that, if it was not, it was important explanatory evidence (s 101(1)(c)) because, in principle, it could explain why the complainant had not run away after the incident, why she did not tell the accomplice's girlfriend about it and why she went into the defendant's car after the incident.

9.7.2 The exclusionary discretion

Evidence of the defendant's bad character which the prosecution propose to adduce under s 101(1)(c) may be excluded by the court under its common law discretion where its prejudicial effect would outweigh its probative value (*R v Sang* [1980] AC 402; see **1.6.2.1**). It is submitted that it can also be excluded under s 78 of PACE 1984 where its admission would have such an adverse affect on the fairness of the proceedings that the court ought not to admit it (see **13.1.3**). Some commentators had argued that Parliament had not intended s 78 of PACE 1984 to apply to the bad character provisions of the CJA 2003 because Chapter 2 of Part 11 of the CJA 2003 (the hearsay provisions) expressly provides that nothing in that chapter prejudices any power of the court to exclude evidence under s 78 of PACE 1984 but there is no equivalent provision for Chapter 1 of Part 11 of the 2003 Act (the bad character provisions). Furthermore, s 101(3) creates an exclusionary discretion in almost identical terms to s 78, which applies only to gateways s 101(1)(d) and s 101(1)(g). If Parliament had intended s 78 to apply to the s 101(1) gateways it would render s 101(3) otiose. However, in *R v Weir* [2006]

1 Cr App 19, the Court of Appeal said that they had no reason to doubt that s 78 PACE 1984 applied to evidence adduced under s 101(1)(f). In *R v Highton* [2006] 1 Cr App R 7, CA, the court stated that, although it had not heard full argument, its inclination was that s 78 applies generally to evidence the prosecution propose to adduce under s 101(1). It would appear that s 78 PACE 1984 applies to evidence adduced under s 101(1)(c).

9.8   Important matters in issue between the prosecution and defence (s 101(1)(d))

Section 101 provides that:

> (1)   *In criminal proceedings evidence of the defendant's bad character is admissible if, but only if—*
>
> . . .
>
> > (d) *it is relevant to an important matter in issue between the defendant and the prosecution*
> >
> > . . .

Unlike the gateways considered so far, only the prosecution can admit evidence of the defendant's bad character under this provision (s 103(6)).

9.8.1   Important matters in issue

The matters in issue between the prosecution and the defence include the facts in issue and any issues of credibility. In addition s 103(1) of the Act provides that the matters in issue between the prosecution and the defendant expressly include:

(a) the question whether the defendant has a propensity to commit offences of the kind with which he is charged; and

(b) the question whether the defendant has a propensity to be untruthful.

Thus, evidence of the defendant's propensity to commit offences and his propensity to be untruthful is deemed to be a matter in issue. The matters in issue between the prosecution and the defence may therefore be summarised as follows:

- the identity of the defendant;
- the *actus reus* of the offence;
- the *mens rea* for the offence;
- any defences;
- the defendant's propensity to commit offences of the type with which he is charged;
- the defendant's propensity to be untruthful; and
- Any issues of credibility.

Section 112(1) defines 'important matter' as a matter of substantial importance in the context of the case as a whole. It is submitted that this definition will encompass all of the main issues between the prosecution and the defence.

9.8.2   The probative value required

Evidence of bad character will be admissible under this provision simply where it is relevant to one or more of the matters in issue. This test for admissibility may be contrasted with the test for the admissibility of the bad character of a person other than the defendant (**10.2**) and the test for the admissibility of the bad character of a co-defendant when adduced by the defendant (**9.9**) where the evidence must have substantial probative value in relation to the matter in issue; mere relevance is insufficient.

9.8.3 Section 101(1)(d): issues to which evidence of bad character is relevant

As noted at the outset, evidence of the defendant's bad character may be admissible where it is a fact in issue, where it is relevant to a fact in issue and where it is relevant to credibility. Evidence of bad character that is itself a fact in issue is admissible under s 98(a) of the Act (see **9.4.2**). Evidence of the defendant's bad character admitted under s 101(1)(d) will therefore be relevant either to a fact in issue or relevant to the defendant's credibility.

9.8.4 Section 101(1)(d): evidence relevant to a fact in issue

Under s 101(1)(d), evidence of the defendant's misconduct may be admitted where it is relevant to:

- the defendant's propensity to commit offences of the type with which he is charged;
- the identity of the defendant;
- the *actus reus* of the offence;
- the *mens rea* for the offence; and
- any defences;

in other words, where it is relevant to proving his guilt. We will consider each in turn.

9.8.4.1 The defendant's propensity to commit offences

At common law, evidence of the defendant's bad character was admissible to prove the defendant's guilt where it had a probative force sufficiently great to make it just to admit it, notwithstanding that it is prejudicial in tending to show that the defendant was guilty of another offence (*DPP v P* [1991] 3 All ER 337, HL). This was known as 'similar fact evidence'. Under the similar fact doctrine, the prosecution was not permitted to adduce evidence tending to show that the defendant had been guilty of criminal acts other that those covered by the indictment, for the purpose of leading to the conclusion that the defendant was a person who was likely from his criminal conduct or character to have committed the offence for which he was being tried (*Makin v Attorney General of New South Wales* [1894] AC 57, PC). Steyn LJ explained the rationale for this rule in *R v Clarke* [1995] 2 Cr App R 425, stating that:

evidence of propensity is excluded as a matter of law because it is regarded as unfair if it is adduced solely for the purpose of proving propensity . . . as a matter of policy the Court regards evidence tendered solely for that purpose as insufficiently relevant to permit its reception.

However, s 103(1), by making propensity to commit the type of offence with which the defendant is charged a matter in issue effectively reverses this principle.

9.8.4.2 Proving a propensity to commit an offence

The defendant's propensity to commit offences of the kind with which he is charged may be established by:

- evidence of previous convictions; and/or
- evidence of misconduct that has not resulted in a criminal conviction.

(a) Evidence of previous convictions

Section 101(1)(d) is supplemented by s 103 which provides that:

(1)   For the purposes of section 101(1)(d) the matters in issue between the defendant and the prosecution include—

   (a) the question whether the defendant has a propensity to commit offences of the kind with which he is charged, except where his having such a propensity makes it no more likely that he is guilty of the offence;

   . . .

(2)   Where subsection (1)(a) applies, a defendant's propensity to commit offences of the kind with which he is charged may (without prejudice to any other way of doing so) be established by evidence that he has been convicted of—

   (a) an offence of the same description as the one with which he is charged, or

   (b) an offence of the same category as the one with which he is charged.

   . . .

(4)   For the purposes of subsection (2)—

   (a) two offences are of the same description as each other if the statement of the offence in a written charge or indictment would, in each case, be in the same terms;

   (b) two offences are of the same category as each other if they belong to the same category of offences prescribed for the purposes of this section by an order made by the Secretary of State.

(5)   A category prescribed by an order under subsection (4)(b) must consist of offences of the same type.

Section 103(2) provides that a defendant's propensity to commit offences of the kind with which he is charged may be established by evidence that he has been convicted of:

- an offence of the same description as the one with which he is charged; or
- an offence of the same category as the one with which he is charged.

An offence is of the same description where the statement of the offence in a written charge or indictment would be in the same terms (s 103(4)). An offence is of the same category where both the previous offence and the offence charged belong to the same category of offences prescribed by the Secretary of State. At the time of writing, the Secretary of State has prescribed two categories:

(i)   The Theft Category (CJA 2003 (Categories of Offences) Order 2004 (SI 2004/3346), Part 1). This category includes all the main offences under the Theft Act 1968 (theft, robbery, burglary, etc), the offence of making off without payment under the Theft Act 1978 and offences of and aiding, abetting, counselling or procuring such offences and attempting to commit any such offences.

(ii) The Sexual Offences (Persons Under the Age of 16) Category (CJA 2003 (Categories of Offences) Order 2004 (SI 2004/3346), Part 2). This category includes 36 sexual offences and offences of aiding, abetting, counselling or procuring such offences and attempting to commit any such offences. The complainant must have been under 16 years of age at the time the offence was committed.

Simply establishing that a conviction is of the same description or category as that charged is not necessarily sufficient in order to establish a propensity to commit the offence. Therefore, a previous conviction will not automatically be admissible as evidence of propensity simply because it falls within the same category.

Propensity may also be established by evidence of previous convictions that neither are of the same description nor of the same category. While s 103(2) permits a propensity to commit the offence to be established by evidence of a previous conviction of the same description or category, it also states that it is without prejudice to any other way of doing so. In *R v Weir* [2006] 1 Cr App R 19, the defendant was charged with an offence of sexual assault by touching a girl under the age of 13 contrary to s 7 of the Sexual Offences Act 2003. The prosecution sought to adduce a previous caution for an offence of taking an indecent photograph of a child contrary to s 1 of the Protection of Children Act 1978 as evidence of a propensity to commit offences of sexual assault on girls under the age of 13. The offence with which the defendant was charged had been categorised by order of the Secretary of State (see the Sexual Offences (Persons Under the Age of 16) Category) (CJA 2003 (Categories of Offences) Order 2004 (SI 2004/3346), Part 2) but the offence in respect of which the defendant had received a caution had not. The Court of Appeal held that the prosecution was allowed to rely upon the previous caution as evidence of propensity despite the fact that it was neither of the same description nor specified in the same category as the offence with which he was charged.

Therefore, the defendant's propensity may be proven by evidence of previous convictions:

- that are of the same description;
- that are of the same category; or
- that are neither of the same description nor the same category.

(b) *Evidence of misconduct other than previous convictions*

As has already been noted, s 103(2) is expressly stated as being without prejudice to any other way of proving the defendant's propensity to commit offences of the kind with which he is charged. Therefore, not only is it possible to establish propensity by reference to previous convictions that are not of the same description or category as the offence charged, but the defendant's propensity may also be established by any evidence of misconduct or disposition towards misconduct, whether or not it resulted in a conviction. It may therefore be established by evidence of:

- misconduct for which the defendant has never been prosecuted;
- misconduct for which the defendant has been prosecuted but was not convicted; or
- misconduct which gives rise to another count on the indictment.

At common law, where a person had been tried for, and acquitted of, an offence on some previous occasion, that did not necessarily mean that the evidence of the commission of that offence would be inadmissible to prove the commission of some other offence at a later date (*R v Z* [2000] 3 All ER 385, HL). In *Z*, the defendant had been tried on three previous occasions for rape and had been acquitted, having run the defence of consent. He was then tried for a fourth rape in which he also ran the defence of consent. There were similarities between his conduct on all four occasions. The House of Lords upheld the trial judge's admission of the evidence of the misconduct that gave rise to the previous charges, notwithstanding that it showed him to be guilty of offences for which he had been acquitted. They held that this was not a breach of the rule against double jeopardy. It is submitted that this doctrine will continue to apply under the new Act.

At common law, where the evidence of misconduct had not resulted in a conviction, whether because a charge was never brought, the defendant was previously acquitted, or it was the subject of another count on the present indictment, evidence of the defendant's misconduct was admissible even if the defendant disputed the facts (*R v Rance* (1976) 62 Cr App R 118). However, there had to be sufficient evidence to justify, as a possibility, a finding by the tribunal of fact that the defendant was guilty of the misconduct alleged to have occurred on that other occasion. For example, in *Harris v DPP* [1952] AC 694, the defendant, a police constable, was indicted on eight counts of larceny, acquitted on the first seven, and convicted on the eighth. The evidence showed that the offences occurred in May, June and July of the same year and that on each occasion the thief had entered the same office in Bradford market by the same method and taken only some of the money found. On the eighth count, the defendant was on duty in the market at the relevant time and was found by detectives near the building shortly after an alarm bell had gone off, which could have warned the thief to hide the money in a nearby bin, where it was found. On the other seven counts, however, the only evidence linking the defendant with the offences was that on the dates in question he was not on leave but was on solitary duty and could have been near the market. The trial judge failed to warn the jury that the evidence on the first seven counts could not, by itself, implicate the defendant on the eighth. The House of Lords allowed the appeal on the grounds that there was no proof that the defendant had been near the office or even in the market at the time of the first seven thefts. It is submitted that these principles will continue to apply under the 2003 Act to any evidence of misconduct adduced under s 101(1)(d) whether it is relevant to the defendant's propensity or another issue.

9.8.4.3 Determining the admissibility of evidence of propensity

Guidance on how to approach the admissibility evidence of propensity was given in *R v Hanson* [2005] 2 Cr App R 21:

(a) Where propensity to commit the offence is relied upon there are essentially three questions to be considered:

    (i) Does the history of conviction(s) establish a propensity to commit offences of the kind charged?

    (ii) Does that propensity make it more likely that the defendant committed the offence charged?

    (iii) Is it unjust to rely on the conviction(s) of the same description or category; and, in any event, will the proceedings be unfair if they are admitted?

(b) There is no minimum number of events necessary to demonstrate such a propensity. The fewer the number of convictions, the weaker is likely to be the evidence of propensity. A single previous conviction for an offence of the same description or category will often not show propensity. But it may do so where, for example, it shows a tendency to unusual behaviour or where its circumstances demonstrate probative force in relation to the offence charged.

(c) Circumstances demonstrating probative force are not confined to those sharing striking similarity. So, a single conviction for shoplifting, will not, without more, be admissible to show propensity to steal. But if the *modus operandi* has significant features shared by the offence charged, it may show propensity.

(d) If there is a substantial gap between the dates of commission of and conviction for the earlier offences, the date of commission should be regarded as generally being of more significance than the date of conviction when assessing admissibility. Old convictions, with no special feature shared with the offence charged, are likely seriously to affect the fairness of proceedings adversely, unless, despite their age, it can properly be said that they show a continuing propensity.

(e) It will often be necessary, before determining admissibility and even when considering offences of the same description or category, to examine each individual conviction rather than merely to look at the name of the offence or at the defendant's record as a whole.

(f) The sentence passed will not normally be probative or admissible at the behest of the prosecution, though it may be at the behest of the defence.

(g) Where the prosecution are relying on a previous conviction to prove propensity the prosecution needs to decide, at the time of giving notice of the application, whether it proposes to rely simply upon the fact of conviction or also upon the circumstances of it. The former may be enough when the circumstances of the conviction are sufficiently apparent from its description, to justify a finding that it can establish propensity, either to commit an offence of the kind charged or to be untruthful. For example, a succession of convictions for dwelling-house burglary, where the same offence is now charged, may well call for no further evidence than proof of the fact of the convictions. In *R v Humphris*, *The Times*, 19 September 2005, the Court of Appeal emphasised that if the prosecution want to adduce more than the evidence of the fact of the conviction they must ensure that they have available the necessary evidence to support what they require. That will normally require the availability of either a statement by the complainant relating to the previous convictions or the complainant to be available to give first-hand evidence of what happened.

Authorities decided under the 2003 Act usefully illustrate the principles enunciated in *Hanson*. In *R v Hanson* [2005] 2 Cr App R 21, CA, one defendant was charged with theft. The prosecution sought to adduce evidence of three previous convictions for theft as evidence of a propensity to steal. All three of the offences were committed within a six-week period, ending three months before the date of the offence charged. The court held that the trial judge was fully entitled to conclude that the offences showed a recent persistent propensity to steal. In *R v Brima* [2006] EWCA 408, the defendant was charged with murder. It was alleged that he had stabbed the deceased with a knife. The trial judge had permitted the prosecution to adduce the defendant's recent previous convictions for assault occasioning actual bodily harm and robbery under s 101(1)(d). On both occasions a knife was used and both offences were committed within the three-year period prior to the date of the murder. The prosecution contended that the appellant had a propensity to commit offences of violence using knives either by inflicting or threatening injury. The Court of Appeal upheld the judge's ruling. In *R v Hanson* [2005] 2 Cr App R 21, CA, one defendant was charged with three counts of rape and two of indecent assault against a nine-year-old girl. The trial judge permitted the prosecution to adduce the defendant's previous conviction dating from 1993 for indecent assault against an 11-year-old girl. He concluded that the earlier offence was of the same description and the same category, within the Categories of Offences Order, as the offences charged. He expressly took into account the length of time since the previous offence and said that 'a defendant's sexual mores and motivations are not necessarily affected by the passage of time'. The Court of Appeal upheld the judge's decision. In *R v Highton* [2006] 1 Cr App R 7, CA, one defendant was charged with cultivating a controlled drug of the genus *Cannabis*. The defendant stated that he had believed the plants in question were a controlled substance and so the only issue at trial was whether or not he was involved in their cultivation. The court held that the judge had been wrong to admit evidence of the defendant's heroin addiction as relevant to an important matter in issue between the prosecution and the defence under s 101(1)(d).

9.8.4.4 Directing the jury

In *R v Hanson* [2005] 2 Cr App r 21, CA, it was held that, in any case in which evidence of bad character is admitted to show propensity, the judge in summing-up should warn the jury clearly against placing undue reliance on previous convictions. Evidence of bad character cannot be used simply to bolster a weak case, or to prejudice the minds of a jury against a defendant. In particular, the jury should be directed:

- that they should not conclude that the defendant is guilty merely because he has these convictions;
- that, although the convictions may show a propensity, this does not mean that he has committed this offence;
- that whether they in fact show a propensity is for them to decide;
- that they must take into account what the defendant has said about his previous convictions; and
- that, although they are entitled, if they find propensity is shown, to take this into account when determining guilt, propensity is only one relevant factor and they must assess its significance in the light of all the other evidence in the case.

In *R v Edwards* [2006] 1 Cr App R 3, CA, it was held that the guidance given in *Hanson* must not be taken as a blueprint, departure from which will result in the quashing of a conviction.

What the summing-up must contain is a clear warning to the jury against placing undue reliance on previous convictions, which cannot, by themselves, prove guilt. It should be explained to the jury why they have heard the evidence and the ways in which that evidence is relevant to and may help their decision. Provided the judge gives such a clear warning, explanation and guidance as to use, the terms in which he does so can properly differ.

9.8.4.5   *Actus reus*, *mens rea* and the rebuttal of defences

At common law, the similar fact doctrine admitted evidence of the bad character of the defendant where it tended to prove that he had committed the *actus reus* or the *mens rea* of the offence or to rebut a defence that was open to him. The same principles will continue to apply under the new Act.

Often the basis on which the evidence was admitted was that there was striking similarity between the present offence and the previous misconduct of the defendant. For example, in *Makin v Attorney-General for New South Wales* [1894] AC 57, PC, Makin and his wife were charged with the murder of an infant child whom they had taken in from its mother for informal adoption, upon the payment by her of a small sum of money which was insufficient for the child's support. When the mother subsequently tried to see the child, there was deceit and evasion by the Makins, and even an attempt to pass off a different child as the child in question. There was also evidence that the baby was received in good health one day in one set of premises, but that two days later the Makins had moved on, surreptitiously and without the baby, to other premises. A child's corpse, wearing the child's clothes, was then found secretly buried in the garden of the first set of premises. There was also evidence that other babies had also been received from their mothers on payment of similarly inadequate sums of money, and that the remains of no less than 13 other children's corpses had been found in three different sets of premises, all occupied at different times by the Makins. The Privy Council held that this evidence was admissible on the grounds that the prosecution, in seeking to prove deliberate killing, were entitled to rely on evidence which negatived the possibility that the child in question had died accidentally or from natural causes. In other words, to find so many bodies of children in the backyards of so many sets of premises all of which had been occupied by the defendant, rendered quite ludicrously incredible any suggestion that this had nothing to do with the accuseds but must have been accidental or coincidental. It is crucial to note that this evidence was not being admitted as evidence of propensity but as evidence of a pattern of behaviour in the light of which an explanation of the child's death as an accident would be untenable.

The same reasoning was employed in the famous 'brides in the bath' case, *R v Smith* (1915) 11 Cr App R 229, CCA. Smith was charged with the murder of B. Smith had purported to marry her and they started living together. In fact he was already married. Both of them made mutual wills. Smith then purchased a bath and installed it into a room without a lock on the door. Although there had been no reason to presume that B suffered from ill health, Smith took her to a doctor and described symptoms that were consistent with epilepsy. The same doctor was then sent for by Smith to find that B was dead in a bath. His defence was that the death had been the result of an epileptic fit while B was bathing. The prosecution, in order to disprove such an explanation, called evidence that Smith had subsequently been through two bigamous ceremonies of marriage with other women, that both of them had died in baths while living with Smith, that the bathroom doors did not lock, that Smith had told a doctor that they had died from epileptic fits and that Smith had on both occasions benefited financially from their deaths because of life assurance he had taken out in respect of them. The court upheld the admission of this evidence. If what happened in this case had happened once only, an explanation based on accident might have been plausible. But when it happened three times, in remarkably similar circumstances and on each occasion to the benefit of the defendant, it gave rise to a very strong inference that the events were so very coincidental that they must have been brought about by design and not accident.

However, striking similarity is not the only way in which the evidence of the defendant's bad character could be relevant to the offence charged. In *DPP v P* [1991] 3 All ER 337, HL, the defendant was convicted on two counts of rape and eight counts of incest which he had committed against his two daughters, B and S. The trial judge found that there were striking similarities between the offences thereby rendering the evidence of one girl admissible in relation to the other. The Court of Appeal overturned the conviction on the grounds that the matters relied upon by the trial judge could not be said to be strikingly similar. The House of Lords held that the evidence had been correctly admitted as similar fact evidence by the trial judge. The essential feature of admissibility of such evidence was that its probative force was so great as to make it just to admit it notwithstanding that it was prejudicial to the defendant in that it indicated that he was guilty of another crime. Although such probative force might be derived from striking similarities in the evidence about the manner in which the crime was committed, it was not restricted to such cases, and the question whether the evidence had sufficient probative value to outweigh its prejudicial effect was one of degree. Since the evidence of both girls described a prolonged course of conduct in relation to each of them involving the use of force and a general domination, including the use of threats, and since there was also evidence that the defendant was involved in payment for abortions in respect of both girls, the circumstances, taken together, gave strong probative force to the evidence of one in respect of the incidents involving the other and were sufficient to make it just to admit that evidence, notwithstanding its prejudicial effect.

Thompson v R [1918] AC 221 is another case where there was sufficient probative value to admit evidence of bad character without there being striking similarity. In that case, the House of Lords held that evidence of the defendant's homosexual inclination was admissible in relation to offences of gross indecency against young boys. The prosecution alleged that he had committed the acts of indecency on two boys on 16 December and then arranged to meet them in the same place on 19 December. On that occasion a police officer was present and confronted the defendant when he approached the boys. The defendant sought to explain the meeting and his payment of money to the two boys as an act of charity on his part and denied that there had been any previous meeting on 16 December. However, on his arrest, the defendant was found in possession of powder puffs. When his lodgings were searched, photographs of young boys in suggestive poses were recovered. The prosecution case was that the meeting of the 19 December was for the same purposes as the meeting of 16 December. Both the powder puffs and the photographs were admitted at trial to disprove both the denial of the meeting on 16 December and the innocent explanation of the meeting on 19 December. The House of Lords upheld the convictions. The powder puffs were admissible as items that were to be used in the intended commission of the offences on 19 December (their Lordships did not explain how). The House of Lords found the photographs were admissible to disprove the defendant's innocent explanation for the meeting as they were evidence of a disposition to commit what they described as unnatural offences.

In *R v Anderson* [1988] QB 678, CA, A was convicted of conspiracy to cause explosions. She said that she knew nothing about any such conspiracy and explained false identification papers and over £1,000 found in her possession on the basis that she was involved in an attempt to smuggle escaped IRA prisoners out of the country. It was held that the prosecution were entitled to cross-examine her about the fact that she was wanted by the police for an unspecified offence in order to show the unlikelihood of choosing her as an escort. The fact that she was wanted by the police would have doubled the risk of detection.

Similarly, in *R v Yalman* [1988] 2 Cr App R 269, CA, the defendant met his father at an airport on his arrival in England. The father was carrying a suitcase containing heroin. The prosecution case was that it was a family-organised importation, but the defendant said that he was unaware of the drugs. It was held that, once there was a prima facie case for the defendant to answer, then evidence that he had used heroin and that scales had been found at his home, which the defendant admitted using to weigh drugs purchased for his own use, was admissible as tending to rebut his assertion that he was an innocent dupe.

9.8.4.6 Identity

The principles that formerly applied to the admission of similar fact evidence in identification cases will continue to apply under the new Act. Evidence of the defendant's bad character could be admitted at common law to prove the identity of the defendant as the person who had committed the offence for which he was being tried if the previous misconduct bore a 'signature' or striking similarity to that offence (*DPP v P* [1991] 3 All ER 337, HL). However, this was not the only way in which similar fact evidence was used to prove identity. In *R v W (John)* [1998] 2 Cr App R 289, the Court of Appeal held that there was no special rule in identity cases requiring a signature or other special feature. Many of the authorities concern cases where the prosecution relied on the facts giving rise to one count on the indictment as evidence in relation to another count on the same indictment, and vice versa. *R v W (John)* was such a case. The Court held that evidence tending to show that a defendant has committed an offence charged in count A may be used to reach a verdict on count B and vice versa, if the circumstances of both offences (as the jury would be entitled to find them) are such as to provide sufficient probative support for the conclusion that the defendant committed both offences, and it would therefore be fair for the evidence to be used in this way, notwithstanding the prejudicial effect of so doing. The same principle applies where the prosecution rely on the defendant's previous convictions to prove his identity as the offender.

Where the similar fact evidence relied upon by the prosecution was the facts giving rise to another count on the same indictment, the Court of Appeal held that the evidence could be approached sequentially or cumulatively, depending on the facts of the case. It is submitted that the same approach will continue to apply under the CJA 2003. Under the sequential approach, the jury, in deciding whether the defendant committed offence A, was invited to have regard to evidence that he also committed offence B. In such cases, the jury must be directed that they must first be sure that, disregarding the similarity of the facts, the defendant had committed offence B (*R v Downey* [1995] 1 Cr App R 547, CA; *R v McGranaghan* [1995] 1 Cr App R 559, CA). The point was succinctly stated by Glidewell J in *McGranaghan* when he said:

> 'An identification about which the jury are not sure cannot support an identification of which the jury are also not sure however similar the facts of the two offences may be.'

The cumulative approach applies to cases where there is evidence that both offences A and B were committed by the same man, but the evidence falls short of proving that that man was the defendant in either case, regarded alone. If there is evidence which entitles the jury to reach the conclusion that it was the same man, even though the evidence in either case does not enable them to be sure who the man was, then they can properly take account of evidence relating to both offences in deciding whether that man was the defendant (*R v Downey* [1995] 1 Cr App R 547).

Evidence of the possession of incriminating articles could also be admitted under the similar fact evidence doctrine to identify the defendant where the articles in question could have been used, even if they are not proved to have been used, in committing the offence charged. In *R v Reading* [1966] 1 WLR 836, CCA, the defendants were charged with robberies which involved the hijacking of lorries. Articles were found in their possession which could have been used in the hijacking, such as car number-plates, walkie-talkie radios and a police uniform. The Court of Criminal Appeal held that evidence of the possession of these articles had been properly admitted in order to confirm the identification of the defendant by witnesses and to rebut the defence of alibi and mistaken identity.

9.8.5 Section 101(1)(d): evidence relevant to credibility

9.8.5.1 Propensity to be untruthful

Section 103 provides that:

> (1)   For the purposes of section 101(1)(d) the matters in issue between the defendant and the prosecution include—
>
> . . .
>
> (b)   the question whether the defendant has a propensity to be untruthful, except where it is not suggested that the defendant's case is untruthful in any respect.

Under s 103(1)(b) evidence of the defendant's propensity to be untruthful will be deemed to be a matter in issue for the purposes of s 101(1)(d) unless it is not suggested that the defendant's case is untruthful in any respect. The prosecution would not suggest a defendant's case is untruthful where, for example, he does not dispute the facts adduced by the prosecution but argues that an essential element of the offence is not made out.

In *R v Hanson* [2005] 2 Cr App R 21, it was held that propensity to untruthfulness is not the same as propensity to dishonesty. Parliament deliberately chose the word 'untruthful' to convey a different meaning, reflecting a defendant's account of his behaviour, or lies told when committing an offence. The court concluded that previous convictions, whether for offences of dishonesty or otherwise, are therefore only likely to be capable of showing a propensity to be untruthful where, in the present case, truthfulness is an issue and, in the earlier case, either there was a plea of not guilty and the defendant gave an account, on arrest, in interview, or in evidence, which the jury must have disbelieved, or the way in which the offence was committed shows a propensity for untruthfulness, for example, by the making of false representations. As with evidence of a propensity to commit offences, there is no minimum number of events necessary to demonstrate a propensity to be untruthful. The fewer the number of convictions, the weaker is likely to be the evidence of propensity.

In *R v Hanson*, it was further held that, in any case in which evidence of bad character is admitted to show propensity to be untruthful, the judge in summing up should warn the jury clearly against placing undue reliance on previous convictions. Evidence of bad character cannot be used simply to bolster a weak case, or to prejudice the minds of a jury against a defendant. In particular, the jury should be directed:

- that they should not conclude that the defendant is untruthful merely because he has these convictions;
- that, although the convictions may show a propensity, this does not mean that he has been untruthful in this case;
- that whether they in fact show a propensity is for them to decide;
- that they must take into account what the defendant has said about his previous convictions; and
- that, although they are entitled, if they find propensity as shown, to take this into account when determining guilt, propensity is only one relevant factor and they must assess its significance in the light of all the other evidence in the case.

In *R v Edwards* [2006] 1 Cr App R 3, CA, it was held that the guidance given in *Hanson* must not be taken as a blueprint, departure from which will result in the quashing of a conviction. What the summing-up must contain is a clear warning to the jury against placing undue reliance on previous convictions, which cannot, by themselves, prove guilt. It should be explained to the jury why they have heard the evidence and the ways in which it is relevant to and may help their decision. Provided the judge gives such a clear warning, explanation and guidance as to use, the terms in which he does so can properly differ.

9.8.5.2   Evidence relevant to credibility other than evidence of a propensity to be untruthful

For evidence to be admitted under s 101(1)(d) as being relevant to the defendant's credibility it is not necessary to show that the evidence establishes a propensity to be untruthful, simply that it is relevant to credibility and that credibility is an important matter in issue. An interesting example arose in *R v Weir* [2006] 1 Cr App R 19. One defendant, a Hindu priest, was charged with the rape of a woman who attended the temple where he worked. The prosecution's case was that over a prolonged period, beginning when she was emotionally vulnerable, the complainant was subjected by the defendant to sexually charged behaviour which on two occasions culminated in rape. The defendant's response was one of complete denial. He did not simply say that there was never any rape but denied that he had behaved improperly at any time. The trial judge allowed the prosecution to call other witnesses who gave evidence that was similar to the complainant's in that it showed that the defendant sought to strike up a relationship with them when they were at a low ebb in their lives, he belittled their former or intended partners, he admired their clothes and suggested what colours they should wear, he acquired telephone numbers and addresses and then telephoned regularly, often late at night. He spoke of dreaming of them, of being married to them in a past life, and of the gods now sending them to him. He offered gifts and did things to their hands and hair in the temple which were inappropriate because they were only done when a girl became a woman or by her husband. Finally he sought to visit each of them at home when they were alone and, only in the case of the complainant, did he succeed. The Court of Appeal upheld the trial judge's ruling as the evidence was relevant to the credibility of the complainant on the one hand and the defendant on the other, which was an important matter in issue between the parties.

9.8.6   The exclusionary discretions

9.8.6.1   Section 101(3) of the Criminal Justice Act 2003

Section 101 provides that:

(3)   *The court must not admit evidence under subsection 1(d) . . . if, on an application by the defendant to exclude it, it appears to the court that the admission of the evidence would have such an adverse effect on the fairness of the proceedings that the court ought not to admit it.*

(4)   *On an application to exclude evidence under subsection (3) the court must have regard, in particular, to the length of time between the matters to which that evidence relates and the matters which form the subject of the offence charged.*

Where the prosecution propose to adduce evidence of the defendant's misconduct under s 101(1)(d) the court must not do so where it appears to the court that the admission of the evidence would have such an adverse effect on the fairness of the proceedings that the court ought not to admit it. The wording of this provision is very similar to s 78 of the PACE 1984 (see **13.1.3**). The key difference is that it is expressed in mandatory ('must not admit') rather than discretionary ('may refuse to allow') terms. It is submitted that because of the clear overlap between the two provisions, s 78 will be otiose to applications to exclude evidence the prosecution propose to adduce under s 101(1)(d).

9.8.6.2   Section 103(3) of the Criminal Justice Act 2003

Where the prosecution rely on previous convictions of the same description or category to prove the defendant's propensity to commit offences of the kind with which he is charged, s 103(3) provides that s 103(2) should not apply where it would be unjust. Section 103 provides that:

> (2) *Where subsection (1)(a) applies, a defendant's propensity to commit offences of the kind with which he is charged may (without prejudice to any other way of doing so) be established by evidence that he has been convicted of—*
> (a) *an offence of the same description as the one with which he is charged, or*
> (b) *an offence of the same category as the one with which he is charged.*
>
> (3) *Subsection (2) does not apply in the case of a particular defendant if the court is satisfied, by reason of the length of time since the conviction or for any other reason, that it would be unjust for it to apply in his case.*

9.8.6.3 The principles to be applied under s 101(3) and 103(3)

In *R v Hanson* [2005] 2 Cr App R 21, CA, it was held that in a conviction case, the decisions required of the trial judge under s 101(3), and s 103(3), though not identical, are closely related. When considering what is just under s 103(3), and the fairness of the proceedings under s 101(3), the judge may, among other factors, take into consideration the degree of similarity between the previous conviction and the offence charged, albeit they are both within the same description or prescribed category. For example, theft and assault occasioning actual bodily harm may each embrace a wide spectrum of conduct. As already noted, this does not, however, mean that what used to be referred to as striking similarity must be shown before convictions become admissible. The judge may also take into consideration the respective gravity of the past and present offences. He must always consider the strength of the prosecution case. If there is no or very little other evidence against a defendant, it is unlikely to be just to admit his previous convictions, whatever they are.

9.8.6.4 The common law discretion

It is submitted that the common law discretion will apply to exclude evidence adduced by the prosecution under s 101(1)(d) where its prejudicial effect outweighs its probative value but in practice it will seldom be relied upon because of the breadth of the discretion under s 101(3).

9.9 Substantial probative value to an important matter in issue between co-defendants (s 101(1)(e))

Section 101 provides:

> (1) *In criminal proceedings evidence of the defendant's bad character is admissible if, but only if—*
>   . . .
>   (e) *it has substantial probative value in relation to an important matter in issue between the defendant and a co-defendant.*

Section 101 is supplemented by s 104 which provides:

>   . . .
> (2) *Only evidence—*
>   (a) *which is to be (or has been) adduced by the co-defendant, or*
>   (b) *which a witness is to be invited to give (or has given) in cross-examination by the co-defendant, is admissible under section 101(1)(e).*

Therefore, only a co-defendant can adduce evidence of the defendant's bad character under s 101(1)(e).

9.9.1 Matters in issue

The matters in issue between the defendant and the co-defendant may include the facts in issue and any issues of credibility, including any propensity to be untruthful. The facts in issue will be a matter in issue where a cut-throat defence is being advanced by the defendant. Section 112(1) defines 'important matter' as a matter of substantial importance in the context of the case as a whole. See, generally, **9.8.1**.

9.9.2   The probative value required

As noted above at **9.8.2**, the probative value required for the defendant's bad character to be admissible under s 101(1)(d) is mere relevance. A stricter test applies to co-defendants. Under s 101(1)(e) the co-defendant must satisfy the court that the evidence of the defendant's bad character has substantial probative value. However, this difference may not be as significant as it might at first appear as the Explanatory Notes to the Criminal Justice Bill stated that the word 'substantial' would only operate to exclude the marginal or trivial.

9.9.3   Section 101(1)(e): evidence relevant to a fact in issue

At common law, the co-defendant could adduce similar fact evidence of the defendant's bad character where it was relevant to his defence. The leading authority prior to the Act was *R v Randall* [2004] 1 WLR 56. R and G were jointly charged with murder. At trial, each defendant gave evidence blaming the other. Under s 1(3)(iii) of the Criminal Evidence Act 1898 (now repealed), each defendant was entitled to cross-examine the other as to his previous convictions. G had a more formidable record, including convictions for offences of violence. The judge had directed the jury that the evidence undermining G's character was only relevant to the issue of credibility and not to the likelihood of G having actually committed the offence. The House of Lords held that the evidence of G's propensity to use and threaten violence was relevant not simply to the issue of R's truthfulness but also to the issue of whether G had inflicted the fatal blows. It is submitted that this principle will continue to apply under the 2003 Act. However, while for common law to be admissible the evidence simply had to be relevant, the Act introduces an enhanced test of relevance which requires that the evidence must be shown to have substantial probative force (see **9.9.2**).

Two further examples of the operation of this principle may be given. In *R v Miller* [1952] 2 All ER 667, the co-defendants were charged with offences in connection with the evasion of customs duties. The defence of one of them, B, was that he was not concerned in the illegal acts and that the offences were all committed by another co-defendant, C, who had masqueraded as B and used B's office for their commission. In pursuance of that defence, therefore, he asked a prosecution witness whether or not the offences stopped when C was sent to prison. It was held that this was a proper question because it was relevant to the defence put forward.

In *R v Douglass* (1989) 89 Cr App R 264, CA, D and P were charged with causing death by reckless driving. A van driven by P collided head-on with another car. D and P were allegedly vying with each other before the accident, D having pulled out into the centre of the road several times to prevent P from overtaking. Their vehicles collided and this caused P's van to hit the oncoming car. P gave no evidence but his counsel, in cross-examination of P's girlfriend, elicited evidence that P had never drunk alcohol in the two years that she had known him. The prosecution suggested that D had been drinking before the accident. Evidence of P's previous convictions, which included offences involving drink, was ruled inadmissible. It was held on appeal that the evidence elicited on behalf of P as to his lack of propensity to have driven as alleged became relevant to the issue of D's guilt. In such a case contradictory evidence as to propensity could be called by D. D should have been allowed to adduce evidence of P's criminal record.

9.9.4   Section 101(1)(e): evidence relevant to credibility

Section 104 provides that:

(1)   *Evidence which is relevant to the question whether the defendant has a propensity to be untruthful is admissible on that basis under section 101(1)(e) only if the nature or conduct of his defence is such as to undermine the co-defendant's defence.*

Under the Criminal Evidence Act 1898, s 1(3)(ii) (now repealed) the defendant was liable to be cross-examined as to his bad character when he had given evidence against any other person charged in the proceedings. In *Murdoch v Taylor* [1965] 574, HL, it was held that 'evidence against' meant either evidence which supports the prosecution's case in a material respect or evidence which undermines the defence for the co-accused. It will be noted that s 104(1) is therefore more restrictive than the previous law in that where the defendant gives evidence in support of the prosecution case, this will not render admissible evidence of his propensity to be untruthful. With the exception of this important distinction, it is submitted that the principles established under the previous case law will be of assistance in interpreting s 104(1).

In *Murdoch v Taylor* [1965] AC 574, HL, it was held that 'evidence against' may be given in either examination-in-chief or cross-examination. Moreover, evidence against need not be given with hostile intent. The intention or state of mind of the person giving the evidence is irrelevant. What is material is the effect of the evidence on the minds of the jury.

On the meaning of 'undermine the co-defendant's defence', see *R v Bruce* [1975] 1 WLR 1252, CA. In that case eight co-defendants were charged with robbery. One of them, M, admitted a plan to rob but denied being a party to the actual robbery. Another, B, denied that there was a plan to rob. The trial judge ruled that B had given evidence against M. The Court of Appeal, however, held that B had not given evidence against M because, despite the contradiction of M, the evidence was more in his favour than against him because it gave to M a different and possibly better defence. Stephenson LJ said that evidence which undermines a co-defendant's defence is only evidence against that co-defendant if it makes his acquittal less likely.

In *R v Varley* [1982] 2 All ER 519, CA, two defendants, D and A, were tried for robbery. D's case was that both he and A had taken part but that his involvement was because of the duress exerted on him by A. The defence of A was that he was not there at all and therefore D's evidence was untrue. A was held to have undermined D's defence. In the course of the Court of Appeal's judgment it was held that a mere denial of participation in a joint venture is not of itself sufficient to rank as evidence against a co-defendant. Where one defendant asserts a view of the joint enterprise which is directly contradicted by the other, such contradiction may be evidence against the co-defendant. In *Varley* this had clearly occurred. The denial of involvement by A directly contradicted D's contention that A had forced him to participate in the robbery and therefore deprived him of a defence. The court also stated that for a denial of participation in a joint venture to undermine the co-defendant's defence, the denial *must* lead to the conclusion that if one did not participate, then it must have been the other who did.

In *R v Crawford* [1998] 1 Cr App R 338, CA, the victim of a robbery alleged that she had been alone in the lavatories of a restaurant with three other women, all of whom had committed the offence. The three were C, her co-defendant, A, and a third woman, L. C's evidence was to the effect that A and L were in the lavatories at the material time, but that she was not. A's evidence was that C and L had committed the robbery while she, A, had been an innocent bystander. It was held that the trial judge had properly allowed A to cross-examine C on her previous convictions, because if the jury accepted C's evidence that only A and L were in the lavatories at the material time, that was very damaging to the credibility of A and made it much less likely that A was simply a passive bystander. It was submitted on appeal that this outcome was in conflict with the proposition in *Varley* that for s 1(3)(iii) to apply a mere denial of participation in a joint venture 'must' lead to the conclusion that if the defendant did not participate, then it must have been the co-defendant who did: this was not a case where it was either C or A who had committed the offence, and if it was not C therefore it must have been A. Rejecting this submission, the Court of Appeal held that in so far as the proposition from *Varley* had been cast in mandatory terms, it went too far: the word 'may' was more appropriate.

9.9.5   The exclusionary discretion

There is no power under the 2003 Act or at common law to exclude evidence once it has been shown to satisfy the test in s 101(1)(e), even if it is prejudicial to a co-defendant. This follows a long-standing principle of English law that the defendant should not be fettered in putting forward his defence to a criminal charge, but should be free to adduce any relevant evidence (see, for example, *Lobban v R* [1995] 1 WLR 877).

9.10   Evidence to correct a false impression (s 101(1)(f))

Section 101 provides:

> *(1)   In criminal proceedings evidence of the defendant's bad character is admissible if, but only if—*
>
> *. . .*
>
> *(f)   it is evidence to correct a false impression given by the defendant*
>
> *. . .*

Only the prosecution can adduce evidence under s 101(1)(f) to correct a false impression (s 105(7)).

Prior to the implementation of the CJA 2003, evidence of the defendant's bad character was admissible both at common law and under the Criminal Evidence Act 1898, s 1(3)(ii) where he had given evidence of his good character. Section 101(1)(f) of the CJA 2003 adopts a similar principle. However, there is one significant difference. Whereas under the previous law evidence of the defendant's bad character was admissible only where good character was asserted, under the CJA 2003 it is admissible where he has given a false impression. It is therefore broader in scope than the previous law.

9.10.1   Giving a false impression

Section 101(1)(f) is supplemented by s 105 which provides:

> *(1)   For the purposes of section 101(1)(f)—*
> *(a)   the defendant gives a false impression if he is responsible for the making of an express or implied assertion which is apt to give the court or jury a false or misleading impression about the defendant;*
> *. . .*
> *(4)   Where it appears to the court that a defendant, by means of his conduct (other than the giving of evidence) in the proceedings, is seeking to give the court or jury an impression about himself that is false or misleading, the court may if it appears just to do so treat the defendant as being responsible for the making of an assertion which is apt to give that impression.*
> *(5)   In subsection (4) 'conduct' includes appearance or dress.*

9.10.1.1 Express and implied assertions

A false impression may be asserted expressly or impliedly. Implied assertions would include the conduct of the defendant, including his appearance or dress (s 105(4), (5)). An example of an implied assertion under the previous law is *R v Samuel* (1956) 40 Cr App R 8, CCA, in which the defendant was charged with the theft of a camera he had picked up after it had been lost. The defendant gave evidence that he had on two previous occasions returned valuable property to its owner. It was held that he had asserted his good character. However, a simple denial of the offence or offences alleged cannot, for the purposes of s 101(1)(f), be treated as a false impression given by the defendant (*R v Weir* [2006] 1 Cr App R 19, CA).

A good example of an express assertion is *R v Wright* [2000] Crim LR 851, which was decided under the old law. The defendant, who was charged with a racially aggravated offence, asserted that he had never entertained racist ideas. It was held that the prosecution had properly been allowed to cross-examine him as to his dismissal from his employment for racist behaviour. In *R v Weir* [2006] 1 Cr App R 19, CA, a decision under the CJA 2003, one defendant, a Hindu priest, was charged with the rape of a woman who attended the temple where he worked. The defendant put himself forward as a man who enjoyed a good reputation as a priest, particularly at a local temple where he had previously been employed, and said he had not behaved inappropriately towards female worshippers. The prosecution was entitled to adduce evidence that the contract of employment at the local temple was brought to an end following complaints about the priest's conduct and to call two women to give evidence as to the priest's inappropriate behaviour towards them.

9.10.1.2 Determining whether the impression given is false

In some cases it will be difficult to determine whether or not the defendant has given a false impression. For example, in *R v Marsh* [1994] Crim LR 52, CA, the defendant was charged with inflicting grievous bodily harm while playing in a rugby match. He wished to adduce evidence that he had no previous convictions. It was held that this would entitle the prosecution to cross-examine him on his disciplinary record of violent play on the rugby field. This case was decided under s 1(3)(ii) of the Criminal Evidence Act 1898 (now repealed) and the issue was whether or not the defendant had asserted his good character. Under s 101(1)(f), the test would have been whether the defendant gave a false impression. It is uncertain how this case would be decided under the 2003 Act.

9.10.1.3 When the defendant is responsible for an assertion

Section 105 provides:

(2) A defendant is treated as being responsible for the making of an assertion if—

    (a) the assertion is made by the defendant in the proceedings (whether or not in evidence given by him),

    (b) the assertion was made by the defendant—

        (i) on being questioned under caution, before charge, about the offence with which he is charged, or

        (ii) on being charged with the offence or officially informed that he might be prosecuted for it, and evidence of the assertion is given in the proceedings,

    (c) the assertion is made by a witness called by the defendant,

    (d) the assertion is made by any witness in cross-examination in response to a question asked by the defendant that is intended to elicit it, or is likely to do so, or

    (e) the assertion was made by any person out of court, and the defendant adduces evidence of it in the proceedings.

(3)   A defendant who would otherwise be treated as responsible for the making of an assertion shall not be so treated if, or to the extent that, he withdraws it or disassociates himself from it.

Therefore, a defendant is treated as being responsible for the making of an assertion where the assertion is made:

- by the defendant in the proceedings (whether or not in evidence given by him);
- by the defendant on being questioned under caution, before charge, about the offence with which he is charged and evidence of the assertion is given in the proceedings;
- by the defendant on being charged with the offence or officially informed that he might be prosecuted for it and evidence of the assertion is given in the proceedings;
- by a witness called by the defendant;
- by a witness in cross-examination in response to a question asked by the defendant that is intended to elicit it, or is likely to do so; or
- by a person out of court, and the defendant adduces evidence of it in the proceedings.

It is submitted that an assertion may be made by the defendant in the proceedings in evidence by his legal representative acting on his instructions and by his conduct or behaviour. A defendant will not be treated as being responsible for the making of an assertion if he withdraws it or disassociates himself from it (s 105(3)). A concession extracted in cross-examination that a defendant was not telling the truth in his examination-in-chief would not normally amount to a withdrawal or disassociation from the original assertion for the purposes of s 105(3) (*R v Renda* [2006] 1 Cr App R 24).

9.10.2   Correcting a false impression

Section 105 provides:

(1)   For the purposes of section 101(1)(f)—

. . .

(b) evidence to correct such an impression is evidence which has probative value in correcting it.

. . .

(6)   Evidence is admissible under section 101(1)(f) only if it goes no further than is necessary to correct the false impression.

Thus, in order to be admissible, the evidence of the defendant's bad character must be capable as a matter of logic of rebutting the false impression. For example, where the defendant is charged with theft and asserts in evidence that he is an honest man, a previous conviction for theft would be admissible under s 101(1)(f), whereas a previous conviction for common assault would not.

9.10.3   Issues to which evidence adduced under s 101(1)(f) is relevant

Where the prosecution adduce evidence of the defendant's bad character under s 101(1)(f) it will be relevant, in principle, to both the defendant's credibility and the facts in issue. For example, where a defendant charged with theft asserts in evidence that he is an honest man, he thereby gives the impression that he is to be believed on oath and is unlikely to have committed the offence. If the prosecution adduce evidence of his previous convictions to correct that false impression, the previous convictions may be relevant and admissible both in relation to his guilt and his credibility.

9.10.4   Exclusionary discretion

Section 101(3) is of no application to evidence of the defendant's bad character adduced under s 101(1)(f). Therefore, evidence of the defendant's bad character which the prosecution propose to adduce may only be excluded by the court exercising its discretion at common law where the prejudicial effect of the evidence would outweigh its probative value (*R v Sang* [1980] AC 402; see **1.6.2.1**) or under s 78 of PACE 1984 (see **13.1.3**) where the admission of the evidence would have such an adverse affect on the fairness of the proceedings that the court ought not to admit it. While there has been some doubt as to whether s 78 of PACE 1984 applies to the bad character provisions of the CJA 2003, in *R v Weir* [2006] 1 Cr App 19, the Court of Appeal said that there was no reason to doubt that s 78 of PACE 1984 applied to evidence adduced under s 101(1)(f). A similar view was expressed in *R v Highton* [2006] 1 Cr App R 7, CA, although the court acknowledged that they had not had the benefit of hearing full argument on the point.

9.11   A defendant's attack on the character of another person (s 101(1)(g))

Section 101 provides:

> (1)   *In criminal proceedings evidence of the defendant's bad character is admissible if, but only if—*
>
> . . .
> > (g)   *the defendant has made an attack on another person's character.*

Only the prosecution can admit evidence of the defendant's bad character under this provision (s 103(6)).

9.11.1   Making an attack on another person's character

Section 101(1)(g) is supplemented by s 106 which provides:

> (1)   *For the purposes of section 101(1)(g) a defendant makes an attack on another person's character if—*
> > (a)   *he adduces evidence attacking the other person's character,*
> > (b)   *he . . . asks questions in cross-examination that are intended to elicit such evidence or are likely to do so, or*
> > (c)   *evidence is given of an imputation about the other person made by the defendant—*
> > > (i)   *on being questioned under caution, before charge, about the offence with which he is charged, or*
> > > (ii)   *on being charged with the offence or officially informed that he might be prosecuted for it.*
>
> (2)   *In subsection (1) 'evidence attacking the other person's character' means evidence to the effect that the other person—*
> > (a)   *has committed an offence (whether a different offence from the one with which the defendant is charged or the same one), or*
> > (b)   *has behaved, or is disposed to behave, in a reprehensible way; and 'imputation about another person' means an assertion to that effect.*

Section 101(1)(g) reflects the previous rule in the Criminal Evidence Act 1898, s 1(3)(ii) (now repealed) which provided that a defendant's bad character could be put to him in cross-examination if 'the nature or conduct of his defence is such as to involve imputations on the character of the prosecutor or the witnesses for the prosecution or the deceased victim of the alleged crime'. In *R v Hanson* [2005] 2 Cr App R 21, CA, it was held that the pre-2003 Act authorities will continue to apply when assessing whether an attack has been made on another person's character to the extent that they are compatible with s 106.

Under s 106 a defendant will therefore be deemed to have made an attack on another person's character in four situations:

- where he adduces evidence attacking another person's character;
- where he asks questions in cross-examination that are intended to elicit such evidence or are likely to do so;
- where evidence is given of an imputation about the other person made by the defendant on being questioned under caution, before charge, about the offence with which he is charged; or
- where evidence is given of an imputation about the other person made by the defendant on being charged with the offence or officially informed that he might be prosecuted for it.

Under s 106(2) evidence attacking the other person's character means evidence to the effect that that person:

- has committed an offence; or
- has behaved, or is disposed to behave in a reprehensible way.

An imputation about the other person means an assertion to that effect. It will be noted that this definition is not the same as the definition for 'bad character' under s 98 of the Act. Evidence of bad character does not include evidence which has to do with the alleged facts of the offence or evidence of misconduct in connection with the investigation or prosecution of the offence. This means that where the defendant alleges that another person committed the offence or that police have behaved improperly, for example by fabricating evidence, he will be deemed to have attacked another person's character even though it was a necessary part of his defence rather than a gratuitous attack. This reflects the position under the previous law (*Selvey v DPP* [1970] AC 304, HL).

There is no requirement that the person on whom the attack is made is a witness in the proceedings.

It will be noted that there are certain similarities between the circumstances in which a defendant will be deemed to have attacked another person's character under s 106 and those where he will be held responsible for giving a false impression under s 105. While s 106 does not expressly refer to a defendant being responsible for an attack made by a defence witness, such evidence would seem to be included as it would be evidence adduced by the defendant. It is unclear whether evidence adduced would extend to cover answers given in cross-examination by the prosecution. However, there are also marked differences between ss 105 and 106. In particular, there is no provision under s 106 which allows the defendant to withdraw or disassociate himself from an attack.

9.11.2 Emphatic denials

Under the previous law, the defendant was not liable to cross-examination as to his bad character if he merely asserted his innocence or denied his guilt, albeit in emphatic terms. It is submitted that the same principle will continue to apply under the 2003 Act. Each case will fall to be decided on its exact facts and circumstances and the exact language used (*R v Levy* (1966) 50 Cr App R 238).

One area of particular complexity concerned those cases in which the defendant challenged the evidence of police officers about alleged confession statements. The prosecution may rely on the defendant's alleged confession to the police during questioning. In such a case, where the defendant denies the offence at trial he will frequently deny that the confession was made. In *R v Britzman* [1983] 1 WLR 350, CA, it was held that a mere denial of a conversation with a police officer in circumstances where this could not be accepted as a mistake or misinterpretation would amount to an imputation on the person alleging that the conversation had taken place. No distinction could be drawn between a defence so conducted as to make specific allegations of fabrication and one in which such allegations arose by way of necessary and reasonable implication.

9.11.3   Relevant to credibility

Evidence obtained by cross-examination under s 1(3)(ii) of the 1898 Act went to credit only. Its sole purpose was to show that the defendant should not be believed on oath (*R v Jenkins* (1945) 31 Cr App R 1). It is submitted that the same is true under s 101(1)(g).

However, it will also be remembered that in *R v Highton* [2006] 1 Cr App R 7, CA, it was held that a distinction had to be drawn between the admissibility of evidence of bad character, which depended upon it getting through one of the 'gateways' in s 101 of the 2003 Act, and the use to which it could be put once it was admitted. The use to which it could be put depended on the matters to which it was relevant rather than upon the gateway through which it was admitted. For example, evidence of bad character adduced because the defendant has made an attack on another person's character (s 101(1)(g)), once it has been admitted, may subsequently become relevant and admissible in relation to an important matter in issue between the defendant and the prosecution (s 101(1)(d)).

9.11.4   The exclusionary discretion

Section 101 provides that:

(3)   *The court must not admit evidence under subsection . . . 1(g) if, on an application by the defendant to exclude it, it appears to the court that the admission of the evidence would have such an adverse effect on the fairness of the proceedings that the court ought not to admit it.*

(4)   *On an applicatrion to exclude evidence under subsection (3) the court must have regard, in particular, to the length of time between the matters to which that evidence relates and the matters which form the subject of the offence charged.*

Where the prosecution propose to adduce evidence of the defendant's misconduct under s 101(1)(g) the court must not do so where it appears to the court that the admission of the evidence would have such an adverse effect on the fairness of the proceedings that the court ought not to admit it. The wording of this provision is very similar to s 78 of PACE 1984 (see **13.1.3**). The key difference is that it is expressed in mandatory ('must not admit') rather than discretionary ('may refuse to allow') terms. It is submitted that the common law discretion to exclude evidence where its prejudicial effect outweighs its probative value will also apply to evidence the prosecution propose to adduce under s 101(1)(g). The discretion under s 78 of PACE 1984 will also apply in principle but in practice it will be otiose because of the overlap with s 101(3).

Under s 1(3)(ii) of the Criminal Evidence Act 1898, the judge had a discretion to refuse to permit cross-examination where an imputation had been cast. It is submitted that the same principles that governed the exercise of that discretion will govern the exercise of the judge's discretion to exclude evidence of the defendant's bad character under s 101(3) or common law.

9.11.4.1   Attacks necessary to the defence

As has been noted, in *R v Britzman* [1983] 1 WLR 350, CA, the court held that no distinction could be drawn between a defence so conducted as to make specific allegations of fabrication and one in which such allegations arose by way of necessary and reasonable implication. The court went on to give the following guidelines regarding the exercise of the judge's discretion in such circumstances:

(a) The Court should exercise its discretion to prevent cross-examination of the defendant where he merely denies, however emphatically or offensively, an incident or the contents of a short interview (as opposed to the denial of a long period of detailed observation extending over hours or a long conversation).

(b) Cross-examination should only be allowed where there is no possibility of mistake, misunderstanding or confusion and the jury will have to decide whether the prosecution witness has fabricated evidence.

(c) In the case of a defendant making wild allegations, allowance should be made for the strain of being in the witness box and the exaggerated use of language resulting from that or from a lack of education or mental stability.

(d) Allowance should also be made for a defendant led into making allegations during cross-examination.

(e) Cross-examination should be disallowed where the evidence against the defendant is overwhelming.

9.11.4.2   Bad character not relevant to credibility

In *R v Powell* [1985] 1 WLR 1364, CA, it was held that the judge was entitled to let the jury know the character of the person making the attack on another. The fact that the defendant's convictions were not for offences of dishonesty was a matter for the judge to take into consideration when exercising his discretion, although it did not oblige the judge to disallow the proposed cross-examination.

9.11.4.3   Similarity of previous misconduct

In *Maxwell v DPP* [1935] AC 309, HL, Viscount Sankey LC said that the trial judge, in the exercise of his discretion under s 1(3)(ii), should disallow cross-examination 'if there is any risk of the jury being misled into thinking that it goes not to credibility but to the probability of (the defendant) having committed the offence with which he is charged'. It is submitted that the same principle will continue to govern the exercise of the judicial discretion under s 101(3) or at common law.

However, the mere similarity of previous offences to those being charged did not mean that the trial judge ought, necessarily, to exercise the discretion (*DPP v Selvey* [1970] AC 304). In *R v Powell* [1985] 1 WLR 1364, CA, the defendant was convicted of knowingly living on the earnings of prostitution. The defendant alleged that the police had fabricated part of the evidence against him. The trial judge allowed cross-examination on his previous convictions, which were for allowing his premises to be used for the purposes of prostitution. It was held that if a deliberate attack is made on a prosecution witness calculated to discredit him, and if there is a real issue about the conduct of an important witness which the jury will have to resolve in order to reach their verdict, then the judge is entitled to let the jury know the character of the person making the attack. The fact that the defendant's convictions were for offences bearing a close resemblance to the offences charged, was a matter for the judge to take into consideration when exercising his discretion, but it did not oblige the judge to disallow the proposed cross-examination.

9.11.4.4   Details of previous misconduct

Given that the sole purpose of cross-examination under s 1(3)(ii) was to undermine the defendant's credibility, the question arose as to whether it should be restricted to the fact of the previous conviction alone, or whether it could include reference to the facts that gave rise to that conviction. In *R v McLeod* [1994] 3 All ER 254, CA, it was held that it was undesirable that there should be prolonged or extensive cross-examination in relation to previous offences, because it would divert the jury from the principal issue in the case, namely the guilt of the defendant on the instant offence. Unless the previous convictions were also admissible as similar fact evidence (see **9.9.4.4** and **9.9.4.5**), prosecution counsel were not permitted to probe or emphasise similarities between the underlying facts of the previous convictions and the instant one. Similarities of defences which had been rejected by juries on previous occasions, and whether or not the defendant pleaded guilty or was disbelieved having given evidence on oath, could be legitimate matters for questions. Those matters did not show a propensity to commit the offence but clearly went to credibility. It was further held that underlying facts that showed particularly bad character over and above the bare facts of the case were not necessarily to be excluded; but that the judge should be careful to balance the gravity of the attack on the prosecution witness with the degree of prejudice to the defendant which would result from the disclosure of the facts in question. The court observed that details of sexual offences against children were likely to be regarded by a jury as particularly prejudicial.

9.12   Stopping the case where evidence is contaminated

Ordinarily it is for the jury to decide whether or not to believe evidence and decide on the weight to be placed on it. At common law it was held in the case of *R v H* [1995] 2 AC 596, that if in the course of the trial it became apparent that evidence had been adduced as part of the prosecution case that no reasonable jury could accept as being free from collusion, then the jury should be directed that it could not be relied upon as corroboration or for any other purpose adverse to the defence. Where this was not so, but the question of collusion had been raised, the judge should draw the attention of the jury to the importance of collusion and tell them that if they were not satisfied that the evidence could be relied upon as free from collusion, it could not be used as corroboration or for any other purpose adverse to the defence. It is submitted that these principles will continue to apply.

However, there may be cases where it is not possible to expect the jury to put such evidence completely out of their minds and the evidence may therefore render the conviction unsafe. Section 107 provides:

(1)   *If on a defendant's trial before a judge and jury for an offence—*
   (a)   *evidence of his bad character has been admitted under any of paragraphs (c) to (g) of section 101(1), and*
   (b)   *the court is satisfied at any time after the close of the case for the prosecution that—*
      (i)   *the evidence is contaminated, and*
      (ii)   *the contamination is such that, considering the importance of the evidence to the case against the defendant, his conviction of the offence would be unsafe, the court must either direct the jury to acquit the defendant of the offence or, if it considers that there ought to be a retrial, discharge the jury.*

(2)   *Where—*
   (a)   *a jury is directed under subsection (1) to acquit a defendant of an offence, and*
   (b)   *the circumstances are such that, apart from this subsection, the defendant could if acquitted of that offence be found guilty of another offence, the defendant may not be found guilty of that other offence if the court is satisfied as mentioned in subsection (1)(b) in respect of it.*

(3)   *. . .*

(4)   *This section does not prejudice any other power a court may have to direct a jury to acquit a person of the offence or to discharge a jury.*

(5)   *For the purposes of this section a person's evidence is contaminated where—*
   (a)   *as a result of an agreement or understanding between the person and one or more others, or*

(b)   as a result of the person being aware of anything alleged by one or more others whose evidence may be, or has been, given in the proceedings, the evidence is false or misleading in any respect, or is different from what it would otherwise have been.

Section 107 confers on the judge a power to direct the jury to acquit the defendant or, if it considers there ought to be a retrial, to discharge the jury where the evidence of the defendant's bad character that has been adduced through gateways s 101(1)(c) to (g) is so 'contaminated' that it would render any conviction unsafe (s 107(1)). In such circumstances, the defendant cannot be convicted of a lesser alternative offence (s 107(2)).

Character evidence is contaminated if it is false or misleading either because of an understanding or agreement between a witnesses in the proceedings and another person (s 107(5)(a)) or because the witness is aware of the allegations of other witnesses in the proceedings (s 107(5)(b)).

9.13   Offences committed when the defendant was a child

Section 108 of the Act provides:

(2)   In proceedings for an offence committed or alleged to have been committed by the defendant when aged 21 or over, evidence of his conviction for an offence when under the age of 14 is not admissible unless—
(a)   both of the offences are triable only on indictment, and
(b)   the court is satisfied that the interests of justice require the evidence to be admissible.
(3)   Subsection (2) applies in addition to section 101.

9.14   Assumption of truth

Section 109 provides that:

(1)   Subject to subsection (2), a reference in this Chapter to the relevance or probative value of evidence is a reference to its relevance or probative value on the assumption that it is true.
(2)   In assessing the relevance or probative value of an item of evidence for any purpose of this Chapter, a court need not assume that the evidence is true if it appears, on the basis of any material before the court (including any evidence it decides to hear on the matter), that no court or jury could reasonably find it to be true.

At common law where an application to exclude similar fact evidence was made, and the submission raised a question of collusion, the judge had to approach the question of admissibility on the basis that the similar facts alleged were true (*R v H* [1995] 2 AC 596).

This principle is reflected in s 109 of the 2003 Act. Under s 109, when determining the admissibility of evidence, the judge must assess the relevance or probative value of evidence on the assumption that it is true. If the evidence takes the form of a previous conviction this provision is uncontroversial. However, where the evidence takes the form of unproven allegations of misconduct, or of allegations of misconduct of which the defendant had previously been acquitted, the court must still accept the evidence as being true. In the latter case this means that the section creates the bizarre presumption that a person must be treated as being guilty of an offence of which he has been acquitted.

It has been held that the mere making of an allegation is capable of being 'evidence' for the purposes of s 109, at least in relation to s 101(1)(d) (*R v Edwards* [2006] 2 Ce App R 4

Crim 3244). Therefore, when a party proposes to adduce an allegation as evidence of misconduct, the court must accept it as being true for the purposes of determining its probative value and thus its admissibility.

9.15 The duty to give reasons

Section 110 provides:

(1)   Where the court makes a relevant ruling—

     (a)   it must state in open court (but in the absence of the jury, it there is one) its reasons for the ruling;

     (b)   if it is a magistrates' court, it must cause the ruling and the reasons for it to be entered in the register of the court's proceedings.

(2)   In this section 'relevant ruling' means—

     (a)   a ruling on whether an item of evidence is evidence of a person's bad character;

     (b)   a ruling on whether an item of such evidence is admissible under section 100 or 101 (including a ruling on an application under section 101(3));

     (c)   a ruling under section 107.

9.16 Rules of procedure

Section 111 allows the creation of rules of court concerning the admission of the evidence of character. By s 111(2) and (3) these rules can (and in the case of the prosecution must) include requirements to serve notice of the intention to adduce evidence of bad character or to elicit such evidence through cross-examination. Section 111(4) provides for making rules concerning costs consequences of failure to comply with the notice requirements created under s 111(2) and (3).

The complete rules are set out in the Criminal Procedure Rules 2005, 35. The main provisions are as follows:

35.4 Prosecutor introducing evidence of defendant's bad character

(1)   A prosecutor who wants to introduce evidence of a defendant's bad character or who wants to cross-examine a witness with a view to eliciting that evidence, under section 101 of the Criminal Justice Act 2003 must give notice in the form set out in the Practice Direction to the court officer and all other parties to the proceedings. Notice under paragraph (1) must be given—

     (a)   in a case to be tried in a magistrates' court, at the same time as the prosecutor complies or purports to comply with section 3 of the Criminal Procedure and Investigations Act 1996; and

     (b)   in a case to be tried in the Crown Court, not more than 14 days after—

          (i)   the committal of the defendant, or

          (ii)   the consent to the preferment of a bill of indictment in relation to the case, or

          . . .

          (iv)   where a person is sent for trial under section 51 of the Crime and Disorder Act 1998 (sending cases to the Crown Court) the service of copies of the documents containing the evidence on which the charge or charges are based under paragraph 1 of Schedule 3 to that Act.

35.5 Co-defendant introducing evidence of defendant's bad character

A co-defendant who wants to introduce evidence of a defendant's bad character or who wants to cross-examine a witness with a view to eliciting that evidence under section 101 of the Criminal Justice Act 2003 must give notice in the form set out in the Practice Direction to the court officer and all other parties to the proceedings not more than 14 days after the prosecutor has complied or purported to comply with section 3 of the Criminal Procedure and Investigations Act 1996.

35.6 Defendant applying to exclude evidence of his own bad character

A defendant's application to exclude bad character evidence must be in the form set out in the Practice Direction and received by the court officer and all other parties to the proceedings not more than 7 days after receiving a notice given under rules 35.4 or 35.5.

In *R v Bovell* [2005] 2 Cr App R 27, CA, it was held that it was necessary for all parties to have, in good time, the appropriate information in relation to previous convictions and other evidence of bad character. That could only be achieved if the rules in relation to the giving of notice were complied with. In *R v Hanson* [2005] 2 Cr App R 21, CA, it was held that in complying with the notice requirements the prosecution should indicate whether it proposes simply to rely upon the fact of conviction or also upon the circumstances of it.

9.17   Handling stolen goods (Theft Act 1968, s 27)

Section 27(3) of the Theft Act 1968 provides:

(3)   *Where a person is being proceeded against for handling stolen goods (but not for any offence other than handling stolen goods), then at any stage in the proceedings, if evidence has been given of his having or arranging to have in his possession the goods the subject of the charge, or of his undertaking or assisting in, or arranging to undertake, or assist in, their retention, removal, disposal or realisation, the following evidence shall be admissible for the purposes of proving that he knew or believed the goods to be stolen goods—*

(a)   *evidence that he has had in his possession, or has undertaken or assisted in the retention, removal or disposal or realisation of, stolen goods from any theft taking place not earlier than 12 months before the offence charged; and*

(b)   *(provided that seven days' notice in writing has been given to him of the intention to prove the conviction) evidence that he has within the five years preceding the date of the offence charged been convicted of theft or of handling stolen goods.*

Section 27(3) allows proof of the defendant's previous convictions to prove that he knew or believed that the goods were stolen. It does not prove his dishonesty (*R v Duffas* (1994) 158 JP 224). The fact that the defendant disputes possession of the goods (or some of them) does not prevent the evidence being admitted under s 27(3) (*R v List* [1966] 1 WLR 9). However, where there are numerous charges, in some of which possession is in dispute and in some of which possession is admitted but knowledge disputed, the judge should consider whether to allow evidence of the previous convictions at all and, if it is allowed, should direct the jury that the previous convictions are only relevant to knowledge and not to any other issue in the case (*R v Wilkins* [1975] 2 All ER 734).

Where the evidence of the previous convictions is admitted, evidence of the details of previous convictions is not admissible (*R v Bradley* (1979) 70 Cr App R 200). However, in *R v Hacker* [1994] 1 WLR 1659, the House of Lords held that the proof of the previous convictions could include proof of such detail of the convictions as was included on the certificate of conviction under PACE 1984, s 73 (see **17.4.1.3**). The certificate of conviction would include details of the subject matter of the conviction, including the property that was handled. Previous convictions that would otherwise be admissible under s 27(3) can be excluded either at common law or under PACE 1984, s 78.

Character evidence: persons other than the defendant in criminal cases

10.1 Evidence of good character

The position with regard to evidence of the good character of a witness is the same in civil and in criminal proceedings. Therefore the rule in *R v Turner* [1975] QB 834 set out at **8.4.2.1** applies equally in criminal proceedings: a party calling a witness cannot call evidence to bolster his credibility.

10.2 Evidence of bad character

The admissibility of evidence of bad character is now governed by s 100 of the CJA 2003 (CJA 2003). Section 100(1) provides:

> (1)   *In criminal proceedings evidence of the bad character of a person other than the defendant is admissible if and only if—*
>   *(a)   it is important explanatory evidence,*
>   *(b)   it has substantial probative value in relation to a matter which—*
>   *(i)   is a matter in issue in the proceedings, and*
>   *(ii)   is of substantial importance in the context of the case as a whole, or*
>   *(c)   all parties to the proceedings agree to the evidence being admissible.*

Therefore, evidence of bad character is generally inadmissible against a person other than a defendant in criminal proceedings. Only evidence that fits within the three situations provided for by s 100(1) will be admissible. Evidence under s 100(1)(a) or (b) also requires the leave of the trial judge before it will be admitted (s 100(4)).

It should be remembered that s 100 protects the character both of prosecution witnesses, witnesses for the defence (other than the defendant) and any other persons. Furthermore, the restriction applies both to the party calling the witness and any party seeking to cross-examine the witness (although it seems unlikely that if a party calling a witness wished to establish that witness's bad character there would not be agreement under s 100(1)(c)).

Section 99(1) abolishes the common law rules governing the admissibility of evidence of bad character, as defined by s 98, with one exception, which is that evidence of the general reputation of a person proving their bad character is still admissible (s 99(2)). See **9.4.1** for further explanation of this rule.

10.2.1   Meaning of bad character

Section 112(1) provides that bad character for non-defendants has the same meaning as that provided for defendants in s 98 (see **9.4.1**). In the context of witnesses in criminal cases this means that it is possible to prove previous convictions, previous misconduct or a disposition to do either of those things.

10.2.2   Important explanatory evidence

Section 100 provides:

> (2)   . . . evidence is important explanatory evidence if—
>   (a)   without it, the court or jury would find it impossible or difficult properly to understand other evidence in the case, and
>   (b)   its value for understanding the case as a whole is substantial.

The text of s 100(2) is identical to s 102, which defines important explanatory evidence admitted against a defendant (see **9.7**) and the same principles apply. An example would be where the prosecution call an accomplice of the defendant to prove the defendant's commission of an offence. It will clearly be necessary to prove the involvement of the accomplice in the commission of the offence to explain his first-hand knowledge of the matters that took place.

10.2.3   Substantial probative value to a matter in issue of substantial importance

Section 100(1)(b) allows proof of the bad character of a person where it has substantial probative value in relation to a matter of substantial importance in proceedings.

10.2.3.1   Substantial importance

Section 100(1)(b)(ii) has the effect of preventing gratuitous attacks, especially on witnesses.

Clearly, facts in issue are always matters in issue of substantial importance. Any allegation that a person committed the offence rather than the defendant, acted in such a way as to afford the defendant a defence such as self-defence or duress, or was in some other way complicit in either the commission of the offence or the false accusation of the defendant, will be admissible subject to the requirement of substantial probative value (see **10.2.3.2**).

It seems equally clear that the credibility of witnesses is a matter in issue, but to what extent is it a matter of 'substantial importance to the case as a whole'? This will depend on the part played in proceedings by the particular witness. In this sense, s 100(1)(b)(ii) reflects the principle identified in *R v Sweet-Escott* (1971) 55 Cr App R 316 (see **8.4.2.2**) that cross-examination as to credit should only be permitted where the questions affect the witness's likely standing after cross-examination. However, as s 100(1)(b) concerns the admissibility of evidence of character generally, the section has extended the *Sweet-Escott* rule beyond cross-examination. The principle in *Hobbs v Tinling & Co Ltd* [1929] 2 KB 1 that cross-examination would not be allowed if the conduct occurred in the distant past or is out of proportion to the matters on which the witness will give evidence is also reflected by s 100(1)(b)(ii).

10.2.3.2   Substantial probative value

Evidence of bad character that has substantial importance to the proceedings as a whole will only be admissible if that evidence also has 'substantial probative value' (s 100(1)(b)(i)). Section 100 provides:

> (3)   In assessing the probative value of evidence for the purposes of subsection (1)(b) the court must have regard to the following factors (and to any others it considers relevant)—
>   (a)   the nature and number of the events, or other things, to which the evidence relates;
>   (b)   when those events or things are alleged to have happened or existed;
>   (c)   where—
>   (i)   the evidence is evidence of a person's misconduct, and
>   (ii)   it is suggested that the evidence has probative value by reason of similarity between that misconduct and other alleged misconduct, the nature and extent of the similarities and the dissimilarities between each of the alleged instances of misconduct;
>   (d)   where—
>   (i)   the evidence is evidence of a person's misconduct,
>   (ii)   it is suggested that that person is also responsible for the misconduct charged, and
>   (iii)   the identity of the person responsible for the misconduct charged is disputed, the extent to which the evidence shows or tends to show that the same person was responsible each time.

Section 100(3) therefore makes general provision for the probative value of the evidence such as the extent to which the evidence of bad character is probative of the character of the witness by reason of the frequency of the misconduct (s 100(3)(a)), the pattern of misconduct (s 100(3)(a)) and the extent to which it is too old to be probative of the witness's current character (s 100(3)(b)). These general provisions will apply whatever the matter in issue is (ie, relevance to a fact in issue or the credibility of the witness).

Section 100(3)(c) makes provision for the proof of the propensity of the witness towards particular misconduct (whether it is the commission of the offence charged, or a tendency to lie or a tendency to act aggressively and to cause fights) by requiring the court to consider the pattern of the offending behaviour. In this sense, the section is adopting the approach of the common law to similar fact evidence. The party wishing to prove the bad character of the witness would seek to do so by showing a pattern of offending that suggests that such misconduct occurred on this occasion. Section 100(3)(d) deals with situations in which the defendant alleges that the witness committed the offence (s 100(3)(d)(ii)) and seeks to prove this by establishing that the offence was committed in the same way in which the offence was committed by the witness on previous occasions.

In determining the probative value of evidence, the court should treat the evidence as though it is true (s 109(1)) unless the evidence before it (possibly adduced at a *voir dire*) establishes that no reasonable tribunal could consider it true (s 109(2)). However, in *R v Bovell* [2005] 2 Cr App R 27, CA, it was doubted whether the mere making of an allegation was capable of being evidence within s 100(1) of the 2003 Act. If an allegation was admitted it would give rise to an excursion into 'satellite' matters which was precisely the sort of excursion a trial judge should be discouraged from embarking upon.

10.2.4   Agreement of the parties

Section 100(1)(c) permits the admission of evidence of the bad character of a witness where all parties agree. Therefore, all co-defendants would have to agree to the admission of the evidence in addition to the prosecution.

10.2.5   Requirement of leave

Section 100(4) provides that save when the parties agree to admit the evidence of bad character under s 101(1)(c), such evidence must not be admitted without leave of the court.

10.3   Complainants in sexual cases

10.3.1   Restriction

The YJCEA 1999, s 41 places separate restrictions on the extent to which a complainant in a sexual offence may be cross-examined about his or her sexual history. Section 41 provides:

(1) *If at a trial a person is charged with a sexual offence, then, except with the leave of the court—*
   (a) *no evidence may be adduced, and*
   (b) *no question may be asked in cross-examination, by or on behalf of any accused at the trial, about any sexual behaviour of the complainant.*
(2) *The court may give leave in relation to any evidence or question only on an application made by or on behalf of an accused, and may not give such leave unless it is satisfied—*
   (a) *that subsection (3) or (5) applies, and*
   (b) *that a refusal of leave might have the result of rendering unsafe a conclusion of the jury or (as the case may be) the court on any relevant issue in the case.*
(3) *This subsection applies if the evidence or question relates to a relevant issue in the case and either—*
   (a) *that issue is not an issue of consent; or*
   (b) *it is an issue of consent and the sexual behaviour of the complainant to which the evidence or question relates is alleged to have taken place at or about the same time as the event which is the subject matter of the charge against the accused; or*
   (c) *it is an issue of consent and the sexual behaviour of the complainant to which the evidence or question relates is alleged to have been, in any respect, so similar—*
      (i) *to any sexual behaviour of the complainant which (according to evidence adduced or to be adduced by or on behalf of the accused) took place as part of the event which is the subject matter of the charge against the accused, or*
      (ii) *to any other sexual behaviour of the complainant which (according to such evidence) took place at or about the same time as that event,*
      that the similarity cannot reasonably be explained as a coincidence.
(4) *For the purposes of subsection (3) no evidence or question shall be regarded as relating to a relevant issue in the case if it appears to the court to be reasonable to assume that the purpose (or main purpose) for which it would be adduced or asked is to establish or elicit material for impugning the credibility of the complainant as a witness.*
(5) *This subsection applies if the evidence or question—*
   (a) *relates to any evidence adduced by the prosecution about any sexual behaviour of the complainant; and*
   (b) *in the opinion of the court, would go no further than is necessary to enable the evidence adduced by the prosecution to be rebutted or explained by or on behalf of the accused.*
(6) *For the purposes of subsections (3) and (5) the evidence or question must relate to a specific instance (or specific instances) of alleged sexual behaviour on the part of the complainant (and accordingly nothing in those subsections is capable of applying in relation to the evidence or question to the extent that it does not so relate).*
(7) *Where this section applies in relation to a trial by virtue of the fact that one or more of a number of persons charged in the proceedings is or are charged with a sexual offence—*
   (a) *it shall cease to apply in relation to the trial if the prosecutor decides not to proceed with the case against that person or those persons in respect of that charge; but*

> (b)   *it shall not cease to do so in the event of that person or those persons pleading guilty to, or being convicted of, that charge.*
>
> (8)   *Nothing in this section authorises any evidence to be adduced or any question to be asked which cannot be adduced or asked apart from this section.*

The CJA 2003, s 112 provides:

> (3)   *Nothing in this Chapter affects the exclusion of evidence—*
>
> . . .
>
> (b)   *under section 41 of the Youth Justice and Criminal Evidence Act 1999 . . .*

The effect of the CJA 2003, s 112(3) is that evidence of a witness's sexual behaviour that has been excluded under the YJCEA 1999, s 41 will not be admissible should it satisfy the requirements of s 100.

10.3.2   Extent of the restriction

> Section 42 of the YJCEA 1999 provides:
>
> . . .
>
> (c)   'sexual behaviour' means any sexual behaviour or other sexual experience, whether or not involving any accused or other person, but excluding (except in section 41(3)(c)(i) and (5)(a)) anything alleged to have taken place as part of the event which is the subject matter of the charge against the accused;
>
> . . .

The restriction imposed by s 41 therefore only relates to questions or evidence about other sexual behaviour; it does not restrict cross-examination about the sexual behaviour that is part of the incident or incidents for which the accused is being tried. In *R v Mukadi* [2003] EWCA Crim 3765, the Court of Appeal stated that it was not possible to define sexual behaviour. Rather, what was meant by the term was a matter of 'impression and common sense'. The behaviour in that case was the act of getting into the car driven by an unknown man who had pulled up alongside the complainant and the exchange of telephone numbers in the car. In allowing the appeal of the defendant, the Court of Appeal concluded that in the circumstances such behaviour was either sexual behaviour relevant to the complainant's consent at a later point (see below) or it was not sexual behaviour and therefore could have been the subject of cross-examination as s 41 did not apply.

If the defence is that the complainant is making false allegations against the accused and the accused seeks to support this by eliciting evidence of false allegations made in the past, s 41 does not apply as the making of false allegations is not 'sexual behaviour' (*R v MH* [2002] Crim LR 73, CA). In *R v C and B* [2003] EWCA Crim 29, the Court of Appeal held that, if the defence wished to question about previous false allegations, it would be necessary to determine whether there was a proper evidential basis for asserting that the allegation in question was (a) made and (b) false. If there was no such evidential basis the effect of questioning would be to prove the falsity of the previous allegation and would therefore be questioning about previous sexual behaviour. It is only if the falsity is shown by other seperate evidence that the previous allegation would not be sexual behaviour. Therefore, if the proof of falsity of the previous allegation wholly depends on cross-examination about sexual behaviour on that previous occasion, the false allegation is sexual behaviour within the meaning of s 41 (*R v H* [2003] EWCA Crim 2367) but if it can be established by evidence of a non-sexual nature, the false allegation is not sexual behaviour.

The previous sexual behaviour does not have to be between the accused and the complainant. However, where the behaviour was with a third person there would have to be very special facts before cross-examination would be permitted.

10.3.3   Restriction on cross-examination

Under s 41 such cross-examination will only be permitted if the court grants leave
(s 41(1)). Leave can only be granted if:

- one of the four qualifying circumstances apply (s 41(2)(a)); *and*
- refusal to grant leave might render a conviction unsafe (s 41(2)(b)).

10.3.3.1   Qualifing circumstances

The four qualifying circumstances, one of which is required before cross-examination can
be permitted, are:

(a) The cross-examination or evidence relates to an issue other than consent
(s 41(3)(a)).

   (i)   Belief in consent is an issue 'other than consent' and therefore if the issue is
belief in consent cross-examination may be permitted (subject to the other
elements of the test) under this section (s 41(1)(b)).

   (ii)   It would also include, for example, the defence that no sexual act took place.
Where there is medical evidence of a sexual act having taken place, the accused
could seek to be allowed to prove that the complainant had had sexual
intercourse with another person at that time.

(b) The cross-examination or evidence relates to the issue of consent and the previous
sexual behaviour took place 'on or about the same time' as the offence (s 41(3)(b)).

   (i)   In *R v A* [2001] 3 All ER 1, HL, it was observed that this meant a matter of hours
rather than days.

   (ii)   It would appear that this category of permissible questioning is aimed at
defences using evidence of the complainant's promiscuity to prove that at the
time of the alleged offence he as likely to have consented to the sexual act in
question.

(c) The cross-examination or evidence relates to the issue of consent and the previous
sexual behaviour in question is very similar either to the alleged offence or other
sexual behaviour at about the same time as the alleged offence (s 41(3)(c)).

   (i)   The exact phrase used by the Act is 'so similar . . . that the similarity cannot
reasonably be explained as a coincidence'.

   (ii)   This is potentially quite complicated but appears to be aimed at evidence of
previous consensual sexual behaviour of a distinctive nature that bears such a
strong similarity to what appears to have taken place during the offence that
this similarity may raise a reasonable doubt as to the complainant's lack of
consent.

   (iii)   For example, evidence that the complainant regularly had sexual intercourse
in a particularly distinctive way with the accused on previous occasions might
be admissible under this circumstance if there was evidence that the sexual act
forming the charge had very similar characteristics.

   (iv)   It is submitted that if the sexual behaviour on the previous and current
occasions were, due to their nature, incapable of being consensual acts, then
such previous behaviour would not be admissible under s 41.

   (v)   Note that s 41(3)(c) relates not only to a similarity between a previous incident
and the alleged offence where the nature of the two incidents could prove
the existence of consent. Under s 41(3)(c)(ii), evidence of previous sexual

behaviour which is similar to behaviour 'at or about the same time' as the alleged offence could also be admitted. In *R v Tahed* [2004] All ER (D) 346 (Feb), where the alleged rape took place within a particular climbing frame at a public park, the conviction was set aside because the trial judge had not allowed cross-examination concerning a similar (consensual) sexual encounter within the same climbing frame three weeks earlier. The trial judge had wrongly considered that the similarity had to be between the acts comprising part of the sexual act and had neglected to consider acts that took place 'at or about the same time'.

    (vi) In *R v Richardson* [2003] EWCA Crim 2754, the Court of Appeal concluded that evidence of a previous relationship and of a relationship after an alleged rape would not be permitted under s 41(3)(c) as the sexual behaviour in question (the relationship in general) would not bear sufficient similarity to the alleged offence.

(d) The cross-examination or evidence is tendered to rebut evidence tendered by the prosecution about the previous sexual behaviour of the complainant and only goes as far as is necessary to rebut that evidence (s 41(5)).

    (i) Note that this exception is not restricted to situations in which the defence is consent.

    (ii) For example, if the prosecution tendered evidence that the complainant had no sexual experience before the act in question, the defence would be able to adduce evidence or ask questions that would establish that he had sexual experience in the past.

Note that no cross-examination will be permitted if its only purpose is to undermine the credibility of the complainant (s 41(4)).

In *R v M* [2004] All ER (D) 103, the Court of Appeal stated that where cross-examination would have the effect of undermining the credibility *and* of supporting the defendant's denial of the complainant's allegations, then such evidence would not be excluded under s 41(4).

Even if the alleged sexual behaviour falls within the four categories of evidence set out in s 41(3) to (5) identified above, such behaviour cannot be admitted unless it relates to specific incidents (s 41(6)). Therefore in *R v White* [2004] All ER (D) 103 (Mar), evidence of previous convictions of the complainant for prostitution were held to have rightly been excluded as such convictions would be too general.

10.3.3.2 Risk of unsafe conviction

The effect of s 41 is that the defence will have to convince the court to allow leave to question about *any* previous sexual behaviour of the complainant. The court cannot grant leave unless persuaded both that there is some particular relevance to the evidence (ie, one of the qualifying circumstances set out above) and that the evidence is probative enough that a failure to allow it to be admitted would put the accused at risk of an unsafe conviction.

In *R v A*, the House of Lords considered the effect of this restriction in light of the right to a fair trial under Article 6 of the ECHR. They recognised that the right to a fair trial included the ability to put forward a full defence and that the restrictions imposed by s 41 of the 1999 Act created a risk that this would not be possible. They therefore invoked s 3 of the Human Rights Act 1998 to interpret s 41 to require that judges should consider the extent to which an accused would be deprived of a material defence and therefore a fair trial as a result of a refusal to grant leave. It would therefore appear that the restriction under s 41 is to be exercised narrowly by the courts.

In *R v Richardson* (above), the Court of Appeal concluded that the strict interpretation of s 41(3)(c) that excluded cross–examination about ongoing sexual relationships between the complainant and the defendant was unfair within the meaning of *R v A* and therefore quashed a conviction where the trial judge, applying s 41(3)(c), had not permitted such cross-examination.

In *R v Mukadi* (above), the issue was whether the complainant had consented to sexual intercourse. The complainant's evidence was that she had gone to the defendant's flat with him, not intending any sexual acts to take place, but that she had allowed him to carry out various sexual acts short of intercourse in the hope that he would then not have full intercourse with her, but that he had subsequently carried out sexual intercourse without her consent. The case for the defendant was that the complainant had willingly consented to all the sexual acts that took place. The Court of Appeal held the behaviour of getting into a car with an unknown person and exchanging telephone numbers a matter of hours before the events alleged would be sufficiently relevant and probative to prove that she may have intended, in going to the defendant's flat, to carry out sexual acts. It was noted that if her evidence had been that she had gone to the defendant's flat willing to engage in sexual activity short of full sexual intercourse, the previous event would not have been particularly probative and therefore probably not admissible. However, as she had stated in evidence that she had not intended to engage in any sexual acts, the previous event was probative not only in proving that she may have been willing to consent but also that her denial of consent was probably untrue. As such, the previous event should have been admitted. *R v Mukadi* therefore illustrates that any analysis of the probative value and therefore of the fairness of refusing to allow questioning will depend on detailed analysis of the issues raised by the evidence of the parties and cannot be determined by simple categorisation of the evidence.

The previous sexual behaviour does not have to have been between the accused and the complainant. However, where the behaviour was with a third person, more cogent evidence of potential consent would be required before cross-examination will be permitted: *R v White* [2004] All ER (D) 103 (Mar).

Hearsay: introduction and hearsay in civil proceedings

11.1 Introduction to hearsay evidence

Chapters 11 and **12** consider the rules relating to hearsay evidence. **Chapter 11** concentrates upon the admissibility of hearsay in civil proceedings. **Chapter 12** considers the admissibility of hearsay evidence in criminal proceedings. However, before considering the admissibility of such evidence, this chapter will identify what is meant by hearsay evidence and the rationale for restricting its admissibility. Understanding what is meant by hearsay and why it has been felt that the rules of evidence should restrict the admissibility of such evidence is vital to understanding the rules themselves.

11.1.1 Out of court statements

The rules relating to hearsay evidence restrict the extent to which statements made out of court will be admitted as evidence. Hearsay statements are not the only 'out of court' statements so it is worth exploring out of court statements generally before looking at hearsay statements in particular.

Take a minute to visualise a trial. It is likely that you will be thinking about a witness in the witness box giving evidence about some matter, perhaps an assault. It is likely that the witness you are thinking about will be an 'eye witness' in that he will be saying what he saw. The reason such a witness is called to give evidence is that he will be the best person available to give such evidence. What makes him the best person is the first-hand experience of the events in question. It makes more sense to call the witness to say what happened than to bring to court someone else the witness spoke to about the incident. Equally, it makes more sense to call the witness than to rely upon a document the witness wrote about the event.

There are a number of aspects to this:

1. The court receives the information with appropriate formality. Testimony is generally given on oath (see **4.2.1**). Even if the witness does not hold religious beliefs, the formality of the court environment and threat of a conviction for perjury form strong encouragements to the witness to give truthful testimony. A person making a similar statement out of court may not feel an equal pressure to be honest.

2. There is less possibility of error. All witnesses can be mistaken in a number of ways. However, when witness B is used to prove what witness A saw by repeating what he has been told by A, we add to A's potential mistakes the chance that B has inaccurately repeated what witness A told him. B could have misheard, misinterpreted, forgotten or distorted what A had said or the account could simply be incomplete. Each extra

person in the chain of communication between the actual witness to the event and the person testifying increases this risk of error.

3. If the testimony is given by the first-hand witness of the event, it will be possible to conduct the most critical examination of the account. A statement made out of court clearly cannot be cross-examined. Further, any possible explanation advanced by the party against whom the evidence is admitted cannot be put to the actual witness if his account is conveyed by another.

4. Where evidence is given by way of a statement made out of court, the tribunal of fact is deprived of an opportunity to assess the demeanour of the person making the statement.

5. Added to this is the risk that inexperienced tribunals of fact, such as juries, may not be sufficiently aware of the weaknesses of out of court statements identified above.

The courts have therefore been resistant to receiving out of court statements as evidence. There is a strong preference for receiving the evidence in court and from the person who had first-hand experience of the matters in question.

There are, however, various reasons for seeking to admit statements made out of court. A party may seek to prove that a statement was made out of court for the following purposes:

(a) To prove the truth of what was said in the out of court statement. The logic in such cases is, 'If A said X then X is true.' If this is the purpose of the statement, it is a *hearsay* statement.

(b) To prove that the statement was made. These statements are called *original* statements. There are a number of reasons why this might be useful in the case:

(i)   to bolster the credibility of a witness by being consistent with his testimony. This is a *previous consistent statement*, which was considered at **6.4**;

(ii)   to undermine the credibility of a witness by being inconsistent with his current testimony. This is a *previous inconsistent statement*, which was considered at **7.7**;

(iii) to prove that the maker held a particular belief or knew a particular fact. The logic is that if a person speaks about a particular thing, he knows of that thing. Therefore a statement, 'Hello, Caroline, have you recovered from your illness?', could prove that the maker *knew* Caroline had been ill as much as it could prove that she had in fact been ill. In so far as it is used to prove Caroline's illness, the tribunal of fact would have to rely on the truth of the statement (or what it implies). In so far as the statement is used to prove that the maker of the statement knew that Caroline was ill, the evidential purpose is to prove a fact (the maker's knowledge) by proving (a) the fact of certain things having been said and (b) that the things said were true (this being achieved by independent evidence): in other words, the statement does not prove the thing alleged (or implied) to be true;

(iv)   to prove that someone other than the maker held a particular belief or knew a particular fact. For example, if the issue in the case was whether the accused acted under duress, evidence that a threat was made to that person would be relevant to prove that the accused *believed* that he had been threatened. It can do this whether or not the threat was genuine or true;

(v)   to prove that words were used because they have a particular legal significance. If I promise to sell you a painting for £100 and then refuse to do so, you could sue me for breach of contract. To prove the contract and its terms you would have to prove that I had made you an offer, which you accepted. To prove the offer, you would have to prove the statement I made out of court: 'I will sell you this painting for £100.' To amount to an offer the promise to sell you a painting for £100 does not have to be true. In fact, if you think about it, most promises in breach of contract cases will have been untrue up to a point: that is why the breach of contract action is being brought. To use a criminal example, it is an offence under s 4 of the Public Order Act 1986 to use 'threatening, abusive or insulting words or behaviour'. If the prosecution allege that the offence was committed by use of threatening words they will have to prove that the words were used. If, for example, the words were 'You bastard, you're dead,' that statement will have to be proved at court. Clearly what is said does not have to be true. The relevance to the case is that the statement was made at all;

(vi) to prove that the maker of the statement lied. Occasionally this sort of statement may overlap with the one above because proof that the maker of the statement lied may be a necessary feature of the case (for example in fraud, misrepresentation or deception cases). On other occasions the lie will be evidence that the maker was conscious of his own guilt and was trying to cover up that guilt (see **Chapter 14** for more detail on the probative value of lies). Obviously, the statement does not have to be true to be a lie!

11.1.2   What is hearsay evidence?

This chapter will first consider what evidence is hearsay and then consider situations in which the courts have concluded statements are not hearsay. The hearsay rule was originally a rule of common law. Many exceptions to the rule evolved because the rule, strictly applied, would lead to the exclusion of much evidence that (a) was highly probative and (b) could not be obtained by other sources. The common law rules have been replaced to a considerable extent in both civil and criminal cases by statute. This chapter will consider both what is meant by hearsay and then how the rule is applied in civil cases. **Chapter 12** will concetrate on the application of the rule in criminal cases.

11.1.2.1   Definition

Hearsay evidence is essentially the use of a statement made out of court to prove something by getting the tribunal of fact to rely upon the truth of what the statement asserts. There is no single definition of hearsay. There are, however, definitions of hearsay in both civil and criminal proceedings and the courts and commentators have also provided definitions.

For civil proceedings, hearsay is defined by the Civil Evidence Act 1995, s 1(2) which provides:

(a)   'hearsay' means a statement made otherwise than by a person while giving oral evidence in the proceedings which is tendered as evidence of the matters stated.

Section 13 provides:

'statement' means any representation of fact or opinion, however made.

In criminal proceedings, the CJA 2003, s 114(1) regulates the admissibility of 'a statement not made in oral evidence in the proceedings . . . as evidence of any matter stated'. CJA 2003, s 115 provides:

(1)   . . . references to a statement or to a matter stated are to be read as follows.
(2)   A statement is any representation of fact or opinion made by a person by whatever means; and it includes a representation made in a sketch, photofit or other pictorial form.

> *(3)   A matter stated is one to which this Chapter applies if (and only if) the purpose, or one of the purposes, of the person making the statement appears to the court to have been—*
>
> *(a)   to cause another person to believe the matter, or*
>
> *(b)   to cause another person to act or a machine to operate on the basis that the matter is stated.*

Further, *Cross & Tapper on Evidence*, 10th edn, OUP, 2004, at p 530, defines the rule against hearsay as:

An assertion other than one made by a person while testifying in the proceedings is inadmissible as evidence of any fact or opinion asserted.

An earlier version of this definition was approved in *R v Sharp* [1988] 1 WLR 7 by Lord Havers (at p 11) although that earlier definition did not contain a reference to opinion evidence.

With one important exception the definitions of hearsay are the same in criminal and civil cases and include:

- a statement;
- that the statement was made out of court (ie, other than as 'oral evidence' or 'testimony'); and
- that the statement is adduced to prove the truth of the matters asserted in it.

As was noted above, where out of court statements are not tendered to prove the truth of the matters asserted but to prove some other fact, the evidence will not be 'hearsay' evidence but 'original' evidence.

11.1.2.2   Implied hearsay

The important difference between the criminal definition of hearsay and that at common law and in civil cases is that the CJA 2003, s 115(3) states that implications from the statements are not hearsay statements if it was not the purpose of the maker to invite that implication.

At common law, implied statements were covered by the rule against hearsay as much as express statements. Therefore in *R v Kearley* [1992] 2 AC 228, HL, statements by unknown people requesting drugs and asking for the defendant, to the extent that they could be admitted as impliedly asserting that Kearley was a drug dealer, were hearsay. In the course of their speeches, their Lordships approved another example of implied hearsay given in *Wright v Doe d Tatham* (1837) 7 Ad & El 313 of a ship's captain who inspects a ship and, having done so, sets sail in the ship with his family. In *Wright*, Parke B suggested that the ship's captain's act was an implied statement as to the seaworthiness of the ship.

At common law, implied hearsay evidence was not without its difficulties. In *Ratten v R* [1972] AC 378, PC, a woman made a telephone call to the police in which she asked for the police in an hysterical manner. Her husband was tried for her murder and the court concluded that the statement was not a hearsay statement. In *Kearley*, the House of Lords concluded that the statement had in fact been an implied hearsay assertion although this was not part of the reasoning of the Privy Council. Furthermore, in contrast to *Wright*, in *Manchester Brewery v Coombs* (1901) 82 LT 347, Farwell J was of the view that the actions of people refusing to drink beer was admissible at common law (and not hearsay) in support of an allegation that the beer was unfit for consumption.

In civil law, the common law position is unaffected. Therefore, implied statements can be hearsay statements.

Section 115(3) of the CJA 2003 has altered the definition of hearsay in criminal cases. By virtue of that section, a statement is not a hearsay statement unless one of the purposes of the statement was to cause the other person to believe the fact in question or to act on the basis that it is true. Therefore, the statements in *Kearley, Ratten* and *Wright* would no longer be hearsay statements. The statute has confirmed the position in *Manchester Brewery*.

However, the CJA 2003, s115(3) has not taken all implied statements out of the ambit of the hearsay rule. Only statements in which there was no intention to convey the relevant fact are removed. Therefore, if a person were deliberately to imply a fact by making a particular statement, that statement is still hearsay. For example, if Anil wishing to give the impression that Ben was in hiding as a result of a crime were to say, 'Well, I would not expect to see Ben on the High Street any time soon,' the statement would still be a hearsay statement if it were established that Anil's purpose was to cause the person to whom the statement was made to believe that Ben was in hiding. The matter was considered in *R v Singh* [2006] All ER (D) 225 (Feb) where the statements were records of mobile phone calls between conspirators to kidnapping. The Court of Appeal rejected the defendant's argument that unintentional implied assertions were inadmissible hearsay. As the maker of the statements in question did not intend to convey the matter for which they were admitted (the defendant's involvement in a criminal conspiracy), they were not 'matters stated' and therefore not hearsay within the meaning of ss 114 and 115. The CJA 2003 had replaced the pre-existing common law on this matter. The effect of this is therefore:

- Where the statement expressly states a fact and the evidence is admitted to prove that fact as true, the statement is (express) hearsay by virtue of s 115.

- Where a fact could be inferred from the express words of the statement (ie, the statement implies that fact), it is necessary to consider the purpose of the maker of the statement:
  - if it appears to the court that the purpose of the maker of the statement was to make another person believe that fact, then the statement is hearsay by virtue of s 115(3)(a) and its admissibility will have to be determined under the CJA 2003;
  - if it does not appear to the court that the purpose of the maker of the statement was to make another person believe that fact, then the statement is not hearsay and will be admissible if relevant (and not inadmissible by virtue of any other rule of evidence).

11.1.2.3   Representations by machines, etc

The rule against hearsay was developed by the common law in the 18th century. It was not therefore particularly well equipped to deal with the technological innovations of the 20th century.

Technological devices produce information that may appear to be statements but which the courts have held occasionally not to be hearsay but real evidence. Whether or not this is so will depend on the extent to which the process of the device is mechanical or is dependent on human input. Where a person types information onto a computer and saves it into a file, it will clearly be as much a statement as if it had been said or written. However, where the courts conclude that the machine or device in question is producing the record automatically, it has been held to be real, not hearsay, evidence. Again, using the definition in *R v Sharp*, we might say that a calculation or automated message is not an 'assertion', nor is the mechanical process asserting any fact.

Consider the following examples:

(a) In *R v Wood* (1982) 76 Cr App R 23, CA, the prosecution had to prove the chemical composition of metal alleged to have been stolen. The Court of Appeal held that the printouts from the computer were not hearsay but real evidence as the computer was performing a calculation that could have been done manually. Note, however, it was still necessary to prove by non-hearsay evidence the formula that had been programmed into the computer and the data that had been fed into it. Once this had been done the computer itself was not making any statement for hearsay purposes. In other words it was the mathematical calculations based on the data that was not hearsay. The data itself would have been hearsay if proved by these printouts.

(b) In *Castle v Cross* [1984] 1 WLR 1372, DC, an intoxometer reading was held not to be hearsay evidence. The reading was a mechanical calculation rather than a statement produced by human agency or interpretation. In contrast to the situation in *Wood,* the machine did not rely upon data fed into it by human agency which would need to be proven by testimony at court.

(c) In *R v Governor of Brixton Prison, ex p Levin* [1997] 3 WLR 117, HL, the mechanical record was of fund transfers made over the Internet. The bank's computer system automatically recorded transactions made. The issue in the case was whether the defendant had used a computer to make such fund transfers. The House of Lords held that the computerised records of the transactions were no more hearsay to prove the fact of such transactions than a photocopy of a fraudulent cheque.

(d) In *Taylor v Chief Constable of Cheshire* [1986] 1 WLR 1479, the Divisional Court held that police officers could give evidence as to what they had seen on a CCTV video of an offence even thought the video had been lost. Rather than the video being an out of court statement it was said by Ralph Gibson LJ to be no different in principle from having witnessed the event when it took place.

The identical definitions of 'statement' in the Civil Evidence Act 1995, s13 and the CJA 2003, s115 require 'representation . . . by a person', which reflects this common law position.

No specific further provision is made for mechanical devices in the Civil Evidence Act 1995. However, the CJA 2003, s 129 provides:

(1)   *Where a representation of any fact—*
   (a)   *is made otherwise than by a person, but*
   (b)   *depends for its accuracy on information supplied (directly or indirectly) by a person, the representation is not admissible in criminal proceedings as evidence of the fact unless it is proved that the information was accurate.*
(2)   *Subsection (1) does not affect the operation of the presumption that a mechanical device has been properly set or calibrated.*

Section 129 regulates statements made by a machine that has received information from a person, such as the computer in *Wood* as opposed to the intoxometer reading in *Castle v Cross*. Section 129(1) reflects the requirement in *Wood* that the information put into a machine has to be proven by non-hearsay evidence. However, it goes further than the requirement in *Wood* of proof of the information by non-hearsay evidence as the accuracy of the information is a pre-condition of admissibility. It would therefore appear to require that the tribunal of law determines the accuracy of the data supplied to such a machine before it can be adduced as evidence in front of the tribunal of fact.

11.1.2.4   Negative hearsay

As we saw from the definitions of hearsay in **11.1.2.1**, a hearsay statement is one that is evidence of any fact asserted. But what if the things that a person states outside of the courtroom are notable not because of what the witness said but because of what the witness did not say. To what extent is this 'evidence of any fact asserted'?

Consider the following example. A theft takes place when some youths are on a hiking trip. The issue is whether the accused, Ed, was in a dormitory when an offence took place. Evidence is given that the person in charge of the trip, Peter, appointed 'Dormitory Monitors' for each dormitory and would call at each dorm asking the monitor who was there. At about the time the theft took place, the prosecution seek to prove that Ed was out of his dormitory.

To what extent should they be able to do so if the evidence they rely on is:

1. that Peter called out to the monitor, 'Is there anyone missing from your dormitory?', to which Michael replied, 'Yes, Ed.';

2. that Peter called out to the monitor, Michael, 'Who is in there with you?' and that Michael replied, 'Me, Adrian, Jack, Steve and Asil.'

The courts have treated these two types of statement completely differently. In both cases the purpose of the statement is to prove that Ed was absent. The first statement does this by proving that what was said (or implied), namely that Ed is absent, was true. In the latter case, nothing has been asserted.

However the courts have taken the view that in the latter case it is not the truth of what was said that proves Ed was absent but the fact of not having said something and, therefore, the evidence that is used to prove Ed was absent is the silence from which absence is inferred.

This concept of proof by the absence of a statement (sometimes confusingly called 'negative hearsay') was recognised (obiter) in *R v Patel* (1981) 73 Cr App R 117, a case concerning illegal immigration, only to arise if:

*   it was proved by an officer responsible for compiling records that a particular method was used for making and storing entries as to the existence of a fact in that record;

*   it was proved by the same officer that due to the process, the absence of a particular entry on the record meant the non-existence of the fact.

For examples of the application of the rule, see:

(a) *R v Shone* (1983) 76 Cr App R 72, CA. There the accused was charged with theft, to prove which the prosecution had to establish that the goods alleged to be stolen had not been legitimately sold on. The prosecution were allowed to call two employees who testified to the system adopted and the absence of a record of onward sale.

(b) *R v Muir* (1984) 79 Cr App R 153, CA. The accused was alleged to have stolen a video recorder but stated in his defence that the recorder had been repossessed by the hire company. The prosecution were allowed to call the district manager of the hire company who gave evidence that if there had been a repossession he would have been informed. This was held to have been original (negative hearsay) evidence. The Court of Appeal held that the district manager could have given evidence that he had checked with his Head Office to determine whether they had any such record. This judgment has been criticised for its inconsistency with the principle in *R v Patel* and *R v Shone* in that the manager did that have personal experience of the system of recording the data, (see, for example, *Blackstone's Criminal Practice, 2006* at F 15.13 and I.H. Dennis, *The Law of Evidence*, 2nd edn, 2002 Sweet & Maxwell at p 573).

11.1.2.5   Significance of hearsay evidence

It will be seen in this chapter and the next that hearsay evidence is subject to restrictions as to its admissibility and, even where admissible, rules of procedure regulating its use. Therefore, it is important to identify whether evidence is hearsay even where it will ultimately be admissible hearsay evidence. If it is not hearsay evidence but original evidence the restrictions and controls identified in this and the next chapter will not apply.

There is an essential two-stage process for considering hearsay issues:

- Is the evidence hearsay evidence at all?
- If it is hearsay, is it admissible under an exception to the rule against hearsay?

If the evidence is admissible hearsay for one purpose, it may still be inadmissible hearsay evidence for other purposes. In such situations the judge will have to direct the jury that they should not rely on the statement as evidence of truth in relation to any other issues. In *R v Nelson* [2004] EWCA Crim 333, the hearsay statement in question was a record of a call made to the police by the defendant's father. The defendant was alleged to have stabbed another man and raised the defence of automatism. The father's call to the police, which was made soon after the incident, showed that the father was aware that a stabbing had taken place and that the defendant might be blamed. It was accepted by the Court of Appeal that such a statement could have been admitted as original evidence (see below) to show that the father may have been aware of the stabbing, which may have proved that the father had been told about it by the defendant, who therefore would not have been suffering from automatism. However, the conviction was quashed because the jury were not directed that they should only use the evidence to decide whether the defendant was not suffering from automatism. They were not directed that they should not use the statement to conclude that the defendant had in fact committed the offence (which would be a hearsay statement because the statement would then be used to prove a fact by virtue of its truth).

The rule against hearsay where it applies does not just prevent a witness from relating what he had heard; it also prevents a witness from adopting as his own knowledge something he has been told. Consider the example of the case of *R v Rothwell* (1994) 99 Cr App R 388, CA. The accused was charged with possession of heroin with intent to supply it. A police officer gave evidence that:

(a) He had seen the accused passing packages to other people and had seen him receive money in return.

(b) He knew that persons to whom the accused passed the money were drug dealers.

(c) He knew this because of his experience in the investigation of drugs offences and prosecutions in the Newcastle area where the events took place.

(d) (In cross-examination) he did not have first-hand experience of seeing the persons in question use drugs.

The Court of Appeal held that the police officer was not able to give such evidence as at this time it was inadmissible at common law. While it was not hearsay evidence in the obvious sense (his testimony was not 'PC Burnes told me that the persons were drug dealers') it was *based* on hearsay evidence (whatever he had in fact been told or heard in court at previous trials that led him to believe that the persons were drug dealers). It was just as inadmissible as if he had repeated every statement on which he was relying when he said that the people were drug dealers.

Nor will the courts allow the hearsay rule to be side-stepped by proving that there was a conversation and then proving what a person immediately did as a result where that would, in effect, suggest to the tribunal of fact what the conversation was about. Using the case of *Rothwell* again, it would not be possible to prove that the police officer giving evidence said that:

(a) He had a conversation with PC Ings.

(b) As a result of that conversation he arrested Rothwell for possession of heroin with intent to supply it.

Quite simply, only the stupidest jury would fail to interpret the conversation as being about supplying heroin in some way, which would almost certainly be hearsay if it had been repeated.

11.1.3   Identifying hearsay evidence

Determining whether a statement is hearsay or original evidence is a skill that requires an understanding of proof and a logical approach to the evidence and, in particular, to relevance.

As the definitions above suggest, identifying hearsay evidence requires the addressing of three questions:

- Is the evidence a statement or assertion at all?
- Was the statement made other than as testimony in the current case?
- Is the statement being used 'as evidence of any fact asserted'; ie, to prove a fact simply by the statement being accepted as true.

If 'yes' to all three questions, the statement is hearsay evidence. If the answer is not 'yes' to all three questions, quite what the evidence is will depend on which of the above questions is answered in the negative.

11.1.3.1   Is the evidence a statement or assertion at all?

This is not generally a difficult stage of the analysis. However, it is worth noting the scope of the statement for these purposes. A 'statement' includes:

(a) both oral and written statements. Matters written in a document are statements for this purpose. This would also include electronic communications;

(b) statements made by gestures or conduct. In *Chandrasekera v The King* [1937] AC 220, PC, for example, a victim of an attack had had her throat cut and could not speak. To illustrate that the accused, a local cowherd, committed the offence, she made gestures and signs (including putting her hands to her head to impersonate a bull) and nodded when asked questions. These gestures were determined to be statements for the purposes of the hearsay rule;

(c) things stated, whether or not there was an intention to communicate that information to another person (therefore a diary entry could be a statement for these purposes).

Note: the word 'statement' is commonly used in procedural rules to refer to a document written in preparation of proceedings. As far as the rule of hearsay is concerned, as can be seen from the analysis above, the word is being used in a much wider sense.

If the out of court fact is not a statement it will either be part of a witness's account of what he saw happen (for example, the accused hitting the victim is probably not a statement) or real evidence (such as a document proved in court not for the content but to prove that a particular type of paper was used).

11.1.3.2   Was the statement 'other than as testimony in the current case'?

Put quite simply, this part of the test requires a distinction between a statement that is made for the first time as testimony and a statement in testimony that is a repetition of something said at another time. A common (if slightly misleading) short-hand term for such a statement is 'out of court'.

Note the following points:

(a) Statements made outside of any court (in the pub, at home, on the street, in a police station, into a tape recorder) are clearly covered by this definition.

(b) Statements made in the witness box in *other* cases are also covered by this definition (*Berkeley Peerage Case* (1811) 4 Camp 401).

(c) Statements made in the courtroom but not in the witness box are also covered by this definition.

(d) Having been sworn does not prevent any of that witness's previous statements and utterances from potentially being hearsay evidence.

(e) However, a witness in a case will have made a statement to those preparing the case that outlines his testimony (a 'witness statement' or 'proof of evidence'). In so far as the witness goes into the witness box and restates what is in that statement as his own testimony, the testimony is not the repetition of an out of court statement. All that document was doing was recording what the witness was intending to say as his evidence. However, if for some reason that statement must be produced before the court, it will be an 'out of court' statement for these purposes. When such statements will be admissible depends on why they are admitted as evidence (see **11.1.4.3** below). See, for example, **6.3** (memory refreshing documents), **6.4** (previous consistent statements) and **7.7** (previous inconsistent statements).

(f) On the other hand, remember that there are certain rules of procedure that allow such earlier statements to stand as the evidence-in-chief of a party (CPR, r 32.5 and s 9 of the Criminal Justice Act 1967, for example: see **4.3**). The effect of these provisions is that these statements become the testimony of the witness in proceedings and cannot therefore be hearsay. This is because formalities and procedures have been complied with: without the required formalities such statements are just like any other 'out of court' statement.

It is important to look carefully at any statement or testimony to distinguish how much of it is (or will be) the testimony of the witness and how much will be the *repetition* of things said outside court. It is only the latter that will be potentially hearsay (ie, to which you need to apply the third stage of the test, see **11.1.4.5**).

Merely because a statement is identified as an 'out of court' statement does not mean that it is automatically inadmissible or even that it is hearsay. It simply means that we need to apply the third stage of the test.

11.1.3.3 'Evidence of any fact asserted'

The really tricky but vital part of hearsay analysis is usually the third stage. It is this stage that distinguishes hearsay out of court statements from 'original' out of court statements.

The term 'hearsay' is only applied to 'out of court' statements or assertions with a particular purpose: those that are used to prove a fact by getting the tribunal to accept that the contents of the statement are true or accurate. If the statement has some other purpose, it will not be 'hearsay' but 'original' evidence. These are the various types of statement identified in **11.1**. By 'purpose' at this point we mean 'evidential purpose' (ie, what it is adduced to prove), not the purpose of the maker of the statement in making it (which is used for determining whether implied statements are hearsay in (CJA 2003, S115(3))

This third stage can be broken down into two further stages:

- What is the relevant purpose of the statement? (Note that it may have more than one.)

- Will the tribunal of fact have to rely on the truth of the statement for that purpose to be achieved?

The key to this part of the test is, therefore, 'purpose': what are you trying to achieve with the evidence? This is a question of logic and proof rather than law.

Consider this example: A's out of court statement is, 'B was on the High Street at 10 pm on Monday.' It has been put in evidence before a jury.

1. Assuming there is no other evidence in the case, if the jury decides that the statement is true or accurate, what does it prove?
2. What could the statement prove without being true or accurate?

If the statement is true, it proves what it says, namely that B was on the High Street at 10 pm on Monday. On these matters, the statement is evidence of those facts and they were asserted in the statement. Therefore for these purposes the statement is hearsay evidence.

In addition, by being true, the statement could also prove, for example, that A (as opposed to B) was on the High Street on Monday. This is done by:

(a) proving the statement above was made;

(b) proving that the statement was true (by use of evidence other than this statement);

(c) arguing that the fact that the statement was made and that it was accurate shows that A was in a position to know that fact and that he was therefore probably on the High Street.

In the second situation the statement is not 'evidence of any fact asserted' because it is not seeking to prove what it states. While it requires the statement to be true to prove something useful in the case, the statement achieves its evidential purpose by being proved to be true by independent evidence. The statement is 'evidence of *knowledge of the facts asserted*'. It is the fact of the particular statement having been made plus proof by other means that the statement was accurate that allows the tribunal of fact to *infer* that the maker of the statement knew (or believed) a particular fact. If the maker's knowledge or belief is relevant, the statement could be relevant *original* evidence.

What could such a statement prove without being true?

The statement can be relevant to prove the following facts without being true (and would therefore be original evidence of these facts):

(a) Facts it can prove by being false could include:

  (i)   B lied about A's presence at 10 pm on Monday;

  (ii) B is prone to misidentify A;

  (iii) B cannot tell the time;

  (iv) etc.

(b) Facts it can prove whether or not the statement is true:

  (i)   A knows B (proved by the fact of having been talking about them);

  (ii) A knows there is a High Street (he mentioned it);

  (iii) A believed B was on the High Street at 10 pm on Monday (A could *believe* this whether or not it was true).

At risk of over-simplification, where the purpose of the evidence is to prove a conclusion by simply proving that the statement was made, the statement is original evidence. Where the purpose of the evidence is to prove a fact by the statement being *true*, the statement is hearsay. The over-simplification is that sometimes (knowledge cases) the conclusion is proved by (1) the fact of the statement having been made and (2) it happening to be true (this being proven by other means). It is still, however, the fact of the statement having been made that determines its non-hearsay nature. The statement is not proving what it states.

While the word 'purpose' is of huge importance, do not overlook the word 'relevant'. Only relevant evidence is admissible. There is no point in determining that the statement could achieve some non-hearsay purpose if that purpose is not relevant in the proceedings. Have another look at **1.3.1.3** in this Manual and in particular the analysis of the cases of *R v Blastland* and *R v Kearley*. In both of those cases statements were determined to be inadmissible hearsay if used to prove that what the maker said was true. In each case they could also have proved what the maker of the statement knew or believed and would be admissible if relevant. In both cases the House of Lords concluded that the state of mind of the maker was not relevant (or not sufficiently relevant) in the case in question. While it might be possible to disagree with the conclusions of the House of Lords in each case on the issue of relevance, the principle that relevance remains an absolute requirement for admissibility is unquestionably correct.

Leaving to one side issues of relevance for the time being, let us go back to the concept of purpose. By identifying the purpose of the evidence we can then work out whether it is 'evidence of the facts stated' or is 'tendered for the truth of its contents' (another way of explaining how hearsay statements can be distinguished from original evidence).

The fact that statements are identified as hearsay does not necessarily mean that they are not admissible. Admissibility is regulated by the CJA 2003 in criminal proceedings and the Civil Evidence Act 1995 in civil proceedings. Other statements, although they would be inadmissible hearsay, could (and should) be proved from other sources such as calling the maker of the statement to give testimony to that effect. Remember that one of the purposes of the rule against hearsay evidence is to ensure that the evidence is given by the most authoritative source. Defining evidence as hearsay does not mean that the conclusion it proves can never be proven by any evidence. It simply means that it cannot be proven by the inadmissible hearsay statement.

11.1.4   Recap

Identifying whether evidence is hearsay is a matter of applying the technique of proof to the facts of a particular case. Case law can illustrate principle but cannot set universal rules that will determine whether a particular statement is hearsay or not.

The process for identifying hearsay evidence is:

(a) Determine whether it is a statement at all.

(b) Determine whether it has been made 'out of court' remembering quite how specific that is.

(c) Determine whether it is evidence of the facts stated by:

   (i)   determining the relevant purpose or purposes of the evidence;

   (ii) determining whether the statement has to be true to achieve those purposes.

(d) If hearsay, determine whether it is admissible or inadmissible hearsay.

11.1.5   Examples of original evidence

The following cases illustrate the approach that the courts have taken in determining whether a statement was hearsay evidence or original evidence. As usual, the cases are illustrations of the application of the principle. In all of the cases, the statements were held not be hearsay but original evidence. While the cases have been put into categories below, that is for illustrative purposes rather than an attempt to define distinct categories. Each turns on its own facts and the purpose of the evidence identified in each case, applying the central principle that the statement must not be used to prove what it alleges. The categories reflect the ways in which statements will prove facts without being 'evidence of a fact asserted' as we identified in **11.1.1** and **11.1.3.2**.

11.1.5.1 Cases in which the truth of the statement is irrelevant

In the following cases the relevant purpose of the evidence is achieved irrespective of the truth or falsity of the statement. Quite simply it is the fact that the statement was made that achieves a relevant purpose in the case. That this is so is generally a matter of the substantive law in question.

Subramaniam v Public Prosecutor [1956] 1 WLR 965, PC: the accused was charged with a terrorism offence and pleaded the defence of duress. He alleged that he had been threatened by terrorists with death if he did not carry ammunition for them. The Privy Council concluded that such statements were not hearsay. The defence of duress applies if a person is threatened, *not* if the person actually faces the harm that has been threatened. In other words it is the *fact* of the threat that is relevant rather than its genuineness or truth. Therefore, the relevant purpose was to prove that the threat had been made, not that it had been a genuine or 'true' threat that the terrorists would in fact carry out.

R v Chapman [1969] 2 QB 436, CA: the accused was charged with driving with excess alcohol. He would have had a defence to the charge if a doctor had objected to the provision of a breath specimen on health grounds. The prosecution were entitled to prove that the doctor did not so object. It was the fact of the lack of objection rather than the genuineness of that lack of objection that was relevant as a matter of substantive law. The purpose of the statement was to show that there was in fact no objection rather than that the doctor was genuinely not objecting. Again it was substantive law that dictated that it was the fact of the lack of objection that mattered.

Woodhouse v Hall (1980) 72 Cr App R 39, DC: the accused was charged with 'acting in the management of a brothel'. The property, which appeared to be a massage parlour, would be a brothel if prostitution was conducted there. The Divisional Court held that this, as a matter of substantive law, would derive not from the actuality of the patrons having sex with the occupants but from the occupants soliciting sex from the patrons. In other words the property was a brothel if sexual acts were *offered* rather than either intended or performed. Therefore, undercover police officers were allowed to give evidence of statements made on the property offering sexual acts. The purpose was to show that sexual acts were offered, not that they were intended or performed.

Ratten v R [1972] AC 378, PC: the accused was charged with the murder of his wife by shooting her. His defence was that his gun went off accidentally. The prosecution were allowed to call evidence from a telephone operator that at the time of the killing a phone call was received from the accused's address in which a woman said in an hysterical and sobbing voice, 'Get me the police, please.' The accused had denied that any such call was made. The Privy Council held that the purpose of the statement was to prove the fact of a phone call and the fact of the hysterical nature of the call, not that the lady wanted the police.

R v O'Connell [2003] EWCA Crim 502: after having been arrested on suspicion of drugs offences, the police intercepted two calls on the defendant's mobile telephone in which the callers impliedly requested drugs. On both occasions, the defendant, who was present at the time, called out that it was not him on the phone but the police and that the callers should end the call. The Court of Appeal stated that what was said by the callers was hearsay evidence (see *R v Kearley* [1992] 2 AC 228 at **1.3.1.3**) but that what the defendant had said in reaction to those calls was admissible original evidence. The defendant's statement showed his reaction to requests on his telephone for drugs and therefore his awareness of his own guilt.

11.1.5.2   Cases in which the purpose was to prove the falsehood of the statement

Mawaz Khan v R [1967] 1 AC 454, PC: two co-defendants were charged with murder. Each had made statements to the police that when the murder took place they were at a particular club. The prosecution were allowed to prove (a) that such statements were made and (b), by other witnesses, that the co-defendants were not at the club. The co-defendants appealed the admissibility of the statements as hearsay evidence. The Privy Council concluded that the statements were not hearsay evidence. The purpose of the statements was not to prove that the co-defendants *were* at the club but to prove the *fact* of having alleged that they were. This fact, combined with the fact that they were elsewhere would be relevant to prove that the co-defendants had lied about where they were (and therefore, potentially, that they were conscious of their guilty involvement in the crime). See also *R v B* [2003] EWCA Crim 2169. For further detail on the evidential value of lies, see **Chapter 14**.

11.1.5.3   Cases in which the purpose is the proof of knowledge of a fact that is either uncontested or proved by other means

To say that a statement is hearsay if it has to be true to achieve its relevant purpose simplifies matters a little too much. A statement does have to be true to achieve its purpose where what the relevant fact is that the person making the statement *knew* a particular fact. This is only achieved by proving it was correctly, accurately or truthfully stated. However, the statement is not being used to prove that truth. Instead, the fact is proved by other means and the statement is simply used to prove that the maker was aware of that fact. Have a look at the two cases that follow.

(a) *Thomas v Connell* (1838) 4 M & W 267: the issue was whether or not the defendant knew that he was insolvent. Proof of a statement in which he said that he was insolvent could prove *knowledge* of that fact. The fact that he was insolvent (another fact in issue in the case) was proved by other evidence.

(b) *R v Blastland* [1986] AC 41: in *Blastland* (referred to above and at **1.4.3.3**) it was accepted that the statements by M that showed he knew that there had been a murder would not be hearsay. While the statement had to true to achieve its purpose, the statement was *not proving the fact it alleged by being true*. Instead, the fact that was alleged (there was a dead boy) was proved by other evidence. The purpose of the statement was to prove that M *knew* that fact. The statement was therefore not hearsay *in so far as it was used to prove that M knew of the death rather than to prove the death occurred*. However, the House of Lords concluded that M's knowledge was not (sufficiently) relevant to the trial issue (ie, whether the accused killed him).

11.2   Admissibility of hearsay in civil cases

Most hearsay evidence is admissible in civil cases and the rules are therefore quite simple. The rules are stated in the Civil Evidence Act 1995. The 1995 Act has created a general rule of inclusion in civil cases, which is set out in s 1:

1. —(1) *In civil proceedings evidence shall not be excluded on the ground that it is hearsay.*

> *(2) In this Act—*
>> *(a) 'hearsay' means a statement made otherwise than by a person while giving oral evidence in the proceedings which is tendered as evidence of the matters stated; and*
>> *(b) references to hearsay include hearsay of whatever degree.*
> *(3) Nothing in this Act affects the admissibility of evidence admissible apart from this section.*
> *(4) The provisions of sections 2 to 6 (safeguards and supplementary provisions relating to hearsay evidence) do not apply in relation to hearsay evidence admissible apart from this section, notwithstanding that it may also be admissible by virtue of this section.*

In other words all hearsay evidence will be admissible in civil proceedings unless it is already admissible under another statute or is one of the common law exceptions preserved under s 7 of the Act. The 1995 Act applies to both documentary and oral statements and to 'multiple hearsay' (ie, where the potentially hearsay statement itself contains or is based on hearsay).

These provisions do not allow the proof of out of court statements made by a person who would not be competent as a witness (s 5 of the 1995 Act: see **Chapter 4**).

The rule of admissibility under s 1 of the 1995 Act and the consequential provisions (set out below) do not apply if the statement is admissible under another statutory exception. Such exceptions include (but are not restricted to):

(a) evidence in connection with the 'upbringing, maintenance or welfare of a child' will be admissible notwithstanding that it is hearsay evidence (Children (Admissibility of Hearsay Evidence) Order 1993);

(b) a copy of any entry in a banker's book is admissible to prove any transactions recorded in it (Bankers' Books Evidence Act 1879, s 3). For more detail, see *Blackstone's Civil Practice*.

11.2.1 The requirement of notice

Where a party proposes to rely upon hearsay evidence, he must comply with the notice requirements set out in s 2 of the 1995 Act. The notice requirements are set out in detail in the *Civil Litigation Manual* or *Blackstone's Civil Practice*. However, in short the main points are:

(a) Failure to give notice:
   (i) does not render evidence inadmissible (s 2(4));
   (ii) can lead the court to make procedural orders (for example, the court could adjourn the hearing and/or order the party who has not complied with the notice requirements to pay costs) (s 2(4)(a));
   (iii) may lead the court to attach less weight to the statement (s 2(4)).

(b) If the hearsay statement will be proved by the oral evidence of a witness (ie, the witness will repeat what he has heard), service of the witness's statement is sufficient notice (CPR, r 33.2(1)).

(c) If the hearsay statement will be proved in a witness statement which will constitute the evidence-in-chief, service of that witness statement amounts to compliance with the notice requirements (CPR, r 33.2(1)). Where the witness statement is going to be used instead of calling the witness, that fact must be identified to the other parties (CPR, r 33.2(2)).

(d) If the hearsay statement is not proved in the way set out above (for example, the hearsay statement will be proved in a document) then a notice should be served on the other parties (CPR, r 33.2(3)). The reason for not calling the witness must be identified in the notice.

11.2.2   The requirement of leave

Generally, leave is not required before such evidence will be admitted. The judge does not have to rule that the hearsay evidence is admissible.

There is one exception to the rule that evidence is admissible without leave. This exception is set out in s 6(2) of the 1995 Act:

> 6.— (2)   A party who has called or intends to call a person as a witness in civil proceedings may not in those proceedings adduce evidence of a previous statement made by that person, except—
>
> (a)   with the leave of the court, or
> (b)   for the purpose of rebutting a suggestion that his evidence has been fabricated.
> This shall not be construed as preventing a witness statement (that is, a written statement of oral evidence which a party to the proceedings intends to lead) from being adopted by a witness in giving evidence or treated as his evidence.

The effect of this is that leave will be required where a party seeks to both:

- call a person as a witness; *and*
- prove that the person has made a previous statement.

It is important to remember the rules relating to previous statements made by a witness. Previous consistent statements are not generally admissible at common law. The effect of s 6 is that they now are generally admissible if the court grants leave. However, some of the types of previous statement have been mentioned specifically in s 6:

(a) *Previous inconsistent statements.* Generally, a party calling a witness would not seek to prove the witness had made a previous *inconsistent* statement; however, this might happen if the witness proves hostile (**6.5**). Section 6(3) provides that ss 3 to 5 of the Criminal Procedure Act 1865 still apply in such situations. The basic rule, therefore, has not changed the circumstances under which such statements can be proved.

(b) *Memory-refreshing documents.* The common law rules concerning the admissibility of such documents as evidence (see **6.3.1**) has not been changed by this section (s 6(4)).

(c) *Statements admitted to rebut a suggestion of previous fabrication.* Such statements (formerly an exception to the common law rule against previous consistent statements: see **6.4.1.2**) are admissible *without leave*.

Any previous statements made by a witness to the proceedings, if admitted, will be evidence of the truth of what is alleged (s 6(5)). At common law such statements were only proof of the consistency of what the witness said (ie, to bolster his credibility).

11.2.3   Proof of a hearsay statement

Although the 1995 Act renders hearsay statements admissible, they still must be proved. Where the statement is oral hearsay (ie, the repetition of what someone *said* elsewhere), the statement is proved by the evidence of the person that heard it.

Where the hearsay statement is contained in a document, the document will be produced at court. The provenance of the document must be established (this is usually described as 'proving' the document). Section 8 provides that a document can be proved by producing it or a copy of it. This does not, however, mean that the document can simply be presented at court (*Ventouris v Mountain (No 2)* [1992] 1 WLR 817). A witness must establish that the document in question has something to do with the case. However, this 'proof' of a document can be achieved by hearsay evidence. In *Ventouris v Mountain (No 2)*, the document in question was a tape recording of conversations between various people on matters relevant to an insurance fraud, which was being litigated. One of the participants to the conversation was G, who was not available to give evidence. A solicitor was allowed to 'prove' the tape recordings as relevant evidence of the conversations by repeating what G had told him about them.

Sections 9 and 10 of the 1995 Act make particular provisions for the admissibility of particular documents without having formally to 'prove' those documents.

(a) Section 9 concerns documents forming part of the records of a business or public authority. Instead of having to call a witness, such a document will be proved if a certificate signed by 'an officer of the business or authority' is produced. 'Records' is defined, by s 9(4) as 'records in whatever form' and 'business' as 'any activity regularly carried on over a period of time, whether for profit or not, by any body . . . or by an individual'. 'Public authority' includes any government department or public undertaking.

(b) Section 10 provides for the admissibility of actuarial tables in personal injuries cases.

11.2.4 Challenging the hearsay statement

Clearly a party against whom a hearsay statement is made has little power to prevent the statement from being admitted. Leave is only required if the statement was made by a witness. Even a failure to comply with the notice requirements will not prevent the statement from being admitted.

However, under the 1995 Act there are a number of ways in which another party can challenge the weight to be attached to the statement.

(a) Where the hearsay statement has been made by a person not called as a witness, any party may call the maker of the statement to cross-examine him if the court grants leave (s 3).

(b) Section 4 lays down guidance upon what weight should be attached to the hearsay evidence. Section 4(2) states that the court may take into consideration the following:

(i)   Whether it would have been reasonable and practical to secure the attendance of the witness rather than using the hearsay statement (s 4(2)(a)).

(ii) Whether the statement was made contemporaneously with the events to which they relate (s 4(2)(b)).

(iii) Whether the hearsay itself is based on the repetition of information from another source ('multiple hearsay') (s 4(2)(c)).

(iv) Any motive the maker has for concealing or misrepresenting matters (s 4(2)(d)).

(v)   How complete the hearsay statement is as an account of the matters (s 4(2)(e)).

(vi) Whether the statement was made by numerous people in collaboration (s 4(2)(e)).

(vii) Why the statement was made (s 4(2)(e)).

(viii)Whether the statement appears to have been produced in a way that would prevent other parties from fully testing or challenging it (s 4(2)(f)). In other words, failure to comply with notice requirements fully will probably lead the court to attach less weight to it. Further, in *Moat Housing v Harris* [2005] EWCA 287 the court stressed that caution should be adopted before admitting evidence of statements of anonymous complaints against a party where that party had not, at that time, been informed of those complaints and would therefore have difficulty answering them.

(c) Where the witness does not attend for cross-examination, provision is made for attacking the credibility of the witness as if he had been called as follows:

(i)   Evidence undermining the credibility of the witness may be called (s 5(2)(a)). This, however, would appear to be subject to the rule of finality (see **7.8.2**). Section 5(2)(a) states that the evidence is admissible for the purpose of attacking the credibility of the maker.

(ii) evidence of previous statements inconsistent with the hearsay statements may be proved (see **7.7**).

11.2.5   Preservation of the common law rules

Section 7 of the 1995 Act preserves some of the common law exceptions. These exceptions concern various statements in documents of a public nature and include:

(a) statements contained in public document (see **11.2.5.1** below);

(b) statements made by deceased persons to prove matters of pedigree (see **11.2.5.2**);

(c) statements made by deceased persons to prove the existence of a public or general right (see **11.2.5.3**);

(d) evidence of a person's general reputation (see **11.2.6**).

Where these exceptions apply there is no need to comply with the notice requirements (**11.2.1**), the leave requirements (**11.2.2**) or the provisions in s 4 concerning the weight to be attached to such documents (**11.2.4**).

11.2.5.1   Statements contained in public documents

At common law hearsay statements in the following types of document were admissible:

- published works dealing with matters of a public nature (such as dictionaries and maps);

- public documents (such as public registers, and returns made under public authority); and

- records (such as the records of courts, treaties, etc).

For detailed explanation of this exception, see *Blackstone's Civil Practice*. However, in outline, the exceptions apply where the document in question is available to the public as of right. 'Public' was stated in *Sturla v Feccia* (1880) 5 App Cas 623 not to mean the whole world but all persons interested in the subject matter in question.

11.2.5.2   Statements made by deceased persons to prove matters of pedigree

A statement made by a deceased person concerning a matter of pedigree (such as marriage, legitimacy, dates of birth, etc) will be admissible (*Butler v Mountsgarret* (1859) 7 HL Cas 633) to prove the truth of the facts stated if:

- the maker of the statement and the person about whom it was made are blood relations or the one is married to a blood relation of the other; and

- the pedigree matter is a fact in issue as opposed to a collateral matter.

11.2.5.3 Statements made by deceased persons to prove the existence of a public or general right

Where the existence of a public right is relevant to an issue, any statement by a deceased person affirming the existence of that public right that was made before the dispute arose shall be admissible to prove the existence of that right (see, for example, *Mercer v Denne* [1905] 2 Ch 638). The statement must relate to rights possessed by the general public or by particular classes of persons, not to those possessed by an individual.

11.2.6 Evidence of a person's general reputation

The rule in *R v Rowton* (1865) Le & Ca 520, 169 ER 1497 provides that the character of a person should be proven by evidence of the general reputation of the person in the community rather than by evidence of specific acts. Proof by this means (honoured by the courts more in the breach than the observance) relies upon statements made by numerous other unidentified people and is therefore proof by hearsay evidence.

The rule in *Rowton* does not establish when evidence of character is admissible, simply how it is proven. For the rules concerning the admissibility of evidence of the character of parties and witnesses in civil cases, see **Chapter 8**.

Hearsay evidence in criminal proceedings

12.1 Criminal Justice Act 2003

The admissibility of hearsay evidence is governed by the CJA 2003. Section 114(1) provides:

(1) In criminal proceedings a statement not made in oral evidence in the proceedings is admissible as evidence of any matter stated if, but only if—

(a) any provision of this Chapter or any other statutory provision makes it admissible,

(b) any rule of law preserved by section 118 makes it admissible,

(c) all parties to the proceedings agree to it being admissible, or

(d) the court is satisfied that it is in the interests of justice for it to be admissible.

'Statement' and 'matters stated' are defined in the CJA 2003, s 115 which was considered at **11.1.2.1**.

Section 114 therefore provides that there are four grounds of admissibility for hearsay evidence. If an out of court statement is a hearsay statement it is not admissible unless it fits within one of those four broad grounds. If, however, the evidence is not hearsay evidence but original evidence, then it does not have to fit within paragraph (a) to (d) to be admissible. Subject to all of the other rules of evidence, original evidence is admissible if relevant.

The four broad grounds for admissibility in s 114(1) are:

- that the statement is admissible under one of the sections of the 2003 Act (or any other statutory provision);

- that the statement is admissible under a preserved common law exception to the rule against hearsay;

- that all of the parties in the proceedings have agreed to the admissibility of the evidence; and

- that, in the absence of such agreement, the court has decided that it is in the interests of justice for the evidence to be admitted.

The CJA 2003 applies to 'criminal proceedings', which are defined in s 140 as 'criminal proceedings in relation to which the strict rules of evidence apply'. In *R v Bradley* [2005] EWCA Crim 20, the Court of Appeal concluded that this meant criminal trials and Newton hearings.

Specific provision is made for rehearings in s 131, which amends the Criminal Appeal Act 1968, sch 2. Paragraph 1 of sch 2 now provides that evidence at a rehearing should be oral if it was given orally at the first trial unless all the parties agree or the witness is unavailable either in the circumstances permitted in the CJA 2003, s 116 (see **12.2.1**) or otherwise unavailable but the court makes a ruling that such evidence is admissible in the interests of justice under the CJA 2003, s 114 (see **12.4**).

12.2 Admissibility under a section of the Criminal Justice Act 2003

The Act provides for the admissibility of evidence in three main situations:

- the maker or the statement is unavailable as a witness (s 116);
- the statement was made in a business or professional document (s 117); and
- the statement is a specific type of previous statement by a witness(ss 119, 120).

It is worth remembering that the CJA 2003, s 114(1)(d) allows the court to admit evidence in the interests of justice if it is not otherwise admissible. Therefore, any technicalities preventing the admissibility of evidence may (but not must) allow the court to admit the evidence under that inclusionary discretion.

12.2.1 Statements where the maker is unavailable as a witness

Section 116 of the CJA 2003 provides:

(1) *In criminal proceedings a statement not made in oral evidence in the proceedings is admissible as evidence of any matter stated if—*

    (a) *oral evidence given in the proceedings by the person who made the statement would be admissible as evidence of that matter,*

    (b) *the person who made the statement (the relevant person) is identified to the court's satisfaction, and*

    (c) *any of the five conditions mentioned in subsection (2) is satisfied.*

(2) *The conditions are—*

    (a) *that the relevant person is dead;*

    (b) *that the relevant person is unfit to be a witness because of his bodily or mental condition;*

    (c) *that the relevant person is outside the United Kingdom and it is not reasonably practicable to secure his attendance;*

    (d) *that the relevant person cannot be found although such steps as it is reasonably practicable to take to find him have been taken;*

    (e) *that through fear the relevant person does not give (or does not continue to give) oral evidence in the proceedings, either at all or in connection with the subject matter of the statement, and the court gives leave for the statement to be given in evidence.*

(3) *For the purposes of subsection (2)(e) 'fear' is to be widely construed and (for example) includes fear of the death or injury of another person or of financial loss.*

(4) *Leave may be given under subsection (2)(e) only if the court considers that the statement ought to be admitted in the interests of justice, having regard—*

    (a) *to the statement's contents,*

    (b) *to any risk that its admission or exclusion will result in unfairness to any party to the proceedings (and in particular to how difficult it will be to challenge the statement if the relevant person does not give oral evidence),*

    (c) *in appropriate cases, to the fact that a direction under section 19 of the Youth Justice and Criminal Evidence Act 1999 (c. 23) (special measures for the giving of evidence by fearful witnesses etc) could be made in relation to the relevant person, and*

    (d) *to any other relevant circumstances.*

(5) *A condition set out in any paragraph of subsection (2) which is in fact satisfied is to be treated as not satisfied if it is shown that the circumstances described in that paragraph are caused—*

    (a) *by the person in support of whose case it is sought to give the statement in evidence, or*

    (b) *by a person acting on his behalf,*

in order to prevent the relevant person giving oral evidence in the proceedings (whether at all or in connection with the subject matter of the statement).

The precursor of the CJA 2003, s 116 was the Criminal Justice Act 1988, s 23 which has been repealed by the 2003 Act. Section 116 allows evidence to be admitted if:

- the statement being repeated would, if it had been stated in court as testimony, have been admissible (in other words this section cannot be used to bypass the rest of the rules of evidence);
- the maker of the statement can be identified; and
- there is a specific good reason for the maker of the statement not to attend at court to give that evidence.

In contrast to the Criminal Justice Act 1988, s 23 the statement admitted does not have to have been made in a document.

12.2.1.1 Oral evidence would have been admissible

The requirement that what has been stated must be admissible evidence is similar but not identical to the position under the 1988 Act. The effect is that the CJA 2003, s 116 allows the use of statements to prove any fact that could have been proven if given as testimony. This could include multiple hearsay (ie, the statement is the repetition of another out of court statement). However, such multiple hearsay is subject to additional restrictions (see **12.5**).

The main effect of the CJA 2003, s 116 is that the repetition of a hearsay statement cannot be used to sidestep any of the other rules of evidence regulating the admissibility or exclusion of evidence. Therefore the mere fact that a person alleges that the defendant is of bad character in an out of court statement does not mean that that statement is admissible, irrespective of the provisions of the CJA 2003, ss 98–112. Equally, irrelevant statements in hearsay statements are no more admissible than irrelevant testimony.

12.2.1.2 Maker of the statement can be identified

The requirement in the CJA 2003, s 116(1)(b) that the maker can be identified was not included in the Criminal Justice Act 1988, s 23. There is therefore no case law applying the requirement. It is the court that must be satisfied as to the identity of the maker, which may therefore require proof of the identity as a pre-condition of admissibility (and may therefore require a *voir dire*). When the court is entitled to be satisfied is unresolved. Consider the following example. Henry is charged with robbery. It is alleged that the crime occurred on a street near a place where a homeless person was sleeping and the homeless person provided the description of the attacker to a passer-by, Irene, but had left by the time the police arrived and could not be found. Could the description by the homeless person be admitted under s 116? Is 'a homeless person' sufficient identity? Would it make a difference if the person was known to people in the area as 'Old Jack'? Would his full name and details be required? It is possible, but far from probable, that the evidence would be admitted in the interests of justice under the CJA 2003, s 114(1)(d) for an 'unidentified' person (see **12.4**).

12.2.1.3 Reasons for admitting the statement

Section 116 of the CJA 2003 is not intended to undermine the principle that persons with knowledge of the facts stated should attend court to give evidence of those matters if they can do so. The section only applies if one of the five good reasons for not doing so apply.

The party seeking to rely upon the document must prove one of the reasons set out in s 116(2) to the satisfaction of the judge. Assuming the principles developed under s 23 of the 1988 Act apply, if it is the prosecution that is seeking to use the document, they must prove the reason beyond reasonable doubt (*R v Acton Justices, ex p McMullen* (1990) 92 Cr App R 98). The defence, when seeking to rely on one of the above reasons, need only prove it on the balance of probabilities (*R v Mattey* [1995] 2 Cr App R 409).

It is the state of the maker of the statement at the time of trial in all of the above situations which is important rather than the state when the statement was made.

None of the conditions for admissibility will apply if it is proven to the court that the condition in question was caused by the person seeking to admit the statement (s 116(5)(a)) or by a person acting on that person's behalf (s 116(5)(b)). It must be proven that the purpose in causing that state was to prevent testimony in the proceedings. It would appear logical that the same rules as to the burden of proof would apply as in relation to proof of the s 116 conditions, but here it is the party challenging rather than seeking the admissibility that must prove the relevant facts. Therefore, where the prosecution seek to challenge the use of a statement by a defendant on the grounds that the defendant, for example, put the maker in fear, that fact should be proven beyond reasonable doubt, as should the purpose of the defendant in causing that fact.

12.2.1.4 Death of the maker

This is clear enough in its meaning.

12.2.1.5 Unfitness of the maker owing to bodily or mental condition

The maker of the statement must be 'unfit to be a witness'. In *R v Setz-Dempsey* [1994] Crim LR 123, the Court of Appeal held that the Criminal Justice Act 1988, s 23 would apply equally where the witness was unable to attend court and where, owing to the physical or mental condition, the witness could not give meaningful testimony. However, the test under the CJA 2003, s 116 means that where special measures can be used to assist the witness in giving testimony either in court or from some other place, the witness would not be 'unfit' (see **Chapter 4** for special measures directions).

In *R v Lang* [2004] EWCA Crim 1701, the Court of Appeal held that the question under the equivalent provision of the Criminal Justice Act 1988 was whether the witness was fit to give evidence and that this was a matter for the trial judge. A judge could, therefore, reach a decision that was different to the medical evidence presented in support of an application. As the relevant language in the CJA 2003, s 116 is 'unfit to be a witness', the same principle would apply.

In so far as the condition of the witness might affect his competence as a witness, this is now governed by the CJA 2003, s 123 (see **12.7.2**).

12.2.1.6 Maker is outside the United Kingdom

There are two aspects to this.

(a) *Outside the UK.* A diplomat resident in this country but who cannot be compelled to attend court is not 'outside the UK' (*R v Jiminez-Paez* [1993] Crim LR 596, CA).

(b) *Securing attendance.* Consider the following points:

(i) That it is not reasonably practicable to do so must be proved. In *R v Bray* (1988) 88 Cr App R 354 the maker of the statement had been suddenly sent to Korea. The prosecution were permitted to admit his statement as evidence of relevant facts. The accused successfully appealed on the grounds that the prosecution had not adduced evidence that it was not reasonably practicable to secure the attendance of the witness.

(ii)   Where a witness is not available at the date of trial, the judge should consider adjourning the case until he is available. However, the judge should consider the practicability of securing attendance on the date of trial (or application to admit the statement) and should not have to look into the future to determine when a witness might be available (*R v French* (1993) 97 Cr App R 421, CA).

(iii)   Note that the test is 'reasonably practical'. This means that it is not necessary to prove that it is not at all possible to get the witnesses to attend. In *R v Maloney* [1994] Crim LR 525, CA, the witnesses were Greek sea cadets and there was evidence that they were at sea, on leave or at college and that formal applications would have to be made to the Greek navy to secure their attendance. The Court of Appeal was satisfied that enough had been done in determining that they were not available for s 23 of the 1988 Act to apply. Clearly, lengthy procedures could have been adopted but these went beyond what was 'reasonably practicable'. The same approach will apply to the CJA 2003.

(iv)   Also as the phrase is 'reasonably practical to secure', a witness who could easily attend court *if he wished to do so* does not necessarily fall within s 116(1)(c). If there are no powers to secure the attendance of an unwilling witness because of the law of the country in which he is located, such a witness will fall within this category. In *R v French*, for example, the witness was Mexican and had already attended to give evidence at a trial that had been adjourned. There was no way of forcing the witness to attend again so the statement could properly have fallen within the identical test under s 23 of the 1988 Act.

(v)   What is 'reasonably practicable' is a matter of fact to be determined in each case. However, in *R v Castillo* [1996] 1 Cr App R 438, the Court of Appeal stressed the following three factors:

- the importance of the evidence the witness could give;
- the expense and inconvenience in securing attendance; and
- the validity of the reasons put forward for not attending.

12.2.1.7   Maker cannot be found

The language of the CJA 2003, s 116(2)(d) has changed from that used in the Criminal Justice Act 1988, s 23. There the test was whether 'all reasonable steps' had been taken. Now the test is 'such steps as it is reasonably practical to take'. As this is the test for the CJA 2003, s 116(2)(c), it is likely that the courts will adopt the same principles in applying this paragraph. The principle that, in determining reasonableness, the seriousness of the charge should not be taken into consideration (*R v Coughlan* [1999] 5 Archbold News 2, CA) will probably continue to remain valid.

12.2.1.8   Maker in fear

Under the Criminal Justice Act 1988 witnesses in fear of giving evidence were governed by s 23(3). Section 116 of the CJA 2003 has extended this category. Any statement made by a person on a previous occasion who is now in fear of giving evidence will be admissible under s 116(2)(e). Section 116(2)(e) applies where the witness refuses to give any evidence, stops giving evidence or gives evidence avoiding reference to particular matters that will be proven by admitting the statement in place of the witness's testimony.

Unlike the other grounds for the application of the CJA 2003, s 116(2) evidence can only be admitted under this paragraph if the judge grants leave. Section 116(4) allows the court, in determining leave, to consider any 'relevant circumstances' but specifically requires consideration of the contents of the statement, the effect of any special measures directions and the risk of unfairness to any party in the proceedings in either admitting or excluding the evidence. The last of those factors (fairness) will be considered in relation to the exclusionary discretions under s 126 (see **12.6.1**). It is also likely that the factors to be considered in relation to the inclusionary discretion under s 114(1)(d) will also be of some relevance.

Section 116(3) of the CJA 2003 requires fear to be widely construed and specifically mentions fear of death or injury to persons other than the maker of the statement and the fear of financial loss. Quite how much wider the definition of fear should extend will have to be resolved by the courts.

It is submitted that the following points made under the Criminal Justice Act 1988, s 23 will also apply under the CJA 2003 s 116.

(a) The judge must conclude that the fear will prevent the maker from giving evidence: *R v Singh* [2003] EWCA Crim 2320.

(b) There is no need to prove that the fear is reasonable or that it was caused by the incident that is being tried (*R v Acton Justices, ex p McMullen* (1990) 92 Cr App R 98). Further, it was resolved in *R v Martin* [1996] Crim LR 589, CA, that it is not necessary to prove that the fear was caused by a particular thing said or done by a particular person. In that case the fear had been triggered by a silent stranger outside the witness's house.

(c) In *R v H* [2001] Crim LR 815, the Court of Appeal stated that the court should consider whether the witness is in fear when the witness is due to give evidence rather than days or weeks beforehand. However, it was recognised that there might be some practical necessity to resolve the matter at the beginning of the trial.

(d) The fear should preferably be established by oral evidence from the witness in fear (*R v H*). However, the evidence of the fear can be given by persons other than the person in fear (*R v Acton Justices, ex p McMullen*). In *R v Rutherford* [1998] Crim LR 490, the court stated that the fear could be proven by witness statement but in *R v Lobban* [2004] EWCA 1099, the Court of Appeal stated that a witness should be produced to give sworn oral evidence and should be subject to cross-examination unless the court concludes that this approach is not appropriate. Where cross-examination by advocates is not permitted, the judge may conduct the questioning having consulted with the legal representatives as to the subject matter to be raised. In *Lobban,* it was also stated that the questioning of a person in fear should take place in court and that the defendant should not be excluded. Other appropriate steps (such as special measures) should be taken to ensure that the person in fear is able to give evidence of that fear.

12.2.2   Statements in business documents

Section 117 of the CJA 2003 Act replaced the Criminal Justice Act 1988, s 24. Section 117 provides:

(1)   In criminal proceedings a statement contained in a document is admissible as evidence of any matter stated if—

(a)   oral evidence given in the proceedings would be admissible as evidence of that matter,

    (b)   *the requirements of subsection (2) are satisfied, and*

    (c)   *the requirements of subsection (5) are satisfied, in a case where subsection (4) requires them to be.*

(2)   *The requirements of this subsection are satisfied if—*

    (a)   *the document or the part containing the statement was created or received by a person in the course of a trade, business, profession or other occupation, or as the holder of a paid or unpaid office,*

    (b)   *the person who supplied the information contained in the statement (the relevant person) had or may reasonably be supposed to have had personal knowledge of the matters dealt with, and*

    (c)   *each person (if any) through whom the information was supplied from the relevant person to the person mentioned in paragraph (a) received the information in the course of a trade, business, profession or other occupation, or as the holder of a paid or unpaid office.*

(3)   *The persons mentioned in paragraphs (a) and (b) of subsection (2) may be the same person.*

(4)   *The additional requirements of subsection (5) must be satisfied if the statement—*

    (a)   *was prepared for the purposes of pending or contemplated criminal proceedings, or for a criminal investigation, but*

    (b)   *was not obtained pursuant to a request under section 7 of the Crime (International Co-operation) Act 2003 (c. 32) or an order under paragraph 6 of Schedule 13 to the Criminal Justice Act 1988 (c. 33) (which relate to overseas evidence).*

(5)   *The requirements of this subsection are satisfied if—*

    (a)   *any of the five conditions mentioned in section 116(2) is satisfied (absence of relevant person etc), or*

    (b)   *the relevant person cannot reasonably be expected to have any recollection of the matters dealt with in the statement (having regard to the length of time since he supplied the information and all other circumstances).*

(6)   *A statement is not admissible under this section if the court makes a direction to that effect under subsection (7).*

(7)   *The court may make a direction under this subsection if satisfied that the statement's reliability as evidence for the purpose for which it is tendered is doubtful in view of—*

    (a)   *its contents,*

    (b)   *the source of the information contained in it,*

    (c)   *the way in which or the circumstances in which the information was supplied or received, or*

    (d)   *the way in which or the circumstances in which the document concerned was created or received.*

As with the CJA 2003, s 116, s 117(1)(a) does not allow the admission of evidence that is inadmissible by other rules of evidence to be presented in a document.

12.2.2.1 Documents to which the CJA 2003, s 117 applies

Section 117 regulates the admissibility of two types of document:

- ordinary business documents, and
- documents prepared for pending or contemplated criminal proceedings or during criminal investigations.

The section does not apply to all documents. To be admissible under the CJA 2003, s 117:

(a) The document must have been created or received by in the course of a trade, business or profession, etc (s 117(2)(a)). Note, therefore, that a letter written by someone in a non-professional capacity but received by someone in a professional/business capacity is covered by the section.

(b) The supplier of the information in the document is shown to have personal knowledge of the facts related (s 117(2)(b)). Section 117(2)(b) also allows the court to infer such personal knowledge from the nature of the document (see *R v Foxley*

[1995] 2 Cr App R 523 and *Vehicle and Operator Agency v Jenkins Transport Ltd* [2003] EWHC 2879 (Admin)).

(c) Where the document represents information that has been passed from person to person, each person receiving the information did so in a trade, business, professional, etc capacity (s 117(2)(c)).

Consider the following example:

Alf is charged with theft of computer parts from Stock Room D of the building where he works as a packer. The prosecution allege that the goods went missing on the evening of 3 March. The computer parts were found in Alf's house and the serial numbers for each part was identified. Consider the following items of evidence:

1. A timesheet recording that Alf was due to pack in Stock Room D on 3 March from 3 pm to 11 pm. The person who filled out the timesheet, Anil, can attend court but cannot remember any details. The system for filling out the sheet is that each stock room has a foreman who informs Anil who was in that room on each day, when they started and when they left.

2. A checklist which records the serial numbers of all parts consigned to each warehouse. On the list the serial numbers for the computer parts found at Alf's house appear in the column headed 'Stock Room D'. A witness can prove that the usual process for recording the information is either for the person compiling the list to look at the parts himself or for him to have a colleague call the numbers out to him.

Both documents relate to hearsay evidence. Furthermore, neither of the documents would be admissible under s 116:

1. The first document is hearsay because its purpose is to prove that Alf had the opportunity to steal the computer parts when they must have gone missing. As Anil is available, the statement cannot be admitted under the CJA 2003, s 116.

2. The second document is hearsay, being an out of court statement admitted to prove that the stolen parts were in Stock Room D. However, it is not possible to prove the identity of the maker so as to comply with the CJA 2003, s 116(1)(b).

We shall see, however, that both documents fall within the CJA 2003, s 117 as they were both created in the course of a business.

There is little question that the filling out of the documents is a business activity. Furthermore, the information supplied in each case can be proven or inferred to be within the personal knowledge of the supplier of the information. The foreman may be inferred to have had personal knowledge of Alf's presence and either Anil himself or one of his colleagues are likely to have had personal knowledge of the serial numbers.

12.2.2.2   Multiple hearsay

Section 117(2)(c) of the CJA 2003 makes particular provision for situations where the information has been received down a chain of communication. However, such 'multiple hearsay' is only admissible if every person who received the *information* contained in the document *received* it in the course of a trade, business, etc. Note that the person who first *supplied* the information does not have to be acting in the course of a trade business or profession, etc. Consider the following examples:

(a) A guest tells a receptionist at a hotel that she saw a man outside room 203. The receptionist writes a note on piece of paper, which is then recorded in a daily log by an unknown employee. The hotel manager reads the daily log and makes an entry in a record book. Only the record book is now available. Can it be used to prove the man was outside room 203?

(b) Same as above but the guest says to the receptionist 'My husband says he saw a man outside room 203'.

In the first situation the record book could be admissible documentary evidence even though its author had no first-hand knowledge of the matters to which it relates. Each person received the information in the course of their business and it is reasonable to suppose that the guest had first-hand knowledge of the matters in question. However, in the second situation, the guest who passes on the information received it from her husband and therefore it has not been received in a trade or business capacity by 'every person through whom it was supplied'.

In the second scenario, it is unlikely that the statement would be admissible as multiple hearsay (see 12.5)

In Alf's case the documents would fall within s 117(2)(c) because the information in both documents (Alf's presence for the first document and the serial numbers for the second document) was received by a person (Anil) in the course of business.

12.2.2.3   Documents prepared for criminal investigations or proceedings

Obviously a police officer or customs officer will be acting in the course of a profession and therefore any document created by them is potentially covered by s 117. Furthermore a police officer recording information given by a member of the public would be receiving such information in the course of his profession. To prevent s 117 from undermining the principle that witnesses attend to give evidence, the information contained in a police notebook as a result of something a witness says (for example) is subject to the same requirements as would be a document created by that witness. Before either can be used instead of the witness, there must be a good reason why the witness himself cannot attend. However, s 117 provides an additional justification for admitting the evidence. Therefore, a s 117 statement created during a criminal investigation or for pending proceedings will be admissible if the maker of the statement is:

- dead;
- physically unfit to be a witness;
- mentally unfit to be a witness;
- abroad and cannot reasonably be made to attend court;
- not reasonably traceable;
- unwilling to give evidence through fear; or
- likely (for justifiable reasons) not to be able to remember the details contained in the statement.

It is the person who supplied the information who must be unable to attend court as a witness or to remember the information and not the person who recorded and received the information.

12.2.2.4   Power to restrict admissibility under the Criminal Justice Act 2003, s 117

Section 117(6) of the CJA 2003 states that the court can direct that any document otherwise admissible under this section (whether or not created for criminal proceedings) will not be admissible. The court may do so if satisfied that the statement is unreliable having regard to the contents of the documents, the source of the information, how the information was supplied or received or the document was created or received (s 117(7)). This power to regulate the admissibility of the evidence focuses on questions of the reliability of the document rather than the effect of admitting the document on the parties in the case. Therefore, an anonymous note scribbled on a piece of paper and left at a police station that alleges that a particular person has committed a crime would not have to be admitted simply because it otherwise complies with the CJA 2003, s 117.

The courts will not, in determining admissibility at this point, consider issues other than reliability, for example whether a defendant is deprived of an opportunity to cross-examine the maker of the document or otherwise challenge its contents. Such matters will be relevant to the general exclusionary discretions (see **12.6.1** below).

12.2.3   Previous inconsistent statements

Whether a previous inconsistent statement is admissible is considered in **Chapter 7** of this Manual at **7.7**. Where such a statement is admissible, s 119(1) of the CJA 2003 provides that the statement is admissible as evidence of the truth of the contents. Before the 2003 Act the document was only admissible to diminish the credibility of the person who made the statement.

In so far as a statement under s 119 is proven by a document and that document therefore becomes an exhibit in the case, s 122 provides that the document should not be taken to the jury room when the jury retires unless either the court considers it appropriate or all the parties in the case agree.

12.2.4   Other previous statements by witnesses

Section 120 of the CJA 2003 also changes the common law in relation to previous statements that are consistent with the testimony that they give at trial. Previous consistent statements were considered in **6.4.2**.

Section 120 of the CJA 2003 applies in relation to previous statements made by someone who does attend court to give evidence as a witness (s 120(1)). None of the statements considered under s 120 will be admissible if the witness does not attend to give evidence (although they could, of course, be admissible if they comply with the requirements of ss 116 to 118).

Section 120 deals with three types of previous statement:

- previous statements admitted to rebut an allegation of fabrication;
- memory–refreshing documents that, by reason of the cross-examination of the witness have become evidence in the proceedings;
- statements of identification or description, etc.

The restriction on the use of the document by the jury when they retire to consider their verdict identified in relation to s 119 applies equally to any document proving a statement under any of the grounds in s 120.

12.2.4.1   Statements in rebuttal of fabrication and memory-refreshing documents

Section 120 of the CJA 2003 provides:

> (2)   If a previous statement by the witness is admitted as evidence to rebut a suggestion that his oral evidence has been fabricated, that statement is admissible as evidence of any matter stated of which oral evidence by the witness would be admissible.
>
> (3)   A statement made by the witness in a document—
> > (a)   which is used by him to refresh his memory while giving evidence,
> >
> > (b)   on which he is cross-examined, and
> >
> > (c)   which as a consequence is received in evidence in the proceedings, is admissible as evidence of any matter stated of which oral evidence by him would be admissible.

These two subsections have not changed the law relating to the admissibility of such evidence (see **6.4.2**). However, the effect of these subsections is that the statements can be used as additional evidence of the facts alleged rather than simply to bolster the credibility of the testimony of the maker.

12.2.4.2   Statements of identification or description, etc

Section 120(4) to (8) of the CJA 2003 provides for the admissibility of three types of statement where the witness gives evidence and adopts the statement as his own and truthful in the course of testimony (s 120(4)(b)).

Section 120 provides:

> (4)   A previous statement by the witness is admissible as evidence of any matter stated of which oral evidence by him would be admissible, if—
> > (a)   any of the following three conditions is satisfied, and
> >
> > (b)   while giving evidence the witness indicates that to the best of his belief he made the statement, and that to the best of his belief it states the truth.
>
> (5)   The first condition is that the statement identifies or describes a person, object or place.
>
> (6)   The second condition is that the statement was made by the witness when the matters stated were fresh in his memory but he does not remember them, and cannot reasonably be expected to remember them, well enough to give oral evidence of them in the proceedings.
>
> (7)   The third condition is that—
> > (a)   the witness claims to be a person against whom an offence has been committed,
> >
> > (b)   the offence is one to which the proceedings relate,
> >
> > (c)   the statement consists of a complaint made by the witness (whether to a person in authority or not) about conduct which would, if proved, constitute the offence or part of the offence,
> >
> > (d)   the complaint was made as soon as could reasonably be expected after the alleged conduct,
> >
> > (e)   the complaint was not made as a result of a threat or a promise, and
> >
> > (f)   before the statement is adduced the witness gives oral evidence in connection with its subject matter.
>
> (8)   For the purposes of subsection (7) the fact that the complaint was elicited (for example, by a leading question) is irrelevant unless a threat or a promise was involved.

The statement will be admitted if it fulfils any *one* of the conditions set out below. They are:

First condition (s 120(5))

The statement is one of identification or description.

This is not restricted to a person but also includes identification or descriptions of objects or places. Therefore a witness attacked on a street could adopt a statement of the precise location and its layout, the appearance of the defendant and of the peculiar knife used in the attack.

Second condition (s 120(6))
There are three requirements:

- the statement was made when the matters were fresh in the witness's memory;
- the witness cannot remember the matters; and
- the witness cannot reasonably be expected to remember the matters.

This condition applies to any witness. The witness would have to testify as to the failure of his recollection of the events. What a witness may reasonably be expected to give evidence of and how well matters must be remembered 'to be able to give oral evidence of them in proceedings' will be matters for the tribunal of law to decide in determining admissibility under this subsection. Clearly, the more intricate or remote the events about which the evidence is to be given, the more reasonable it is for the witness not to remember them. However, where the court is concerned with traumatic events there may be difficult arguments as to whether such events should be more or less memorable. It is likely, given the language used, that the courts will have to have regard to what it is reasonable for the particular witness to remember rather than to adopt any objective standard.

Third condition (s 120(7), (8))
The third condition expands the common law rule that recent complaints by victims of sexual offences are admissible to bolster the credibility of the testimony of the complainant to cover victims of non-sexual offences. The requirements for the application of s 120(7) are:

- the witness is the alleged victim to an offence being tried (s 120(7)(a), (b));
- the statement is a complaint to any person that the offence has been committed (s 120(7)(c));
- the complaint was made as soon as could reasonably be expected after the alleged offence (s 120(7)(d));
- there was no pressure or threat leading to the complaint (s 120(7)(e)) although it can have been the result of leading questions (s 120(8)); and
- the witness has given some testimony on the offence (s 120(7)(f)) although one would assume by virtue of the second condition (s 120(6)) not detailed testimony.

Therefore, the CJA 2003, s 120(7) can only be used to prove statements by the victim of the crime who gives evidence of that crime. The crime no longer has to be a sexual offence and the statement is admissible to prove the truth of what was alleged in the statement. The following principles from the common law on previous complaints are likely to continue to apply:

(a) the subsection applies to statements made in private, such as entries in a diary not intended to be seen by any other person (*R v B* [1997] Crim LR 220);

(b) what is 'as soon as could reasonably be expected' is a question for the judge (*R v Cummings* [1948] 1 All ER 551, CA). However, s 120(7)(d) has removed the common law test of 'first reasonable opportunity', which the courts had, in any event, interpreted to allow some delay (*R v Valentine* [1996] 2 Cr App R 213, CA). On the other hand pre-CJA 2003 case law on this area was exclusively concerned with sexual offences. What is reasonable to expect of a victim of a crime without the perceived social stigma of a sexual offence will be different.

12.3   Admissibility under preserved common law exceptions

Section 118(1) of the CJA 2003 preserves the following common law exceptions to the rule against hearsay:

- public information;
- evidence of reputation;
- *res gestae*;
- confessions;
- admissions by agents;
- common enterprise;
- expert evidence.

Otherwise all of the common law rules concerning the admissibility of hearsay evidence in criminal proceedings are abolished by the CJA 2003, s 118(2).

12.3.1   Public information

Section 118(1) provides the following description of the common law rules preserved:

Public Information etc.

(1) Any rule of law under which in criminal proceedings—

- *(a)   published works dealing with matters of a public nature (such as histories, scientific works, dictionaries and maps) are admissible as evidence of facts of a public nature stated in them,*
- *(b)   public documents (such as public registers, and returns made under public authority with respect to matters of public interest) are admissible as evidence of facts stated in them,*
- *(c)   records (such as the records of certain courts, treaties, Crown grants, pardons and commissions) are admissible as evidence of facts stated in them, or*
- *(d)   evidence relating to a person's age or date or place of birth may be given by a person without personal knowledge of the matter.*

Whether a document is 'public' is a question of degree and does not require proof that the document had to be of relevance to the whole world. Rather, it was necessary that it concerned all the people interested in the matter in question (*Sturla v Freccia* (1880) 5 App Cas 623). For details of the types of document that fit within this exception, see *Blackstone's Criminal Practice*, at F 16.25 to F 16.27.

12.3.2   Reputation

Section 118(1), paragraphs 2 and 3 preserve the following rules:

Reputation as to character

(2) Any rule of law under which in criminal proceedings evidence of a person's reputation is admissible for the purpose of proving his good or bad character.

Note

The rule is preserved only so far as it allows the court to treat such evidence as proving the matter concerned.

Reputation or family tradition

(3) Any rule of law under which in criminal proceedings evidence of reputation or family tradition is admissible for the purpose of proving or disproving—

- *(a)   pedigree or the existence of a marriage,*
- *(b)   the existence of any public or general right, or*
- *(c)   the identity of any person or thing.*

Note

The rule is preserved only so far as it allows the court to treat such evidence as proving or disproving the matter concerned.

Proof of the character of a person by reputation is only permitted where the proof of the character in question is admissible evidence: see, generally, **Chapters 8, 9 and 10**.

12.3.3   *Res gestae*

Section 118(1) states the rule which it preserves under the heading '*res gestae*' as follows:

(4)   *Any rule of law under which in criminal proceedings a statement is admissible as evidence of any matter stated if—*

(a)   *the statement was made by a person so emotionally overpowered by an event that the possibility of concoction or distortion can be disregarded,*

(b)   *the statement accompanied an act which can be properly evaluated as evidence only if considered in conjunction with the statement, or*

(c)   *the statement relates to a physical sensation or a mental state (such as intention or emotion).*

Paragraph 4 is not intended to define the *res gestae* rule, merely to identify it. The definition of *res gestae* is a matter for the common law.

Statements forming part of the *res gestae* fall into a number of different categories. The phrase '*res gestae*' is used by the law to identify the event in question. The various *res gestae* exceptions loosely conform to a principle that the statement must be made at or about the same time as the matter to which it relates. In other words, there is some requirement of contemporaneity. Quite what the statement relates to for each exception varies, as shall be seen below. The logic of these exceptions is that statements made at the time of the event or matter are less likely to be made up or distorted than statements made at a later point.

12.3.3.1   Statements contemporaneous to an emotionally overpowering event

This category of *res gestae* statement is one that is made by someone as an event is taking place and where the event is dominating or overwhelming the mind of the person making the statement.

The test for admissibility for this type of *res gestae* statement is set out in *R v Andrews* [1987] AC 281 where a man was attacked and mortally wounded by two others. The prosecution called police officers to give evidence that the victim told them that Andrews was one of the attackers. Clearly this was a hearsay statement adduced to prove that fact. The House of Lords held that nonetheless the statement was admissible under the *res gestae* exception. In doing so Lord Ackner defined the test of admissibility (at p 300) as follows:

1.   The primary question which the judge must ask himself or herself is — can the possibility of concoction or distortion be disregarded?

2.   To answer that question the judge must first consider the circumstances in which the particular statement was made, in order to satisfy himself or herself that the event was so unusual or startling or dramatic as to dominate the thoughts of the maker so that his utterance was an instinctive reaction to that event, thus giving no real opportunity for reasoned reflection. In such a situation the judge would be entitled to conclude that the involvement or the pressure of the event would exclude the possibility of concoction or distortion, providing that the statement was made in conditions of approximate but not exact contemporaneity.

Therefore:

(a) The primary test is whether concoction or distortion can be disregarded.

(b) This test is passed if the judge concludes (ie, it is proved to him that):

  (i)   There was an 'unusual or *startling* or dramatic' *event*.

  (ii) That event therefore *dominated the thoughts* of the maker of the statement.

  (iii) As a result of that domination of the thoughts, the statement was an 'instinctive reaction' to the event. In other words, the statement was *spontaneous*.

  (iv) The statement was *approximately contemporaneous*.

Lord Ackner made the following additional points:

(a) On the issue of spontaneity Lord Ackner said:

  (i)   The statement must be 'so closely associated with the event . . . that it can fairly be said that the mind of the declarant was still dominated by the event'.

  (ii) The judge must be satisfied that the 'event, which provided the trigger mechanism was still operative'.

  (iii) That the statement is a response to a question is only a factor to consider in deciding whether the statement was sufficiently spontaneous.

(b) The judge should consider any factors other than the passage of time that might, in the circumstances of each case, support any argument that the statement was concocted or distorted. In *R v Andrews*, for example, it was alleged that the victim had a malicious motive to fabricate evidence against Andrews. In such cases the judge must be satisfied that there was no possibility of any concoction or distortion having regard to the allegations of malice.

(c) Generally any risk that the person hearing and repeating the statement has made an error goes to the weight not the admissibility of the statement. However, where a special feature is alleged to have caused the mistake such as drunkenness (as was the case in *R v Andrews*) or short sightedness, the judge must 'consider whether he can exclude the possibility of error'. If not, it would seem the judge may have to exclude the statement.

Note the importance of proof of these matters. Whether or not a particular statement fits within this exception will have to be established by evidence. In *Teper v R* [1952] AC 480, PC, the statement was made to a police officer by an unknown person. It was held that as it was not known who had made the statement, it was *unlikely* to be possible to rely on this exception. This is because it is unlikely that it will be possible to prove that the maker's mind was dominated by the event if it is not known who the maker is. However, there may be circumstances in which there is evidence to suggest that the statement was made by an unknown person whose mind was dominated. This will be a matter of proof in each case.

The statement must be approximately contemporaneous. This will be a question of fact in each case. In *Tobi v Nichols* [1988] RTR 343, a statement made 20 minutes after a collision was determined not to be sufficiently contemporaneous. However, it was also considered that the event was not sufficiently mind-dominating. It is submitted that there is a correlation between the nature of the event and how long after it a statement may be roughly contemporaneous. The more traumatic the event, the better the argument that it is still dominating the mind of the maker at a later point. In *R v Carnall* [1995] Crim LR 944, for example, a statement made an hour after a murderous assault was held to have been rightly admitted. As the statement must be a reaction to or part of the event, statements made before the event in question cannot be part of this category of *res gestae* exception (*R v Newport* [1998] Crim LR 581).

There are no particular requirements that the person who made the statement is dead or unavailable at the time of trial (*R v Nye* (1977) 66 Cr App R 252). Even statements made by the accused can be part of the *res gestae* and therefore admitted by either party. In *R v Glover* [1991] Crim LR 48, the accused said 'I am David Glover . . . we will not think twice about shooting you and your kids.' As the trial issue was identity, the prosecution were allowed to call this statement as part of the *res gestae*. However, in *R v Andrews*, Lord Ackner observed that it would be wrong to use this *res gestae* exception to avoid calling the witness in question so as to deprive other parties of an opportunity to cross-examine the maker of the statement. In *Attorney-General's Reference (No 1 of 2003)* [2003] 2 Cr App Rep 453, the Court of Appeal ruled that there was no requirement that a witness was unavailable before a statement made by that witness would be admissible under the doctrine of *res gestae*. However, where the prosecution sought to rely on a *res gestae* statement made by a person who could be called as a witness but whom the prosecution did not propose to call, the trial judge had a discretion under s 78 of PACE 1984 to exclude the *res gestae* statements. In deciding whether to do so the court would have regard to the circumstances in which the statement was made and how easy it would have been to call the witness.

12.3.3.2 Contemporaneous statements accompanying an act

Such statements must be:

(a) approximately contemporaneous to the act. In *Howe v Malkin* (1878) 40 LT 196, it was said that such a statement was admissible because it was mixed up with the event in question;

(b) made by the person performing the act (*Peacock v Harris* (1836) 5 Ad & El 449); and

(c) the act should itself be relevant to the issues in the case (in *R v McCay* [1990] 1 WLR 645, the statement 'It's number 8,' was made at the same time as a person was identified in an identification parade).

12.3.3.3 Contemporaneous statements relating to the maker's physical or mental state

A statement made by a person in which he refers to his current physical state will be admissible to prove that physical state.

The statement can prove the physical state but not its cause (*R v Gloster* (1888) 16 Cox CC 471). Therefore in *R v Thomson* [1912] 3 KB 19 statements by a woman that she had recently operated upon herself were not admissible to prove the cause of a miscarriage.

The statements do not have to be made at the exact time that the feelings are being experienced: whether a statement is contemporary to the feeling is a question of degree. In *Aveson v Lord Kinnaird* (1805) 6 East 188, statements made by a woman as to symptoms she said she had been suffering for some time were admitted to prove that not only was she suffering those symptoms when she made the statement but also that she had suffered them some days earlier.

So far as the maker's state of mind is concerned, statements revealing that a person was of a particular frame of mind could be original evidence (eg *Thomas v Connell* (1838) 4 M & W 267, as confirmed by the approach of the courts in *R v Blastland* [1986] AC 41, and *R v Kearley*). This is probably the best approach to cases from which a state of mind is inferred (ie, because A said a particular thing we can infer a particular state of mind or particular emotional state). Clearly, however, where a person expressly states that he is of a particular state of mind (such as 'I hate that man,' or 'I believe he is the one who stole my watch') there can be little doubt that the statement is hearsay evidence.

However, such a statement will be admissible as an exception to the rule against hearsay evidence if it is sufficiently contemporaneous. Statements of one's state of mind at an earlier time are not admissible (*R v Moghal* (1977) 65 Cr App R 56).

A particular difficulty arises from this rule where a statement of a contemporaneous fact is used to prove what happened at a later date. The usual case is one in which the statement reveals the intention of the maker and the issue is whether the maker later acted on that intention. Consider the following cases:

(a) *R v Buckley* (1838) 13 Cox CC 293: a statement made by a police officer that he intended to keep a watch on the accused was admitted to prove that he had later been keeping a watch on the accused when he was murdered.

(b) *R v Moghal* (above): a statement made by S that she intended to kill R was held to be admissible to prove that she and not the accused had killed R even though the statement had been made six months before.

(c) *R v Callender* [1998] Crim LR 337: statements made by a person two weeks before he was arrested on explosives charges that he intended to carry false explosive devices for publicity purposes was held not to be admissible.

The case law in this area appears confused. It is submitted that the best view to take of cases about current intentions is that such statements of intention are admissible under this exception but only if relevant. If the statements are not sufficiently relevant, they should not be admitted. This was the view taken in *R v Blastland* in which the statement in *R v Moghal* was criticised as insufficiently relevant. For a further criticism of *R v Callender*, see *Blackstone's Criminal Practice*, 2006, at F16.31.

12.3.4   Confessions and admissions

Section 118(1), paragraph 5 provides for the continued operation of the admissibility of confessions and mixed statements as an exception to the rule against hearsay. Confession evidence is dealt with in detail in **Chapter 13**. Mixed statements are considered at **6.4.2.4**.

Section 118(1), paragraph 6 provides for the continued operation at common law of the rule whereby admissions made by an agent (*R v Turner* (1975) 61 Cr App R 67) or a person appointed by the defendant to answer questions on the defendant's behalf (*Williams v Innes* (1808) Camp 364) will be admissible in evidence against the defendant. The agency must be proven by evidence independently of the agent's assertions (*R v Evans* [1981] Crim LR 699).

12.3.5   Common enterprise

Paragraph 7 of s 118(1) preserves:

(7)   *Any rule of law under which in criminal proceedings a statement made by a party to a common enterprise is admissible against another party to the enterprise as evidence of any matter stated.*

Where, in the course of committing a crime, A makes a statement which proves that B was also committing the same crime, the common law allows such matters to be admitted as proof of the fact that B committed the crime. This rule should be contrasted with the rule that generally a confession is only admissible against the person who makes it and not another person.

Before a statement will be admissible under this exception, however, it must be established that:

• there was a common criminal purpose or enterprise; and

• the statement was made to pursue or further that purpose.

12.3.5.1 Common purpose

A common purpose is wider than a conspiracy. In *R v Jones* [1997] 2 Cr App R 119, CA, for example, the doctrine was applied to the offence of evading the prohibition on the importation of drugs (drug smuggling) even though there was no charge of conspiracy on the indictment. However, there does have to be some common element of commission of the offence. In *R v Gray* [1995] 2 Cr App R 100, there had been an allegation of a 'network' between various co-accused as to insider dealing but each accused was charged with separate offences. The Court of Appeal concluded that, in the absence of some allegation that the offences had been committed jointly, the rule did not apply. Usually such an allegation would arise from the way in which the accused persons were charged. Therefore even if there does not have to be conspiracy charged, the rule will generally only apply where the parties are jointly charged, whether as principals or as secondary parties. The court did leave open the possibility that future cases may involve a common purpose even if the various parties were charged with separate offences but did not explain how that might be the case.

The existence of the common purpose must be proved by evidence independent to the statement to be admitted under the exception (*R v Blake* (1844) 6 QB 126). In other words, what is said in the statement cannot prove that there was a common purpose and the jury should be directed that they cannot rely on the statement itself to prove the existence of such a common purpose (*R v Williams* [2002] EWCA Crim 2208). However, the court can conditionally admit the evidence of the statement subject to proof at some later stage of the common purpose (*R v Governor of Pentonville Prison, ex p Osman* [1990] 1 WLR 277). If the existence of a common purpose cannot subsequently be proven by independent evidence, the statement will have to be excluded from the case against any co-accused (*R v Donat* (1985) 82 Cr App R 173) and, in jury trials, a direction will have to be given directing the jury to ignore the evidence or they may have to be discharged.

12.3.5.2 Furtherance of the common purpose

A statement made after the criminal purpose has been achieved or one that simply explains what another member has done without advancing it in any way, will not be 'in furtherance' of the common purpose and therefore not admissible (*R v Walters* (1979) 69 Cr App R 115; *R v Steward* [1963] Crim LR 697).

What is capable of being a statement in furtherance of a common purpose will depend on the facts of the case. In *R v Devonport* [1996] 1 Cr App R 221, the statement concerned the intended division of proceeds from a drug deal. This was treated as in furtherance of the common purpose. However, in *R v Blake* (1844) 6 QB 126, a cheque proving that B had received his share of the proceeds from a conspiracy was held not to be in furtherance of the common purpose. In the former case the statement assisted or encouraged the commission of the offence whereas in the latter case it was simply a consequence of it.

Where the evidence that is alleged to prove the common purpose is a document, it will be necessary to prove (a) it was either made in a particular (and relevant) way or to have been found in an incriminating way, and (b) that it suggests the involvement of the defendants in the common purpose (*R v Jenkins* [2003] Crim LR 107). Merely producing the document without proving it in this way will not render it admissible as evidence of the common purpose.

The courts have interpreted what furthers the purpose quite loosely. In *R v Ilyas* [1996] Crim LR 810, the diary of A was admitted to prove that B, C and D had received stolen cars, Latham J appearing to extend the definition to documents 'created *in the course of*, or furtherance, of the conspiracy'.

12.3.6   Expert evidence

Section 118(1), paragraph 8 preserves:

> (8)   *Any rule of law under which in criminal proceedings an expert witness may draw on the body of expertise relevant to his field.*

Expert evidence is considered in detail in **Chapter 16**. There it will be seen that experts are, understandably, entitled to rely upon hearsay in the sense that they can rely on the observations and writings of other experts in their field of expertise.

However, the rule that the data upon which the expert's opinion is based has to be proven by admissible evidence has been relaxed by the CJA 2003, s 127, which provides that an expert can base his opinion on information contained in a statement prepared for criminal purposes if the fact that the expert will do so is notified to the other parties. The other parties have the opportunity to object to such a use of the statement. Where such a statement is used, s 127(3) provides that the statement becomes evidence of its contents.

12.4   Admissibility in the interests of justice

Section 114(1)(d) of the CJA 2003 provides that the court may admit hearsay evidence in the absence of the agreement under s 114(1)(c) or any specific statutory or common law rule in s 114(1)(a) and (b) where to do so would be in the interests of justice.

Section 114(2) provides:

> (2)   *In deciding whether a statement not made in oral evidence should be admitted under subsection (1)(d), the court must have regard to the following factors (and to any others it considers relevant)—*
> > (a)   *how much probative value the statement has (assuming it to be true) in relation to a matter in issue in the proceedings, or how valuable it is for the understanding of other evidence in the case;*
> > (b)   *what other evidence has been, or can be, given on the matter or evidence mentioned in paragraph (a);*
> > (c)   *how important the matter or evidence mentioned in paragraph (a) is in the context of the case as a whole;*
> > (d)   *the circumstances in which the statement was made;*
> > (e)   *how reliable the maker of the statement appears to be;*
> > (f)   *how reliable the evidence of the making of the statement appears to be;*
> > (g)   *whether oral evidence of the matter stated can be given and, if not, why it cannot;*
> > (h)   *the amount of difficulty involved in challenging the statement;*
> > (i)   *the extent to which that difficulty would be likely to prejudice the party facing it.*

In *R v T* [2006] All ER (D) 174 (Jan), it was stated that a judge, in determining whether to admit evidence in the interests of justice under s 114(1)(d), does not have to consider all 9 of the s 114(2) factors in all cases. It is a matter for the judge, having regard to any factors identified in the course of argument and to any factors he considers relevant, to consider the interests of justice test.

Some of the factors under the CJA 2003, s 114 concern the probative value of the hearsay evidence. Under s 114(2)(a) the court must assume that the statement is true when assessing its probative value. This means that the question for the court is how much impact it would have on the case if accepted by the jury, not whether they are likely to accept it as true. However, under paragraphs (e) and (f) the court can also consider any evidence of the reliability of both the maker of the statement and the circumstances of the making of the statement.

Other factors concern the importance of the evidence to the trial process. Paragraph (a) requires the court to consider the impact of the evidence on the trial and paragraph (b) requires consideration of alternative means of proving the facts the statement would prove. Paragraph (c) requires consideration of the matter that is proven to the trial issues. Therefore, hearsay evidence going to a collateral issue, such as the credibility of a witness, that is not admissible under any other rule in the CJA 2003 is less likely to be admissible than hearsay evidence relevant that directly proves one of the facts in issue. However, hearsay evidence that confirms or supports a complainant's case may well be considered to require admission in the interests of justice (*R v Xhabri* [2005] EWCA Crim 3135.)

Given that hearsay evidence is intended not to substitute oral evidence, the court is required to consider the availability of other oral evidence (s 114(2)(g)) and the difficulties of challenging the evidence given the lack of the opportunity to cross-examine the maker (s 114(2)(h)).

A final type of consideration concerns the extent to which the evidence could cause prejudice to the party facing it (paragraph (i)).

The court will probably use many of the principles developed in exercising the exclusionary powers under the Criminal Justice Act 1988, ss 25 and 26, which required consideration of similar factors (but note that in *R v Xhabri* [2006] 1 Cr App R 26, no such case law was cited during the judgment). The following issues in particular may be of use:

(a) Where such a statement is admitted instead of calling the maker to give evidence, it will often not be possible to controvert it by cross-examination. Therefore, the only way to challenge the statement will often be by the accused giving evidence. However, the accused may wish not to do so. The fact that the accused would be put under pressure to give evidence as a result of the statement to be admitted will not dictate where the 'interests of justice' lie (*R v Cole* [1990] 2 All ER 108; *R v Gokal* [1997] 2 Cr App R 266).

(b) Whether the 'interests of justice' test can cause difficulties where there is more than one accused. In such circumstances, admitting the evidence may cause difficulties for one accused while not admitting the evidence may cause difficulties for another. For example, in *R v Duffy* [1999] 1 Cr App R 307, CA, two accused, D and H, were charged with murder and robbery. The statement by the son of the victim suggested D had attempted to dissuade H from killing the victim. The prosecution sought to prove the statement, which H opposed under s 26 of the Criminal Justice Act 1988 on the ground that H would not be able to cross-examine the maker of the statement. The trial judge declined to grant leave to admit the statement. D, who had therefore been deprived of support for her defence, appealed. The Court of Appeal allowed her appeal. In doing so they contrasted the interests of justice of each accused. On the one hand, while H could not cross-examine the maker of the statement, he could still have controverted the statement by giving evidence himself. In contrast D had suffered by the decision not to admit the evidence as she was deprived of support for her evidence. Therefore, the interests of justice should have favoured D over H and the statement should therefore have been admitted. In *R v Lake Estates Watersports Ltd* [2002] EWCA Crim 2067, the Court of Appeal considered that the trial judge should have had regard to the late stage in the proceedings at which the prosecution had sought to admit a statement. The court concluded that the statement should not have been admitted as the defendant had been deprived of a chance to call an expert witness to rebut the evidence contained in the statement.

(c) The quality of the evidence will be an important factor in determining whether or not to grant leave. Where the evidence is of marginal value, the court may decide not to admit it (see, for example, *R v Patel* (1993) 97 Cr App R 294, CA), whereas if the evidence is clear and precise it is more likely to be admitted (*R v Fairfax* [1995] Crim LR 949).

(d) In *Neill v North Antrim Magistrates' Court* [1992] 1 WLR 1221, it was stated that if the statement contains evidence of identification, the court will generally be reluctant to admit it. Such evidence would be particularly difficult to challenge effectively given that the witness cannot be cross-examined.

(e) Furthermore, the court will take into consideration the importance of the evidence. Where the evidence of the witness is central to the case, the approach of the courts has varied. In cases such as *R v French* (1993) 97 Cr App R 421, the courts have been reluctant to admit evidence where there is no other evidence on the issue. However, in cases such as *R v Dragic* [1996] 2 Cr App R 232, the courts have shown willingness to admit statements even when they are the only source of evidence on a crucial issue. The extent to which the statement provides the only evidence on a crucial issue would appear to be a strong factor.

(f) Furthermore, the court will have regard to the extent to which the loss of the opportunity to cross-examine the maker of the statement conflicts with the right to a fair trial under Article 6 of the ECHR and, in particular, Article 6(3)(d) which provides for the accused's right to cross-examine witnesses: see *R v Thomas* [1998] Crim LR 887, CA in which regard to Article 6(3)(d) did not lead to the exclusion of evidence and *R v Radak* [1999] 1 Cr App R 187, CA, in which the court excluded a s 23 statement that it regarded as an essential link in the prosecution case. In *R v KM, The Times*, 2 May 2003, the Court of Appeal overturned a conviction which was wholly based on a statement by a complainant witness who had been mentally unfit to attend. To base all of the prosecution case on evidence that the accused could not cross-examine was considered to be a breach of Article 6 of the ECHR. However, in *R v Xhabri* [2006] 1 Ce App R 26, the Court of Appeal had regard to the fact that defence counsel would have had difficulty mounting any effective cross-examination of the maker of the statements in question and that the lack of any ability to cross-examine the maker did not cause any particular unfairness to the defendant in that case. Furthermore, the court concluded that Article 6 applied when considering the power to exclude evidence under s 126 rather than the power to admit it in the interests of justice under s 114(1)(d).

Consider again the situation of the homeless person at **12.2.1.2**. It was noted there that the statement of the person would not be admissible under the CJA 2003, s 116 as the maker was not identifiable. Nor would the statement of identification be admissible under the CJA 2003, s 120 as the maker did not give evidence. Nor would the statement fit within any of the preserved common law exceptions. Could the statement be admitted under s 114(1)(d)? There would be no certainty that it would: the evidence concerns an important issue in the case (s 114(2)(a)), namely identity, and nothing is known of the maker of the statement that would allow his credibility as a witness to be properly challenged (s 114(2)(e) and (h)). On the other hand, if, for example, the victim was unable to make an identification of her attacker, there may be no other evidence on this important matter (s 114(2)(a), (b), (c) and (g)).

In *R v Xhabri*, the defendant, an Albanian, was charged with kidnapping a Latvian woman and then forcing her to work as a prostitute. One of the statements that the prosecution relied upon was made by two Albanians to the victim's father which were testified to by the victim's father. According to the father, the Albanians told him, amongst other things, that the victim had disappeared from the flat in which she was staying with the defendant. The Court of Appeal concluded that this statement was not admissible. It is likely that this was because, if the disappearance of the victim was within the personal knowledge of the Albanians, it would not be admissible under s 116 because the makers were unidentified and, if not, their personal knowledge of that fact would not have been admissible under s 121 (see **12.5** below). However, the court concluded that it had been admissible under s 114 as it confirmed a significant part of the victim's account of what had happened. Although the court did not specifically cite s 114(1)(d), it seems that this would be an example of evidence not otherwise admissible in the interests of justice.

12.5 Multiple hearsay

Consider the following example. Eric sees Frank one evening in a particular place where a robbery has occurred and says to Devon, 'Frank was near No 10 Gerrard Street last night.' Devon repeats this to Charlie. None of the people mentioned receives the information in any professional or business capacity. Clearly, Eric could testify that he saw Frank: that is his personal experience. Devon could (in principle) also give evidence, under s 116(2), of what he heard Eric say if there is a reason why Eric is not available. But could Charlie also repeat the statement made by Devon?

The problem that is posed is that of multiple hearsay. Section 117 of the CJA 2003 makes specific provision for multiple hearsay contained in documents and received by people acting in the course of a trade, business, etc. For situations other than that, s 121 provides:

(1) *A hearsay statement is not admissible to prove the fact that an earlier hearsay statement was made unless—*
   (a) *either of the statements is admissible under section 117, 119 or 120,*
   (b) *all parties to the proceedings so agree, or*
   (c) *the court is satisfied that the value of the evidence in question, taking into account how reliable the statements appear to be, is so high that the interests of justice require the later statement to be admissible for that purpose.*
(2) *In this section 'hearsay statement' means a statement, not made in oral evidence, that is relied on as evidence of a matter stated in it.*

Section 121(1) requires consideration of the admissibility of the two hearsay statements: the first-hand hearsay statement (in our case what Devon said) and the second-hand hearsay statement (what Eric said). If either of those two statements is admissible under the CJA 2003, ss 117, 119 or 120, then both are admissible. In our case neither is. Therefore, the statement would only be admissible if all the parties agree to its admissibility (s 121(1)(b)) or it is in the interests of justice to admit it (s 121(1)(c)).

Note that the interests of justice test for these purposes is different to that in s 114. This test specifically links the interests of justice to the probative value of the evidence and does not require consideration of other factors. Furthermore, the CJA 2003 does not make clear whether the two tests are mutually exclusive. It would seem logical that, in defining this specific inclusionary power for multiple hearsay, Parliament intended the test in s 114 not to apply but the matter may be open to argument in the appellate courts.

Consider Frank's case with the following alternatives:

- Devon is a police officer, who wrote a note of what was said that somehow comes into the possession of Charlie other than in the course of business;
- Eric gives evidence at trial and testifies that he and Frank were at a football match in another town at the time;
- Eric gives evidence but has difficulty remembering exactly where he saw Frank at the time but does remember having seen him that evening.

In each of these situations the statement would become admissible. In the first situation Devon's notebook would be admissible evidence under s 117. In the second situation, Eric has made a previous inconsistent statement that could be admissible under s 119 and in the third case the statement by Eric could be admissible under s 120(4). Therefore, for all three statements Charlie could give evidence as to the whole chain of statements. Charlie can prove Devon's statement under s 116. Devon's statement could be admitted as evidence of any fact of which admissible evidence could be given. By virtue of s 121, that includes what Eric said.

Another of the hearsay statements admitted in *R v Xhabri* was the testimony of a police officer who had spoken to two unidentified individuals who had visited a police station and spoken to him. These individuals told him where the victim lived and that she was being held there against her will. They did not have personal knowledge of these facts so the material information (the details told to them by the victim) would have to be proven by hearsay evidence (what they told the police officer the victim had said to them). This therefore meant that the evidence would only be admissible if it complied with one of the three requirements of s 121(1). As the victim had given evidence of what she had said to these two people and the Court of Appeal concluded it was admissible under s 120(4), (7) (previous complaint of a crime), one of the two statements was admissible under s 120 and therefore the multiple hearsay was admissible under s 121(1)(a). The court also considered it likely that the evidence could have been admitted under s 121(1)(c) (the interests of justice ground) as well, given its evidential value was so high. The court did not consider whether the statement received by the police officer could also have been admissible under s 117. If made in a document, this may also have rendered the report by the informants admissible under s 121(1)(a).

12.6 Exclusion of the evidence

12.6.1 General discretions to exclude evidence

Section 126(1) of the CJA 2003 creates a general discretion to exclude hearsay evidence and s 126(2) preserves the operation of the exclusionary discretions that apply to criminal law generally in relation to such evidence.

Section 126(1) states:

(1) In criminal proceedings the court may refuse to admit a statement as evidence of a matter stated if—

    (a) the statement was made otherwise than in oral evidence in the proceedings, and

    (b) the court is satisfied that the case for excluding the statement, taking account of the danger that to admit it would result in undue waste of time, substantially outweighs the case for admitting it, taking account of the value of the evidence.

The exclusion applies to any hearsay evidence that would otherwise be admitted in criminal proceedings. Therefore, it could restrict the admissibility of hearsay evidence admitted under a common law exception preserved under s 118 as much as under any hearsay admitted under the CJA 2003. The section also applies to restrict hearsay evidence irrespective of which party is seeking to adduce it.

The meaning of the subsection is less than clear. There are two possibilities:

(a) There is a broad discretion to exclude evidence if the case for admitting the evidence is 'substantially outweighed' by the case for excluding it. The 'waste of time' and 'value of the evidence' are merely factors to be taken into account among other factors in exercising this discretion.

(b) There is a narrow discretion to exclude evidence where the risk of time being wasted creates a case for excluding the evidence that substantially outweighs the case for admitting it, having regard to the value of the evidence.

The authors of *Blackstone's Guide to the Criminal Justice Act 2003*, Oxford University Press, 2004 favour the broader ground not least because of the need to provide the safeguards of the Article 6 right to fair trial. In addition to this, if the narrow interpretation is correct there is no specific provision within the CJA 2003 for the exclusion of evidence on the grounds that the evidence jeopardises the right to a fair trial or that it is contrary to the interests of justice. Evidence admitted under the Criminal Justice Act 1988, ss 23 and 24 could be excluded under ss 25 and 26 of that Act, having regard to the interests of justice. These provisions were interpreted to preserve the right to a fair trial. There might be a strong argument that the discretion under the CJA 2003, s 126 was intended by Parliament to continue that protection. That it was s 126 that protected a defendant's Article 6 rights was confirmed in *R v Xhabri* [2006] 1 Cr App R 26.

On the other hand, the CJA 2003, s 126(2) expressly retains the exclusionary discretions that apply the criminal law in general. Section 126(2) provides:

(2) Nothing in this Chapter prejudices—

    (a) any power of a court to exclude evidence under section 78 of the Police and Criminal Evidence Act 1984 (c. 60) (exclusion of unfair evidence), or

    (b) any other power of a court to exclude evidence at its discretion (whether by preventing questions from being put or otherwise).

It is possible that the control over hearsay evidence that was effected by ss 25 and 26 of the Criminal Justice Act 1988 will now be achieved by use of PACE 1984, s 78 and the common law power to exclude evidence where its probative value is outweighed by its prejudicial effect.

Whether it is the CJA 2003, s 126 or PACE 1984, s 78 that allows for the exclusion of evidence in the interests of ensuring a fair trial, it is likely that the principles developed in applying the Criminal Justice Act 1988, ss 25 and 26 will continue to be adopted. These principles are set out at **12.4** above.

12.6.2 Stopping a case

In addition to the power to exclude evidence, the CJA 2003, s 125 provides the court with the power to stop a case where the evidence admitted poses the danger of an unsafe conviction.

Section 125 provides:

(1) *If on a defendant's trial before a judge and jury for an offence the court is satisfied at any time after the close of the case for the prosecution that—*
    (a) *the case against the defendant is based wholly or partly on a statement not made in oral evidence in the proceedings, and*
    (b) *the evidence provided by the statement is so unconvincing that, considering its importance to the case against the defendant, his conviction of the offence would be unsafe,*
    the court must either direct the jury to acquit the defendant of the offence or, if it considers that there ought to be a retrial, discharge the jury.
(2) *Where—*
    (a) *a jury is directed under subsection (1) to acquit a defendant of an offence, and*
    (b) *the circumstances are such that, apart from this subsection, the defendant could if acquitted of that offence be found guilty of another offence, the defendant may not be found guilty of that other offence if the court is satisfied as mentioned in subsection (1) in respect of it.*
(3) . . .
(4) *This section does not prejudice any other power a court may have to direct a jury to acquit a person of an offence or to discharge a jury.*

This section applies only to prosecution evidence (s 125(1)) and only where the case is based 'wholly or partly' on hearsay evidence (s 125(1)(b)). Where that is the case the court must consider both the probative value of the evidence and the importance that it has in determining trial issues. If the court considers it to have minimal probative value to the degree that, due to its importance to the trial issues, it poses the risk of an unsafe conviction, then the court must not simply exclude the evidence but must either direct the jury to acquit the defendant or must discharge the jury and order a retrial. This power is more extensive than the power to acquit following a submission of no case to answer as it can be exercised at any time after the close of the prosecution case.

Where the defendant is acquitted, by virtue of this section, of an offence to which a lesser verdict could be returned, that lesser verdict must not be returned if it also depends on the unconvincing hearsay evidence which has been withdrawn (s 125(2)). Therefore, if the hearsay evidence that is unconvincing relates to the identity of a defendant alleged to have intentionally caused grievous bodily harm on the victim contrary to the Offences Against the Person Act 1861, s 18 the withdrawal of the evidence would not permit a conviction for an offence contrary to the Offences Against the Person Act 1861, s 20. However, if the evidence related to the intention to cause such an injury to the victim, the acquittal for the s 18 offence would not necessarily preclude the jury from continuing to consider the s 20 offence.

12.7 Procedural issues

12.7.1 Documents

A document must be 'proven' before it will be admissible. This means that the significance of the document to the trial issues must be established. Generally, a document is proved by a witness who testifies as to its significance (ie, that the witness wrote it or where the witness found it). However, the CJA 2003, s 133 makes further provision for proof of hearsay in documents:

Where a statement in a document is admissible as evidence in criminal proceedings, the statement may be proved by producing either—

    (a) the document, or

    (b) (whether or not the document exists) a copy of the document or of the material part of it, authenticated in whatever way the court may approve.

Therefore, even if the original exists, the court may accept in evidence a copy or a part of a copy of it.

12.7.2 Capacity

Hearsay evidence should not be used to sidestep the rules on competence of witnesses (see **Chapter 4**). Therefore, the CJA 2003, s 123 creates rules that regulate how the court should proceed when the issue of the competence is raised:

    (1) Nothing in section 116, 119 or 120 makes a statement admissible as evidence if it was made by a person who did not have the required capability at the time when he made the statement.

    (2) Nothing in section 117 makes a statement admissible as evidence if any person who, in order for the requirements of section 117(2) to be satisfied, must at any time have supplied or received the information concerned or created or received the document or part concerned—

        (a) did not have the required capability at that time, or

        (b) cannot be identified but cannot reasonably be assumed to have had the required capability at that time.

    (3) For the purposes of this section a person has the required capability if he is capable of—

        (a) understanding questions put to him about the matters stated, and

        (b) giving answers to such questions which can be understood.

    (4) Where by reason of this section there is an issue as to whether a person had the required capability when he made a statement—

        (a) proceedings held for the determination of the issue must take place in the absence of the jury (if there is one);

        (b) in determining the issue the court may receive expert evidence and evidence from any person to whom the statement in question was made;

        (c) the burden of proof on the issue lies on the party seeking to adduce the statement, and the standard of proof is the balance of probabilities.

This section does not apply in relation to statements admitted as exceptions to the rule against hearsay preserved under the CJA 2003, s 118.

Those classes of evidence that are primarily directed at first-hand hearsay (ss 116, 119 and 120) simply provide that the maker of the statement must be 'capable' of giving evidence when the statement is made for the statement to be admissible. Capability is defined in s 123(3) in similar terms to the competence test under the YJCEA 1999, s 53(3), namely the witness must be able to understand questions put to him and able to give understandable answers to them.

Section 123(2) of the CJA 2003 applies the same test of competence to all persons involved in the transfer of information under the CJA 2003, s 117, that is to say, the supplier of the information and any person who received the information, or created any document containing the information or received any document with the information in it. The relevant time for each person is the point at which they supplied, created or received the information or document. As tracing all persons in a chain of communication would be potentially impossible, s 123 requires the court to consider whether any identifiable person was not capable (s 123(2)(a)) and whether any unidentifiable person 'cannot reasonably be assumed to have the required capability at that time'. It seems likely on the language of paragraph (b) that the courts will be willing to presume that a person was capable unless there is evidence that prevents that being reasonably assumed.

Section 123(4) of the CJA 2003 makes provision for the proof of the capability of the person in question. The issue should be tried in the absence of the jury (s 123(4)(a)) and the burden of proof is upon the party seeking to prove competence on the balance of probabilities irrespective of whether it is the prosecution or defence seeking to adduce the hearsay statement. Clearly, the court cannot (in contrast to practice under the YJCEA 1999, s 53) make its own inquiries as to the competence of the maker, at the time of the making of a statement, given the statement was made some time in the past. The court will be reliant on such direct and circumstantial evidence of the maker's mental state at that time as it can obtain. Note that s 123(4) (b) appears to limit who may testify as to the maker's mental state to experts and the person to whom the statement was made. Alternatively, s123 (4)(b) could be interpreted not to restrict the source of these two types of witness. It is submitted that the latter is the better view: there is no logical reason why other informed witnesses could not testify to relevant facts on such a matter.

12.7.3   Attacking the credibility of the maker of the statement

As was noted at the start of **Chapter 11**, one of the main problems with hearsay evidence is that it is not possible to test the reliability of the statement, or the credibility of the person who made the statement, by cross-examination. Section 124 of the CJA 2003 makes provision for challenges to the credibility of hearsay statements:

(1)   *This section applies if in criminal proceedings—*
    (a)   *a statement not made in oral evidence in the proceedings is admitted as evidence of a matter stated, and*
    (b)   *the maker of the statement does not give oral evidence in connection with the subject matter of the statement.*
(2)   *In such a case—*
    (a)   *any evidence which (if he had given such evidence) would have been admissible as relevant to his credibility as a witness is so admissible in the proceedings;*
    (b)   *evidence may with the court's leave be given of any matter which (if he had given such evidence) could have been put to him in cross-examination as relevant to his credibility as a witness but of which evidence could not have been adduced by the cross-examining party;*
    (c)   *evidence tending to prove that he made (at whatever time) any other statement inconsistent with the statement admitted as evidence is admissible for the purpose of showing that he contradicted himself.*
(3)   *If as a result of evidence admitted under this section an allegation is made against the maker of a statement, the court may permit a party to lead additional evidence of such description as the court may specify for the purposes of denying or answering the allegation.*
(4)   *In the case of a statement in a document which is admitted as evidence under section 117 each person who, in order for the statement to be admissible, must have supplied or received the information concerned or created or received the document or part concerned is to be treated as the maker of the statement for the purposes of subsections (1) to (3) above.*

And the CJA 2003, s 119(2)(c) provides:

(2)   *If in criminal proceedings evidence of an inconsistent statement by any person is given under section 124(2)(c), the statement is admissible as evidence of any matter stated in it of which oral evidence by that person would be admissible.*

Section 124 of the CJA 2003 applies to any hearsay evidence admitted in criminal proceedings. It therefore also applies where the evidence was admitted under one of the exceptions to the rule against hearsay preserved in s 118 as much as it applies to other statements admissible under other sections of the CJA 2003. However, s 124 does not apply where the maker of the statement gives evidence. It, therefore, does not apply where the hearsay statement is admitted under ss 119 or 120. Nor will it apply to hearsay statements admitted under s 118 where the maker is called as a witness (for example where the defendant made a *res gestae* statement and gives evidence at trial as happened, for example, in *R v Glover,* referred to at **12.3.3.3**). In so far as the statement is admitted under s 117, evidence relevant to the credibility of any of the persons involved in the transfer of the information is potentially admissible under this section (s 124(4)).

Section 124(2) makes provision for the challenge of the person in three ways that reflect what could have been done had that person given evidence but in a way that makes allowance for their absence:

(a) Section 124(2)(a) allows evidence which would have been admissible as relevant to his credibility as a witness to be adduced (for example, proof of his bad character under the CJA 2003, s 100 or proof of other facts permitted by the rule against finality).

(b) Section 124(2)(b) allows evidence to be given of a matter which could have been put in cross-examination as relevant to his credibility even though, had the maker actually been a witness at trial, such evidence could not have been adduced. Remember that the rules concerning cross-examination allowed questions to be asked affecting the credit of a party but the rule of finality provided that only some of those matters could be proved in evidence if the witness denied the facts alleged during cross-examination. Because the maker of the statement is not present to give evidence, the questions cannot be put to him. Therefore, s 124(2)(b) allows the evidence to be put before the tribunal of fact. However, to maintain the distinction between those things admissible as exceptions to the rule against finality and those matters which are not, evidence of matters which do not fit within any of those exceptions are only admissible with the leave of the court. For the rule of finality, see **7.8.2** and **Chapter 4**.

(c) Section 124(2)(c) allows proof of previous inconsistent statements. As the maker of the statement is not present to give evidence, the procedure for establishing inconsistency under the Criminal Procedure Act 1865, ss 3, 4 and 5 cannot be adopted. Therefore, a statement inconsistent with the hearsay statement admitted is admissible as of right.

Section 124(3) of the CJA 2003 allows any party to counter the attacks on the credibility of the maker of the statement under s 124(2) by proof of further evidence. The most likely ways in which this could occur would be by proof of previous consistent statements admissible as evidence of rebuttal of an allegation of fabrication under s 120(2) or evidence to disprove the evidence of the defendant's bias, criminality, reputation for untruthfulness or mental instability that would have been admitted as an exception to the rule of finality under s 124(2)(b). Where a party has admitted evidence under s 124(2)(c) to impeach the credibility of the maker of a statement as a substitute for cross-examination, s 124(3) would appear to allow another party (most probably the person who adduced the hearsay statement in the first place) to adduce evidence to counter any such challenge. In so far as this would appear to undermine the rule of finality and that rule's aim to prevent extensive expenditure of time and resources on collateral issues, it should be remembered that the court has the discretion under the CJA 2003, s 126 to exclude evidence having regard to the danger that admitting it would be an 'undue waste of time'.

12.7.4   Rules of court

Section 132 of the CJA 2003 provides for the making of rules of court to regulate the process of proof of hearsay evidence, in particular about procedure to be followed and conditions for admissibility of such evidence (s 132(2)) and the provision of notices (s 132(3)). Section 132(4) provides that a failure of a party to challenge the admissibility of evidence under the notice procedure can amount to agreement as to the admissibility of that evidence.

The effect of failure to comply with the notice provisions is dealt with by the CJA 2003, s 132(5):

> (5)   If a party proposing to tender evidence fails to comply with a prescribed requirement applicable to it—
>   (a)   the evidence is not admissible except with the court's leave;
>   (b)   where leave is given the court or jury may draw such inferences from the failure as appear proper;
>   (c)   the failure may be taken into account by the court in considering the exercise of its powers with respect to costs.
> (6)   In considering whether or how to exercise any of its powers under subsection (5) the court shall have regard to whether there is any justification for the failure to comply with the requirement.
> (7)   A person shall not be convicted of an offence solely on an inference drawn under subsection (5)(b).

CPR, r 34 regulates the notice provisions under the CJA 2003. The rule applies to evidence admitted on all of the grounds under s 114 of the Act and therefore includes evidence admitted as an exception to the rule against hearsay preserved under s 118 by virtue of s 114(1)(b). The notice procedure is as follows:

(a) the prosecution must give notice (under r 34.3) in the Crown Court within 14 days of committal to the Crown Court or an equivalent and in a magistrates' court as part of the disclosure process;

(b) the defendant must give notice of hearsay evidence within 14 days of the prosecution complying or purporting to comply with its obligation (r 34.4);

(c) opposition to hearsay evidence must be given within 14 days of receipt of notice (r 34.5)

The court has the power to vary notice (r 34.7) and any party may waive their entitlement to notice (r 34.8). The court, in exercising the power to vary notice will have to have regard to the overriding objective of dealing with cases justly (rr 1.1 and 1.3).

12.8   Other statutory exceptions to the rule against hearsay in criminal cases

With the exception of confessions (which are covered in **Chapter 13**) the statutory exceptions to the rule against hearsay in criminal cases all relate to documentary evidence. Other statutes have created exceptions to the rule against hearsay, including:

(a) the Bankers' Books Evidence Act 1879, ss 3 and 4, which provide for the use of bankers books to evidence banking transactions;

(b) the Magistrates' Courts Act 1980, ss 5A–5F, which creates comprehensive rules for the admissibility of documentary evidence at committal proceedings in the magistrates' court;

(c) The Criminal Justice Act 1967, s 9, which provides that the written statement of a witness shall be admissible 'as evidence to the like extent as oral evidence' of the maker. This will only happen, however, if no other party has objected to the use of the statement instead of calling the witness. See **4.3.1.1**;

(d) The Theft Act 1984, s 27(4), which provides for the proof of facts by statutory declarations relating to goods in transmission.

The above list is far from comprehensive. See *Archbold* for a more extensive list and *Blackstone's Criminal Practice*, for a more extensive consideration of documentary evidence in criminal cases.

Confessions and illegally or improperly obtained evidence

13.1 Confessions

The admissibility of a confession is governed by PACE 1984.

13.1.1 The definition of confession

Section 82(1) of PACE provides that:

'confession' includes any statement wholly or partly adverse to the person who made it, whether made to a person in authority or not and whether made in words or otherwise.

This is a very wide definition. However, the leading case, *R v Sat-Bhambra* (1988) 88 Cr App R 44, notes that there is a restriction on confessions to the extent that the statement must have been adverse *when made*. Therefore, statements that were favourable when made, eg false alibis, but later proved to be adverse are not confessions: *R v Park* (1995) 99 Cr App R 270.

The whole statement is admissible, therefore a statement that is partly exculpatory and partly adverse (ie, mixed) cannot be divided and is taken as one confession: *R v Garrod* [1997] Crim LR 445. See **6.2.4.2** for more detail on mixed statements.

13.1.1.1 Section 76(1), PACE 1984

Section 76(1), PACE 1984 provides that:

In any proceedings a confession made by an accused person may be given in evidence against him in so far as it is relevant to any matter in issue in the proceedings and is not excluded by the court in pursuance of this section.

Generally speaking, confession must be based on facts that are known by the person who makes it. In *R v Hulbert* (1979) 69 Cr App R 243, the defendant was charged with handling stolen goods and confessed that the person from whom she bought the goods told her that they were stolen. This confession could not prove that the goods were stolen, but only went to Hulbert's knowledge of the goods.

If a confession made by an accused person is evidence against him, it follows that the tribunal of fact must be satisfied that the accused was the person who made the admission before they can use the statement as confession evidence against him. Thus, where the evidence of the identity of the maker of a confession comes from the confession itself, logic would seem to dictate that the confession should not be admitted. However, in *R v Ward* [2001] Crim LR 316, the accused denied being the person to whom a certain police officer had spoken on a particular occasion. It was held that the accused's statement to the police officer, giving his name and address, was admissible as a confession proving that the accused was the person to whom the officer had spoken. The Court of Appeal recognised that there was some circularity in its reasoning.

13.1.1.2   The confession is only admissible against the defendant who made it

A confession made by one defendant is generally not evidence against a co-defendant. However, when the statement is made in the presence of the co-accused and he acknowledges the incriminating parts so as to make them, in effect, his own, the statement will be admissible against both parties. Note also that evidence that a co-accused gives on oath is evidence for all purposes, including being evidence against the accused: *R v Rudd* (1948) 32 Cr App R 138.

Where X makes adverse statements about Y, X is entitled to have the whole confession statement admitted even when parts incriminate Y: *R v Pearce* (1979) 69 Cr App R 365. Y is only protected by a direction by the judge to state that the confession is not evidence against Y.

The question of whether a statement should be edited was raised in *R v Silcot* [1987] Crim LR 765, where it was suggested that the trial judge had a discretion whether to order editing. However, in *Lobban v R* [1995] 2 All ER 602, the Privy Council held that the discretion to exclude by balancing the probative value and prejudicial effect applies only to prosecution evidence and there is therefore no discretion in regard to defence evidence. This case was decided before the Human Rights Act 1998. It is possible that were the case to be heard now, the result might be different.

13.1.2   Statutory restrictions on admissibility of confessions (s 76(1), PACE 1984)

Section 76(1) is subject to subsection 76(2) which provides grounds on which such evidence will be excluded. Further, ss 78 and 82(3) provide discretionary grounds by which a confession may be excluded. The prosecution do not have to prove the admissibility of a confession unless:

* the defence raised an argument under s 76(2); or
* the court requires proof of admissibility.

The standard of proof is beyond reasonable doubt.

Further, the Codes of Practice provided for under PACE 1984 give weight to this issue. Section 67(11), PACE 1984, provides that the court *shall* take account of the codes in determining any question (where relevant) arising in any proceedings.

13.1.2.1   The first barrier to admissibility, s 76(2) and (3), PACE 1984

(2)   If, in any proceedings where the prosecution proposes to give evidence of a confession made by an accused person, it is represented to the court that the confession was or may have been obtained—

(a)   by oppression of the person who made it; or

(b)   in consequence of anything said or done which was likely, in the circumstances existing at the time, to render unreliable any confession which might be made by him in consequence thereof, the court shall not allow the confession to be given in evidence against him except insofar as the prosecution proves to the court beyond reasonable doubt that the confession (notwithstanding that it may be true) was not obtained as aforesaid.

(3)   In any proceedings where the prosecution proposes to give in evidence a confession made by an accused person, the court may of its own motion require the prosecution as a condition of allowing it to do so, to prove that the confession was not obtained as mentioned in subsection (2).

13.1.2.2   Making an objection under s 76

The leading case, pre-PACE 1984, in relation to the admissibility of confessions was *Adjodha v The State* [1982] AC 204, PC. In this case Lord Bridge indicated that the confession should not be opened to the jury and the issue of admissibility would be resolved by a *voir dire*. A confession could be excluded where its 'voluntariness' was in doubt.

After PACE 1984 was enacted the procedure in *Adjodha* was followed. However, the case of *R v Sat-Bhambra* made no reference to *Adjodha* and did not see the defendant's position as one of choice. If there was to be an objection under s 76, the time to take the objection was before the confession was given in evidence. The court went on to state that where a confession was admitted, following an objection or not, if during the course of the trial it emerged that the issue of admissibility was in doubt, the judge was precluded from reopening the s 76 issue. However, the judge could direct the jury in several ways:

- to disregard the statement;
- direct their attention to the matters which might affect the weight attached to the confession; or
- if the matter could not be solved by a suitable direction, he could discharge the jury.

The judge's power to do the above derives from the preservation of the common law, under s 82(3), PACE 1984, to take such steps that are necessary to prevent injustice.

13.1.2.3   Oppression and reliability in s 76(2)

Oppression is defined in s 76(8) of PACE 1984 as 'torture, inhuman or degrading treatment, and the use or threat of violence (whether or not amounting to torture)'.

In *R v Fulling* [1987] QB 426, Lord Lane held that 'oppression' was to be given its ordinary dictionary meaning:

The Oxford English Dictionary as its third definition of the word runs as follows: 'exercise of authority or power in a burdensome, harsh, or wrongful manner; unjust or cruel treatment of subjects, inferiors, etc., or the imposition of unreasonable or unjust burdens'.

There is no reference to Article 3 of the ECHR, nor are the words 'the use or threat of violence' further defined in PACE 1984. 'Torture' is a criminal offence under s 134, Criminal Justice Act 1988 and 'violence' or 'force' is broadly defined in s 8, Public Order Act 1986 (where it includes violent conduct to property and person).

In *R v Paris* (1992) 97 Cr App R 99, CA, the fact that the defendant had a solicitor present did not deprive the interview of its oppressive character. The police had continued to shout at the suspect even though he had denied the charge over 300 times.

In *R v Parker* [1995] Crim LR 223, CA, and *Re Proulx* [2001] 1 All ER 57, it was held that any breach of the PACE Codes of Practice would not automatically exclude the confession. It was important to look at the context in which the term oppression was used to judge whether or not the confession had been obtained by oppression.

The assessment as to the nature of 'oppression' varies according to the character and attributes of the accused. In *R v Miller* [1986] 1 WLR 1191, it was said per Watkins LJ that it might be oppressive to put questions to an accused who is known to be mentally ill so as to 'skilfully and deliberately' induce a delusionary state in him. In *R v Seelig* [1992] 1 WLR 128, Henry J took account of the fact that the accused was an 'experienced merchant banker' and was 'intelligent and sophisticated' when he assessed whether he had been questioned in an oppressive way.

When considering the issue of the reliability of a confession, reference to pre-PACE 1984 law may be made to see whether the test has been passed. *R v Phillips* (1988) 86 Cr App R 18,

CA relates to inducements: promises of bail and taking further offences into consideration, leading to unreliable confession. *R v Prager* (1972) 56 Cr App R 151 states 'questioning which by its nature or duration…excites hope (such as hope of release) or fears, or so affects the mind of the subject that his will crumbles and he speaks when otherwise he would have stayed silent'.

Therefore, s 76 (2)(b), unlike s 76 (2)(a), may be inadmissible *without any impropriety*.

The case of *R v Barry* (1992) 95 Cr App R 384 sets out some useful guidelines when considering the reliability of a confession taken during police interview:

1. Identify the thing 'said or done' (the judge must take into account everything 'said or done' by the police).

2. Ask whether or not the thing 'said or done' was likely in the circumstances to render unreliable any confession made in consequence.

3. Ask whether the prosecution have proved beyond reasonable doubt that the confession was not obtained in consequence of the thing 'said or done'.

(1) and (2) are objective and the third step is a question of fact. See Code C, PACE 1984.

The words 'said or done' do not include anything said or done by the person making the confession: *R v Goldenberg* (1989) 88 Cr App R 285, CA. In this case a heroin addict was interviewed at a time when he may have been withdrawing from the effects of heroin. The police agreed that they would not have interviewed him if they had known he was withdrawing. However, the fact that the section states 'in consequence of' meant that a causal link had to be shown between what was said and done and therefore it followed that the words 'said or done' were limited to something external to the person making the confession.

Breaches of PACE Code C can amount to 'things done'. Examples include a failure to caution a suspect (*R v Doolan* [1988] Crim LR 747, CA) or improper denial of access to a solicitor (*R v McGovern* (1991) 92 Cr App R 228, CA). The test is whether the breach is significant: see *R v Delaney* (1989) 88 Cr App R 338, CA, where a confession made at the end of an interview which had not been recorded in accordance with Code C was ruled inadmissible. In *R v M* [2000] 8 Archbold News 2, M's solicitor, by intervening in the interview in an attempt to secure a confession, rendered the resultant confession unreliable.

13.1.2.4 Mentally handicapped persons

Section 77, PACE 1984 states 'the court shall warn the jury that there is a special need for caution before convicting the accused in reliance on the confession'. If the judge fails to give this warning it is likely that the conviction will be quashed: *R v Lamont* [1989] Crim LR 813, CA. See **5.5**.

The provisions for mentally handicapped and mentally disordered persons can be found in PACE Code C and are summarised in Annex E.

13.1.2.5 Confessions tendered by a co-accused

In *R v Myers* [1998] AC 124, HL, it was held that where the accused has made a confession, and that that confession is relevant to the defence of a co-accused, then the co-accused will be allowed to adduce evidence of that confession unless the way in which it was obtained would have rendered it inadmissible at the hands of the prosecution by virtue of PACE 1984, s 76(2). However, where a confession is inadmissible for the prosecution under PACE 1984, s 78, it could still be admissible for the co-accused. A modified version of this rule has been put on a statutory footing in PACE 1984, s 76A which was inserted by the CJA 2003. Section 76A provides:

(1) *In any proceedings a confession made by an accused person may be given in evidence for another person charged in the same proceedings (a co-accused) in so far as it is relevant to any matter in issue in the proceedings and is not excluded by the court in pursuance of this section.*

(2) *If, in any proceedings where a co-accused proposes to give in evidence a confession made by an accused person, it is represented to the court that the confession was or may have been obtained—*

    (a) *by oppression of the person who made it; or*

    (b) *in consequence of anything said or done which was likely, in the circumstances existing at the time, to render unreliable any confession which might be made by him in consequence thereof, the court shall not allow the confession to be given in evidence for the co-accused except in so far as it is proved to the court on the balance of probabilities that the confession (notwithstanding that it may be true) was not so obtained.*

13.1.3 The discretion(s) to exclude

Section 78, PACE 1984 provides that:

(1) *In any proceedings the court may refuse to allow evidence on which the prosecution proposes to rely to be given if it appears to the court that, having regard to all the circumstances, including the circumstances in which the evidence was obtained, the admission of the evidence would have such an adverse effect on the fairness of the proceedings that the court ought not to admit it.*

(2) *Nothing in this section shall prejudice any rule of law requiring a court to exclude evidence.*

Section 82(3), PACE 1984 preserves the common law discretion to exclude evidence pre-PACE 1984 and provides that:

Nothing in part of this Act shall prejudice any power of a court to exclude evidence (whether by preventing questions being put or otherwise) at its discretion.

13.1.3.1 Section 78 and the *voir dire*

A *voir dire* is necessary in the Crown Court to determine whether a confession should be excluded under s 78. However, s 78 has no application when magistrates are acting as examining justices, ie, in committal proceedings (Criminal Procedure and Investigations Act 1996, sch 1, para 26).

13.1.3.2 Deprivation of rights under the 1984 Act and Code C

The discretion to exclude a confession is likely to be exercised when deliberate impropriety or bad faith has obtained the confession and this has resulted in unfairness. Therefore, the fact that there has been a breach of the Code or a defendant's rights have been infringed by the actions of the police does not automatically lead to exclusion under s 78. Since the Human Rights Act 1998, the courts should be more 'rights oriented' in their application of s 78. One obvious example of this is where a confession has been obtained after an unjustified refusal of access to a solicitor.

13.1.3.3 Rights of access

A person who is arrested and held in custody at a police station has a right, at his request, to consult with a solicitor at any time, privately (s 58, PACE 1984). Article 6(3), ECHR requires that consultation must take place out of the hearing of a third party (in particular a police officer): *Brennan v UK* (2002) 34 EHRR 507. In the magistrates' court it is not a statutory right but it is a common law right to have access to a solicitor as soon as is reasonably practicable.

The right is a right to advice and not to be present during interview; however, Code C, para 6.8 states that if the detainee has requested a solicitor and the solicitor is present before the interview starts, the detainee *must* be allowed to have the solicitor present during the interview.

The police may refuse access on the ground that allowing a particular individual access to the detainee may prejudice the investigation: *R (Thompson) v Chief Constable of the Northumberland Constabulary* [2001] 1 WLR 1342. In *Samuel* [1988] QB 615, the Court of Appeal stated that if the police seek to deny access to a solicitor they must show more than a substantial risk of their fears being realised. If delay is authorised, the reasons must be given and noted in the custody record.

13.1.4 Effects of excluding a confession

Section 76(4), (5) and (6) provides that:

(4) *The fact that a confession is wholly or partly excluded in pursuance of this section shall not affect the admissibility in evidence—*

  (a) *of any facts discovered as a result of the confession; or*

  (b) *where the confession is relevant as showing that the accused speaks, writes or expresses himself in a particular way, of so much of the confession as is necessary to show that he does so.*

(5) *Evidence that a fact to which this subsection applies was discovered as a result of a statement made by an accused person shall not be admissible unless evidence of how it was discovered is given by him or on his behalf.*

(6) *Subsection (5) applies—*

  (a) *to any fact discovered as a result of a confession which is wholly excluded in pursuance of the section; and*

  (b) *to any fact discovered as a result of a confession which is partly so excluded, if the fact is discovered as a result of the excluded part of the confession.*

These provisions have no effect in committal proceedings, as examining magistrates cannot rule on the admissibility of a confession.

The effect of s 76(4) to (6) is that, even where the confession is excluded, facts discovered as a result of the confession are admissible. However, the prosecution cannot prove that those facts were discovered due to the making of the excluded confession. If the confession is excluded under s 78, then s 76(4) to (6) cannot be invoked. However, the common law principles of relevance will apply should the prosecution wish to admit facts arising from the confession. Furthermore, any evidence obtained as a result of a confession excluded under s 78 may also be subject to a s 78 argument.

13.2 Illegally or improperly obtained evidence other than confessions

It is well established that a judge has, under his overriding duty to ensure a fair trial, a discretion to exclude evidence that may be admissible prosecution evidence where the prejudicial effect of the evidence outweighs its probative value. This principle is applied on a case by case basis.

Where the police or state has obtained evidence unlawfully or improperly, a s 78 application may be made to exclude the evidence. In *R v Sang* [1980] AC 402, the House of Lords held that at *common law* the court did not have a discretion to exclude this type of evidence unless its probative value was outweighed by its prejudicial effect or the evidence could be equated with a confession. An example of the latter is where a defendant was induced into providing a specimen, which was then used to show that he was unfit to drive: *R v Payne* [1963] 1 WLR 637.

Under both case law and recent legislation, the defendant is not *entitled* to have unlawfully obtained evidence excluded simply because it has been so obtained,

R v P [2002] 1 AC 146 and the Regulation of Investigatory Powers Act 2000. Therefore, any s 78 application to exclude unlawful or improperly obtained evidence must turn on its facts.

In *R v Khan (Sultan)* [1997] AC 558, the House of Lords upheld the Court of Appeal decision that evidence obtained by a bugging device, attached by the police to a private house without the knowledge of the owner, was admissible. Lord Nolan (at p 582) stated that the significance of any breach of any relevant law or convention will normally be determined by its effect on the fairness of the proceedings rather than its irregularity or unlawfulness. This case went to the European Court: *Khan v UK* [2000] Crim LR 684. The case was that there had been a breach of Article 8, respect for private life and therefore a breach of Article 6(1), fair trial. The court decided that there was no breach of Article 6, despite finding that the UK had violated Article 8. Since this decision, the Regulation of Investigatory Powers Act 2000 now governs the actions of the police for covert surveillance.

In *R v Smurthwaite; R v Gill* (1994) 98 Cr App R 437, CA, the court held that entrapment itself did not result in the exclusion of evidence but laid down a number of criteria that should be followed by the police, the first criterion being whether the officer enticed the defendant to commit an offence he would not otherwise have committed. *R v Loosely; Attorney General's Reference (No 3 of 2000)* [2002] 1 Cr App R 29 reviewed the issue of entrapment and Lord Hoffman stated that the more appropriate remedy in cases of entrapment would be staying the prosecution as an abuse of process rather than excluding the evidence. For further comment on abuse of process, see *R v Latif; R v Shahzad* [1996] 2 Cr App R 92, HL.

Lies and silence

14.1 Introduction

In the last chapter we considered how the courts will use confessions obtained (usually but not exclusively) by police officers investigating a criminal offence. Clearly not all persons questioned will confess. Others may seek to lie to deflect the police from investigating them further. So to what extent can the court use the fact either that someone remained silent or lied?

Consider the following scenario:

Ollie is alleged to have stolen a car. When arrested by the police he is in possession of a car radio (that, it later turns out, is the same as the car radio that has been taken from the stolen car). Ollie refuses to say anything about the radio when asked to do so by the police. Ollie is taken to the police station. He is interviewed and says that he does not know anything about the car in question and that when it went missing he was at work. The police tell him (correctly) that they found his wallet in the back of the car. He asks to see his solicitor and, having taken the solicitor's advice, he refuses to answer any other questions.

What if anything does Ollie's conduct prove? How might the following situations change the way in which a tribunal of fact might treat Ollie?

(a) At trial, Ollie alleged that he lied about his whereabouts because he was visiting his girlfriend, of whom his parents do not approve and he didn't want them to know. He found the radio on the road.

(b) In addition to (a) above, his solicitor advised him not to answer any questions because the police officer interviewing him had a reputation for planting evidence.

(c) Instead of (a) and (b) above, Ollie alleges at trial that he did not answer questions because his solicitor advised him that he had a right to remain silent and that it was for the police to obtain all the evidence to prove the case against him without his help.

(d) Instead of (a) to (c) above, Ollie gives no evidence at trial in his own defence but his barrister has cross-examined the police witnesses to suggest that the wallet was planted in the car by racist police officers (Ollie is black and has been in trouble with the police before).

The detail of the answers to these questions will be considered below. However, for the time being, it is worth considering the issues that the questions have raised:

(a) What is the evidential value of a lie? Does it show that the liar is guilty of the offence about which he has lied? Should it be admitted in evidence in a criminal trial?

(b) What is the evidential value of refusing to answer questions or allegations at the time of arrest and questioning?

(c) What is the effect of raising a defence for the first time at trial? Does it show that the accused was trying to hide his defence from the prosecution until he put it before the jury? If so, does that mean that he is more likely to be guilty?

(d) What if the refusal to explain or answer questions is due to legal advice?

(e) What does the fact that an accused person does not testify in his own defence prove? Does this show that he is conscious of his own guilt?

(f) Does it make a difference if a person does not testify but gets his lawyer to advance the defence through cross-examination?

Before looking at these areas in more depth, it should be noted that what this chapter looks at is the evidential value of lies or silence on the part of a party. It is not about the evidential value of the thing that the party lied or was silent about. Consider the example above. Ollie was found with a car radio like the one from the car and his wallet was found in the car. These are items of circumstantial evidence unaffected by the law covered in this chapter. They are admissible in so far as they are relevant. What this chapter considers, amongst other things, is the evidential value of *failures to explain those other items of admissible evidence*. Do not mistake the two (it is very easy to do so).

As is common with the rules of evidence, we shall see that there is a very different approach between the civil and the criminal courts. We shall consider the civil rules first.

14.2 Civil cases

The common law governs the position in civil cases in respect of both lies and silence. The courts have treated the silence or lie like any other item of evidence: it is admissible if it is relevant to a fact in issue and the weight to be attached to it is a matter for the tribunal of fact and will depend on the facts and issues in each case. Examples include:

- *Bessela v Stern* (1877) 2 CPD 265 in which the plaintiff confronted the defendant over a promise to marry her. The defendant's silence was treated as admissible evidence to prove that there had been such a promise because he would have denied that fact if it had not been true.

- *Wiedmann v Walpole* [1891] 2 QB 534 in which the defendant did not reply to an accusatory letter written by the plaintiff. The court held that the letter was not admissible as evidence that the accusations were true. The failure to reply to the letter simply did not go far enough in proving that the accusation was true. There were a number of reasons why a person might not reply to such a letter.

- *Francisco v Diedrick The Times*, 3 April 1998 where a plaintiff had made out a prima facie case, the defendant's failure to testify was circumstantial evidence that supported the plaintiff's case.

14.3 Lies in criminal cases

The evidential value of lies, as opposed to silence, in the face of accusation or questioning, is governed by the common law. Evidence of lies is generally admissible. The statements alleged to be lies will be admissible as original, as opposed to hearsay evidence (see **10.1.3.3**). The rules set out below apply to lies told both outside of court and in the witness box. Further research: see Specimen Direction 27 at www.jsboard.co.uk and *Blackstone's Criminal Practice*, 2006, F1.12.

14.3.1   Directing the jury on lies

Where a lie is admitted, the judge will ensure that the jury is given careful guidance as to how they should deal with it as evidence. The leading case is *R v Lucas* [1981] QB 720, where Lord Lane CJ said (at p 724) that the jury must be directed that to be capable of being evidence against the accused the lie must be:

- deliberate;
- concerned with a material issue in the case;
- motivated by a realisation of guilt and fear of the truth;
- shown to be untrue.

All four matters must be identified to the jury in summing up and they must be told that before they use the alleged lie as evidence of the accused's guilt, they must be satisfied beyond reasonable doubt that the statement is a lie (*R v Burge* [1996] 1 Cr App R 163).

On the issue of the motive for the lie, Lord Lane said:

The jury should in appropriate cases be reminded that people sometimes lie, for example, in an attempt to bolster up a just cause, or out of shame or out of a wish to conceal disgraceful behaviour from their family.

Clearly, a statement made by the defendant that is alleged to be untrue will potentially be a lie within the meaning of *Lucas*. However, what if the statement is made by another person in the presence of the defendant? In *R v Collins* [2004] EWCA Crim 33, C and B were arrested together on suspicion of having recently kidnapped H. When B was asked where he had been he told the police officers (in C's presence) that both he and C had been at a particular public house. However, in interview and at trial C maintained that he had been with H but that he had not kidnapped him. At trial the judge gave a *Lucas* direction against C. The Court of Appeal quashed C's conviction. The court concluded that where a question was asked and an untrue answer was given in the presence of a defendant, the jury could conclude that his reaction to that question and answer could amount to his adoption of that answer, if the jury were satisfied that (a) the question called for some response from the defendant and (b) that by his reaction the defendant had adopted the answer made. In the circumstances of that case the jury had not been properly directed to adopt that approach and in any event there was not sufficient evidence adduced at trial for the jury to reach such a conclusion from the question and answer posed. Clearly, whether this is the case or not will depend on the particular facts of each case.

14.3.2   When a *Lucas* direction is required

The direction set out above is not always necessary. A *Lucas* direction is only required where lies are of direct relevance to the offence charged, eg false alibi (*R v Smith* [1995] Crim LR 305). In *R v Burge* [1996] 1 Cr App R 163 the Court of Appeal identified four situations in which such a direction would be necessary:

(a) where the accused raised an alibi;

(b) where the judge has directed the jury to look for supporting evidence for particular witnesses and has made reference to potential lies as corroboration (on the need for the judge to issue such a direction, see **Chapter 5**);

(c) where the prosecution have sought to rely on an alleged lie as evidence of the accused's guilt;

(d) where the prosecution have not explicitly sought to rely on the alleged lie but there is a real danger that the jury will do so.

Situation (d) mentioned in *R v Burge* clearly places an obligation on the trial judge to consider the likely effect of any untrue statements made during or before trial. In *R v Nash* [2004] EWCA Crim 164, no *Lucas* direction was given. The defendant was charged with criminal damage, it being alleged that he had fired pellets from an airgun at car windows. The only evidence against the defendant was that (a) he was seen near the scene of the crime acting suspiciously, (b) he denied owning an air rifle and (c) an air rifle was found at his flat. The Court of Appeal concluded that, in such circumstances, a direction should have been given as there was a real danger that the jury might use the defendant's lie as evidence of guilt even though the prosecution did not so rely upon it.

The list identified in *R v Burge* is not exhaustive. In *R v Jefford* [2003] EWCA Crim 1987, the Court of Appeal noted that the categories identified in *Burge* did not reduce the general principle that a direction is required where there is a danger that the jury may regard the fact that the defendant has told lies as probative of his guilt. In any such situation, a *Lucas* direction may be required. In *Jefford*, the need for the direction arose as a result of the significance that the judge attached to potential lies and inconsistencies even though the prosecution had placed no particular reliance upon those lies.

Although it should generally be clear whether such situations arise in each case, this may not always be so. The court in *R v Burge* stated that the judge and counsel should consider the need for a *Lucas* direction before the judge starts summing up. Further, the Court of Appeal would generally be unwilling to overturn a conviction due to the lack of a *Lucas* direction if defence counsel did not identify the need for one at trial. This is because the lawyers and the trial judge are in a better position than the Court of Appeal to evaluate the issues and to determine whether a *Lucas* direction should have been given in any particular case. If the lawyers did not identify the need for a direction at trial, the Court of Appeal is unlikely to conclude that the absence of a direction renders a conviction unsafe (*R v McGuinness* [1999] Crim LR 318).

On some occasions where the jury rejects the accused's account (ie, concludes he is lying) they will have no choice but to convict. In such circumstances, there is no need for the judge to direct the jury in respect of the lie (*R v Patrick* [1999] 6 Archbold News 4). Clearly, as the effect of rejecting the defence case is the conviction of the accused, there is little purpose to be served by also considering whether the lie is evidence that the accused was guilty of the offence.

14.4 Silence in criminal cases

Parliament has created a number of rules that allow the failure of the accused to answer allegations to be admitted as evidence of the accused's guilt.

It is not difficult to understand why a lie might prove that a person is guilty of an offence. A lie suggests that the person lying is trying to cover up for their guilty behaviour. But what about a refusal to answer questions or to explain matters? Clearly, it is possible to infer from such silence that the suspect does not have an explanation that will stand up to scrutiny. However, there are numerous reasons why a person might refuse to answer questions or explain incriminating evidence and being guilty is only one of them. Therefore, as we shall see, the courts have sought to ensure that juries are carefully directed only to use silence as evidence if any innocent explanations have been rejected.

Furthermore, using the silence of the accused as evidence of guilt offends some fundamental principles of the criminal justice process. Clearly, such evidence runs contrary to the right to silence and the privilege against self-incrimination. These principles are enshrined in Article 6 of the ECHR. For this reason the statutory provisions set out below have been the subject of regular scrutiny to determine whether they comply with the right to a fair trial.

Instead of a single rule relating to inferences from silence, Parliament has provided different rules for inferences to be drawn in respect of silence at different stages in the criminal process. These stages are dealt with below.

14.4.1 Silence upon being questioned

Inferences may be drawn in certain circumstances if the accused has not explained his defence at an early opportunity; see, generally, *Blackstone's Criminal Practice*, 2006, F19. Before considering when this might happen, it is worth making sure that you understand the powers of the police to question suspects. Have a look at the *Criminal Litigation and Sentencing Manual*, **Chapter 2**, and *Blackstone's Criminal Practice*, 2006, D7.52.

14.4.1.1 The Criminal Justice and Public Order Act 1994, s 34

Section 34 of the Criminal Justice and Public Order Act 1994 states:

(1) *Where, in any proceedings against a person for an offence, evidence is given that the accused—*
   (a) *at any time before he was charged with the offence, on being questioned under caution by a constable trying to discover whether or by whom the offence had been committed, failed to mention any fact relied on in his defence in those proceedings; or*
   (b) *on being charged with the offence or officially informed that he might be prosecuted for it, failed to mention any such fact,*

   . . .
(2) *Where this subsection applies—*

   . . .
   (c) *the court, in determining whether there is a case to answer; and*
   (d) *the court or jury, in determining whether the accused is guilty of the offence charged, may draw such inferences from the failure as appear proper.*

Section 34 places a suspect under an obligation to explain his potential defence under specified circumstances. These circumstances will be discussed in more detail below. The duty is not absolute. There is no automatic sanction for failing to explain a defence: the failure to mention a fact simply allows the tribunal of fact the option of treating that failure as something that can strengthen the prosecution case.

14.4.1.2 No inference will be drawn if the fact relied on is true

In *R v Wisdom* (CA, 10 December 1989) it was stated that no inference should be drawn under s 34 if the fact in question has been shown to be true. This was approved in *R v Webber* [2004] 1 All ER 770.

14.4.1.3 The timing of the duty to explain

The court can draw inferences from the accused's failure to explain defences in two situations:

- upon being questioned, but only if—
  - the accused has been cautioned,
  - the accused has not yet been charged with the offence;
- upon being charged with the offence.

Therefore, not all questions asked by a police officer are covered by s 34. There are situations in which questioning is possible both before caution and after charge (for detail, see Code C of the PACE Codes of Practice). However, in such situations s 34 will not apply. To the extent that the prosecution seek to rely on a failure to provide answers to questions in those non-s 34 situations the common law rules apply (see below).

The text of the caution is:

You do not have to say anything. But it may harm your defence if you do not mention when questioned something which you later rely on in court. Anything you do say may be given in evidence. (PACE Code C, para 10.4)

It is likely that the second situation (failure to mention facts in response to charge) would arise in the sort of situations where the police did not feel that there was a need to question the accused because they have sufficient evidence to charge the defendant. It would be rare for an inference to be drawn in this situation as under para 16.1 of Code C, even if the police have sufficient evidence to charge, they should only do so if 'the person has said all he wishes to say'. However, s 34(1)(b) will also apply if no inferences can be drawn from the interview because it has been excluded under s 78 (see **Chapter 13**). In those circumstances, inferences can be drawn from the failure to mention a defence on charge even though the accused was questioned fully prior to charge (*R v Dervish* [2002] 2 Cr App R 105).

Note that s 34 applies to situations in which the prosecution will be commenced other than by charging the accused (see the *Criminal Litigation and Sentencing Manual*, **Chapter 2**). In such circumstances the obligation to explain facts arises upon the accused being told he will be prosecuted.

14.4.1.4   The fact that is not mentioned must later be relied upon as part of a defence

This is a very important feature of s 34. Inferences cannot be drawn simply because the accused did not answer questions during interview (or upon caution). They may only be drawn if the accused:

- relies on a fact in his defence; and
- did not mention that fact when questioned under caution or charged.

In other words, it is the last-minute use of a defence (or facts supporting a defence) that leads to the inference rather than the simple exercise of the right to silence. But in what circumstances has a person relied upon a fact in his defence? Where the accused gives evidence, this is relatively simple. But what if either the accused does not give evidence or the question as to s 34 inferences arises before the accused has had an opportunity to do so (for example during a submission of no case to answer)?

Think again about the case concerning Ollie at **14.1**. Have a look at situations (a) and (d) identified there. In which of the two situations does Ollie rely on a fact in his defence?

In situation (a), it is clear that Ollie has relied upon an alibi defence (he was visiting his girlfriend) and also that he found the radio on the road. In addition to any adverse inferences that might result from having lied, he could be subject to adverse inferences under s 34.

Situation (d) has presented more difficulty for the courts. To what extent does a defendant rely on a fact if he does not give evidence or call any witnesses? Does cross-examination of the police witnesses that the wallet was planted amount to reliance upon a fact? In *R v Webber* [2004] 1 All ER 770, the House of Lords considered the meaning of 'fact' within s 34 at some length. Lord Bingham said (at [33]) that the word 'fact' in s 34: 'should be given a broad and not a narrow or pedantic meaning. The word covers any alleged fact which is in issue and is put forward as part of the defence case: if the defendant advances at trial any pure fact or exculpatory explanation or account which, if it were true, he could reasonably have been expected to advance earlier, s 34 is potentially applicable.' For this reason, the House concluded that a party relies on a fact within the meaning of s 34 not only when the defendant gives evidence of that fact but also when the defendant's advocate 'puts a specific and positive case to prosecution witnesses, as opposed to asking questions intended to probe or test the prosecution case' and that was the case whether or not the witness in question accepted the allegation put to them by defence counsel.

It is therefore necessary to distinguish between cross-examination that tests the prosecution evidence (such as suggesting that an identification witness was mistaken) and cross-examination that suggests a positive defence (putting to the same witness that the accused was at another place at the time of the offence). The former will not amount to reliance on a fact under s 34 but the latter probably will.

The use of the phrase 'facts relied on in defence' may appear to give the prosecution and the court an opportunity to invoke s 34 whenever there is a small detail raised by the defendant at trial that he did not mention during a previous interview. However, in *R v Brizzalari* [2004] EWCA Crim 310, the Court of Appeal recognised that it was a matter for the trial judge to determine whether facts mentioned by the defendant were sufficiently important to fall within s 34.

14.4.1.5 The failure to mention the fact must be unreasonable

Section 34 states that a fact which is not mentioned must be 'a fact which in the circumstances existing at the time the accused could reasonably have been expected to mention'.

In many cases, the defendant will have a reason for having failed to answer questions which should be presented to the jury and which the jurors must consider. In *R v Cowan* [1996] 1 Cr App R 1, a case concerning s 35 of the 1994 Act, which also allows adverse inferences to be drawn unless there are good reasons for the defendant's silence, it was noted that there would have to be evidence before the jury of the reasons for silence. It was not possible for counsel simply to give those reasons in the absence of an evidential foundation.

In *R v Nickolson* [1999] Crim LR 61, the Court of Appeal held that a suspect could not be expected to give an innocent explanation of potentially incriminating evidence that was not presented to him at interview.

In *R v Turner* [2004] 1 All ER 1025, the Court of Appeal stated that, where possible, the prosecution should challenge the defendant about any unmentioned fact in cross-examination and give the defendant an opportunity to provide an explanation.

It would appear that s 34 will not apply if the accused mentioned the fact in a prepared statement even if he then refuses to answer questions (*R v Ali* [2001] All ER (D) 16).

Have another look at the scenarios concerning Ollie at **14.1**. Now consider situations (a), (b) and (c). In which of those situations should the jury be allowed to draw an adverse inference from Ollie's failure to explain his defence at the police station?

In relation to situation (a), the reason Ollie did not give the real explanation was fear of his parents. It will be a matter for the jury as to whether they believe this explanation. If not, they may decide that he did not give his defence because he was guilty. Note the similarity of approach adopted in relation to the lie he told: the jury will have to decide whether his reason for lying or not mentioning a fact was a consciousness of guilt. It should also be noted that no explanation appears to have been given for the failure to explain the radio. As he has not put forward any reason for failing to mention how he came by the incriminating radio, the jury would simply have to decide whether his failure to mention the finding of the radio was evidence that he might be guilty of the offence. In other words, where the defendant attempts to give an explanation for his failure to mention facts at trial, the jury will have to undertake a more complicated analysis before drawing adverse inferences against him.

In situations (b) and (c) Ollie's failure to put forward defences at the police station *are* explained at trial. However, the jury is not bound to accept the reasons he gives. Even legal advice does not determine whether or not inferences should be drawn. In *R v Condron* [1997] 1 Cr App R 185, two suspects being investigated for drug offences had been interviewed under caution but both remained silent. At trial the two accused put forward innocent explanations of all the prosecution evidence, which explanations could have been given at the police station. They also testified that their solicitor had advised them not to answer questions because he felt that they were suffering from heroin withdrawal. The police (acting on the advice of the police doctor) had decided the suspects were fit to be interviewed. The jury was directed that they could draw an inference from the failure of the accused to explain their defences at the police station. The Court of Appeal affirmed their convictions. Legal advice could not determine whether or not s 34 applied. Instead, the jury should have regard to the reasons given by the accused (including legal advice) and consider whether it is the legal advice or the consciousness of guilt that is the reason for the failure to mention the fact. The matter was taken to the European Court of Human Rights (*Condron & Condron v UK* [2000] Crim LR 677) where it was decided that it was necessary that the jury be directed that they should only draw an adverse inference if they concluded (beyond reasonable doubt) that the *only* reason for failing to mention the fact was that the suspect had no answer to the questions (or none that would stand up to cross-examination). See *R v Daly* [2002] 2 Cr App R 201 and *R v Petkar* [2004] 1 Cr App R 270.

In *R v Argent* [1997] Crim LR 346, the Court of Appeal stated that the jury should take into consideration the circumstances in which advice was given and the personality of the accused in deciding the real reason for remaining silent. It was also said that the reasons for the legal advice should not determine whether or not adverse inferences should be drawn. The jury should not be concerned with the correctness of the advice but its impact upon the accused's conduct at the police station. Therefore it is not the fact (or the accuracy) of the legal advice that determines whether or not it amounts to a good reason for remaining silent. Rather, the jury will have to consider whether the advice was the cause of the silence or whether it was some other matter and should only infer guilt where they conclude that the other reason was the guilty mind of the accused. As it was put by the Court of Appeal in *Beckles* [2005] 1 Cr App R 23, the jury should be told to consider whether the defendant had 'genuinely and reasonably relied' on the legal advice given to him. There is no real difference between situations (b) and (c) except in so far as the jury is likely to accept one or the other as more or less likely to have influenced Ollie's decision. The fact that the advice in situation (c) is clearly wrong (in that it overlooks s 34) is simply a matter for the jury to take into account.

As legal advice can (but not must) be a good reason for failing to mention a fact it will occasionally be necessary to prove what legal advice was given. The accused could testify as to what his legal adviser told him (this would not be hearsay evidence because it is admitted to prove the fact not the truth of the advice: see **Chapter 11**). However, it may be necessary to call the legal adviser to testify as to what advice he gave to assist in deciding whether the decision to remain silent was really based on the legal advice given (*R v Roble* [1997] Crim LR 449). In *R v Bowden* [1999] 4 All ER 43, it was said that where the accused or his solicitor had given evidence as to not just the fact of advice having been given to keep silent but also the reasons for that advice, the accused 'voluntarily withdrew the veil of privilege and having done so could not resist questioning directed to the nature of that advice and the factual premises on which it was based' (per Lord Bingham CJ at p 47). While it is not generally permissible for one party to enquire into the legal advice that another has received (see legal professional privilege in **Chapter 18**), it is possible for this rule to be waived and following *R v Bowden* the giving of evidence as to the legal advice received constitutes such waiver. The witness (whether the solicitor or his or her client) could be cross-examined about that advice.

14.4.1.6   The nature of the questioning

Section 34 only applies if the questioning relates to whether or by whom the offence has been committed. A failure to explain other matters cannot be used to support an inference under s 34 (although it may do so at common law: see **14.4.1.10**).

14.4.1.7   Who must conduct the questioning

While s 34(1) refers to a constable, the section also applies to 'persons (other than constables) charged with the duty of investigating offences or charging offenders' (s 34(4)) (*R v Ali* [2001] EWCA Crim 83). Where questioning is conducted by someone who does not have a duty of investigating offences the rules at common law apply.

14.4.1.8   Access to legal advice

When questioning takes place in an 'authorised place of detention' (which includes but is not limited to a police station: see s 38(2A)) then no inferences can be drawn if the suspect was not allowed an opportunity to consult a solicitor (s 34(2A)) (see *Murray v United Kingdom* (1996) 22 EHRR 29). If the accused declines the right to consult a solicitor, it would appear that inferences could be drawn (as the opportunity has been allowed) although the matter has not been determined by case law. However, if the police exercise the power to delay access to legal advice under s 58 of PACE 1984 (see **Chapter 13**) then inferences could not be drawn from the failure to mention a fact.

14.4.1.9   The effect of the failure to mention the fact

Where the jury decide that there has been a failure to mention a fact in the circumstances set out above they may draw 'such inferences as appear proper' (s 34(2)). However, in *R v Petkar* [2004] 1 Cr App R 270, the Court of Appeal accepted that the trial judge should give guidance as to what inferences might be drawn in each case.

14.4.1.10   Direction to the jury

There will always be a need to direct a jury when the judge concludes that the defendant has relied upon a fact and that the jury could conclude the failure to mention it was unreasonable. However, in *R v Mountford* [1999] Crim LR 575, the Court of Appeal held that if the defence is raised for the first time at trial and the reasons for not mentioning it earlier were so related that the rejection of the defence would necessarily involve a rejection of the reasons, then a direction to the jury was unnecessary. Mountford's defence was that a prosecution witness (W) had committed the offence and that he had not mentioned this before trial out of fear of that witness. If the jury rejected the defence ('W did it') they must necessarily reject the reasons for not mentioning that defence ('W would kill me for saying so') and so a direction would serve no purpose. However, in *R v Daly* [2002] 2 Cr App R 201, the Court of Appeal doubted that s 34 required any such restriction and thought that the direction should be given in all cases. Further in *R v Webber* [2004] 1 All ER 770, the House of Lords questioned the judgment in *R v Mountford*, noting that the jury could find assistance in deciding whether to believe W or Mountford from considering why Mountford had not offered the explanation he did at an earlier point.

Where the prosecution have not sought to rely on section 34 the judge should not invite the jury to draw an adverse inference from the alleged failure of the accused to mention a defence without first discussing the matter with counsel (*R v Khan* [1999] 2 Archbold News 2).

The full specimen direction can be obtained from the Judicial Studies Board website (www.jsboard.co.uk). In essence the jury should be directed that:

(a) A suspect is not bound to answer police questions.

(b) An inference from silence cannot prove guilt on its own.

(c) The prosecution must have established a case to answer before any inference may be drawn.

(d) It is for them to decide whether the defendant could reasonably be expected to have mentioned the defence. If they think the defence should have been mentioned then the jury may, but not must, draw inferences against the accused.

(e) They can draw an inference *only* if satisfied that the defendant was silent because he had no answer or none that would stand up to investigation. See *R v Daly* [2002] 2 Cr App R 14.

The judge should identify the facts it is alleged the accused has relied upon that give rise to this inference (*R v Chenia* [2003] 2 Cr App R 83). Simple reference to a general failure to answer questions at interview creates the risk that the jury will convict on the silence at interview alone rather than on the failure to mention a fact later relied on in defence: *R v Turner* [2004] 1 All ER 1025.

The judge in summing up should not only identify any reasons given by the defendant for failing to mention a fact but should do so as part of the direction on s 34 rather than when summing up on the defence case: *R v Petkar* [2004] 1 Cr App R 270.

14.4.1.11   The position at common law

Section 34 will not apply if:

- The person questioning is not a police officer or authorised investigator.
- The questioning or accusation does not take place under caution.
- The questioning takes place after the accused has been charged.
- The accused does not rely on a fact in his defence.
- The questioning did not concern whether or by whom an offence had been committed.
- The failure to mention the fact now relied upon was not unreasonable.

As noted above, if s 34 does not apply, the common law rules on inferences from silence may apply (*R v McGarry* [1999] 1 WLR 1500). However, the common law rules will be of limited application because:

(a) A person could only be subject to adverse inferences arising from his failure to answer questions or accusations if:

(i)   the accused had not been cautioned; and

(ii) the questioner/accuser and the accused were on equal terms: *Parkes v R* [1976] 1 WLR 1251.

(b) Where the person questioning or making accusations is a police officer or equivalent they will not be on equal terms (*Hall v R* [1971] 1 WLR 298) although an obiter dictum in *R v Chandler* [1976] 1 WLR 585 suggested that a person might be on equal terms with a police officer if he was accompanied by a solicitor. Furthermore, in *R v Horne* [1990] Crim LR 188, CA an unprompted accusation was made by a victim of an attack in the presence of the defendant and police officers. The Court of Appeal ruled that the defendant's failure to respond to that accusation had been rightly admitted.

The main situation in which the common law rule will apply is where the person making the accusations or asking the questions is another member of the public (as was the case in *Parkes v R*).

14.4.1.12 'Counterweight' directions

If the accused does not advance a new defence or new facts in support of a defence at trial, s 34 will not apply. Because the accused was questioned under caution the common law rules concerning inferences do not apply either.

However, s 34(3) allows the prosecution to prove the silence under questioning (a 'no-comment' interview) before or after the accused relies on a fact. This is a pragmatic rule allowing to prove the accused's interview as an ordinary part of the prosecution case rather than requiring the prosecution to reopen their case when the accused later raises a new fact or defence and therefore triggers s 34. It is very rare in practice for an interview (other than those excluded under ss 76 or 78 of PACE 1984) not to be proved during the prosecution case.

Where the prosecution have proved the interview but the accused does not then advance any new defence or facts, the tribunal of fact will have heard or read the interview and may draw an adverse inference of their own accord. In such situations not only should the judge not issue a s 34 direction, he should also issue a further direction (a 'counterweight direction') that the jury should not hold the accused's silence against him (*R v McGarry*). However, the judge should have regard to whether on the particular facts there is any real risk that the jury would draw an adverse inference in the absence of any comment by the judge on the matter (*R v La Rose* [2003] EWCA Crim 1471). Where, for example, a direction will be made under s 35 (see **14.4.5** below) the jury would have been sufficiently warned about the right to remain silent, so any further direction would simply be confusing.

14.4.2 Silence upon confrontation about particular types of incriminating evidence

There are two inferences of a similar nature. Both arise when a person is confronted about particular types of incriminating evidence. Unlike inferences under s 34, they do not arise because the accused later relies upon a defence which he has not mentioned at an earlier point but simply because he does not offer an explanation when invited to do so. In other words, it is the simple exercise of the right to silence in incriminating circumstances that gives rise to the inferences.

14.4.2.1 Failure to account for objects, substances or marks

Section 36 of the Criminal Justice and Public Order Act 1994 provides:

> *(1) Where—*
>> *(a) a person is arrested by a constable, and there is—*
>>> *(i) on his person; or*
>>> *(ii) in or on his clothing or footwear; or*
>>> *(iii) otherwise in his possession; or*
>>> *(iv) in any place in which he is at the time of his arrest,*
>> *any object, substance or mark, or there is any mark on any such object; and*
>> *(b) that or another constable . . . reasonably believes that the presence of the object, substance or mark may be attributable to the participation of the person arrested in the commission of an offence specified by the constable; and*

(c)   the constable informs the person arrested that he so believes, and requests him to account for the presence of the object, substance or mark; and

(d)   the person fails or refuses to do so,

then if, in any proceedings against the person for the offence ... evidence of those matters is given, subsection (2) below applies.

(2)   Where this subsection applies—

(a)   ...

(b)   ...

(c)   the court, in determining whether there is a case to answer; and

(d)   the court or jury, in determining whether the accused is guilty of the offence charged,

may draw such inferences from the failure or refusal as appear proper.

(3)   Subsections (1) and (2) above apply to the condition of clothing or footwear as they apply to a substance or mark thereon.

In addition to the above points, it should be noted:

(a) Section 36 allows the court to draw adverse inferences from the failure to explain the object, substance or mark only if the accused has been arrested and the effect of the failure to explain the incriminating object, etc, has been explained to the accused. Note, however, that the object, substance or mark itself is evidence in its own right and there are no particular rules or conditions for its admissibility (other than the usual rules of evidence).

(b) The inference can only be drawn if the suspect has been told of the reasons for suspicion and of the effect of failing to comply with this section (s 36(4)). The officer does not have to identify the precise offence. In *R v Compton* [2002] EWCA Crim 2835, CA, it was considered sufficient that the police officer had said that he was investigating 'drug trafficking'.

(c) Code C sets out the text of the special warnings that should be given to the accused under s 36 at para 10.5A.

(d) Section 36 applies to questions raised by customs and excise officers as well as police officers (s 36(5)). However, in contrast to s 34, other officers with a duty of investigating offences are not specifically mentioned. It would therefore appear that only confrontations or questions about objects, substances or marks by police or customs officers will lead to adverse inferences.

(e) Where the accused was in a place of authorised detention, inferences are only possible if the accused was offered access to a solicitor. This is likely to be a common feature of s 36 inferences as the section only arises upon arrest, at which stage the police should generally take a suspect to a police station before questioning him.

14.4.2.2   Failure to account for presence at the scene of a crime

Section 37 of the 1994 Act provides:

(1)   Where—

(a)   a person arrested by a constable was found by him at a place at or about the time the offence for which he was arrested is alleged to have been committed; and

(b)   that or another constable investigating the offence reasonably believes that the presence of the person at the place at that time may be attributable to his participation in the commission of the offence; and

(c)   the constable informs the person that he so believes, and requests him to account for that presence; and

(d)   the person fails or refuses to do so,

then if, in any proceedings against the person for the offence, evidence of those matters is given, subsection (2) below applies.

> *(2)   Where this subsection applies—*
>
> >   *(a)   ...*
> >   *(b)   ...*
> >   *(c)   the court, in determining whether there is a case to answer; and*
> >   *(d)   the court or jury, in determining whether the accused is guilty of the offence charged,*
>
> *may draw such inferences from the failure or refusal as appear proper.*

The points noted in relation to s 36 above apply equally to s 37. However, the text for the special warning is at Code C, para 10.5B.

14.4.3   Refusal to give body samples

Body samples are used to prove issues by scientific evidence, usually be DNA profiles. During the investigation of a crime samples or substances such as blood or semen might be taken, for example from the scene of the crime or from a victim. To prove that the accused committed the offence, the DNA profile of the sample and a profile from a sample taken from the accused must be matched.

The taking of bodily samples is governed by ss 62 and 63 of PACE 1984. This is covered in more detail in **Chapter 15**. However, at this point it is worth noting that bodily samples are defined in two classes:

(a) Non-intimate samples: such samples can be taken without the consent of the owner in certain circumstances (s 63). If the conditions for taking such a sample without consent do not apply and the owner declines to consent without good reason, the court may draw inferences of guilt from that refusal at common law (*R v Smith* (1985) 81 Cr App R 286).

(b) Intimate samples: such samples cannot be taken without the consent of the owner in any circumstances. However, if the owner refuses to consent to the taking of such samples without good cause the court may draw such inferences from that refusal as appear proper. These inferences can be used in determining the issue of guilt and in determining whether there is a case to answer.

14.4.4   Failure to disclose the defence case

The inferences that we have already considered all relate to pre-trial investigation. Those that follow all relate to the trial process itself.

The Criminal Procedure and Investigations Act 1996, s 5 places the accused under an obligation to disclose his defence by way of a defence statement. See the ***Criminal Litigation and Sentencing Manual***, *Blackstone's Criminal Practice*, or *Archbold*, for the detailed rules of procedure. In outline, a defence statement should set out in general terms the nature of the accused's defence and matters with which he takes issue with the prosecution case and the basis of any such dispute (s 5(6)). The logic of this procedure is that the accused is then committed to the defence to be run at trial. Where the accused intends to rely on an alibi defence (ie, that he was at some other specific place at the time of the offence) there are additional obligations. Section 11 of the 1996 Act makes provision for any failure on the part of the accused to comply with his obligations under s 5. The court may draw inferences when deciding the guilt of the accused *but not when deciding whether there is a case to answer* if the accused:

• does not give a defence statement;

• gives the defence statement late;

- runs a defence at trial which is inconsistent with that in his defence statement;
- seeks to establish an alibi without having complied with the additional notice requirements for alibi defences.

In summary proceedings, the giving of a defence statement is voluntary (s 6) but must comply with the requirements in s 5 as to the form and content of the statement. However, under s 11 inferences can be drawn if the accused:

- gives the defence statement late;
- runs a defence at trial which is inconsistent with that in his defence statement;
- seeks to establish an alibi without having complied with the additional notice requirements for alibi defences.

The accused cannot be convicted solely on the basis of an inference under s 11 (s 11(10)). The court should take care to ensure that the jury is properly directed as to the nature of any discrepancy and the reasons that the accused may give for it (*R v Wheeler* (2000) 164 JP 565). There may be particular difficulties where the accused states that the defence statement was not drafted under his or her instructions (in other words that a solicitor drafted it) and that therefore that its contents do not reflect his or her intended defence. It is not possible to force the accused to sign the statement (*R (Sullivan) v Crown Court at Maidstone* [2002] 1 WLR 2747, CA). However, under the Criminal Procedure and Investigations Act 1996, s 6E(1) where an accused's solicitor purports to give a defence statement on behalf of the accused there is a rebuttable presumption that it was given with the accused's authority.

There is no specimen direction concerning inferences under s 11 but it would appear likely that such a direction should contain the features of an adverse inference direction: that the inconsistency is proven, deliberate, material and motivated by a consciousness of guilt.

14.4.5   Failure to testify

The traditional right of an accused not to testify has been modified by s 35 of the Criminal Justice and Public Order Act 1994, which provides:

> (1)   At the trial of any person for an offence, subsection . . . (3) below applies unless—
>   (a)   the accused's guilt is not in issue; or
>   (b)   it appears to the court that the physical or mental condition of the accused makes it undesirable for him to give evidence;
>   . . .
> (3)   Where this subsection applies, the court or jury, in determining whether the accused is guilty of the offence charged, may draw such inferences as appear proper from the failure of the accused to give evidence or his refusal, without good cause, to answer any question.

Such inferences can only be drawn if the accused has either been warned by the court of the effect of the failure to give evidence (s 35(2)) or has stated that he will give evidence and then fails to do so (s 35(1)). The text of any warnings to the accused is set out in the *Practice Direction (Criminal: Consolidated)* [2002] 3 All ER 904, para 44. The section applies to a person who refuses to answer questions in evidence unless the refusal is justified (under s 35(5)):

(a) on the grounds of legal privilege (see **Chapter 18**),

(b) because another statute excludes the evidence that would be contained in the answer; or

(c) because the court rules that the question need not be answered.

Note that inferences can only be drawn when determining whether the accused is guilty. Inferences cannot be used to determine whether there is a case to answer, not least of all because the accused has not had the opportunity to give evidence by that point in proceedings (*Murray v DPP* [1994] 1 WLR 1, HL).

Section 35 allows the judge to direct the jury (or requires the magistrates) to take into account the failure of the accused to testify if the conditions in s 35(1) are satisfied and the warnings have been issued under s 35(2). Further, the prosecution are entitled to comment on the failure of the accused to testify.

14.4.5.1   The accused's guilt is not in issue

There are situations in which the accused could give evidence in his 'defence' even though his guilt is not in issue. The most obvious example is a 'Newton' hearing at which the issue is not whether the accused committed a particular crime but how serious his commission of the offence was so that an appropriate sentence can be passed: see the ***Criminal Litigation and Sentencing Manual***, *Blackstone's Criminal Practice*, D18.2 or *Archbold*.

14.4.5.2   'Physical or mental condition'

There must be evidence that the physical or mental condition of the accused is such that an inference should not be drawn (*R v A* [1997] Crim LR 883).

In *R v Friend* [1997] 1 WLR 1433, F was tried for murder. He did not give evidence and sought to avoid a s 35 inference on the grounds that he had a mental age of nine (he was 15 years old). The judge did invite the jury to draw an inference under s 35 on the grounds that, in light of the fact that he had been able to give a clear account of what he said had happened before trial, his mental age did not make it undesirable that he give evidence. The conviction was upheld by the Court of Appeal. In so far as F would have had any special needs in giving evidence the court could have met these needs so the prejudice of having to give evidence could be accommodated. However, this case was subsequently referred back to the Court of Appeal by the Criminal Cases Review Commission, with new evidence from expert psychologists that F had suffered from Attention Deficit Hyperactivity Disorder during his childhood and that, at the time of his trial, this was 'unrecognised, undiagnosed and untreated'. His symptoms included 'poor attentional control, distractibility, difficulty attending and staying on task, poor response inhibition [and] hyperactivity'. Defence counsel from the trial supplied a note to the effect that F was not called as a witness because he was 'simply incapable of giving a coherent account of himself when in consultation'; even so, one expert felt that at the trial 'it is unlikely that the severity of these problems was fully appreciated'. The new expert observed that 'aside from having difficulty following the proceedings, it is unlikely that Mr Friend would have coped satisfactorily with giving evidence for prolonged periods in the witness box'. The court concluded that the conviction was unsafe as the trial judge would not have ruled that any adverse inference could be drawn from F's failure to testify. See *R v Friend* [2004] EWCA Crim 2661.

14.4.5.3   The direction to the jury

In *R v Cowan* [1996] 1 Cr App R 1, CA, Lord Taylor stated that a direction to the jury should contain the following elements:

(a) The accused has a right not to give evidence but he has been warned that a failure to do so may lead to the jury drawing inferences.

(b) A failure to give evidence cannot on its own prove guilt but it can assist in deciding whether the accused is guilty.

(c) If a reason for not testifying has been advanced the jury should consider it and:
  (i)   If they accept the reason advanced, they cannot draw any inference against the accused.

(ii) If they reject they reason advanced, they may draw an inference but are not obliged to do so.

(d) If the jury conclude that the only sensible explanation for his decision not to give evidence is that he has no answer to the case against him, or none that could have stood up to cross-examination, then it would be open to them to hold against him his failure to give evidence. It is for the jury to decide whether it is fair to do so.

There is a specimen direction for judges when dealing with s 35 (see www.jsboard.co.uk). The House of Lords observed in *Becouarn* [2006] 1 Cr App R 2 that it appears to have stood the test of time but that 'trial judges have full discretion to adapt even a tried and tested direction if they consider that to do so gives the best guidance to a jury and fairest representation of the issues'.

In *R v Birchall* [1999] Crim LR 311, CA, a conviction was overturned where the trial judge had not required the jury to decide whether the prosecution had established a prima facie case before they could draw an inference, such consideration being an absolute requirement before an inference could be drawn under s 35.

Note that the jury can be invited to infer the fact of guilt from the failure to testify if a prima facie case has been made out. Lord Mustill described the matter in this way in *Murray v DPP* (a case concerning Northern Ireland legislation with provisions that were materially the same):

If ... the defendant does not go on oath ... the fact finder may suspect that the defendant does not tell his story because he has no story to tell or none which will stand up to scrutiny; and this suspicion may be sufficient to convert a possible prosecution case into one which is actually proved.

Lord Mustill also said that whether such inferences should be drawn depended upon whether the accused should be able to give his own account of the particular matter in question. Developing this point, the Court of Appeal concluded in *R v McManus* [2001] EWCA Crim 2455 that a direction under s 35 was inappropriate where there was no factual dispute in the case. The only issue in that case was whether a particular property could in law constitute a 'disorderly house', the facts that supported such a conclusion being agreed between the defence and prosecution. The accused's testimony could not have assisted on this matter so a s 35 inference was inappropriate.

14.4.5.4 Tactical dilemmas

Whilst s 35 did not remove the right of a defendant to remain silent, it did generate a significant tactical dilemma for defendants with a bad character. Under the Criminal Evidence Act 1898, there were strict limitations governing when evidence of the bad character of the accused could be given at trial. With a couple of exceptions, this could only happen during cross-examination of the accused. Thus, if the accused did not testify at trial, the chances of any bad character evidence being given were greatly reduced. A defendant with previous convictions had to choose: 'do I testify in support of my defence and run the risk of being cross-examined on my bad character OR do I keep out of the witness box?' The latter choice would mean that the bad character evidence was unlikely to emerge but the defence case was weakened. It was effectively a lose–lose situation for such defendants, as recognised by the House of Lords in *Becouarn* [2006] 1 Cr App R 2.

With the advent of the new provisions on a defendant's bad character in the CJA 2003 (ss 101–113), it is no longer possible for a defendant to avoid evidence of his bad character being adduced simply by making a tactical decision not to testify at trial. His previous convictions can now come out typically as part of the prosecution case, regardless of whether or not he goes into the witness box. To that extent, the dilemma for such defendants has been simplified – either testify and be exposed to cross-examination about your story or do not testify, do not face cross-examination but run the risk of an adverse inference being drawn.

14.4.6   Failure to call evidence

At common law it is permissible for the judge to comment on the failure of the accused to call a particular witness. The principle is that the judge should exercise care before doing so and the comments made to the jury should not generally invite the court to equate the failure to call the witness with the accused's account being untrue (*R v Weller* [1994] Crim LR 856). It is especially important that no comment should be made about the failure to call a witness if there may be a valid reason for not calling the witness (*R v Couzens* [1992] Crim LR 822, CA).

PACE 1984, s 80A, provides that the failure to call a spouse should not be commented upon by the *prosecution* (the spouse of an accused person not being compellable on his behalf under s 80 of that Act: see **Chapter 4**). However, there is no prohibition on the *judge* commenting on the failure to call a spouse. However, in *R v Naudeer* [1984] 3 All ER 1036, the Court of Appeal took the view that great care should be exercised by the judge before any such comment was made.

14.4.7   Conclusion on inferences from silence in criminal cases

There are two broad categories of inference:

(a) Silence before a criminal prosecution is commenced:
  (i)   silence under questioning (Criminal Justice and Public Order Act 1994, s 34);
  (ii) failure to explain objects substances or marks on the suspect's person (Criminal Justice and Public Order Act 1994, s 36);
  (iii) failure to explain presence at the scene of the crime (Criminal Justice and Public Order Act 1994, s 37);
  (iv) failure to provide bodily samples (PACE 1984, s 62).

(b) Silence after a criminal prosecution has been commenced:
  (i)   failure to produce a defence statement (Criminal Procedure and Investigations Act 1996, s 11);
  (ii) failure of the accused to testify in his own defence (Criminal Justice and Public Order Act 1994, s 35);
  (iii) failure to call witnesses (common law).

There are many differences between the various sections but the essential difference between the two categories is that silence before commencement of a prosecution case can be used to raise a case for the accused to answer while silence after commencement cannot.

All of the inferences in criminal cases, however, have certain common features whether as a result of statute or common law. While expressed differently in different situations, the common features are that:

(a) Before an inference can be drawn it must be established that the motive for the failure must be a realisation of guilt rather than some other reason (and the jury should be told that they must rule out any other reason).

(b) The tribunal of fact is never obliged to draw an inference in any of the above cases: the facts simply establish that an inference may rather than must be drawn.

(c) The inference can never prove guilt on its own.

15

Identification evidence

15.1 Introduction

We have already looked at situations where the fact-finders may need to be alerted to the possible danger of relying on a particular source of evidence — see **Chapter 5**. Usually, this happens on a case-by-case, witness-by-witness, basis. But there is one whole category of evidence where it is thought that the risk of unreliability is much greater than normal, or at least greater than the inexperienced fact-finder would expect. This is identification evidence. Courts have tried to minimise the danger by requiring a warning to be given by the judge to the jury where a case turns on such disputed evidence. We shall look first at the rationale behind the concerns (**15.2**) and next at the methods now used to deal with them (**15.3 to 15.8**). Finally, we will look at how evidence is produced to prove identification in court and the procedures that must be followed (**15.9**).

15.2 Identification evidence and miscarriages of justice

Intuitively, most people consider that identification evidence is very reliable and accurate. Indeed, identification witnesses themselves often think so and come into the witness box convinced that they have identified the criminal correctly. That there are dangers in over-reliance on such evidence has been plain since at least the early 20th century and the case of Adolf Beck. Beck was twice convicted wrongly (in 1896 and 1904) of offences of fraud. In the 1870s, when Beck claimed to have been in South America, a 'John Smith' was convicted in England of several frauds. Each offence alleged that Smith had become intimate with a woman, persuaded her to put valuable jewellery into his possession, and then disappeared. In 1895, several more women were called as witnesses at a new trial. The offences seemed identical. Each woman identified the accused, this time Adolf Beck. The prosecution even called two police officers to testify that Adolf Beck and John Smith were the same man. Beck was convicted and sentenced to seven years' imprisonment. After his release, the offences started again. In 1904, Beck was again convicted on the word of several women, each of whom claimed to have been intimate with him. Whilst Beck was held in custody, awaiting sentence, John Smith was caught committing another offence. Smith's appearance matched the descriptions given by the women, which included the fact that their seducer was circumcised. Prison records from the 1870s indicated that 'John Smith' was circumcised. Beck was not circumcised. Beck was released, pardoned and received a substantial sum in compensation. Following this case, the Court of Criminal Appeal was set up and the first set of general instructions on the conduct of identification parades was issued.

However, miscarriages of justice continued to occur in cases based upon identification evidence. As Lord Devlin has pointed out:

In 1912 a man on a charge of murder was identified by no less than 17 witnesses, but fortunately was able to establish an irrefutable alibi. In 1928 Oscar Slater, after he had spent 19 years in prison . . . had his conviction for murder quashed; he had been identified by 14 witnesses. Nevertheless, cases continued to be left to the jury as if they raised only a simple issue between the identifier and the accused as to which was telling the truth . . . In 1974 two shattering cases of mistaken identity came to light within four weeks of each other. (Patrick Devlin, *The Judge*, 1981.)

15.3 The special need for caution — *Turnbull* warnings

In May 1974, Lord Devlin was invited to chair a committee to investigate the law and procedure on identification and his committee's report (*Report to the Secretary of State for the Home Department of the Departmental Committee on Evidence of Identification in Criminal Cases*) was published in April 1976. It made several recommendations for changes to the gathering of identification evidence and its treatment in the courtroom, all of which were intended to be effected by statute. However, as Lord Devlin has observed:

The Court of Appeal decided to forestall legislation by giving in July 1976 . . . a comprehensive judgment laying down a new approach . . .

That judgment was given in *R v Turnbull* [1977] QB 224 by Lord Widgery CJ. The 'new approach' is as follows (see pp 228–30 of the report):

(a) *First, whenever the case against an accused depends wholly or substantially on the correctness of one or more identifications of the accused which the defence alleges to be mistaken, the judge should warn the jury of the special need for caution before convicting the accused in reliance on the correctness of the identification or identifications. In addition he should instruct them as to the reason for the need for such a warning and should make some reference to the possibility that a mistaken witness can be a convincing one and that a number of such witnesses can all be mistaken. Provided this is done in clear terms the judge need not use any particular form of words.*

(b) *Secondly, the judge should direct the jury to examine closely the circumstances in which the identification by each witness came to be made. How long did the witness have the accused under observation? At what distance? In what light? Was the observation impeded in any way, as for example by passing traffic or a press of people? Had the witness ever seen the accused before? How often? If only occasionally, had he any special reason for remembering the accused? How long elapsed between the original observation and the subsequent identification to the police?*

(c) *Was there any material discrepancy between the description of the accused given to the police by the witness when first seen by them and his actual appearance?*

(d) *If in any case, whether it is being dealt with summarily or on indictment, the prosecution have reason to believe that there is such a material discrepancy they should supply the accused or his legal advisers with particulars of the description the police were first given. In all cases if the accused asks to be given particulars of such descriptions, the prosecution should supply them. Finally, he should remind the jury of any specific weakness which had appeared in the identification evidence.*

(e) *Recognition may be more reliable than identification of a stranger; but even when the witness is purporting to recognise someone whom he knows, the jury should be reminded that mistakes in recognition of close relatives and friends are sometimes made.*

(f) *When the quality (of the identifying evidence) is good, as for example when the identification is made after a long period of observation, or in satisfactory conditions by a relative, a neighbour, a close friend, a workmate and the like, the jury can safely be left to assess the value of the identifying evidence even though there is no other evidence to support it: provided always, however, that an adequate warning has been given about the special need for caution.*

(g) *When, in the judgment of the trial judge, the quality of the identifying evidence is poor, as for example when it depends solely on a fleeting glance or on a longer observation made in difficult conditions, the situation is very different. The judge should then withdraw the case from the jury and direct an acquittal unless there is other evidence which goes to support the correctness of the identification. This may be corroboration in the sense lawyers use that word; but it need not be so if its effect is to make the jury sure that there has been no mistaken identification.*

(h) *The trial judge should identify to the jury the evidence which he adjudges is capable of supporting the evidence of identification. If there is any evidence or circumstances which the jury might think was supporting when it did not have this quality, the judge should say so.*

(i) *Care should be taken by the judge when directing the jury about the support for an identification which may be derived from the fact that they have rejected an alibi. False alibis may be put forward for many reasons . . . It is only when the jury is satisfied that the sole reason for the fabrication was to deceive them and there is no other explanation for its being put forward can fabrication provide any support for identification evidence. The jury should be reminded that proving the accused has told lies about where he was at the material time does not by itself prove that he was where the identifying witness says he was.*

Note that identification evidence given by police officers has no special status. Typically, officers receive training in observation and they might be thought to possess greater ability to identify people than is possessed by ordinary members of the public. However, in *Reid v R* (1990) 90 Cr App R 121, the Privy Council stated that:

. . . experience has undoubtedly shown that police identification can be just as unreliable and is not therefore to be excepted from the now well established need for the appropriate warnings.

This remains the position, even where the police witness claims to have recognised the accused at the scene of crime, having known him previously (see *R v Bowden* [1993] Crim LR 379).

15.4 Form of a *Turnbull* warning

When a trial judge directs a jury about identification evidence, in the summing-up, there is no set form of words that is needed for the *Turnbull* warning. In *Mills v R* [1995] 1 WLR 511, the Privy Council stated that *Turnbull* was not a statute and did not require the incantation of a formula. A judge has:

a broad discretion to express himself in his own way when he directs a jury on identification. All that is required . . . is that he should comply with the sense and spirit of the guidance in . . . *Turnbull* . . .

Notwithstanding the discretion that a judge clearly has, there is a specimen direction (number 30) formulated by the Judicial Studies Board:

This is a trial where the case against the defendant depends wholly or to a large extent on the correctness of one or more identifications of him which the defence alleges to be mistaken. I must therefore warn you of the special need for caution before convicting the defendant in reliance on the evidence of identification. That is because it is possible for an honest witness to make a mistaken identification. There have been wrongful convictions in the past as a result of such mistakes. An apparently convincing witness can be mistaken. So can a number of apparently convincing witnesses.

You should therefore examine carefully the circumstances in which the identification by each witness was made. How long did he have the person he says was the defendant under observation? At what distance? In what light? Did anything interfere with the observation? Had the witness ever seen the person he observed before? If so, how often? If only occasionally, had he any special reason for remembering him? How long was it between the original observation and the identification to the police? Is there any marked difference between the description given by the witness to the police when he was first seen by them and the appearance of the defendant?

See further the JSB website, www.jsboard.co.uk/criminal.

15.5   Poor quality identification evidence — submissions of no case

You have seen, in **15.3** points (g) to (i), how the Court of Appeal in *R v Turnbull* [1977] QB 224 recognised that identification evidence may sometimes be of poor quality. The suggestion was that cases based on such weak evidence should be stopped on a submission of no case to answer unless there was some evidence which might support the accuracy of the identification.

At the conclusion of the prosecution evidence in a trial, the defence may make a submission of no case to answer. Generally, such submissions are governed by the principles set out in *R v Galbraith* [1981] 1 WLR 1039 but in cases where evidence of identification is disputed, the submission will be based upon *R v Turnbull*:

(a) Where there is no identification evidence at all, the judge's decision is simple. The submission succeeds.

(b) Where there is identification evidence but it is of poor quality and is unsupported by other evidence, again the judge should withdraw the case from the jury. First, the judge should assume the identification evidence to be honest (that is, he does not need to form a view about the credibility of the prosecution witness). Then if the judge considers that the identification evidence has a base which is so slender that it is unreliable and thus not sufficient to found a conviction, he should uphold the submission and order the defendant's acquittal on the charge. See, for example, *Daley v R* [1993] 4 All ER 86.

(c) Where there is identification evidence of poor quality but which is potentially supported by other evidence, the judge will allow the case to go to the jury. The judge should tell the jury what other evidence is capable of supporting the accuracy of the identification. See **15.6**. According to *R v Akaidere* [1990] Crim LR 808, a judge should not tell a jury that the identification evidence is of poor quality and the case would have been withdrawn if there was no supporting evidence. The reason for this ban is that, whilst it is for the judge to decide if there is evidence *capable* of supporting the identification, it is a question of fact for the jury to decide whether it does support it. The jury might be inappropriately influenced in their decision if they knew of the judge's view.

We shall consider how identification evidence may be supported in **15.6**.

15.6   Support for poor quality identification evidence

One possible form of support was specifically considered in *R v Turnbull* [1977] QB 224 —the fact that the defendant had put forward a false alibi (see point (i), **15.3**). If a defendant's alibi is rejected as a lie, this fact can offer support but a careful direction is required (*R v Keane* (1977) 65 Cr App R 247). It does not follow that, because an alibi has been rejected by the jury as false, the defendant was wherever the identification witness says he was. The jury should consider if there is a reason why the defendant might have offered a false alibi, consistent with his innocence. An example might be where he was with a girlfriend and did not want his wife to find out about it, so offered a different, false, alibi. You will see the parallel with the general treatment of lies by the accused; *R v Lucas* [1981] QB 720, **14.3.1**.

In the absence of other sources of evidence to support a poor quality identification (for example, D's fingerprints on the murder weapon), the judge should consider whether several identification witnesses may support each other. If they have each been hampered in their observation (eg, passengers on a night bus passing an incident on the street), the judge may have to withdraw the case from the jury and direct an acquittal. If they have observed in satisfactory conditions (eg, several spectators at a sunny daytime football match observe an assault by a fellow spectator), then their evidence may be presented to the jury as capable of supporting each other's identification evidence. In that situation, the judge should also direct the jury that several honest witnesses can all be mistaken. See *R v Weeder* (1980) 71 Cr App R 228; also *R v Breslin* (1985) 80 Cr App R 226.

In some situations, several identification witnesses may offer mutual support even though they have each witnessed a different incident, where it is alleged that each incident involved the same offender.

15.7 Situations where a *Turnbull* warning may be unnecessary

As you know by now, the concern that lay behind the decision in *R v Turnbull* [1977] QB 224 was that an identification witness may be mistaken but be persuasive because he appears to be sincere and convincing. In fact, he is sincere and has probably convinced himself that his identification is accurate. But he may still be wrong. The *Turnbull* warning is intended to alert the jury to the danger of being misled. But what if *mistaken* identification is not an issue at the trial? This may arise in three ways.

(a) There may be no possibility of mistake. If so, there is no need for a *Turnbull* warning. One example is when the only person who could be the offender is the defendant. In *R v Slater* [1995] 1 Cr App R 584, an offence took place in a nightclub and the accused accepted that he had been there. The accused was 2 metres tall and the Court of Appeal noted that there was no evidence to suggest that anyone remotely similar in height to the accused was present in the nightclub where the offence took place; no *Turnbull* warning was needed. Conversely, in *R v Thornton* [1995] 1 Cr App R 578, an offence occurred at a wedding reception. The accused accepted that he was at the reception. There were a number of people present who were dressed similarly to the accused (black leather jacket, black trousers) and several people were allegedly involved in the offence. The Court of Appeal thought that a mistaken identification was clearly possible; a *Turnbull* warning should have been given.

(b) Where the defence allege that the identification witness is lying. In this situation, mistake is simply not a live issue for the jury to consider. The issue now is simply the veracity of the witness. Does the jury believe the identification witness or not? In *R v Courtnell* [1990] Crim LR 115, the Court of Appeal accepted that point but noted that if there was evidence that might support the contention of mistaken identification, the judge should direct the jury accordingly, even though the defence had not raised that issue at the trial. In *R v Courtnell*, there was no such evidence and the judge had not erred in omitting a *Turnbull* direction. Similarly, in *R v Cape* [1996] 1 Cr App R 191, the defendants were alleged to have been involved in a fight in a pub. The pub landlord, who knew the men, testified that they were so involved. The defendants admitted being in the pub at the time but denied involvement; they suggested the landlord was lying and motivated by a grudge. The issue for the jury was simply whether they accepted the evidence of the landlord as truthful; that did not call for a *Turnbull* warning.

In *Beckford v R* (1993) 97 Cr App R 409, the Privy Council reiterated the need to consider carefully all of the issues before the jury. Beckford and two co-accused were tried for murder. The sole witness to the crime identified all three men as being present. At trial, the accused all ran alibi defences and alleged that the witness was lying because either (i) he was a compulsive and inveterate liar or (ii) he was susceptible to mental aberrations (having previously been a patient in a mental hospital). The Privy Council considered that there were two questions for the jury to address:

(i)   Is the witness honest? This was at the heart of the defence case. If the jury found he was not honest, they would disregard his evidence.

If the jury found him to be an honest witness, they would need to consider (and be directed on) a second question.

(ii) Could the witness be mistaken? If this was a possibility, on the evidence, it would require a *Turnbull* direction from the judge. The direction should then be given even if the defence did not rely on the possibility of mistake.

(c) Where the evidence does not identify a person. Where an eyewitness gives evidence only of *description* (for example, clothing or general characteristics), this is not identification evidence. In *R v Gayle* [1999] 2 Cr App R 130, the Court of Appeal noted that the danger of an honest witness being mistaken about distinctive clothing, or the general description of a person he has seen (eg, short or tall, black or white, direction of movement) is minimal. What the jury need to concentrate upon is the honesty of the witness.

Where the prosecution try to prove that a defendant was present at a particular place by calling witnesses who will say that they saw *a man* driving a car, and they can identify *the car*, then a full *Turnbull* warning is not needed. The prosecution will need to produce other evidence to prove that the defendant was driving the car at the material time. This was the view taken by the Court of Appeal in *R v Browning* (1991) 94 Cr App R 109. The explanation for the distinction between identification of a person and of a car was said to be that, whereas people may change their appearance frequently (eg, facial expression or bodily posture), cars do not change their shape, colour or size (unless of course they are altered deliberately). Nevertheless, a jury should still be directed about any difficulties regarding observation of the car (eg, if the witness was a driver who got a fleeting glance of the car whilst being overtaken).

15.8   Appeals and identification evidence

A failure to observe the *Turnbull* guidelines will often lead to a successful appeal: see *R v Hunjan* (1979) 68 Cr App R 99. Indeed, the Privy Council said, in *Reid v R* (1990) 90 Cr App R 121, that they had:

no hesitation in concluding that a significant failure to follow the identification guidelines as laid down in *Turnbull* . . . will cause a conviction to be quashed because it will have resulted in a substantial miscarriage of justice . . . If convictions are to be allowed upon uncorroborated [unsupported] identification evidence there must be strict insistence upon a judge giving a clear warning of the danger of a mistaken identification which the jury must consider before arriving at their verdict. It is only in the most exceptional circumstances that a conviction based on uncorroborated identification evidence will be sustained in the absence of such a warning.

An example of such 'exceptional circumstances' may be found in *Freemantle v R* [1994] 3 All ER 225. Here, the Privy Council said that if the identification evidence was of exceptionally good quality, this would be an exceptional circumstance. Amongst the factors which the Privy Council thought showed the exceptionally good quality of the identification evidence, was a dialogue between the accused, Freemantle, and one of the eyewitnesses, Campbell. Campbell shouted to the man he saw, 'Freemantle me see you'; the man's reply was regarded as an implied acknowledgement of the accuracy of that identification. See also *Scott v R* [1989] AC 1242.

15.9   Establishing a link between the accused and the crime

15.9.1   Ways to make a link

Suppose that a defendant (or suspect) denies being the offender, there are several ways to produce evidence which can show that he is the offender. For example:

- visual identification by an eyewitness;
- aural (voice) identification by an ear witness;
- prints left at the crime scene — these could be prints made by fingers, palm, foot or even ear;
- fibres left at the crime scene;
- DNA left at the crime scene;
- handwriting left at the crime scene;
- fingerprints, etc, or property from the crime scene which have been found to match ones found on the defendant or on his clothing, among his possessions or in his house.

We now need to consider what must be done in order to turn any of these pieces of information into admissible evidence that could be used in a trial. In all of these situations, there will be a witness as to the facts. This person must make a witness statement to say 'I heard something', 'I saw someone', 'I found this letter', 'I picked up this cigarette butt', and so on. A comparison must then be made between that information and the defendant (or suspect).

Comparison by an eye or ear witness is usually done by letting the witness see or hear the suspect in controlled conditions (for example, an identification parade). In order to insulate the witness from attack in cross-examination at trial, the witness should give a description of the person he saw or heard *before* comparing his recollection with the suspect's appearance or voice. See Code D, para 3.1.

Finders will need to send their discoveries elsewhere for testing. They should protect their discoveries by sealing them in plastic bags, to avoid possible contamination. Such bags must be labelled so that the expert making the comparison can show the connection between what he is testing and what was found. Defence counsel may object at trial either that a discovery has been contaminated by coming into contact with other material, or that there is no evidence to link the sample tested in a laboratory by an expert witness to what was found at the crime scene.

In the case of prints, fibres, DNA or handwriting, comparison must be made with a specimen obtained from the suspect. DNA and fingerprints may already be available to the police, following the suspect's conviction on an earlier occasion. Otherwise, a specimen must be obtained now. We will consider how that happens in **15.9.6**. Once we have the specimen, we need an expert to make the comparison. If there is a sufficient match, we will have our evidence of identity. The expert witness must provide an expert report, to be disclosed to the defence and used at trial. The probative value of that evidence will vary from case to case. A fingerprint or DNA match may be very probative but some fibres or types of glass, for example, may be in very common use and so have a low probative value. If they were rare, for example pieces of handblown medieval glass from a church window, the match would have a higher probative value. Even with a good match and uncommon material, we have only circumstantial evidence to link the suspect to the crime scene. This means that the match may be explained away at trial by the defence, or somehow shown to be less probative. For example, in the trial of several youths for the murder of Damilola Taylor at the Old Bailey in 2002, the prosecution alleged that the fatal injury to the victim was caused by a shard from a glass bottle. Fragments of the bottle were recovered at the crime scene. One of the accused youths possessed a pair of trainers on which was found a tiny piece of glass. Scientific tests showed it to match the type of glass which had been found at the crime scene. Thus, the police had evidence to make a link between the youth and the crime scene. At trial, the defence explained this apparently damaging match by showing that the youth had visited the crime scene a day or two after the death of Damilola Taylor. This was confirmed by police officers who were present at the time. The piece of glass could have got onto his trainer then, quite innocently. There are other ways to challenge expert evidence (on identification and other matters) which we will consider in **Chapter 16**.

15.9.2 Admissibility and exclusion of evidence

Quite apart from the risks which attach to identification evidence in general (to which the *Turnbull* direction relates), questions arise as to the ways in which identification evidence should be (a) gathered and (b) presented in court. Some forms of identification evidence, eg, dock identifications, are thought to carry such a risk of prejudice to the accused that the courts have frequently excluded such evidence. Exclusion is at the court's discretion either at common law or under PACE 1984, s 78 (see **13.1.3**). In general the courts have sought to ensure that identification evidence is gathered in 'controlled circumstances' and to this end a code of practice (Code D) has been laid down by virtue of s 66 of the 1984 Act. Some aspects of the admissibility of identification evidence have already been dealt with in **Chapters 5** and **11** of this Manual.

Many Court of Appeal decisions illustrate that non-compliance with Code D may be an important factor in deciding whether to exclude the evidence pursuant to s 78 of the 1984 Act. See, for example, *R v Leckie* [1983] Crim LR 543; *R v Gall* (1990) 90 Cr App R 64 and *R v Conway* [1990] Crim LR 402.

However, breaches of Code D do not automatically lead to the exclusion of the identification evidence. See *R v Quinn* [1990] Crim LR 581; *R v Penny* [1992] Crim LR 184; *R v Palmer* [2002] EWCA Crim 2645; *R v Alan Jones, Tina Jones* [2005] EWCA Crim 3526. For example, in *R v Forbes* [2001] AC 473, the House of Lords held that two street identifications by an eyewitness had been rightly allowed in as evidence at a trial, notwithstanding non-compliance with Code D.

Whether there is a breach of Code D or not, s 78 of the 1984 Act would need to be considered. For example, evidence of a street identification, in the absence of an identification parade, *might* be excluded. In the final analysis, the fairness of allowing the other identification evidence to be called will depend on a variety of factors which are usually taken into consideration under s 78.

15.9.3 Cases where the link between the accused and the crime is based upon an eyewitness

This topic is dealt with generally in Code of Practice D, issued under PACE 1984. Code D can be found in *Blackstone's Criminal Practice* Appendix 2, or the *Archbold Supplement*. Code D and the Annexes A–D are particularly important. The current Code D came into effect on 1 January 2006. In considering the use to be made of an eyewitness, we must start by distinguishing between two situations:

   (i) where an eyewitness identifies the accused as the offender in court, while giving evidence at the trial (see **15.9.3.1**); or

   (ii) where an eyewitness identifies the accused as the offender before the trial begins (see **15.9.3.2**).

15.9.3.1 In-court eyewitness identification (usually called dock identification)

Dock identification should not generally be allowed (*R v Howick* [1970] Crim LR 403). The reason for this ban is the lack of probative value of a dock identification. It is easy for a witness to 'identify' the alleged criminal when he is standing rather obviously in the dock and the exercise adds little or nothing to a previous act of identification. In the absence of a previous identification by that witness, to allow a dock identification would flout the basic principles that govern the production of identification evidence (through an identification parade, for example).

A dock identification may be permissible when a defendant refuses to attend a parade (*R v John* [1973] Crim LR 113, CA) or renders a parade impracticable, eg, by changing his appearance (*R v Mutch* [1973] 1 All ER 178, CA).

There is no logic in making a distinction between a dock identification in a Crown Court and in a magistrates' court. However, in road traffic offences it is usually necessary to prove that the defendant was the driver of the car at the time of the offence. Generally, there is no dispute that the accused was the driver but a failure to call any evidence on that issue is likely to result in an acquittal. In summary trials for road traffic offences, the custom has evolved where a witness (usually a police officer) is asked, 'Do you see the driver in court?' Because of the sheer number of such offences which are tried by magistrates, if there had to be an identification parade in every case where the accused did not expressly admit that he was the driver, 'the whole process of justice in a magistrates' court would be severely impaired' (*Barnes v Chief Constable of Durham* [1997] 2 Cr App R 505). Thus, it seems that in this type of case the onus is on the accused to raise the issue of disputed identification before the trial starts, and seek an identification procedure.

15.9.3.2 Out of court eyewitness identification

The obvious way to avoid the prejudice of a dock identification is to refer to an out of court identification made in less prejudicial circumstances. Code D lays down a regime for ensuring this (so far as is possible): see, in particular, Code D, para 3. All forms of out of court identification would seem to be admissible either as prior consistent statements (under the principle in *R v Christie* [1914] AC 545), under the rules in *R v Osbourne* [1973] QB 678 or under the CJA 2003, s 120(4) and (5) (see **6.4.2**). See also *R v Rogers* [1993] Crim LR 386 confirming the admissibility of a street identification.

When the *identity* of the *suspect* is *known* to the police *and* he is *available*, four forms of identification procedure may be used to confirm or refute identification. In a *video identification*, the witness is shown images of a suspect, together with images of at least eight other people who resemble the suspect. The images may be moving or still (see Code D, Annex A). An *identification parade* puts the suspect into a line-up of at least eight other people who resemble the suspect as far as possible (see Annex B). *Group identification* is less formal — the suspect is put into an informal group of people, perhaps walking through a shopping centre or in a queue at a bus station (see Annex C). *Confrontation* involves a direct confrontation between witness and suspect. This will usually take place in a police station and the witness shall be asked, 'Is this the person?' (see Annex D).

If the suspect does not dispute identification by a witness, no identification procedure is necessary unless the officer in charge of the investigation considers it would be useful (Code D, paras 3.12 and 3.13). If identification is disputed, an identification procedure shall be held if practicable unless, in all the circumstances, it would serve no useful purpose in determining the suspect's involvement in the offence (para 3.12). There will be no such useful purpose where it is not disputed that the suspect is already well-known to the eyewitness, or there is no reasonable possibility of the witness making an identification. For example, in *R v Abbott* [2006] EWCA Crim 151, two witnesses to a robbery described the height and build of the robbers, their clothing, which included balaclavas and ski masks, and their eyes which were either 'light-coloured' or 'blue'. A had deep brown eyes. The Court of Appeal held that there had been no need to hold an identification procedure (nor give a *Turnbull* warning) as this was not an eyewitness identification case. Although A disputed involvement, no witness purported to identify him and a parade would have served no useful purpose; his involvement was shown purely through circumstantial evidence such as fingerprints. *R v Robinson* [2005] EWCA Crim 3307 is a curious example of a situation where an identification procedure served a useful purpose. R denied involvement in a robbery and sought to challenge that he had been correctly identified in almost every conceivable way. One of the three other alleged robbers became a Crown witness and picked out R on an identification parade. That was probative evidence because the fellow robber had only known R by sight and by his nickname of 'Rambo'; the Crown needed to establish that 'Rambo' and Robinson were one and the same.

If an identification procedure is to be used, the officer in charge of the case will consult with the identification officer as to the suitability and practicability of holding either a video identification or an identification parade. (An identification officer is the officer responsible for the arrangement and conduct of identification procedures, usually an inspector: para 3.11). A video identification will normally be offered to the suspect unless it is not practicable or an identification parade or a group identification would be practicable and more suitable (paras 3.14 and 3.16). The suspect may refuse the offered procedure and may then make representations as to why a different procedure should be used. The identification officer shall then offer an alternative procedure if one is suitable and practicable. If the suspect refuses or fails to take part in any practicable identification procedure, arrangements may be made for covert video identification or covert group identification (para 3.21). As a last resort, if none of the other procedures are practicable, a confrontation may be arranged. See *R v Nolan (Mercedes)* [2005] EWCA Crim, where M refused to participate in a video parade, the officer then compiled a series of still photos which did not require M's active involvement. M changed her mind about participating in the video procedure although it is unclear whether this happened (and the police officer was told) before or after her photo was picked out by the witness. The Court of Appeal held that the officer had acted properly in the circumstances of the case. The court did observe, however, that:

the inspector running the [identification] procedure should consider carefully any timely and clearly communicated change of mind on the part of a suspect, resulting in an agreement by him or her to cooperate. If it is still reasonably possible to organise a fair video/moving image identification procedure without materially endangering the willingness of the witnesses to cooperate or otherwise prejudicing the identification procedure, the inspector should consider whether fairness dictates that he should revert to a video/moving image identification. Whether or not he should accede to a request/change-of-mind of this kind will always depend on the circumstances of the case.

If an eyewitness makes an identification after an identification parade has ended, the suspect and his solicitor should be informed. The police should also consider whether to give the witness a second opportunity at a parade (Code D, Annex B, para 20). Where two witnesses were put into the same room after taking part in a parade, and only one had identified the suspect, but later the second made a statement doing so, neither witness's evidence had to be excluded. See *R v Willoughby* [1999] 2 Cr App R 82, where the Court of Appeal held that merely 'firming-up' a tentative identification at a parade does not come within the ambit of what is now Annex B para 20. As to the witness who had not previously identified the suspect, the court observed that even if para 20 is breached, so long as the breach is relatively minor and innocent (eg, no coaching has occurred), the trial judge may decide not to exclude that evidence under s 78 of the 1984 Act. See, by way of contrast, *R v Ciantar* [2005] EWCA Crim 3559, where an eyewitness who attended a video identification some six weeks after a fatal stabbing did not pick out anyone at the time but immediately afterwards told the investigating officer that she had been nervous and scared during the procedure and that the man whose image was numbered five 'had a look about him that frightened [her] and reminded [her] of the guy at [the restaurant]'. C's image was number five. She had not picked him out as she thought that she needed to be 100 per cent sure before doing so. The witness's evidence was allowed in the trial following a *voir dire*. The Court of Appeal held that the trial judge had been correct not to put it to the jury as a positive identification but rather as a 'qualified' identification whose weight was less than that of a positive identification. For further guidance on 'qualified' identifications, see *R v George* [2002] EWCA Crim 1923.

When the *identity* of the *suspect* is *known* to the police but he is *not available*, the identification officer may arrange a video identification. The suspect will be 'unavailable' if not immediately available to participate in a procedure and will not become available within a reasonably short time. Failure or refusal to participate may be treated as not being available (see Code D, para 3.4 and 3.21).

When the *identity* of the *suspect* is *not known* to the police, then clearly the steps outlined above cannot be taken. To discover the identity of the suspect an eyewitness may be taken to a particular neighbourhood (usually shortly after the alleged offence) to make a street identification (if possible) or given an opportunity to look through police photographs. See Code D, paras 3.2 and 3.3.

15.9.4 Cases where the link between the accused and the crime is made by recognition of voice

An alleged recording of an accused's voice should be heard by the jury but expert evidence on it should also be presented (see *R v Bentum* (1989) 153 JP 538; *R v Robb* (1991) 93 Cr App R 161).

In *R v Deenik* [1992] Crim LR 578, a witness testified to recognising the accused's voice (as that of the person who had committed the offence) on overhearing the accused being interviewed. It was held that it was not necessary to exclude the evidence merely because the accused was unaware that the witness was listening to the interview. The Court of Appeal has said that where a witness identifies a suspect by hearing his voice, Code D has no application and there is no obligation to hold a voice identification parade. However, reference to Code D shows that a witness attending an identification parade may ask to hear any member speak (see Code D, Annex B, para 18).

In any event, what the judge should do is to direct the jury using a suitably adapted form of *Turnbull* warning. Research suggests that identification by voice is less reliable than visual identification, so the warning should be in stronger terms. See further, *R v Hersey* [1998] Crim LR 281; *R v Gummerson* [1999] Crim LR 680; *R v Roberts* [2000] Crim LR 183.

A tape of the perpetrator's voice may be played to the jury, if the accused has given evidence, so they may form their own judgement of the opinions of the experts. This was stated by the Court of Appeal in *R v Bentum* (1989) 153 JP 538 and approved by the Court of Appeal in Northern Ireland in *R v O'Doherty* [2003] 1 Cr App R 5. This is the position, notwithstanding that experts called for both prosecution and defence in *R v O'Doherty* had expressed the view that there are dangers in playing tapes to juries. The Northern Ireland Court of Appeal also said that where expert evidence is given of voice analysis, the evidence should normally deal with both auditory and acoustic analysis. Where a tape is played, the jury should be given a specific warning about the danger of relying upon their own untrained ears. The evidence of Dr Nolan, a Reader in Phonetics at the University of Cambridge, was effectively ignored in so far as he rejected the notion that there was any benefit in playing a tape to the jury. For example, 'jury members were already inevitably under psychological bias from the very fact that [the accused] was in the dock and had been confidently identified by a police officer of his acquaintance.' Dr Nolan made a comparison with identification parades, where the purpose of requiring at least eight other participants was to give a degree of protection to an innocent suspect. 'The jury were in effect given a line-up of one and asked "Is this the person or not[?]".' The Northern Ireland Court of Appeal rejected those concerns, and made a comparison with the case law on the playing of videotapes to a jury (see **12.9.5**). It might be that identical concerns could be raised about that, too.

15.9.5 Cases where the link between the accused and the crime is based upon security film/photographs, etc

The jury can look at a CCTV film or a still photograph and form their own view as to whether the person shown is the accused sitting in the dock. See *Kajala v Noble* (1982) 75 Cr App R 149, DC; and *R v Dodson and Williams* [1984] 1 WLR 971. According to *R v Blenkinsop* [1995] 1 Cr App R 7 a full *Turnbull* warning would not be appropriate in such cases. However, it may be preferable to call a witness who knows the accused and recognises him on the film (in which case a *Turnbull* hearing would generally be appropriate).

R v Fowden [1982] Crim LR 588, *R v Grimer* [1982] Crim LR 674, *Taylor v Chief Constable of Cheshire* [1987] 1 All ER 225 and *R v Caldwell* (1994) 99 Cr App R 73 deal with the situation where witnesses (usually police officers) who know the accused are called upon to identify him as the person caught on film, etc. The propositions which emerge from these cases are:

(a) Where there are several witnesses, they should not be allowed to view the film, etc together but should be asked to view the film individually and state whether they recognise the person on the film (see also Code D, Annex A).

(b) At trial, attempts should be made not to reveal to the jury that the witness knows the accused through previous encounters in the course of investigations into other criminal offences.

(c) A *Turnbull* warning should be given to the jury.

All of these cases were considered and approved by the Court of Appeal in *Attorney-General's Reference (No 2 of 2002)* [2002] EWCA Crim 2373, [2003] Crim LR 192.

In *R v Stockwell* (1993) 97 Cr App R 260, the Court of Appeal accepted that the opinion evidence of a facial-mapping expert is admissible, particularly in cases where there is a possibility that the person caught on the film was disguised. However, one must take care that the opinion evidence of a facial-mapping expert stays within acceptable bounds. It is acceptable to call such an expert at trial to demonstrate to a jury particular characteristics or a combination thereof, with the aid of specialist enhancement techniques if appropriate. It is not acceptable for such an expert to offer an estimate of probabilities or to state the degree of support provided by particular facial characteristics. These are subjective opinions and will be inadmissible until such time as a 'national database or agreed formula or some other such objective measure is established': see *R v Gray* [2003] EWCA Crim 1001.

In *R v Clarke* [1995] 2 Cr App R 425, the Court of Appeal held that evidence of facial mapping by way of video superimposition (of police photographs of the accused upon photographs of the offender taken by a security camera) was admissible as a species of real evidence to which no special rules applied.

In *R v Clare* [1995] 2 Cr App R 333, the Court of Appeal accepted that a police officer, who had viewed a security video of a crowd disturbance at a football match over 40 times (having the facility to stop the video and examine it in slow motion), had thereby become an expert on that video so as to justify calling him to give evidence interpreting the video and the role and identification of the person caught on the video. In *R v Thomas* (1999) LTL 22/11/99, the Court of Appeal held that there is no obligation on the prosecution to put the accused on an identification parade before people on whom neither the police nor the Crown ever intend to rely as identification witnesses. Before T was put on trial for four bank robberies, a police officer studied CCTV videos and single-frame shots of the robberies 'repeatedly'. The Court of Appeal said that the officer had 'acquired special knowledge that the [trial] court did not possess'; in effect, he had become an 'expert' and there was no purpose in seeing if he could pick out T on a parade.

In *R v McNamara* [1996] Crim LR 750 the Court of Appeal held that where a jury requested a view of the accused to compare with a man on a video, no inference could properly be drawn if the accused chose to absent himself from the dock.

Where a crime has been seen by an eyewitness as well as being recorded on a surveillance video, the witness may be allowed to view the video and to amend his witness statement in the light of what he sees on it (see *R v Roberts* [1998] Crim LR 682).

Where a security tape exists, and it shows an offence being committed, but does not show the accused who is now on trial, that tape is material evidence which must be disclosed to the defence. See *Sangster v R* [2002] UKPC 58.

15.9.6   Cases where the link between the accused and the crime is made by fingerprints or DNA profiles

The problem here is primarily how fingerprints or body samples can *properly* be obtained from the accused. The governing statutory provisions in this regard are to be found in PACE 1984, ss 61 to 65 (as amended) and supplemented by Code D, para 4 (fingerprints) and para 6 (body samples).

15.9.6.1   Taking fingerprints

Expert evidence on fingerprints is likely to be excluded if there are less than eight matching ridge characteristics. If there are no exceptional circumstances, the prosecution should not attempt to introduce such evidence. A judge would also consider whether there were any dissimilar characteristics between the print and that taken from the accused, and the size, quality and clarity of the print relied upon. See, for example, *R v Buckley* (1999) 163 JP 561.

PACE 1984, s 61 states:

(1) *Except as provided by this section no person's fingerprints may be taken without the appropriate consent.*

(2) *Consent to the taking of a person's fingerprints must be in writing if it is given at a time when he is at a police station.*

(3) *The fingerprints of a person detained at a police station may be taken without the appropriate consent if—*

    (a) *he is detained in consequence of his arrest for a recordable offence; and*

    (b) *he has not had his fingerprints taken in the course of the investigation of the offence by the police.*

    . . .

(4) *The fingerprints of a person detained at a police station may be taken without the appropriate consent if—*

    (a) *he has been charged with a recordable offence or informed that he will be reported for such an offence; and*

    (b) *he has not had his fingerprints taken in the course of the investigation of the offence by the police.*

    . . .

(6) *Any person's fingerprints may be taken without the appropriate consent if—*

    (a) *he has been convicted of a recordable offence;*

> (b) he has been given a caution in respect of a recordable offence which, at the time of the caution, he has admitted; or
>
> (c) he has been warned or reprimanded under section 65 of the Crime and Disorder Act 1998 (c 37) for a recordable offence.
>
> (7) In a case where by virtue of subsection (3), (4) or (6) above a person's fingerprints are taken without the appropriate consent—
>
> (a) he shall be told the reason before his fingerprints are taken; and
>
> (b) the reason shall be recorded as soon as is practicable after the fingerprints are taken.
>
> [(7A) to (9) omitted]

The definition of 'recordable offence' includes *all* offences punishable by imprisonment. See the National Police Records (Recordable Offences) Regulations 1985, SI 1985/1941.

Section 65 of the 1984 Act has the following definitions:

> *'fingerprints'* include palm prints;
>
> *'appropriate consent'* means—
>
> (a) in relation to a person who has attained the age of 17 years, the consent of that person;
>
> (b) in relation to a person who has not attained that age but has attained the age of 14 years, the consent of that person and his parent or guardian; and
>
> (c) in relation to a person who has not attained the age of 14 years, the consent of his parent or guardian.

Expert evidence may also be given of comparisons of ear prints: *R v Dallagher* [2003] 1 Cr App R 11.

15.9.6.2   Body samples (DNA profiles)

The governing provisions are PACE 1984, ss 62 and 63, as amended by the Criminal Justice and Public Order Act 1994. These are set out below. Section 62 deals with intimate samples and s 63 deals with non-intimate samples.

'Intimate sample' means (a) a sample of blood, semen or any other tissue fluid, urine or pubic hair; (b) a dental impression; (c) a swab taken from a person's body orifice other than the mouth; (*'intimate search'* means a search which consists of the physical examination of a person's body orifices other than the mouth).

'Non-intimate sample' means (a) a sample of hair other than pubic hair; (b) a sample taken from a nail or from under a nail; (c) a swab taken from any part of a person's body other than a part from which a swab taken would be an intimate sample; (d) saliva; (e) a skin impression which means any record of the skin pattern and other physical characteristics or features of the whole or any part of the foot or of any other part of the body.

Section 62 of the 1984 Act provides:

> (1) . . . an intimate sample may be taken from a person in police detention only—
>
> (a) if a police officer of at least the rank of inspector authorises it to be taken; and
>
> (b) if the appropriate consent is given.
>
> (1A) An intimate sample may be taken from a person who is not in police detention but from whom, in the course of the investigation of an offence, two or more non-intimate samples suitable for the same means of analysis have been taken which have proved insufficient—
>
> (a) if an officer of at least the rank of inspector authorises it to be taken; and
>
> (b) if the appropriate consent is given.
>
> (2) An officer may only give an authorisation under subsection (1) or (1A) above if he has reasonable grounds—
>
> (a) for suspecting the involvement of the person from whom the sample is to be taken in a recordable offence; and
>
> (b) for believing that the same will tend to confirm or disprove his involvement.
>
> [(3) to (9A) contain various procedural rules about the taking of intimate samples.]

(10) Where the appropriate consent to the taking of an intimate sample from a person was refused without good cause, in any proceedings against that person for an offence—
  (a) the court, in determining whether . . . there is a case to answer; and
  (b) the court or jury, in determining whether that person is guilty of the offence charged,
  may draw such inferences from the refusal as appear proper.

For the definition of 'recordable offence', see the note following s 61 in **15.9.6.1**.
Section 63 of the 1984 Act provides:

(1) Except as provided by this section, a non-intimate sample may not be taken from a person without the appropriate consent.
(2) Consent to the taking of a non-intimate sample must be given in writing.
(2A) A non-intimate sample may be taken from a person without the appropriate consent if two conditions are satisfied.
(2B) The first is that the person is in police detention in consequence of his arrest for a recordable offence.
(2C) The second is that—
  (a) he has not had a non-intimate sample of the same type and from the same part of the body taken in the course of the investigation of the offence by the police, or
  (b) he has had such a sample taken but it proved insufficient.
(3) A non-intimate sample may be taken from a person without the appropriate consent if—
  (a) he is being held in custody by the police on the authority of a court; and
  (b) an officer of at least the rank of inspector authorises it to be taken without the appropriate consent.
(3A) A non-intimate sample may be taken from a person (whether or not he is in police detention or held in custody by the police on the authority of a court) without the appropriate consent if—
  (a) he has been charged with a recordable offence or informed that he will be reported for such an offence; and
  (b) either he has not had a non-intimate sample taken from him in the course of the investigation of the offence by the police or he has had a non-intimate sample taken from him but either it was not suitable for the same means of analysis or, though so suitable, the sample proved insufficient.
(3B) A non-intimate sample may be taken from a person without the appropriate consent if he has been convicted of a recordable offence.
(3C) A non-intimate sample may also be taken from a person without the appropriate consent if he is a person to whom section 2 of the Criminal Evidence (Amendment) Act 1997 applies (persons detained following acquittal on grounds of insanity or finding of unfitness to plead).
(4) An officer may only give an authorisation under subsection (3) above if he has reasonable grounds—
  (a) for suspecting the involvement of the person from whom the sample is to be taken in a recordable offence; and
  (b) for believing that the sample will tend to confirm or disprove his involvement.
[(5) to (11) contain various procedural rules about the taking of non-intimate samples. See also Code D, para 6.]

Section 63 (especially s 63(3A) and (3B)) brings the position with regard to obtaining *non-intimate* samples into line with the position relating to obtaining fingerprints (see above). Thus a *non-intimate* sample can be taken from a person for the first time without the appropriate consent in a variety of circumstances, for example, whenever the person has been convicted of a recordable offence (s 63(3B)). Even where a non-intimate sample cannot be taken without the appropriate consent, the refusal to consent may form the basis for an inference of guilt at common law (see **14.4.3**). Section 63(3C) and s 63(9A) were inserted by the Criminal Evidence (Amendment) Act 1997.

Section 64 of the 1984 Act makes provision for the destruction of samples where suspects are eventually cleared of any offence — see Code D, Annex F. Regarding the effect of breaches of these statutory rules, see *R v Nathaniel* [1995] 2 Cr App R 565, in which it was held that the trial judge should have applied PACE 1984, s 78, to exclude evidence obtained from a blood sample which should have been destroyed. Lord Taylor CJ said:

> To allow that blood sample to be used in evidence . . . when the sample had been retained in breach of statutory duty and in breach of undertakings to the accused must . . . have had an adverse effect on the fairness of the proceedings.

Subsequently, the House of Lords has drawn a distinction between, on the one hand, trying to use a DNA profile as evidence in a trial when it should have been destroyed (as was the position in *R v Nathaniel*) and using such a profile as part of a criminal investigation. The position is governed by different parts of s 64 — s 64(3B)(a) and (b), respectively. In *R v B (Attorney-General's Reference (No 3 of 1999))* [2001] 1 Cr App R 475, the House of Lords considered the use of a DNA profile from a man (B) acquitted of burglary. The profile had been placed on the national DNA database but, contrary to s 64(3B)(b), was not removed following his acquittal. Subsequently, the profile provided a match with DNA obtained from a rape victim. B was arrested and one of his hairs was removed, legally but without his consent. The hair provided another DNA match. At trial, the prosecution did not rely on the first DNA profile. B was convicted and appealed. The House of Lords held that the 1984 Act did not stipulate a consequence for a breach of s 64(3B)(b) and that the subsection did not legislate that evidence obtained as a result of the prohibited investigation was inadmissible. Section 64(3B)(b) had to be read in conjunction with s 78 of the 1984 Act. Section 64(3B)(b) prohibited the use of a sample liable to destruction for the purposes of any investigation of other offences. It would not prohibit the use of any evidence resulting from such investigation in any subsequent criminal proceedings. The House also considered Article 8 of the ECHR and concluded that its interpretation of s 64(3B)(b) did not contravene the convention.

15.9.6.3   Adducing evidence of DNA profiles

In *R v Doheny* [1997] 1 Cr App R 369, the Court of Appeal laid down the following guidelines as regards the adducing (in court) of DNA evidence:

(a) The scientist should adduce the evidence of the DNA comparisons between the crime stain and the defendant's sample together with his calculations of the random occurrence ratio.

(b) Whenever DNA evidence is to be adduced the Crown should serve on the defence details of how the calculations have been carried out which are sufficient to enable the defence to scrutinise the basis of the calculations.

(c) The Forensic Science Service should make available to a defence expert, if requested, the databases upon which the calculations have been based.

(d) Any issue of expert evidence should be identified and, if possible, resolved before trial. This area should be explored by the court in the pre-trial review.

(e) In giving evidence the expert will explain to the jury the nature of the matching DNA characteristics between the DNA in the crime stain and the DNA in the defendant's blood sample.

(f) The expert will, on the basis of empirical statistical data, give the jury the random occurrence ratio — the frequency with which the matching DNA characteristics are likely to be found in the population at large.

(g) Provided that the expert has the necessary data, it may then be appropriate for him to indicate how many people with the matching characteristics are likely to be found in the United Kingdom or a more limited relevant sub-group, for instance the Caucasian, sexually active males in the Manchester area.

(h) It is then for the jury to decide, having regard to all the relevant evidence, whether they are sure that it was the defendant who left the crime stain, or whether it is possible that it was left by someone else with the same matching DNA characteristics.

(i) The expert should not be asked his opinion on the likelihood that it was the defendant who left the crime stain, nor when giving evidence should he use terminology which may lead the jury to believe that he is expressing such an opinion.

(j) It is not appropriate for an expert to expound a statistical approach to evaluating the likelihood that the defendant left the crime stain, since unnecessary theory and complexity deflect the jury from their proper task.

(k) In the summing-up careful directions are required in respect of any issues of expert evidence, and guidance should be given to avoid confusion caused by areas of expert evidence where no real issue exists.

(l) The judge should explain to the jury the relevance of the random occurrence ratio in arriving at their verdict and draw attention to the extraneous evidence which provides the context which gives that ratio its significance, and to that which conflicts with the conclusion that the defendant was responsible for the crime stain.

(m) In relation to the random occurrence ratio, a direction along the following lines may be appropriate, tailored to the facts of the particular case:

'Members of the jury, if you accept the scientific evidence called by the Crown this indicates that there are probably only four or five white males in the United Kingdom from whom that semen stain could have come. The defendant is one of them. If that is the position, the decision you have to reach, on all the evidence, is whether you are sure that it was the defendant who left that stain or whether it is possible that it was one of that other small group of men who share the same DNA characteristics.'

Opinion evidence

16.1 General rule

You may recall an occasion when someone (a parent or teacher perhaps) said to you, 'When I want your opinion, I'll ask for it!' In the courtrooms of England and Wales, the approach is effectively the same. In civil and criminal cases, the opinions of witnesses are not generally admissible.

Opinions, and conclusions, are for the court to reach, based upon the information placed before it. If a conclusion on a point of law is required, the court will base its conclusion upon the legal arguments put before it by the advocates. Any factual conclusion will be based upon the evidence in the trial (or other form of hearing). Any witness should normally be confined to stating the facts.

When reaching conclusions of fact, the court should make its decisions for itself. So, a rule evolved that a witness should not be asked questions, or offer answers, which require the witness to venture an opinion on a fact in issue. To do so could appear to exert improper influence over the court. This is sometimes known as the 'ultimate issue' rule.

There is also a risk that the court might be unaware of the factual basis (or lack of it) on which the witness's opinion is founded. What the court really needs are the original facts, upon which the witness's opinion is based.

Finally, in situations where the court is quite capable of forming an opinion on the fact in issue, it would be a waste of time to allow a witness to state his opinion on that fact.

Any description of the rule against opinion evidence, even if it is supported with examples, fails to give a true impression of the impact of the rule upon the questioning of witnesses. An objection to a particular question is often made on the basis that the witness is being invited to state opinion. Sometimes the question itself is really nothing more than comment on the witness's evidence.

The general rule excluding opinion evidence is subject to two important exceptions. These arise in cases where the court lacks the witness's competence to form an opinion on a particular issue. That may arise through (a) lack of the necessary direct knowledge or (b) lack of the necessary expertise.

16.2 Witnesses of fact who offer their opinion

Statements of opinion by an eyewitness (E) to the facts in issue are often really a convenient way of stating several facts. Thus, an assertion by E that the defendant was drunk is a convenient way of stating the various facts which E saw (or heard or smelt) which led him to form that opinion. Such a statement will generally be admissible as long as a proper appraisal of the facts does not call for any special expertise.

In civil cases this exception has been put into statutory form: the Civil Evidence Act 1972, s 3(2):

It is hereby declared that where a person is called as a witness in any civil proceedings, a statement of opinion by him on any relevant matter on which he is not qualified to give expert evidence, if made as a way of conveying relevant facts personally perceived by him, is admissible evidence of what he perceived.

If a degree of precision is required, then a witness's best guess or estimate by itself will probably not do. In a case concerning a road accident it will often be necessary to consider the speed at which the vehicles involved were travelling and E may be allowed to state his opinion on this issue. However, if the charge is driving over the speed limit or driving with an amount of alcohol in the blood which exceeds the maximum prescribed by law, precision is needed. See, for example, the Road Traffic Regulation Act 1984, s 89 (see **5.2.2**), which states that it is insufficient to use the opinion of just one witness to prove a speeding case.

16.3   Expert opinion evidence

16.3.1   General principle

There are many situations in which an issue the court is required to determine is so far removed from the court's experience that it needs the opinions of experts to help it determine the issue in question. When such need arises the opinion of an expert *is* admissible. This was recognised as long ago as *Folkes v Chadd* (1782) 3 Doug KB 157. The converse is also true: if an issue calls for expert evidence, the evidence of a non-expert should not be admitted: see *R v Inch* (1989) 91 Cr App R 51.

It is not possible to list all the matters in respect of which expert evidence is required; some matters (eg, medical and scientific) obviously call for the opinions of experts. However, the line between matters which do call for expert evidence and matters which do not is often extremely fine (especially in relation to psychiatric evidence) and the courts consider the question most carefully. In *R v Turner* [1975] QB 834, CA at p 841 Lawton LJ put the point very effectively in this way:

The fact that an expert witness has impressive scientific qualifications does not by that fact alone make his opinion on matters of human nature and behaviour *within the limits of normality* any more helpful than that of the jurors themselves; but there is a danger that they may think it does. (Emphasis added.)

In a similar vein, note the views of the Australian Northern Territory Supreme Court on the absence of need for expert help in assessing the credibility and likelihood of fabrication for a normal nine year-old boy (see case commentary on *The Queen v Joyce* [2005] NTSC 21, [2006] Crim LR 276).

So, expert evidence will usually be excluded if it merely offers an opinion on normal human behaviour. But this sometimes begs the question, 'What is normality?' In a development from the position in *R v Turner*, expert evidence may now be called not merely where the accused is alleged to be suffering from a recognised mental illness, but also if it could show that the accused is suffering from a personality disorder which would tend to affect the reliability of the confession or other evidence. See, for example, *R v Pinfold* [2004] 2 Cr App R 5.

There are particular difficulties in criminal cases when there *is* evidence of *abnormality* but the central issue in the case turns on the application of an objective test. By definition the 'reasonable man' cannot be assumed to be abnormal. In so far as an expert's evidence would *only* be relevant if such an assumption could be made then it would appear to be inadmissible. You should refer to practitioner works to review the (sometimes contradictory) case law on this subject. It has affected such issues as duress, recklessness and provocation.

Expert evidence is probably encountered most frequently in civil cases (and there are many rules of civil procedure which relate to expert evidence — see the *Civil Litigation Manual*). We saw earlier that witnesses of fact can express their opinion on an issue, even though it may be an 'ultimate issue' for the court to decide. The same is true for an expert witness. In civil cases, this is established by the Civil Evidence Act 1972, s 3(1) and (3):

> *(1)   Subject to any rules of court made in pursuance of this Act, where a person is called as a witness in any civil proceedings, his opinion on any relevant matter on which he is qualified to give expert evidence shall be admissible in evidence . . .*
>
> *(3)   In this section 'relevant matter' includes an issue in the proceedings in question.*

Sometimes, an expert may seem to trespass into ultimate issues in criminal cases, for example, *R v Stockwell* (1993) 97 Cr App R 260 — an early use of facial mapping evidence. There is no statutory equivalent of the Civil Evidence Act 1972 to permit experts in criminal cases to offer their opinions on ultimate issues but it seems to be a matter of the form that questions take now, rather than their substance. See further, *Blackstone's Criminal Practice*, 2006.

16.3.2   Who is an expert?

Where a matter calls for expert evidence, only a suitably qualified expert can give it. Indeed, the starting point in examining in chief an expert witness is to establish his expertise. But this does not necessarily mean that there must be formal qualifications. Examples are *R v Silverlock* [1894] 2 QB 766 — a solicitor who had for many years studied handwriting as a hobby (handwriting expert); *Ajami v Comptroller of Customs* [1954] 1 WLR 1405 — a banker with 24 years' experience of Nigerian banking law (foreign law expert). (Matters of *foreign* law are generally treated as calling for expert evidence.) However, it will not be easy to satisfy a judge that a witness is an expert in a field if he lacks formal qualifications. See, for example, *R v Stockwell* (1993) 97 Cr App R 260, where the 'expert' in facial mapping had 'no scientific qualifications, no specific training, no professional body and no database'.

It has sometimes been said that an expert witness would be disqualified from giving evidence in a trial if he had an interest in the proceedings (see, for example, *Liverpool Roman Catholic Archdiocesan Trustees Inc v Goldberg (No 3)* [2001] 1 WLR 2337). Such a situation might arise where the expert is an employee of one of the litigants, or is related to one. It ought to be clear that the expert owes an overriding duty to the court, not to himself or to a litigant (see, for example, CPR, r 35.3). Currently, the position is that a litigant who wishes to call an expert as a witness should disclose to the other litigant(s) and the court any interest that the expert has, or may seem to have. That interest will not automatically disqualify the expert, although disqualification may be required on the facts of the particular case. It has been said that it is 'the nature and extent of the interest or connection which matters, not the mere fact of the interest or connection' (see Nelson J in *Armchair Passenger Transport Ltd v Helical Bar plc* [2003] EWHC 367). Apparent bias is not enough to disqualify an expert from being called as a witness.

The key questions are:

- Does the person have relevant expertise?
- Is he aware of the overriding duty as an expert to the court, and willing and able to fulfil it?

If allowed to testify, the interest or connection may still be relevant to the weight of the evidence given by the expert. In conclusion, 'it is always desirable that an expert should have no actual or apparent interest in the outcome of the proceedings in which he gives evidence', according to Lord Phillips MR in *R (Factortame Ltd) v Secretary of State for Transport, Local Government and the Regions (No 8)* [2003] QB 381.

We must also note the recent decision of Collins J in *Meadow v General Medical Council* [2006] EWHC 146. Sir Roy Meadow had given expert evidence in several 'battered baby' trials. Following successful appeals by women such as Sally Clark and Angela Cannings (see **16.3.3** below), the professional body of Sir Roy Meadow – the General Medical Council – found him guilty of serious professional misconduct and struck him off its register of medical practitioners. On his application for judicial review of those decisions, the Administrative Court held that expert witnesses ought to have immunity from suit arising out of the evidence given to a court. To have no immunity was likely to have a serious impact on the administration of justice by making experts reluctant to become involved with litigation as witnesses. However, such immunity would be limited so that if a judge felt that the expert's conduct had fallen below what was expected of him and merited some disciplinary action, the judge could refer that conduct to the appropriate disciplinary body. The effect of this judgment is to impose a preliminary hurdle upon such disciplinary proceedings. In the absence of the judge taking an adverse view of the expert's conduct, neither a complaint to the professional body nor its own initiative may lead to disciplinary proceedings.

16.3.3   Status of expert evidence

Expert evidence should be treated like the evidence of any other witness. It is a misdirection to tell a jury that they must accept it. See, for example, the speech of Lord Diplock in *R v Lanfear* [1968] 2 QB 77. However, in *R v Anderson* [1972] 1 QB 304 it was held that it would equally be a misdirection to tell a jury that it could disregard expert evidence which had been given by only one witness and which, if accepted, dictated one answer. See also, to the same effect, *R v Bailey* (1978) 66 Cr App R 31.

In civil cases, it has been said that:

even though it is always for the judge rather than for the expert witness to determine matters of fact, the judge must do so on the basis of the evidence, including the expert evidence. The mere application [by a judge] of 'common sense' cannot conjure up a proper basis for inferring that an injury must have been caused in one way rather than another when the only relevant evidence is undisputed scientific evidence which says that either way is equally possible.

See Lord Rodger of Earlsferry in *Fairchild v Glenhaven Funeral Services Ltd* [2002] 3 All ER 305, HL. Similarly, where two or more experts have been called as witnesses:

'a coherent reasoned opinion expressed by a suitably qualified expert should be the subject of a coherent reasoned rebuttal'. This does not mean that the judgment should contain a passage which suggests that the judge has applied the same, or even a superior, degree of expertise to that displayed by the witness. He should simply provide an explanation as to why he has accepted the evidence of one expert and rejected that of another. It may be that the evidence of one or the other accorded more satisfactorily with facts found by the judge. It may be that the explanation of one was more inherently credible than that of the other. It may simply be that one was better qualified, or manifestly more objective, than the other. Whatever the explanation may be, it should be apparent from the judgment.

See Lord Phillips of Worth Matravers MR in *English v Emery Reimbold and Strick Ltd* [2002] 3 All ER 385.

The dilemma for judges (and other fact-finders) in relying on expert evidence is well illustrated in the case of Angela Cannings (*R v Cannings* [2004] 2 Cr App R 7), a mother convicted of the murders of two of her children on the basis of expert evidence as to sudden infant deaths. Quashing her convictions, the Court of Appeal observed that:

> Not so long ago, experts were suggesting that new born babies should lie on their tummies. That was advice based on the best-informed analysis. Nowadays, the advice and exhortation is that babies should sleep on their backs . . . This advice is equally drawn from the best possible known sources. It is obvious that these two views cannot both simultaneously be right . . . [R]esearch in Australia [suggests] that the advice that babies should sleep on their backs had not achieved the improvement in the rate of cot deaths attributed to modern practice . . . Our point is to highlight the fact that even now contrasting views on what might be thought to have been settled once and for all are current.

16.3.4   Upon what can an expert base an opinion?

An expert's opinion will be based upon much more than the facts of the particular case he is considering. It will be based on the expert's experience and any information that he has obtained from extraneous sources such as textbooks, articles and journals. Such information (often referred to as secondary facts) is not treated as hearsay but simply as part of the basis for the expert opinion. Obviously the facts of the particular case on which the opinion is given (the primary facts) should be proved by admissible evidence (whether or not by the expert).

For example, an expert valuer of antiques may be called to give opinion evidence of the value of certain Chinese vases. The opinion may be based on his own knowledge of previous sale prices of similar vases; it may also be based on secondary facts — reports of sales at foreign auction rooms, or books published for the antiques trade specialist. However, if the valuation is based on the 'primary fact' that these vases date from the era of the Ming dynasty in China and are in excellent condition, these primary facts must themselves be proved by admissible evidence. This might be done either by this witness testifying about what he observed when looking at the vases (maker's marks, absence of cracks, chips, etc) or by calling other witnesses who have examined the vases. Thus, our expert may need dual expertise — first, on current saleroom prices for excellent quality Ming vases; secondly, how to identify an 'excellent quality Ming vase'. See, generally, *English Exporters (London) Ltd v Eldonwall Ltd* [1973] Ch 415 and *H v Schering Chemicals Ltd* [1983] 1 WLR 143. Compare *R v Bradshaw* (1986) Cr App R 79, in which 'as a concession to the defence' a psychiatrist was allowed to base his opinion as to the accused's mental state upon statements made out of court by the accused (ie, hearsay).

In *R v Jackson* [1996] 2 Cr App R 420 the Court of Appeal held that although, strictly speaking, an expert witness should not give an opinion based on scientific tests which had been made by assistants (in the expert's absence), maximum use should be made of written statements and formal admissions in proving such tests where it is not disputed that the tests were properly carried out.

A good example of the difference between primary and secondary facts is *R v Abadom* (1983) 76 Cr App R 48. A was charged with robbery. An expert gave opinion evidence that glass found on A's shoes came from a window which had been broken during the robbery. Samples of glass taken from the shoes and the window had the same refractive index. The expert stated that, according to statistics produced by the Home Office Research

Establishment, the chances of the glass being from two distinct sources were minimal. A was convicted and appealed on the grounds that the statistics were hearsay. The Court of Appeal held that the statistics were secondary facts supporting the expert's opinion. So long as the primary facts (ie, that the samples compared were (a) glass taken from A's shoes and (b) glass from the robbery scene and they shared the same refractive index) were proved by admissible evidence, the expert could (indeed should) state why he arrived at his opinion on those facts.

Secondary facts cannot be introduced as evidence in the absence of an expert's opinion. For example, on a drink-driving charge a defendant who is not a medical expert cannot refer to a medical journal to support his defence. See *Dawson v Lunn* [1986] RTR 234. Note that the CJA 2003, s 127 allows proof of the primary facts through hearsay evidence in criminal cases.

16.3.5   Advance notice of expert evidence

16.3.5.1   Civil proceedings

The Civil Evidence Act 1972, s 2(3), made provision for rules of court to be made in relation to advance notice of expert evidence in civil cases. By CPR, r 35.13, a party who fails to disclose an expert's report may not use the report at the trial or call the expert to give evidence orally unless the court gives permission.

A party should be sure that he wishes to use the expert's report as evidence in his case *before* disclosing it to the other side. CPR, r 35.11, provides that *any* party to whom such a report is disclosed can put it in evidence. In general an expert's advice which is sought by a party for the purposes of pending or contemplated litigation would be protected from disclosure (at any stage of the proceedings) by legal professional privilege (see **Chapter 18** of this Manual) but r 35.11 makes it clear that the privilege is lost once the report has been disclosed under the advance notice procedure.

Even where a party relies on legal professional privilege in respect of an expert's opinion, it should be remembered that there is no property in a witness. A party who chooses not to use an expert's evidence can claim privilege in respect of the expert's opinion given to that party but he cannot muzzle the expert. Other parties to that litigation are entitled to instruct the expert and seek his opinion (subject to the procedural restrictions): see *Harmony Shipping Co SA v Saudi Europe Line Ltd* [1979] 1 WLR 1380, CA.

The amount of expert evidence which can be used in civil cases is affected by CPR, r 35.7(1), which provides:

Where two or more parties wish to submit expert evidence on a particular issue, the court may direct that the evidence on that issue is to be given by one expert only.

Unless the parties agree on the expert under this rule, the court may select an expert from a list submitted by the parties, or direct how the expert should be selected. Once selected, each instructing party may give instructions to the expert, sending a copy to the other instructing parties.

16.3.5.2   Criminal proceedings

The prosecution are obliged to disclose their expert evidence to the defence (see the ***Criminal Litigation and Sentencing Manual***). The defence are also obliged to disclose such evidence. In the Crown Court, rules require any party proposing to adduce expert evidence to furnish the other parties with a written statement of the expert's finding or opinion. Such party then, *on request* in writing by any other party, must provide a copy of, or opportunity to examine, the record of any observation, test or calculation on which the finding or opinion is based. See the Criminal Procedure Rules, r 24.

A party may elect not to comply with the rules on disclosure if that party has reasonable grounds for believing that compliance might lead to intimidation or attempted intimidation of an expert witness or to interference with the course of justice. In those circumstances, the party must give notice of the grounds for non-compliance to the other parties. If the rules are not complied with in other circumstances, the expert evidence can only be used with the court's permission.

16.3.6   Opinion evidence and the hearsay rule

16.3.6.1   In civil proceedings

In civil proceedings, hearsay statements are rendered admissible by the Civil Evidence Act 1995, subject to ss 5 and 6(2) of the Act. 'Statement' is defined in s 13 of the Act for the purpose of civil proceedings as 'any representation of fact *or opinion* however made' (emphasis added). Accordingly, the fact that opinion evidence is presented as hearsay will not generally affect its admissibility in civil cases. This will apply to both expert opinion evidence (typically in the form of an expert report) and also to statements of opinion by witnesses of fact (where covered by CEA 1972, s 3(2)).

16.3.6.2   In criminal proceedings

By the Criminal Justice Act 1988, s 30:

(1)   *An expert report shall be admissible as evidence in criminal proceedings, whether or not the person making it attends to give oral evidence in those proceedings.*

(2)   *If it is proposed that the person making the report shall not give oral evidence, the report shall only be admissible with the leave of the court.*

(3)   *For the purpose of determining whether to give leave the court shall have regard—*

　　(a)   *to the contents of the report;*

　　(b)   *to the reasons why it is proposed that the person making the report shall not give oral evidence;*

　　(c)   *to any risk, having regard in particular to whether it is likely to be possible to controvert statements in the report if the person making it does not attend to give oral evidence in the proceedings, that its admission or exclusion will result in unfairness to the accused or, if there is more than one, to any of them; and*

　　(d)   *to any other circumstances that appear to the court to be relevant.*

(4)   *An expert report, when admitted, shall be evidence of any fact or opinion of which the person making it could have given oral evidence.*

　　In this section 'expert report' means a written report by a person dealing wholly or mainly with matters on which he is (or would if living be) qualified to give expert evidence.

(4A)   *Where the proceedings mentioned in subsection (1) above are proceedings before a magistrates' court inquiring into an offence as examining justices this section shall have effect with the omission of—*

　　(a)   *in subsection (1) the words 'whether or not the person making it attends to give oral evidence in those proceedings', and*

　　(b)   *subsections (2) to (4).*

This section applies to statements of fact *and* opinion in the expert report. The effect is clear. It creates a hearsay exception specifically directed at expert reports. When the expert attends as a witness the report is admissible without leave. However, where the expert is not available as a witness the court's leave to use the report is required.

There is no specific provision applicable to criminal cases to allow out of court statements which are essentially shorthand for facts perceived (cf. the Criminal Evidence Act 1972, s 3(2)). However, the CJA 2003, ss 114 and 115 allow out of court statements to be used in evidence, whether they are statements of fact or opinion.

16.3.7 Guidance for experts

There is quite detailed provision covering the form and content of expert reports and the duty of expert witnesses in civil litigation – see CPR, r 35 and *Blackstone's Civil Practice* 2006, **Chapter 52**. Guidance on expert evidence in *criminal* proceedings has been given by the Court of Appeal in two recent cases. First, in *R v Harris and others* [2006] 1 Cr App R 5, the Court approved of and reiterated the guidance given in the *Ikarian Reefer* case [1993] 2 Lloyds Reports 68:

- Expert evidence given to a court should be, and be seen to be, the independent product of the expert, uninfluenced as to form or content by the exigencies of litigation.

- The expert witness should offer independent assistance to the court by stating his objective unbiased opinion on matters within his expertise, and should never become in effect an advocate for a litigant.

- The expert should make it clear if a particular question or issue falls outside his expertise.

- The facts or assumptions upon which the expert's opinion is based must be stated. Material facts which detract from his opinion should be included.

- If the expert feels that he has been supplied with insufficient data properly to research a matter, then his opinion will be provisional and should be identified as such.

- Following exchange of reports, an expert may change his mind on a material matter. If so, the other party or parties (and the court where appropriate) should be told without delay.

Subsequently, in *R v Bowman* [2006] EWCA Crim 417, the court added further guidance on the content of the report. The report (whether the only one or a supplementary one) should:

- disclose all qualifications and the range of expertise relevant to the opinions expressed in the report;

- state –
  - the substance of the instructions received by the expert,
  - the questions asked of the expert,
  - what materials have been provided ,
  - which documents, evidence and assumptions have had a material effect upon formation of the opinion;

- state who did any measurements, tests, etc, what methodology was used and what supervision there was;

- if there is a range of opinion on any matter, summarise the range of opinion and the reasoning supporting it. Any negative material, facts or conflicting opinions should be set out;

- contain extracts from the literature in the relevant field which may assist the court;

- state that the expert has complied with their duty to provide the court with independent assistance by way of objective unbiased opinion on matters within their expertise and acknowledge that, if the expert's opinion changes, all parties (and, where appropriate, the court) will be informed.

The Court of Appeal concluded that the guidance was 'designed to help build up a culture of good practice' amongst experts. The Criminal Procedure Rules Committee issued a consultation paper in 2005 with the aim of making provisions for criminal litigation similar to those which exist in the Civil Procedure Rules. The consultation period closed in January 2006 so we may expect some details to go into the Criminal Procedure Rules, r. 33, in due course. One of the more controversial elements, as recognised by the Criminal Procedure Rules Committee was the suggestion that a single joint expert might be appointed, where appropriate.

Judgments as evidence of the facts on which they are based

17.1 Introduction

How might a case which has already been decided be relevant to a current case?

The judgment in the earlier case may have established a legal principle or precedent that is relevant to the legal issues in the current case.

Alternatively, the parties and the issues in the two cases may be the same. It may be necessary to refer to the judgment in the earlier case to prevent unnecessary repetition of litigation. In a civil case, we might refer to the concept of *res judicata*, and say that the earlier case establishes an issue estoppel (or a cause of action estoppel) between these litigants. Legal certainty requires an end to litigation. Likewise, in a criminal case, the accused can enter a special plea, either *autrefois acquit* or *autrefois convict*, to prevent successive proceedings for the same crime. This principle is often described in criminal cases as the rule against double jeopardy. For more information, you should consult the practitioner texts concerned with these topics.

A third possibility is that the facts that were proved in the earlier case may be relevant to the facts in issue in the current case.

17.2 General rule

The general rule is that such judgments are inadmissible if offered in later trials as evidence of the facts upon which they were based. This rule is often regarded as having been established in a civil case: *Hollington v F Hewthorn and Co Ltd* [1943] KB 587 (hence, the rule is often referred to as the rule in *Hollington v Hewthorn*). Mr Hollington brought a civil claim for damages for the death of his son in a road accident. His cause of action was the allegedly negligent driving of the defendant's employee. The court held that it was not possible to call evidence of the employee's conviction for driving without due care and attention on that specific occasion in order to prove the facts on which that conviction was based. To succeed on the issue of negligence, Mr Hollington had to call evidence, starting from scratch. The driver's conviction did not weigh in the scales at all — it was simply inadmissible and so unusable as evidence.

One consequence of this judgment was that proceedings in the civil courts were often extended unnecessarily because (unless the facts were admitted by the convicted party) the same issues had to be proved all over again. The inconvenience of this general rule is obvious. A further unfortunate consequence was that in some civil trials, matters which had already been established beyond reasonable doubt (in a criminal trial) were not found to be established to the lower standard of proof, on the balance of probabilities. That inconsistency was a matter for serious concern (although, in fairness, we should observe that the evidence in the two trials might have been different).

An example of the sort of problem thrown up by this rule is found in *Hinds v Sparks* [1964] Crim LR 717. Hinds had been tried for and convicted of a robbery and had appealed unsuccessfully to the Court of Criminal Appeal. Later, a journalist, Sparks, published a statement asserting that Hinds had committed a robbery some years previously. Hinds sued Sparks for defamation. The law of defamation requires the defendant to prove the truth of his assertion. Sparks was unable to produce any evidence to support his assertion, other than the robbery conviction. Unfortunately, the rule in *Hollington v Hewthorn* made that evidence inadmissible to show Hinds had committed a robbery. Hinds won his claim.

There are now a number of exceptions to the rule in civil and criminal proceedings. With one exception, these relate to the admissibility of previous convictions. In only one example is the conviction conclusive evidence of the facts upon which it was based (see Civil Evidence Act 1968, s 13, **17.3.3** below). We shall look at the exceptions in civil cases, then criminal cases.

17.3 Use of a previous judgment as evidence of the facts in civil cases

17.3.1 Use of a criminal conviction as evidence of the facts upon which it was based in a subsequent civil case

The Civil Evidence Act 1968, s 11, reverses the actual decision in *Hollington v F Hewthorn and Co Ltd* [1943] KB 587 (ie, the conviction for driving without due care would now be admissible evidence in the civil trial to help Mr Hollington prove negligence). It therefore creates a major exception to the general rule. Section 11 puts the legal burden of proof on to the party (let us call him X) who denies that the person convicted of the offence in question did commit it. Section 11 does not say that the conviction is conclusive of the facts; it simply creates a rebuttable presumption.

The Civil Evidence Act 1968, s 11 states:

(1) *In any civil proceedings the fact that a person has been convicted of an offence by or before any court in the United Kingdom or by a court-martial there or elsewhere shall (subject to subsection (3) below) be admissible in evidence for the purpose of proving, where to do so is relevant to any issue in those proceedings, that he committed that offence, whether he was so convicted upon a plea of guilty or otherwise and whether or not he is a party to the civil proceedings; but no conviction other than a subsisting one shall be admissible in evidence by virtue of this section.*

(2) *In any civil proceedings in which by virtue of this section a person is proved to have been convicted of an offence by or before any court in the United Kingdom or by a court-martial there or elsewhere—*

    (a) *he shall be taken to have committed that offence unless the contrary is proved; and*

    (b) *without prejudice to the reception of any other admissible evidence for the purpose of identifying the facts on which the conviction was based, the contents of any document which is admissible as evidence of the conviction, and the contents of the information, complaint, indictment or charge-sheet on which the person in question was convicted, shall be admissible in evidence for that purpose.*

(3) *Nothing in this section shall prejudice the operation of section 13 of this Act or any other enactment whereby a conviction or a finding of fact in any criminal proceedings is for the purposes of any other proceedings made conclusive evidence of any fact.*

(4) *Where in any civil proceedings the contents of any document are admissible in evidence by virtue of subsection (2) above, a copy of that document, or of the material part thereof, purporting to be certified or otherwise authenticated by or on behalf of the court or authority having custody of that document shall be admissible in evidence and shall be taken to be a true copy of that document or part unless the contrary is shown.*

See, generally, *Blackstone's Civil Practice*, 2006, **Chapter 47**.

17.3.2 Challenging a conviction

Remember, X is the party against whom the presumption in s 11 will operate. How should X go about rebutting this presumption? This question has been considered by the courts on several occasions. The prevailing view is that it will not avail X simply to challenge the technical correctness of the conviction. X must prove either:

- that he (or whoever else was convicted) did not commit the crime; or
- that the crime was not committed at all.

The practical consequence of s 11 is that it is extremely difficult for a party to challenge successfully the presumption that the person convicted did in fact commit the offence in question. One need simply note the different standards of proof involved in securing the criminal conviction (beyond reasonable doubt) and in the civil trial (balance of probabilities). See *Stupple v Royal Insurance Co Ltd* [1971] 1 QB 50; *Taylor v Taylor* [1970] 1 WLR 1148; and *Wauchope v Mordechai* [1970] 1 WLR 317.

It has been said (in *Brinks Ltd v Abu Saleh (No 1)* [1995] 4 All ER 65 by Jacob J) that a convicted defendant must adduce fresh evidence which 'entirely changes the aspect of the case' in order to be permitted to contest a civil action based on the same facts. Others have since argued that this requirement to adduce fresh evidence which 'entirely changes the aspect of the case' is a very difficult one to surmount and, if it were applied generally, the effect would be to prevent a convicted defendant from ever contesting a civil claim. The matter was considered in *J v Oyston* [1999] 1 WLR 694.

The defendant O was convicted by a jury of raping J, and indecently assaulting her. Subsequently, J sued the defendant for damages. O now wished to call evidence about J (the claimant/complainant), which had not been produced at his criminal trial, although it had been put before the Court of Appeal when he appealed unsuccessfully against his conviction. J asserted that to allow O to call evidence which was intended to show that no crime had been committed would constitute an abuse of process and should not be allowed. Smedley J rejected that assertion. Smedley J ruled that it was entirely legitimate for O to seek to disprove allegations of rape and indecent assault, notwithstanding his convictions for both offences. In effect, J wanted to stop O from doing precisely that which s 11(2)(a) permitted him to do. That would be quite contrary to the intention of Parliament as enshrined in s 11 and as interpreted by Lord Diplock in *Hunter v Chief Constable of the West Midlands Police* [1982] AC 529. It may be difficult for a party successfully to rebut a presumption under s 11, but it must be a matter for that party to decide whether or not he wants to attempt it.

Conversely, it seems that where a *claimant* seeks to re-litigate a matter which has already been determined against him by a criminal court (that is, a convicted defendant seeks to challenge the correctness of the conviction by initiating a civil claim against the prosecuting authority), the claim is likely to be struck out as an abuse of process under

CPR, r 3.4(2)(b). See *Hunter v Chief Constable of the West Midlands Police* (and cf. Civil Evidence Act 1968, s 13, below).

Section 11 only applies to subsisting convictions. If a party in a civil claim wishes to use a conviction under s 11, the civil proceedings should be adjourned until any pending criminal appeal has been heard: see *Re Raphael* [1973] 1 WLR 998. A party seeking to rely on s 11 should state this clearly in the appropriate statement of case (see the ***Drafting Manual***). This should include details of the conviction and the issue to which it is relevant. Section 11(4) allows a certified copy of the conviction, indictment, etc to be used to prove the facts on which the conviction was based.

An interesting example of s 11 being considered appears in *Raja v Van Hoogstraten* [2005] EWHC 1642. VH had originally been convicted of the manslaughter of the claimant, R; two associates of VH were convicted of R's murder. The conviction of VH was subsequently quashed on appeal but the issue in the present (civil) litigation turned on whether VH had instigated his two associates to murder the claimant. R's representatives sought to rely upon the murder convictions of the two men under the Civil Evidence Act 1968, s 11 to show that they had killed R; the judge having ruled that no such reliance could be placed upon VH's quashed (and thus not 'subsisting') manslaughter conviction. VH was refused leave to amend his defence to include a rebuttal of the murder convictions, on the grounds (a) that it was so late in the proceedings as to be unfair on the claimant to allow the amendment (estimated to expand the length of trial from 6 to 12 weeks) and (b) that the task for a defendant seeking to rebut a conviction under s 11 was to prove on the balance of probabilities that the person convicted was innocent. Simply alleging (as here) that the conviction is unsafe will not do. Furthermore, the evidence offered in support did not 'show an arguable case (let alone a case with any real prospect of success)' that the convicted individuals were not guilty of R's murder.

17.3.3 Use of convictions in defamation cases

A convicted criminal might try to use libel proceedings to reopen a criminal case which resulted in his conviction (in a similar vein to Mr Hinds, **17.2**). Section 11 would not prevent this because it only creates a rebuttable presumption. Now, in this situation a defendant could try to persuade the judge that the claim should be struck out as an abuse of process (under CPR, r 3.4; cf. *Hunter v Chief Constable of the West Midlands Police* [1982] AC 529, **17.3.2**). That application might or might not succeed. This specific situation was addressed by s 13 of the Civil Evidence Act 1968, which creates an irrebuttable presumption that the person convicted of the crime did in fact commit it.

The Civil Evidence Act 1968, s 13 states:

(1) *In an action for libel or slander in which the question whether a person did or did not commit a criminal offence is relevant to an issue arising in the action, proof that, at the time when that issue falls to be determined, that person stands convicted of that offence shall be conclusive evidence that he committed that offence; and his conviction thereof shall be admissible in evidence accordingly.*

(2) *In any such action as aforesaid in which by virtue of this section a person is proved to have been convicted of an offence the contents of any document which is admissible as evidence of the conviction, and the contents of the information, complaint, indictment or charge-sheet on which that person was convicted, shall, without prejudice to the reception of any other admissible evidence for the purpose of identifying the facts on which the conviction was based, be admissible in evidence for the purpose of identifying those facts.*

(3) *For the purposes of this section a person shall be taken to stand convicted of an offence if but only if there subsists against him a conviction of that offence by or before a court in the United Kingdom or by a court-martial there or elsewhere.*

The effect of s 13 is that an action in defamation will be struck out if it is based on the defendant's assertion that the claimant committed an offence for which the claimant has been convicted. In other words, in defamation cases a person convicted of an offence is *conclusively* presumed to have committed it. Some care still needs to be taken, though — s 13 does not give publishers carte blanche to make *general* attacks on the character of convicts (see *Levene v Roxhan* [1970] 1 WLR 1322).

17.3.4   Use of a criminal acquittal as evidence of the facts upon which it was based in a subsequent civil case

An acquittal is not covered by any exception in the Civil Evidence Act 1968, so it appears that the rule in *Hollington v Hewthorn* still applies: the acquittal is inadmissible evidence if it will be used to show that the criminal defendant did not commit the offence. This may be justified by reference once more to the different standards of proof which apply in the two trials. See further, *Blackstone's Civil Practice*.

17.3.5   Use of a civil judgment as evidence of the facts upon which it was based in a subsequent civil case

There is no *general* provision allowing for previous civil judgments to be used as evidence of the facts on which they were based. However, s 12 of the Civil Evidence Act 1968, allows a very limited range of civil judgments to be used as evidence of the facts on which they are based. See *Blackstone's Civil Practice*, 2006, **Chapter 47**.

17.4   Use of a previous judgment as evidence of the facts in criminal cases

17.4.1   Use of a criminal conviction as evidence of the facts upon which it was based in a subsequent criminal case

Until relatively recently the common law rule excluding judgments as evidence of the facts on which they are based was of general application in criminal cases. For example, where A was charged with handling stolen goods, it was not permissible to prove that B was convicted of the theft of the goods in question to show that the goods were stolen. You may wonder why a rule established in a civil case (*Hollington v Hewthorn*) should hold sway in criminal cases, too. In fact, the rule in criminal cases pre-dates *Hollington v Hewthorn*. The example that you have just read is taken from *R v Turner* (1832) 1 Mood CC 347.

For convictions, the rule has been changed by PACE 1984, s 74. A distinction needs to be drawn between (a) convictions of the accused and (b) convictions of persons other than the accused.

17.4.1.1   Convictions of the accused

PACE 1984, s 74(3), as amended by the CJA 2003, provides:

> *In any proceedings where evidence is admissible of the fact that the accused has committed an offence, if the accused is proved to have been convicted of the offence —*
>
> *(a)   by or before any court in the United Kingdom; or*

(b)   by a Service court outside the United Kingdom,
he shall be taken to have committed that offence unless the contrary is proved.

The general rule is that evidence that the accused has previously offended is inadmissible at his trial (see **Chapter 9**). This is so, regardless of whether or not the accused was actually convicted of the earlier offence. In exceptional situations, the fact that the accused has previously offended *may* be relevant and admissible (see CJA 2003, s 101). Where one of these exceptional situations applies, the prosecution can take advantage of s 74(3). This provision works in the same way as the Civil Evidence Act 1968, s 11(2). It sets up a rebuttable presumption that the accused did indeed commit the previous offence.

Section 74(3) does *not* deal with questions of admissibility. All it says is that, where it is relevant and admissible to prove that D committed an offence, the act of adducing evidence that he has been convicted of it results in a rebuttable presumption. It will then be for D to try to prove, on a balance of probabilities, that he did not commit the offence.

So, remember what we are looking for. These are situations where it is relevant and admissible to show that the accused has previously *committed* an offence. In such situations, if the prosecution prove his conviction for the earlier offence, they can rely on s 74(3) to reverse the burden of proof on that fact. This still begs the question, How does the prosecution prove the conviction? See **17.4.1.3**.

17.4.1.2   Convictions of persons other than the accused

In 1972, the 11th Report of the Criminal Law Revision Committee had recommended the abolition of the rule in *Hollington v Hewthorn* in criminal proceedings. The committee apparently thought that it was recommending simply that a conviction would be admissible in evidence to deal with the situation 'where it was necessary as a preliminary matter for it to be proved that a person other than the accused had been convicted of an offence' (see *R v O'Connor* (1986) 85 Cr App R 298, per Taylor J). This would ease the burden on the prosecution in the following situations, for example:

- in a trial for handling stolen goods, in order to prove that the goods were stolen the prosecution could prove the conviction of the thief;
- in trials for harbouring offenders, the prosecution could prove the conviction of the offender.

PACE 1984, s 74(1) and (2) (as amended by CJA 2003, Sch 36), provides:

(1)   In any proceedings the fact that a person other than the accused has been convicted of an offence by or before any court in the United Kingdom or by a Service court outside the United Kingdom shall be admissible in evidence for the purpose of proving that that person committed that offence, where evidence of his having done so is admissible, whether or not any other evidence of his having committed that offence is given.

(2)   In any proceedings in which by virtue of this section a person other than the accused is proved to have been convicted of an offence by or before any court in the United Kingdom or by a Service court outside the United Kingdom, he shall be taken to have committed that offence unless the contrary is proved.

That seems quite straightforward. The effect of s 74(2) is very similar to the effect of the Civil Evidence Act 1968, s 11(2), in civil cases. That is, it puts the legal burden of proof on the party who denies that the convicted person committed the offence in question (of course the *standard* of proof in a criminal case will vary according to whether that party is the prosecution or the defence). Prior to the amendment of s 74(1) by the CJA 2003, the judicial interpretation of this provision had caused considerable practical difficulties, with several cases going to the Court of Appeal (see, for example, *R v Robertson* (1987) 85 Cr App

R 304). In its amended form, s 74(1) does not say in what circumstances a conviction will be admissible to prove that a non-defendant has committed an offence, it simply says that, when such a matter may be put before the court (and see in particular, CJA 2003, s 100), evidence of a conviction for the offence is admissible to show its commission by that person.

It remains to be seen how the amended version of s 74(1) is treated by the courts. Previous case law on the original subsection indicated that it was 'a provision that should be sparingly used' (see *Robertson*). It should also be noted that the exclusionary discretion in PACE 1984, s 78 was often relied upon by defendants who were opposing use of the provision by the prosecution.

It should be noted that s 74(1) only provides a short cut for proving matters which otherwise may be proved by calling a witness. For example, in a case where one of several defendants has entered a guilty plea, the prosecution can then call the former co-defendant to testify for the Crown against the rest. In that event the remaining defendants can then cross-examine the former co-defendant, on both the facts and his credibility. The trial judge may also warn the jury to take care when assessing the evidence of the former co-defendant. By using s 74(1) instead, the opportunity of cross-examination and the need for a 'care' warning are both removed. It is arguable that this situation could deny the accused a fair trial, contrary to the ECHR, Article 6. Perhaps this is why the Court of Appeal said (in *Robertson* and subsequent cases) that s 74(1) is to be used sparingly.

17.4.1.3 Proving a conviction

This is a two-limb process that can be done using PACE 1984, s 73(1) and (2).

One limb is that the prosecution must call a witness to produce the certificate of conviction. What qualifies as a certificate is explained in s 73(2). The other limb is that the prosecution must call a witness to say that the person named in the certificate is the accused in the dock. It could be the same witness for both limbs, usually a police officer. It was noted in *Pattison v DPP* [2005] EWHC 2938 (Admin) that where D denies he is the person named on the certificate, that fact must be proved beyond a reasonable doubt. There were three clear ways to do this:

- an admission by or on behalf of D;
- fingerprint evidence;
- evidence of someone present in court for the previous conviction.

(See *Derwent Justices, ex Heaviside* [1996] RTR 384.)

The court in *Pattison* identified a fourth way – matching D's personal details with those on the certificate. Even where the details are common, a match can establish a prima facie case that D was the person convicted. In the absence of any contradictory evidence offered by D, that should be sufficient for the court to find the issue proved (helped, possibly, by an adverse inference under the Criminal Justice and Public Order Act 1994, s 35).

Section Z provides:

(1) *Where in any proceedings the fact that a person has in the United Kingdom been convicted or acquitted of an offence otherwise than by a Service court is admissible in evidence, it may be proved by producing a certificate of conviction or, as the case may be, of acquittal relating to that offence, and proving that the person named in the certificate as having been convicted or acquitted of the offence is the person whose conviction or acquittal of the offence is to be proved.*

(2) *For the purposes of this section a certificate of conviction or of acquittal—*

   (a) *shall, as regards a conviction or acquittal on indictment, consist of a certificate, signed by the proper officer of the court where the conviction or acquittal took place, giving the substance and effect (omitting the formal parts) of the indictment and of the conviction or acquittal; and*

(b)   shall, as regards a conviction or acquittal on a summary trial, consist of a copy of the conviction or of the dismissal of the information, signed by the proper officer of the court where the conviction or acquittal took place or by the proper officer of the court, if any, to which a memorandum of the conviction or acquittal was sent;

and a document purporting to be a duly signed certificate of conviction or acquittal under this section shall be taken to be such a certificate unless the contrary is proved.

17.4.1.4   What does the conviction prove?

Where a conviction is introduced into evidence in a trial, the judge must be careful to direct the jury as to:

* to what issue in the trial it relates; and
* what is the effect of the conviction.

First, it is important for judge and counsel to be clear on the exact issue to which the conviction is said to be relevant. If it is liable to be misused by the jury, the judge should probably exclude evidence of the conviction, using PACE 1984, s 78. Secondly, the conviction is *not* conclusive evidence that an offence was committed by anyone. That is shown by s 74(2), which creates a rebuttable presumption. It was confirmed in *R v Dixon* [2001] Crim LR 126 that if the defendant testifies that no such offence was committed, it is for the jury to decide whose account to believe.

By PACE 1984, s 75(1):

Where evidence that a person has been convicted of an offence is admissible by virtue of section 74 above, then without prejudice to the reception of any other admissible evidence for the purpose of identifying the facts on which the conviction was based—

(a)   the contents of any document which is admissible as evidence of the conviction; and

(b)   the contents of the . . . indictment . . . on which the person in question was convicted, shall be admissible in evidence for that purpose.

17.4.2   Use of a criminal acquittal as evidence of the facts upon which it was based in a subsequent criminal case

This situation is unaffected by PACE 1984. If the acquittal is that of the defendant, D, then generally it will be inadmissible as evidence in the current trial. However, facts involved in the offence of which D was acquitted may be relevant and the acquittal admissible (see *R v Z* [2000] 2 AC 483; *R v Hay* (1983) 77 Cr App R 70; *R v Terry* [2005] QB 996).

If the acquittal is of someone other than the accused, generally it is inadmissible. Again, it may be relevant to an issue in the current case. An example may occur if the credibility of a witness is challenged (and the witness has previously testified for the prosecution in a trial where he allegedly fabricated a confession) (see *R v Cooke* (1987) 84 Cr App R 286). The general principle is illustrated by the decision of the Privy Council in *Hui Chi-ming v R* [1992] 1 AC 34. A man was killed. D1 and D2 were charged with his murder. D1, the alleged killer, was tried first. The jury acquitted him of murder but convicted him of manslaughter. At D2's trial, as an accomplice to murder, the defence wanted to use evidence of D1's acquittal for murder. The trial judge ruled that it was inadmissible. The ruling was upheld by the Privy Council on appeal because the verdict of the first jury was irrelevant, being only evidence of their opinion. You may feel that this produces exactly the same result as *Hollington v Hewthorn*, nearly 50 years earlier, and could also be criticised. It may make more sense if you bear in mind that there are often seemingly inconsistent verdicts involving different parties to a single crime. Also, an acquittal simply records a failure by the prosecution to prove their case beyond a reasonable doubt. It does not do the opposite and prove that D is innocent. Of course, in a case like that above, it would have been better for justice to have held a single trial of D1 and D2 before the same jury on the same evidence.

17.4.3 Use of a civil judgment as evidence of the facts upon which it was based in a subsequent criminal case

Owing to the lower standard of proof in civil trials, any finding of fact would seem to be insufficiently probative to be admissible as evidence in a criminal trial.

18

Privilege and public policy

18.1 Introduction

Most of the rules of evidence involve analysis of the probative value of the evidence and lead to the exclusion of evidence that will not, for various reasons, be valuable in this way. We have seen that there are occasional wider social, political or moral considerations (for example the exclusion of 'unfair' evidence under s 78 or improperly obtained confessions even though they are not prejudicial). However, generally, the main concern of the rules of evidence in both civil and criminal cases is ensuring that the evidence that goes before the tribunal of fact will assist in proving the case. Even when policy reasons for excluding evidence arise, those policies (such as fairness or proportionality) are aspects of the interests of justice. In such cases competing aspects of the interests of justice have to be weighed against each other (such as unfair procedures versus accurate trial verdicts under PACE 1984, s 78).

The rules of evidence considered in this chapter reflect this concern to ensure that the interests of justice do not lead to admitting evidence that will cause a greater damage to society. With 'privileged' evidence, the concern for broader interests of justice outside the particular case have been taken to outweigh the interests of justice in the particular case. In the case of public policy exclusion the interests of justice are weighed against other social and moral questions (for example, national security).

Both privilege and public policy arguments are most likely to arise during the disclosure/discovery procedure both in civil cases (see the *Civil Litigation Manual* or *Blackstone's Civil Practice*, 2006, **Chapter 48**) and in criminal cases (see the *Criminal Litigation and Sentencing Manual*, *Blackstone's Criminal Practice*, 2006 or *Archbold*, 2006).

18.2 Privilege

In broad terms the privileges which follow allow one (or in the case of 'without prejudice' correspondence either) party to prevent evidence from being put before the court on specific grounds. The types of privilege covered in this chapter are:

- the privilege against self-incrimination;
- legal professional privilege;
- 'without prejudice' correspondence.

18.2.1   Privilege against self-incrimination

The privilege against self-incrimination influenced the development of the rules of evidence and procedure in a number of areas (particularly the exercise of the right to silence (**Chapter 14**) and the compellability of witnesses (**Chapter 4**)). The principle is also enshrined in Article 6(1) of the ECHR.

The privilege has a more general application. No person is obliged to reveal a fact if doing so renders it reasonably likely that proceedings will be commenced that expose him to the risk of any criminal charge or sanction (*Blunt v Park Lane Hotel Ltd* [1942] 2 KB 253). In explaining the above test in *R v Boyes* (1861) 1 B & S 311, Cockburn J said that the risk of prosecution and punishment must be 'real and appreciable with reference to the ordinary operation of the law in the ordinary course of things; not a danger of an imaginary and unsubstantial character'.

The rule does not apply where the risk posed is a civil liability (Witnesses Act 1806) or criminal liability under foreign law (*King of Two Sicilies v Willcox* (1851) 1 Sim NS 301; Civil Evidence Act 1968, s 14) but can extend to penalties under EC law (*Rio Tinto Zinc Corporation v Westinghouse Electric Company* [1978] AC 547).

The privilege extends not only to the evidence that the person might give but to documents, items or information that the person is requested to provide during proceedings.

18.2.1.1   'Real and appreciable danger'

The evidence, etc, must *create* the risk of incrimination. If there is already strong evidence against the witness on the matter to which the privilege is said to relate, the privilege will not apply (*Khan v Khan* [1982] 2 All ER 60).

Furthermore, if the risk can be avoided, the privilege will not apply. So in *AT&T Istel v Tully* [1993] AC 45, HL, an offer by the CPS not to prosecute the defendant in respect of any frauds revealed was held to be sufficient protection for the defendant to prevent the privilege from applying.

Where the sanction or punishment that is faced is trivial, the court may also conclude that there is no real and appreciable danger (*Rank Film Distributors Ltd v Video Information Centre* [1982] AC 380).

18.2.1.2   To whom does the privilege apply?

In criminal cases the privilege only applies to the person asserting it. In other words, A could not exercise the privilege on the grounds that his answer would incriminate B (this is implicit from *R v Pitt* [1983] QB 25 where a witness was treated as compellable to give evidence against her spouse: this would not have been the case if she could have asserted a privilege against incriminating her spouse).

In civil cases the privilege does extend to spouses (Civil Evidence Act 1968, s 14(1)(b)) but no further.

Companies can be covered by the privilege (*Triplex Safety Glass Co Ltd v Lancegaye Safety Glass* [1939] 2 KB 395). However, in such circumstances the privilege excuses an employee of the company from giving testimony (or disclosing evidence) that would incriminate the company; it does not excuse him from incriminating an employee of the company (*Rio Tinto Zinc v Westinghouse Electric*) other than himself.

18.2.1.3   Privileged evidence that is revealed

If a witness answers questions without claiming the privilege the evidence can be used against the witness in subsequent proceedings (*R v Coote* (1873) LR 4 PC 599). However, if the witness does claim privilege and is wrongly refused (and therefore forced to answer), the evidence must be excluded in the subsequent proceedings (*R v Garbett* (1847) 1 Den CC 236).

18.2.1.4   Statutory exceptions

The privilege is subject to numerous statutory exceptions. First of all the privilege does not protect the accused in criminal proceedings from answering questions in respect of those proceedings (Criminal Evidence Act 1898, s 1(2)).

In the following situations evidence that reveals criminal conduct may be admitted in specific types of proceeding (the type of proceeding being illustrated in each situation below). However, in each situation, there are restrictions on the extent to which the information revealed can be used in subsequent criminal proceedings:

(a) Theft Act 1968, s 31(1): in proceedings concerning the recovery or administration of property, the execution of any trust or an account for property or dealings with property, a person has no privilege against answering questions simply because doing so would reveal he may have committed an offence under the Theft Act 1968. However, any statement or testimony made is not admissible in a subsequent prosecution under the Theft Act 1968. This protection also extends to the spouse of the witness. If the evidence poses a real risk of both a Theft Act and a non-Theft Act prosecution the court will apply the privilege against self-incrimination (*Renworth Ltd v Stephansen* [1996] 3 All ER 244) with the effect that the person is not obliged to answer the question.

(b) The same provision exists in the Criminal Damage Act 1971, s 9 relating to the same types of civil action, but the criminal offences to which it relates are criminal damage offences.

(c) Children Act 1989, s 98: in proceedings concerning the care, supervision or protection of children, a person cannot refuse to answer questions on the grounds that that person or his spouse would be incriminated. Again, however, such evidence will not be admissible in subsequent proceedings other than perjury proceedings (s 98(2)). It has been suggested that this protection extends to oral or written statements made before trial (*Oxfordshire County Council v P* [1995] 2 All ER 225; *Cleveland County Council v F* [1995] 2 All ER 236). However, in *Re G (A Minor)* [1996] 2 All ER 65, the Court of Appeal stated that the protection under s 98(2) should be restricted to evidence in the proceedings and not pre-trial statements. However, the court recognised that the criminal courts were not bound by that view. In *A Chief Constable v A County Council* [2003] 1 FLR 579, the court took the view that statements made by parents to expert witnesses appointed by the court would be covered by s 98(2) privilege and therefore would not be admissible in subsequent criminal proceedings.

(d) Criminal Justice Act 1987, s 2: the Director of the Serious Fraud Office has broad powers to investigate persons in respect of offences of serious or complex fraud (ie, those under Part 1 of that Act). Persons investigated can be required to answer questions or provide documentation. Such evidence can only be used at a later trial if the person is being prosecuted for the offence of providing false information under s 2 or subsequently makes a statement inconsistent with it (ie, as a previous inconsistent statement: see **6.3.6**).

(e) Insolvency Act 1986: various statements a person must make under this Act could be incriminating. Section 433(1) of the Act provides that such statements may be used in evidence against the person who made them in subsequent proceedings.

Section 433(2), however, provides that in subsequent criminal proceedings such statements may only be admitted (or questions asked about them) if the person who made the statement has already admitted evidence relating to that statement. This restriction does not apply in relation to perjury and related proceedings or criminal proceedings under the Insolvency Act itself.

(f) Similar restrictions to those under the Insolvency Act apply in relation to investigations under the Companies Act 1985, ss 434 and 447 and various other statutes in Sch 3 to the YJCEA 1999.

In so far as any other statute appears to have revoked the privilege against self-incrimination without any restriction upon the extent to which statements made can be used in subsequent criminal proceedings, there is a potential breach of Article 6(1) of the ECHR, but this is not always so. In *Brown v Stott* [2001] 2 WLR 817, the Privy Council recognised that Article 6 rights are subject to a limited qualification. Where there was a clear public interest in revoking the privilege, the statutory provision would not necessarily be held to be incompatible with Article 6. In *Office of Fair Trading v X* [2003] 2 All ER (Comm) 183, the High Court upheld powers to search premises and to question persons present about items found during the search where the statutory framework for such searches included guarantees of a suspect's rights.

18.2.2 Legal professional privilege

Both civil and criminal litigation depends upon parties having access to effective legal advice. This in turn depends upon a party and his lawyer being able to communicate freely and without fear that the content of the discussion will be used by the other side. Furthermore, legal professional privilege is a function of Article 6 of the ECHR (*S v Switzerland* (1991) 14 EHRR 670; *Foxley v United Kingdom* (2001) 31 EHRR 25).

There are two classes of legal professional privilege, which broadly are:

(a) communications between a lawyer and his client (also known as 'lawyer–client privilege' or 'legal advice privilege');

(b) communications between the lawyer or client on the one hand and third parties on the other where such communication relates to pending or contemplated litigation: *Waugh v British Railways Board* [1980] AC 521 (also known as 'litigation privilege').

Under both classes the privilege applies to communication with solicitors, barristers, foreign lawyers and in-house legal advisers (*Re Duncan* [1968] P 306; *Alfred Compton Amusement Machines Ltd v Customs & Excise Commissioners* [1974] AC 405).

18.2.2.1 Lawyer–client privilege

Communications between a lawyer and his client for the purposes of obtaining or giving legal advice are privileged whether or not litigation is contemplated (*Greenough v Gaskell* (1833) 1 My & K 98).

The privilege clearly covers any requests for advice from a client to a lawyer and any advice given by the lawyer to the client. However, unlike litigation privilege (**18.2.2.2**) this privilege does not attach to communications between a lawyer or a client and a third party to the lawyer–client relationship. Therefore, in *Wheeler v Le Marchant* (1881) 17 Ch D 675, no lawyer–client privilege could be attached to communications between a solicitor and a surveyor, the purpose of which communication was to provide advice concerning land included in a will. Therefore, factual information communicated to a solicitor for the purpose of advice will not be protected when provided by a third party even if the third party was responding to a request for that information by the solicitor for the purpose of giving advice. In *Three Rivers District Council v Bank of England (No 3)* [2003] QB 1556, the Court of Appeal ruled that internal communications between employees of the Bank of England would not be covered by lawyer–client privilege even though some of those communications were to and from employees responsible for seeking legal advice from the Bank's solicitors. It was only the communication between employees at the Bank on the one hand and the Bank's solicitors on the other that were covered by the privilege.

Lawyers do not restrict their advice and communication to explanation of the law. In *Belabel v Air India* [1988] Ch 317, Lord Taylor said at p 330:

In most solicitor and client relationships, especially where a transaction involves protracted dealings, advice may be required [as] appropriate on matters great or small at various stages. There will be a continuum of communication and meetings between the solicitor and client . . . Where information is passed by the solicitor or client to the other as part of the continuum aimed at keeping both informed so that advice may be sought and given as required, privilege will attach . . . Moreover, legal advice is not confined to telling the client the law; it must include advice as to what should prudently and sensibly be done in the relevant legal context.

Even if between a solicitor and a client, only communications for the purposes of 'legal advice' are covered by this privilege. Therefore, the purpose of any communication must be considered. In *Three Rivers District Council v Bank of England (No 4)* [2004] 3 WLR 1274, the House of Lords ruled that, in addition to advice on legal rights and obligations, this privilege could also attach to advice on the presentation of evidence at an inquiry or tribunal which is not a court of law as long as the advice is given in the 'legal context' to which Lord Taylor referred in *Belabel v Air India*. Their Lordships attached importance to the impact of such an inquiry on legal rights (Lord Scott at [43]) or the legal content of the inquiry (Lord Scott at [44] and Lord Carswell at [116]). Therefore, communications between the Bank of England and its solicitors were privileged even if the purpose related solely to the presentation of evidence to the Bingham Inquiry investigating the collapse of BCCI. The inquiry was an ad hoc investigation initiated by the government.

However, lawyers do not restrict their advice to legal matters. What if the purpose of the communication in question is mixed? In *Belabel v Air India* [1988] Ch 317, the Court of Appeal observed that whether communication was for the purposes of legal advice had to be interpreted broadly. In *Hellenic Mutual War Risks Association (Bermuda) Ltd v Harrison (The Sagheera)* [1997] 1 Lloyd's Rep 160, Rix J stated that documents would be privileged if the *dominant* purpose of the retainer (the employment of the lawyer) was the provision of legal advice. In *Three Rivers District Council v Bank of England (No 3)*, the Court of Appeal accepted without argument that 'purpose' in *Greenough v Gaskell* meant 'dominant purpose'. Therefore, before lawyer–client privilege will attach to any communication, it must be established to have been predominantly about 'legal advice' in the broad sense of the phrase identified in *Three Rivers District Council v Bank of England (No 4)* (above).

The courts will not adopt a rigid or technical approach to determine whether one or more item is covered by lawyer–client privilege. As was noted above, in *Belabel* it was stated that the 'continuum' of communication rather than each individual communication is to be assessed when determining its purpose. However, in *United States of America v Philip Morris Inc*, *The Times*, 16 April 2004, the Court of Appeal questioned the simple analysis of all communications under a solicitor's retainer and noted that *Belabel* had not created any rule that the 'continuum of communication' had to be entirely privileged or without privilege. In fact it was stated in *Belabel* that whether documents produced to note or record meetings would be covered by lawyer–client privilege would depend on whether they were 'part of that necessary exchange of information of which the object is the giving of legal advice as and when appropriate' (at p 332). The Court of Appeal in *USA v Morris* approved a decision of the judge at first instance not to award lawyer–client privilege to a series of communications but rather to order disclosure of all communications and to leave it to the respondent parties to claim privilege over any particular document when required. The effect of this judgment would appear to be to limit the extent of privilege to those documents which either requested or gave privileged advice or (in the words used in *Belabel*) were 'necessary exchange of information of which the object is the giving of legal advice'.

Where the communication was intended to be passed on to other parties, such communications will not be privileged (*Conlon v Conlon's Ltd* [1952] 2 All ER 462).

18.2.2.2   Third party or litigation privilege

The second class of legal professional privilege is aimed primarily at communications with potential experts or witnesses of fact although the rule is not restricted to persons in such classes. The object of this class is to extend privilege to communications with a third party to the lawyer–client relationship in certain limited circumstances.

Note that this class of privilege applies if there is communication between a third party and *either* the lawyer or the client.

This privilege will arise where the communication concerned pending or contemplated litigation. Where the communication takes place before any dispute has arisen it is highly unlikely that it will be privileged (*Wheeler v Le Marchant* (1881) 17 Ch D 675, CA). In *Re Highgrade Traders Ltd* [1984] BCLC 151, Oliver LJ at p 172 used the expression 'if litigation is reasonably in prospect' to define whether litigation was pending or contemplated and in *Mitsubishi Electric Australia Pty Ltd v Victorian WorkCover Authority* [2002] VSCA 59 an Australian court defined the test as 'a real prospect of litigation as distinct from a mere possibility'. This approach was approved in *United States of America v Philip Morris Inc, The Times*, 16 April 2004, where it was noted that 'a mere possibility' of litigation being commenced would be inadequate.

In *Waugh v British Railways Board* [1980] AC 521, it was held that the dominant purpose of the communication had to be litigation. In that case the document in question was a report by an accident investigator that had been prepared so that the defendants could assess their liability in a crash and so that they could take steps to prevent any such accident from happening again. The House of Lords held that the two purposes had been of equal weight so the document was not privileged. Quite what the dominant purpose of a document or communication is will depend on the facts of each case.

In *Re L (A Minor) (Police Investigation: Privilege)* [1997] AC 16, the House of Lords held that this type of privilege only applies in adversarial proceedings and therefore would not apply to advice concerning investigations and inquiries (but see *Three Rivers District Council v Bank of England (No 4)* [2004] 3 WLR 1274 (above), where it was accepted that communications in respect of a judicial enquiry formed by the government would be privileged). Furthermore, in *United States of America v Phillip Morris Inc* (above), it was stated that the prospect of a party being required to produce documents at the trial between two other parties did not amount to litigation for these purposes and therefore no privilege would attach to communication about such matters.

18.2.2.3   The effect of legal professional privilege

Communication falling under either class will not be admissible at trial unless the party who has the privilege waives it (see **18.2.2.4** below). The privilege renders the communications inadmissible and immune from discovery. However, it does not prevent documents or items in the possession of the lawyer or third party from being admissible nor does it prevent the lawyer or third party from being called as a witness of fact on some matters (see **18.2.2.5** below). Furthermore, there are two exceptions to the rule that communications are privileged (see **18.2.2.6** below).

The privilege is that of the client, not of the lawyer or third party (*Schneider v Leigh* [1955] 2 QB 195).

The communication will remain privileged after the proceedings to which they relate has ended and will also pass to successors in title (*Minet v Morgan* (1873) 8 Ch App 361).

18.2.2.4   Waiver of privilege

As the privilege is that of the client, only he can waive it. Where the alleged waiver was made in excess of the powers of the person doing so, privilege will not have been waived: *GE Capital v Sutton* (2004) 2 BCLC 662. Equally, waiver that is effected by compulsion will not cancel the privilege (*British American Tobacco (Investments) Ltd v United States of America* [2004] EWCA Civ 1064). The court will look carefully at the circumstances of the waiver to determine whether and exactly how much of the privilege has been waived (*Great Atlantic Insurance Co v Home Insurance Co* [1981] 1 WLR 529).

Where a client has purported to waive privilege in respect of one matter or communication but not in respect of others, the court may infer that other communications have been waived (*General Accident Fire & Life Assurance Corporation Ltd v Tanter* [1984] 1 WLR 100). In large documents, the court will apply the waiver to the whole document unless parts of it are deemed to be distinct and severable in their nature (*British Coal Corporation v Dennis Rye Ltd (No 2)* [1988] 3 All ER 816).

Particular difficulties arise when a party is forced to give evidence as to the nature of discussions with his lawyer. This is most likely to be the case where the accused remains silent as a result of legal advice when questioned by the police and the prosecution in a criminal case seek to rely on s 34 of the Criminal Justice and Public Order Act 1994 (see **14.4.1.1**). To explain that such silence was not motivated by a consciousness of guilt, the lawyer may have to give evidence. In *R v Bowden* [1999] 2 Cr App R 176, the Court of Appeal held that calling the lawyer in this way meant that the lawyer could be cross-examined as to the detail and reasons for the advice given and that it would be inappropriate for legal professional privilege to restrict this.

18.2.2.5   Limits on the scope of privilege

The privilege applies to the communications between lawyer and client, not to facts that were perceived during the solicitor/client relationship such as the client's identity (*Studdy v Sanders* (1823) 2 Dow & Ry KB 347) or the fact of the client having attended the solicitor's office to receive advice (*R v Manchester Crown Court, ex p R, The Times*, 15 February 1999). In *R (Hoare) v South Durham Magistrates' Court* [2005] RTR 4, the Divisional Court held that a solicitor could be called to prove the identity of his client and the fact of a previous conviction (at which the solicitor was present) without offending lawyer–client privilege.

Furthermore, documents or items do not become privileged simply because they are in the possession of a party's lawyer (*Dubai Bank v Galadari* [1989] 3 All ER 769). In *R v Peterborough Justice, ex p Hicks* [1977] 1 WLR 1371, the defendants were charged with forgery offences. The Court of Appeal refused to quash a warrant to search the party's solicitor's offices for allegedly forged documents stating that the solicitor had no better right to resist the warrant than the person upon whose behalf he held them. Therefore, whether the documents can be withheld depends on whether the client has some right other than legal professional privilege to keep them. This can be seen by contrasting the following two cases in which experts had received items of evidence for the purposes of advising a party and in which litigation privilege was alleged:

(a) In *R v King* [1983] 1 WLR 411, CA, it was held that a subpoena was properly issued to the prosecution requiring a handwriting expert, who had been retained by the defence, to produce documents containing the defendant's handwriting but which may have incriminated the accused.

(b) In *R v R* [1994] 4 All ER 260, CA, it was held that DNA samples that had been sent to an expert for his advice should not have been admitted. The DNA samples could not have been taken from the accused without his consent (**15.4.3**).

Note, in the two cases the items of evidence were admissible to prove facts in their own right. Equally, an expert whose expert opinion is privileged could be called by the other party to prove facts as opposed to opinions he has perceived (*Harmony Shipping Co SA v Saudi Europe Line Ltd* [1979] 1 WLR 1380, CA).

Facts related to a lawyer as part of his instructions will be privileged. However, if the lawyer perceives facts while acting for a client where those facts were not communicated to him or her by the client, those facts will not be privileged. In *Brown v Foster* (1857) 1 Hur & N 736, the plaintiff brought an action for malicious prosecution having been acquitted of embezzlement. In the course of the embezzlement trial, it was alleged that he had not made an entry in a ledger and the charge had been dismissed when it was revealed that an entry in a ledger had in fact been made. The defendant in the malicious prosecution proceedings was allowed to call the plaintiff's barrister in the embezzlement proceedings to say that the day before the ledger was admitted as evidence, there was no such entry. This was a fact perceived by the barrister rather than information received from the plaintiff under privileged instructions.

18.2.2.6   Exceptions to legal professional privilege

The privilege applies absolutely. There is no general power to override the privilege because of public interest considerations (*R v Derby Magistrates' Court, ex p B* [1995] 3 WLR 681). However, the privilege is subject to two qualifications set out below which reflect public interest concerns:

(a) *Legal professional privilege does not apply to communications made in pursuance of a crime or fraud* (*R v Cox and Railton* (1884) 14 QBD 153). In *Crescent Farm (Sidcup) Sport Ltd v Sterling Offices Ltd* [1972] Ch 553, it was stated that fraud went beyond the tort of deceit and included 'all forms of dishonesty such as fraudulent breaches of contract, fraudulent conspiracies, trickery and sham contrivances' (per Goff J). Clearly, a lawyer will regularly be exposed to the criminal past of a client and will even have to advise them that future conduct might be unlawful in some way. However, in *Barclays Bank plc v Eustice* [1995] 4 All ER 411, CA, a distinction was drawn between legal advice as to the legal affect of what had happened and advice as to how to carry out a fraudulent unlawful purpose in the future. However, the timing of the criminal conduct does not fully determine the matter. Advice as to the potential illegality of future conduct will still be privileged (*Butler v Board of Trade* [1971] Ch 680). The test is whether the communication was made in pursuance of the fraud or crime (*R v Snaresbrook Crown Court, ex p DPP* [1988] QB 532).

The issue for the court to determine is whether it was the purpose of the lawyer *or* the client to pursue a fraud or crime. *R v Central Criminal Court, ex p Francis & Francis*, HL concerned the powers of search and seizure under s 10 of PACE 1984. The House stated that s 10 reflected the common law on legal professional privilege. The police, during a drugs investigation, had obtained orders requiring solicitors to produce documentation concerning the buying and selling of properties by a suspect and his family. The solicitors argued that the transactions and communications concerning them were privileged. However, the House concluded privilege would not apply if the intention of furthering a criminal purpose was that of the holder of the document or of any other party.

Merely instructing a lawyer to advance a case that may be proven to be untrue is not the furthering of a fraud or crime (*Snaresbrook Crown Court, ex p DPP*). However, where there is an agreement to pervert the course of justice that can be proven by evidence that is independent of the proof of the case in question, privilege will not attach to communication made in pursuance of that agreement (*R (Hallinan Blackburn Gittings and Nott) v Middlesex Guildhall Crown Court* [2005] 1 WLR 766). In *Kuwait Airways Corporation v Iraqi Airways Co, The Times*, 25 April, 2005, the Court of Appeal held that if the alleged fraud was one of the issues in the case in question, there would have to be strong prima facie evidence of such fraud before privilege would be overruled.

(b) *Litigation privilege does not apply in non-adversarial proceedings*. In any proceedings concerning the upbringing of children, the welfare of the child is the court's paramount consideration (s 1(1) of the Children Act 1989). In *Oxfordshire County Council v M* [1994] 2 All ER 269, the Court of Appeal held that the welfare of the child required that communications with third parties should not be subject to privilege. In children cases such communications will generally address various aspects of the welfare of the child such as his physical, educational or emotional needs or harm the child may or may not have suffered. The court was also influenced by the fact that such third parties were appointed by the court in any event. The position was confirmed by the House of Lords in *Re L (A Minor) (Police Investigation: Privilege)* [1996] 2 WLR 395. There the House noted the investigative nature of children proceedings and the requirement of leave for third parties to be instructed. It was therefore held to be inappropriate for third-party privilege to apply in cases resolved using inquisitorial procedures. In *Three Rivers District Council v Bank of England (No 4)* [2004] 3 WLR 1274, the House of Lords reiterated the restriction of litigation privilege to adversarial proceedings but noted that the inquisitorial nature of the CPR invited a reappraisal of litigation privilege.

18.2.2.7 Proving evidence by other means

The privilege attaches only to the communications or documents set out above. The facts contained in the communications or documents are not covered by the privilege. Therefore if the fact can be proved by other means, other parties may attempt to do so. The extent to which the court must let them do so depends upon whether it is a criminal or civil case:

(a) *Criminal cases*: once the information has been made available to the prosecution, the accused's privilege is lost. For example:

   (i) A note from the accused to his barrister that was found on the floor had been properly used in cross-examination (*R v Tompkins* (1977) 67 Cr App R 181, CA).

   (ii) The written account from the accused to his solicitor was accidentally sent to the prosecution. It had properly been used by them at trial (*R v Cottrill* [1997] Crim LR 56, CA).

However, the court will consider whether the evidence has been obtained unfairly and should therefore be excluded under s 78 of PACE 1984 (*R v Cottrill* and *R v Willis* [2004] All ER (D) 287).

(b) *Civil cases*: the position is now governed by CPR, r 31.20, which provides:

> Where a party inadvertently allows a privileged document to be inspected, the party who has inspected the document may use it or its contents only with the permission of the court.

In deciding whether or not to grant permission, the court will have regard to pre-CPR case law concerning the granting of injunctions to restrain the use of such evidence. Injunctions were generally granted where the documents had been obtained by fraud (*Ashburton v Pape* [1913] 2 Ch D 469) or obvious error (*Goddard v Nationwide Building Society* [1987] QB 670, CA) but what if the mistake is not obvious? In *International Business Machines Corporation v Phoenix International (Computers) Ltd* [1995] 1 All ER 413 numerous documents were made available by the defendant to the plaintiff. These documents included documents that were clearly privileged in principle. However, the plaintiff's solicitors took the view that privilege had been waived in respect of the documents and told the defendant's solicitors this. The defendant therefore applied for an injunction restraining such use and seeking their return. The court held that the test was whether a reasonable solicitor would have realised that privilege had not been waived. In doing so the court would take into account the extent to which privilege was claimed in respect of other documents, the nature of the case, of the documents and the way in which discovery (disclosure) had taken place thus far. On that basis the documents in question were clearly privileged.

However, the advent of the CPR has led to a stricter approach. In *USP Strategies v London General Holdings, The Times*, 30 April, 2004, it was held that when a party obtains possession of communications to which an unwaived privilege attaches, the normal starting point is to order that the privileged material shall not be used and that any discretion to allow the use of such material should not be exercised merely to allow probative evidence to be admitted. However, in extreme cases, the court could refuse to make an order restraining use of such evidence on the basis that use of such evidence furthers the public interest that justice is properly administred (*ISTIL Group Inc v Zahoor* [2003] 2 All ER 252).

Note also that paragraph 608(f) of the Code of Conduct for the Bar restricts the extent to which a barrister may use a document which has come into his possession by 'some means other than the normal and proper channels'. If the barrister accidentally reads such a document and then realises that he should not have done so, he may withdraw if he:

• would be embarrassed in the discharge of his duties by knowing what was revealed in the document; and
• he can do so without jeopardising the client's interests.

18.2.3   'Without prejudice' communications

It was noted above (**18.2.2.1**) that where the communication was intended to be passed on to other parties, such communications will not be privileged (*Conlon v Conlon's Ltd* [1952] 2 All ER 462 (see also *Paragon Finance plc v Freshfields* [1999] 1 WLR 1183)). Generally, communications between parties are not privileged (after all, the main purpose of the privilege is to prevent other parties from knowing the strength of the party's case). However, this principle is subject to an exception where the parties are seeking to settle the case by negotiation. In such situations parties need not fear that their admissions or concessions during negotiation will be seen by the tribunal of fact should they fail to settle. This ground of excluding evidence resembles legal professional privilege but is different, not least of all because the protection can only be waived by agreement between both parties.

Such communication is generally referred to as 'without prejudice' correspondence. As a matter of good practice those words should be clearly marked on any letters that are not intended to go before the judge. However:

(a) The court is not bound to hold correspondence to be 'without prejudice' whenever the words are used (*Buckinghamshire County Council v Moran* [1990] Ch 623).

(b) The court is not bound to hold that correspondence without those words can never be 'without prejudice' (*Chocoladefabriken Lindt & Sprungli AG v Nestle Co Ltd* [1978] RPC 287).

(c) The real test is whether the correspondence is part of negotiations genuinely aimed at settlement (*South Shropshire District Council v Amos* [1986] 1 WLR 1271).

The rule prevents the correspondence from being admissible at trial (either on the matter of liability or on the issue of remedies). However, there are limited circumstances in which such correspondence will be admissible:

(a) If the negotiations reach settlement, the correspondence can be used as evidence of what was agreed (*Walker v Wilshire* (1889) 23 QBD 335; *Tomlin v Standard Telephones & Cables Ltd* [1969] 1 WLR 1378). It is not evidence on any other matter, nor is the agreement between the claimant and the first defendant admissible in respect of the dispute between the claimant and another defendant on exactly the same matter (*Rush & Tompkins Ltd v Greater London Council* [1989] AC 1280, HL). The reaching of an agreement is not necessarily recognition of the truth of the allegations to which it relates and should not therefore be allowed to prove anything other than the *fact* of agreement. However, where one of the parties who reached a settlement brings proceedings against a third party for a contribution to the damages in the main claim and the without prejudice correspondence refers to the degrees of contribution, the correspondence can be referred to on that issue (*Gnitrow Ltd v Cape plc* [2000] 1 WLR 2327).

(b) Where subsequent proceedings relate to wholly different subject matter and the correspondence reveals evidence on that different subject matter then the correspondence will be admissible whether or not a settlement was reached (*Muller v Linsley & Mortimer The Times*, 8 December 1994).

(c) Where correspondence is marked 'without prejudice save as to costs' the court may, in limited circumstances, refer to the correspondence when determining costs issues. This detailed procedure is governed by CPR, Part 36 (see *Blackstone's Civil Practice*, 2006) and in family proceedings by r 2.69 of the Family Proceedings Rules 1991, SI 1991/1247, and the case law deriving from *Calderbank v Calderbank* [1976] Fam 93. This will necessarily only apply where there was no settlement as the point of the analysis is to determine whether the party in question received a better order from the court than was offered by the other party and should therefore have the costs of the litigation paid by the other party.

(d) In proceedings relating to children, any admissions made by a parent concerning any harm that a child has suffered, whether made in an attempt to settle proceedings before trial of for other reasons will be admissible as evidence (*Re D (Minor)* [1993] 2 All ER 693).

18.3 Public policy exclusion

The rules we have examined in this chapter so far have concerned the inadmissibility of evidence because one or both parties has asserted a privilege in respect of it. These privileges exist because of a concern to maintain the integrity of the litigation process and the interests of justice above and beyond the needs of the particular case. However, there is also a rule of more general application that restricts the extent to which otherwise admissible evidence can be revealed to parties and admitted as evidence. The rationale for this rule is that there are other public policy reasons for keeping evidence out of court than its impact upon the interests of justice.

This area of law is also commonly known as public interest immunity (or PII).

18.3.1   The general rule

The test of public policy exclusion is simply a matter of balancing the interest of justice in disclosing the evidence in question, on the one hand, against the public policy for excluding it, on the other hand (*Conway v Rimmer* [1968] AC 910). The claim of public policy exclusion should be decided by the courts.

The mere fact that a government agency or the prosecution alleges that it is not in the public interest for evidence in their possession to be revealed does not determine whether or not it should be (*R v Ward* [1993] 1 WLR 619 and the Criminal Procedure and Investigations Act 1996, Part I). Further, if no party requests that the evidence be excluded on public policy grounds the court may (and should) consider whether to do so if necessary (*Duncan v Cammell Laird & Co Ltd* [1942] AC 624).

The public interest for these purposes is not determined by the class of document or source of information in question. Although such an approach had previously been adopted in relation to documents such as high-level government papers, the House of Lords stated in *Burmah Oil Co v Bank of England* [1980] AC 1090 that 'class' claims should be evaluated and decided on their merits just like any other type of document. Therefore, public interest immunity from disclosure or use will not automatically be granted in respect of a document merely because it is diplomatic correspondence or a confidential economic report, for example. In 1996 the Lord Chancellor issued a statement (1997 147 NLJ 62) that government departments would no longer seek exclusion simply on the grounds that the document fell into a particular class. Instead, ministers will:

> . . . focus directly on the damage that disclosure of sensitive documents would cause . . . Ministers will only claim immunity when they believe that disclosure . . . will cause real damage or harm to the public interest. Damage will normally have to be in the form of a direct and immediate threat to the safety of an individual or to the nation's economic interest or relations with a foreign state, though in some cases the anticipated damage might be indirect or longer term, such as damage to a regulatory process.

Therefore, a balancing exercise must be conducted in all cases. The fact that evidence from a particular class of source is more or less regularly excluded than that from other classes of source simply reflects the importance that is often attached to such sources when that balancing exercise is conducted rather than any absolute rule as to whether or not they should be excluded.

While in civil cases the interest of justice may vary from case to case, in criminal cases it has been said that where evidence may prove the accused's innocence or prevent a miscarriage of justice, the balance comes down heavily in favour of disclosure (*R v Keane* [1994] 1 WLR 746, CA). This does not prevent the court from having to consider the potential value of the evidence: the decision not to disclose material to the defence on the grounds of public interest immunity may undermine the right of the defendant to a fair trial in accordance with Article 6 of the ECHR. The European Court has recognised that the withholding of some information about prosecution investigative procedures is permissible without breaching the right of the accused to a fair trial (*Klass v Federal Republic of Germany* (1978) 2 EHRR 214, 232). However, in *Rowe and Davis v United Kingdom* (2000) 30 EHRR 1, the European Court of Human Rights stated that only such withholding of evidence as was strictly necessary would be consistent with a fair trial. In *R v H, R v C* [2003] UKHL 2847, the House of Lords considered the process for determining whether material in the possession of the prosecution could be withheld from the defence on the grounds of public interest immunity. As part of the identification of a seven-stage process for determining such disclosure issues (see **18.3.4.1** below), the House defined the test for public interest immunity in two stages:

1   Is there a real risk of serious prejudice to an important public interest (and, if so, what) if full disclosure of the material is ordered? If No, full disclosure should be ordered.

2   If the answer to . . . [2] is Yes, can the defendant's interest be protected without disclosure or disclosure be ordered to an extent or in a way which will give adequate protection to the public interest in question and also afford adequate protection to the interests of the defence?

18.3.2   The effect of public policy exclusion

Where evidence is excluded for reasons of public policy, no party can waive that right. The failure of any interested party to claim that evidence ought to be excluded on the grounds of public policy is simply a factor that the courts will consider in balancing the public policy against the interests of justice. In this sense the evidence is different to evidence excluded under one of the privileges set out in **18.2** above, as in privilege cases, the exclusion of the source of evidence depends upon a claim by someone that the evidence is privileged.

Further, it is the fact or information that is excluded on public policy grounds rather than the means of proving it as is the case where privilege is asserted (ie, the source or document itself) (*Rogers v Home Secretary* [1973] AC 388). Therefore, in contrast to evidence excluded on the grounds of a privilege, information excluded on the grounds of public policy cannot be proved by some other route (for the contrast, see **18.2.2.7**).

18.3.3   Examples

The following cases are all examples of the exercise of the principle of public policy exclusion. The list is not comprehensive. For further cases see *Blackstone's Criminal Practice*, 2006, at F9.1 to F9.8, *Archbold*, 2006, 12–34 to 12–44. While 'class' claims no longer determine whether or not evidence will be admitted, the type of document or type of information contained in the document tends to raise similar concerns and issues.

18.3.3.1   National security, affairs of state and foreign policy interests

It was this type of claim of public policy exclusion that previously led to automatic exclusion by class of document. However, in Sir Richard Scott V-C's *Report of the Inquiry into the Export of Defence Equipment and Dual-Use Goods to Iraq and Related Prosecutions* (House of Commons Paper 115, 95/96, at G18.86) the use of class claims even in relation to national security interests was criticised, leading to the Lord Chancellor's statement (at **17.3.1** above). Therefore, any statement even that national security evidence should be excluded as a matter of course has to be looked at critically. However, the trend has been for such evidence to be excluded. For example:

(a) In *Duncan v Cammell Laird & Co Ltd* [1942] AC 624, the court refused to order the disclosure of plans for a submarine that sank during trials.

(b) In *Burmah Oil Co v Bank of England* [1980] AC 1090, the bank's refusal to produce confidential records of dealings with banks and other businesses was upheld. The refusal was at the request of the government on the grounds of national economic interests.

(c) In *Buttes Gas and Oil Co v Hammer (No 3)* [1981] 1 QB 223, information relating to a company's dealings with a foreign state would not be revealed where that country was in a border dispute with its neighbour. The public interest served by refusing to disclose the evidence was international comity.

18.3.3.2 Police information

Information that has been used during investigations will often be of potential benefit to the accused in criminal proceedings or to parties taking action against the police in respect of their policing. Examples include:

(a) In *Evans v Chief Constable of Surrey* [1988] QB 588, a report sent to the DPP by the police was held not to be disclosable in a civil action as it was held to be important to preserve the freedom of communication between the police and the DPP. Equally where the police have obtained evidence during a criminal investigation, the court must balance the confidentiality of such information obtained under the exercise of compulsory powers on the one hand against the basic public interest in assuring a fair trial on full evidence in any subsequent civil proceedings on the other: *Marcel v Commissioner of Police for the Metropolis* [1992] Ch 225, CA; and *Taylor v Director of the Serious Fraud Office* [1999] 2 AC 177. In *Frankson v Home Office* [2003] EWCA Civ 655, the Court of Appeal rejected the argument that statements made to police officers under caution would necessarily be excluded in the public interest. There is therefore no general public interest in maintaining the confidentiality of statements made to prosecuting authorities that will outweigh the interest of a fair trial, although the court did leave open the possibility that an overriding public interest in non-disclosure could arise in specific cases.

(b) In *R v Horseferry Road Magistrates' Court, ex p Bennet (No 2)* [1994] 1 All ER 289, it was recognised that communications between prosecuting authorities in different countries could potentially be excluded, although the evidence was admitted on that occasion as it showed that the accused had been unlawfully returned to the jurisdiction.

(c) In *R v Chief Constable of the West Midlands, ex p Wiley* [1995] 1 AC 274, it was held that whether or not statements made in the course of police complaints investigations should be excluded depended on the facts of each case.

(d) Where a criminal case appears to have been based upon informant evidence the courts have generally held that the identity of informants should not be disclosed although it may be ordered if it is necessary to establish the innocence of the accused (*Marks v Beyfus* (1890) 25 QBD 494). There is no general rule, however, that such evidence should not be disclosed; it is simply that generally, the anonymity of the informant has been deemed to weigh heavily in the balance (*R v Keane* (above)). In *R v Agar* [1990] 2 All ER 442, the accused's case was that the informant and the police had cooperated in setting up the accused by inviting him to the informant's house and then planting evidence there. The Court of Appeal held that the defence should have been entitled to cross-examine the police officers as to whether the informant had told them that the accused was due to visit his house.

(e) A similar approach has been adopted in relation to persons who have allowed their houses to be used as police surveillance posts (*R v Rankine* [1986] QB 861). In *R v Johnson*

(Kenneth) (1989) 88 Cr App R 131, the Court of Appeal stated that before the court can admit evidence from a surveillance, two matters should be proved (as a minimum):

(i) A police officer in charge of the observations (no lower in rank than sergeant) testifies that *before the observation took place* he spoke to the occupiers of the premises to be used about their attitude to the observation, including the risk of disclosure of the use of the premises.

(ii) A police officer of the rank of at least chief inspector testifies that *immediately before trial* he visited the place of the observation and spoke to the occupiers at that time about their attitude to the disclosure of its use as an observation post at trial.

Where the court rules that the identity of informants or the details of information held by the police must be revealed, the prosecution may decide not to proceed on the charges in question. In this way they can preserve their sources.

18.3.3.3   Other confidential information

The approach of the courts in such cases rather depends on the issues being litigated (ie, the interests of justice) on the one hand and the source of information and the importance of confidentiality (the public interest in exclusion) on the other. The results have therefore varied considerably, for example:

(a) *D v National Society for the Prevention of Cruelty to Children* [1978] AC 171, in which exclusion was granted in respect of anonymous reports made to the NSPCC concerning child abuse to children;

(b) *Science Research Council v Nassé* [1980] AC 1028, in which public policy exclusion was unsuccessfully sought in respect of documents used to determine promotion applications for employees;

(c) *Lonhro Ltd v Shell Petroleum Company Ltd* [1980] 1 WLR 627, in which information given in confidence to a government inquiry concerning a matter of foreign policy was held to have been properly excluded;

(d) *Re M (A Minor) (Disclosure of Material)* [1990] 2 FLR 36, in which social services reports and case notes concerning a child in care were not disclosable. (However, such immunity does not operate against a guardian appointed for the child by the court in Children Act 1989 proceedings. Such a guardian can be ordered by the court to have access to all social service records under s 42 and no immunity would prevent such disclosure.);

(e) *R v Hampshire County Council, ex p K* [1990] 2 All ER 129, in which Social Services Department records were held not to be disclosed unless the judge ordered so;

(f) *Lonrho plc v Fayed (No 4)* [1994] QB 775, in which a taxpayer's tax returns held by the Inland Revenue were held potentially to be subject to public interest immunity as they had been obtained from the taxpayer by compulsion.

18.3.3.4   Journalistic sources

The Contempt of Court Act 1981, s 10, makes general provision as to the circumstances in which a journalist may be required by court order to reveal sources of information. Section 10 provides:

No court may require a person to disclose, nor is any person guilty of contempt of court for refusing to disclose, the source of information contained in a publication for which he is responsible, unless it be established to the satisfaction of the court that disclosure is necessary in the interests of justice or national security or for the prevention of disorder or crime.

Therefore, a journalist is not generally under an obligation unless the evidence is necessary for one of four purposes: the interests of justice, national security, prevention of crime or prevention of disorder. The effect is that journalistic sources are covered by public policy exclusion and must be weighed against the other reason for revealing the source, of which one is the interests of justice, a phrase that has been interpreted narrowly (*Secretary of State for Defence v Guardian Newspapers* [1985] 1 AC 339). In *X Ltd v Morgan-Grampian (Publishers) Ltd* [1991] 1 AC 1, the interests of justice were defined as the protection of important legal rights or the protection against serious legal wrongs. Disclosure must be necessary for those purposes; therefore, important factors will include the significance of the evidence and the difficulty of obtaining the information from other sources.

The 'prevention of disorder or crime' ground has been interpreted to relate to crime in general not specific crimes (*Re an Inquiry under the Companies Securities (Insider Dealing) Act 1985* [1988] AC 660). Therefore, the section cannot be used in this way to force a journalist to disclose sources so that they can be called as witnesses in the case unless this is in the 'interests of justice'.

18.3.4   Determining whether to exclude evidence

As noted at the start of this chapter, whether or not evidence will be disclosed is a question of procedure rather than the rules of evidence. You should therefore refer to the *Criminal Procedure* and the *Civil Procedure Manuals* for detail. However, in outline the procedures are as follows.

18.3.4.1   Criminal cases

Public policy exclusion will generally arise as part of the disclosure proceedings relating to unused material (ie, evidence the prosecution will not rely upon). Under ss 3 and 7 of the Criminal Procedure and Investigations Act 1996, the prosecution are under an obligation to disclose material at the primary disclosure stage which might reasonably be considered to undermine the prosecution case or assist the defence case. The 1996 Act also provides the making of applications to the court to determine whether the evidence ought to be revealed. The extent to which the defence should be involved in such applications or should be informed depends on the degree of sensitivity of the material in question. There are three possibilities:

1. For the least sensitive class of material, the prosecution must inform the defence of the application (and the defence will be allowed to participate at the hearing) and of the class of material to which it relates at the very least.

2. For more sensitive material (where the prosecution allege that harm would be caused to a public interest by merely identifying the material in question), the prosecution must inform the defence of the application and the defence can make representations about the procedure to be adopted for determining the public interest immunity issue. However, the prosecution do not have to reveal the nature of the material and the defendant and his representatives are not permitted to attend the hearing of the application.

3. For the most sensitive cases (those in which the public interest to be protected would be threatened merely by revealing the fact of an application), the prosecution may apply to the court without notifying the defence of the application at all.

As the decision not to disclose evidence to the defence threatens the right to a fair trial, the process for determining what evidence should be revealed should itself safeguard the right to a fair trial protected by Article 6(1) of the ECHR. In *Rowe and Davis v United Kingdom* (2000) 30 EHRR 1, the European Court of Human Rights stated, at paragraph 61, 'any difficulties caused to the defence by a limitation on its rights must be sufficiently counter-balanced by the procedures followed by the judicial authorities'.

In *R v H* [2003] 1 WLR 411, the House of Lords considered the procedures under the Criminal Procedure and Investigations Act 1996 in the light of developing practice in the UK courts and European jurisprudence. The result of this consideration was a seven-stage process to be adopted when the prosecution opposed the disclosure of evidence on the grounds of public interest. The court must:

1. Identify and consider the material that the prosecution seek to withhold.

2. Determine whether the material is such as may weaken the prosecution case or strengthen that of the defence. (Disclosure does not have to be ordered for evidence that does not do one or the other.)

3. Determine whether there is a real risk of serious prejudice to an important public interest if full disclosure of the material is ordered. (If no serious prejudice, disclosure should be ordered.)

4. Determine whether the defendant's interest can be protected without disclosure or limited disclosure can be ordered that will both give adequate protection to the public interest and also to the interests of the defence. The court may have to consider what measures can be taken to offer adequate protection for the defence short of full disclosure.

5. Consider whether measures proposed in answer to (4) represent the minimum derogation necessary to protect the public interest in question. (The court is under a duty to get as close as possible to full disclosure while offering adequate protection for the interest in question.)

6. Consider whether any order for limited disclosure under (4) or (5) above may render the trial process unfair to the defendant. (If the trial process is rendered unfair fuller disclosure should be ordered even if this leads the prosecution to discontinue the proceedings so as to avoid having to make disclosure.)

7. Keep the fairness of the trial process under constant review during the trial in light of the order for limited disclosure. (The House noted that it was important that the answer to (6) should not be treated as final.)

The House therefore recognised that not only is there an issue of whether or not evidence ought to be disclosed, but also that the court ought to consider ways in which evidence could be partially disclosed. The balance between disclosure and public interest immunity can therefore be achieved not simply by ordering or refusing disclosure of evidence but also by altering the way in which evidence is disclosed. The House noted, in particular, possibilities such as formal admissions of some or all of the facts the defence seek to prove with the evidence, disclosure short of full disclosure by the preparation of summaries or extracts of evidence, or the provision of edited or anonymised documents.

The House also noted that occasionally a fair trial would require that the defendant was represented at disclosure hearings of the more sensitive types. In such cases, as noted above, the defendant and his representatives may not even be informed of the application. The House therefore approved the practice of appointing 'special counsel' to argue the defendant's case for disclosure at such hearings. However, special counsel would only be appointed in exceptional circumstances. Special counsel would not be acting for the defendant and therefore would not be under any obligation to report to him about matters revealed during the disclosure hearing. However, special counsel would be in a position to challenge the prosecution case from the defence perspective so as to ensure that the adversarial nature of the trial process was safeguarded.

Where the person holding the information is not a party to the proceedings he may make an application to the court to rule that the information should be excluded. Alternatively, such matters fall to be resolved when the third party is the subject of a witness summons requiring him to attend court to produce the document or information.

18.3.4.2   Civil cases

CPR, r 31.19(1) makes detailed provision for determining whether evidence should be revealed. Such applications may be made without notice and will not generally be served on the other party unless the court orders otherwise. Where the information is sought from a non-party to the proceedings the application is made under CPR, r 31.17 (see also *Blackstone's Civil Practice*, 2006, **Chapter 48**).

INDEX